e-HRM

As with other parts of business, technology is having a profound effect on the world of work and management of human resources. Technology is a key enabler for faster, cheaper and better delivery of HR services and in some cases can have a transformational as well as unintended negative effect.

Designed for the digital era, *e-HRM* is one of the first textbooks on these developments. It incorporates the most current and important HR technology related topics in four distinct parts under one umbrella, written by leading scholars and practitioners drawn from across the world. All the chapters have a uniform structure and pay equal attention to theory and practice with an applied focus. Learning resources of the book include chapter-wide learning objectives, case studies, debates on related burning issues, and the companion website includes lecture slides and a question bank.

Mohan Thite is an Associate Professor in HRM at Griffith University, Australia, with over 30 years of professional and academic experience in HR. He has worked extensively in the IT industry as HR professional, researcher and consultant. His key research interests and publications are in Strategic Human Resource Management (SHRM), Digital HRM, International HRM, Global talent management and mobility. He is the Founding Editor-in-Chief of *South Asian Journal of HRM*.

"Mohan Thite has again done a masterful job in this volume at providing both breadth on the growing digital HR agenda and depth on specific topics. He has amassed an all-star team of digital HR thinkers who focus their insights by sharing how these new digital HR concepts can be taught to the next generation . . . By understanding technology, HR professionals may help shape both a business and HR digital agenda. This marvelous anthology offers insights that may further this agenda"

Dave Ulrich, *Rensis Likert Professor, Ross School of Business, University of Michigan, and Co-Founder and Principal, The RBL Group, USA*

e-HRM
Digital Approaches, Directions & Applications

Edited by Mohan Thite

LONDON AND NEW YORK

First published 2019
by Routledge
2 Park Square, Milton Park, Abingdon, Oxon OX14 4RN

and by Routledge
711 Third Avenue, New York, NY 10017

Routledge is an imprint of the Taylor & Francis Group, an informa business

© 2019 selection and editorial matter, Mohan Thite; individual chapters, the contributors

The right of Mohan Thite to be identified as the author of the editorial material, and of the authors for their individual chapters, has been asserted in accordance with sections 77 and 78 of the Copyright, Designs and Patents Act 1988.

All rights reserved. No part of this book may be reprinted or reproduced or utilised in any form or by any electronic, mechanical, or other means, now known or hereafter invented, including photocopying and recording, or in any information storage or retrieval system, without permission in writing from the publishers.

Trademark notice: Product or corporate names may be trademarks or registered trademarks, and are used only for identification and explanation without intent to infringe.

British Library Cataloguing-in-Publication Data
A catalogue record for this book is available from the British Library

Library of Congress Cataloging-in-Publication Data
A catalog record for this book has been requested

ISBN: 978-1-138-04394-7 (hbk)
ISBN: 978-1-138-04397-8 (pbk)
ISBN: 978-1-315-17272-9 (ebk)

Typeset in Bembo
by Sunrise Setting Ltd., Brixham, UK

Visit the companion website: www.routledge.com/cw/thite

This book is lovingly dedicated to

- my wife and soul mate, Anjana, and
- our children and the centre of our existence, Pallavi and Parag

who are also my no-holds-barred critics to keep me in balance.

Contents

List of figures	ix
List of tables	x
List of contributors	xii
Foreword and forward thinking on digital HR	xvi
DAVE ULRICH, RENSIS LIKERT PROFESSOR, ROSS SCHOOL OF BUSINESS, UNIVERSITY OF MICHIGAN AND PARTNER, THE RBL GROUP	

1	**Electronic/digital HRM: A primer**	1
	MOHAN THITE	

PART I
Key approaches to e-HRM   23

2	**Strategic management approach to technology-enabled HRM**	25
	MARK L. LENGNICK-HALL, CYNTHIA A. LENGNICK-HALL & DERRICK McIVER	
3	**Soft systems thinking approach to e-HRM project management**	42
	MOHAN THITE & NMK BHATTA	
4	**Agile approach to e-HRM project management**	57
	NMK BHATTA & MOHAN THITE	

PART II
Key directions in e-HRM   73

5	**Big data and e-HRM**	75
	TOBIAS M. SCHOLZ	
6	**HR metrics and analytics**	89
	MARTIN R. EDWARDS	
7	**Cloud computing and e-HRM**	106
	VINIT GHOSH & NACHIKETA TRIPATHI	

8 Social media and e-HRM 123
CHRISTOPHER J. HARTWELL

9 Gamification and e-HRM 140
TOBIAS M. SCHOLZ

PART III
e-HRM applications 151

10 e-Talent in talent management 153
SHARNA WIBLEN

11 e-Recruitment and selection 172
ANNA B. HOLM & LARS HAAHR

12 e-Performance and reward management 196
KENT V. RONDEAU

13 e-Learning and development 214
CHARISSA TAN

PART IV
Problems and prospects 233

14 Strategic evaluation of e-HRM 235
RALF BURBACH

15 Information security and privacy in e-HRM 250
SHANKAR SUBRAMANIYAN, MOHAN THITE & S. SAMPATHKUMAR

16 Future directions in electronic/digital HRM 268
MOHAN THITE

Index 283

Figures

0.1	Overall logic for digital and business impact	xvii
0.2	Phases of HR digital agenda	xviii
3.1	IT system development life cycle	45
3.2	Key success factors in the systems development life cycle	48
3.3	People capability maturity model	50
4.1	Agile Scrum process diagram	62
4.2	Gieles and van der Meer's HR→T Talent Management Model under Agile	64
10.1	Example 'digital footprint' report	161
11.1	Recruitment and selection process: Tasks with subtasks	173
15.1	Overview on ISMS	254
16.1	Framework of digital HR strategy	276

Tables

0.1	Use of technology to innovate HR practices	xviii
1.1	Competency portfolio of the digital workforce	6
1.2	Examples of digital tools in HR applications	10
2.1	Corporate vs. business unit strategies—strategic HRM issues	27
2.2	Strategic human resource management levels	27
2.3	Key strategic HRM concepts	28
3.1	Emotional maturity and five deadly sins of project management	43
4.1	Principles of Agile methodology	59
4.2	Key terms in Agile Scrum	63
4.3	Key skills and competencies of Agile personnel	65
4.4	Design thinking principles of learning organisations	66
5.1	Moneyball: The art of winning an unfair game	80
5.2	Disconnect between algorithms and automated applicant shortlisting	81
5.3	Big data in HRM: Literature review	81
6.1	HR analytics case study on turnover analyses	91
6.2	Statistical analyses tools	93
6.3	Example HR metrics	95
6.4	Predicting graduate performance simulation	97
6.5	HR analytic competency frameworks	100
7.1	Evolution of HR technologies	108
7.2	Key features of cloud computing	110
8.1	Twelve types of social media users	126
8.2	Recommended social media policy sections	129
8.3	Comparison of two approaches to social media screens	131
10.1	Talent conceptualisations	155
10.2	Justification for technology-enabled talent identification	162
11.1	Key steps, processes and considerations in e-recruitment	180
11.2	Key steps, processes and considerations in e-selection	186
13.1	Learner-centred psychological principles	216
13.2	Comparing training with learning	217
13.3	Advantages and disadvantages of e-learning	222
13.4	Research guidelines for e-learning design	222
14.1	Benefits of using e-HRM	238
14.2	Key success factors for e-HRM implementation	240
14.3	Potential negative outcomes of e-HRM	241

15.1	Role of IT and HR in mitigating data breaches and cyber security threats	258
15.2	Key dimensions of privacy principles	261
15.3	Privacy principles listed in Australia's Privacy Act 1988	262
16.1	Evolution of the HR function	271

Contributors

NMK Bhatta is a Professor of Information Systems in the Indian Institute of Management Indore. He has extensive technical experience in the development/maintenance and certification of avionics software and has worked in the IT industry in several senior positions including in one of the largest global IT services companies. He managed several major global software projects end to end and implemented Agile Methodology. He is a Certified Agile Scrum Master from Scrum Alliance, USA, Agile Certified Practitioner from PMI, USA, and an Agile Trainer. He consults in the field of transformation to Agile and Business Excellence.

Ralf Burbach is Head of Hospitality Management at the Dublin Institute of Technology. Following a managerial career in the hospitality industry, he has been working in academia since 2001. His research and publication interests include electronic HRM, global talent management, international hospitality operations, and vocational/dual education systems. Dr. Burbach is the President-elect at the European chapter of the Council on Hospitality Restaurant and Institutional Education. He is a chartered member of the Chartered Institute of Personnel and Development and a member of the Irish Hospitality Institute. In addition, Dr. Burbach serves on the Hospitality Skills Oversight Group for Ireland.

Martin R. Edwards is currently a Reader in HRM and Organisational Psychology at the King's College London Business School. Martin's academic interests include researching social and multiple identities in organizations, the role of employee/employer branding, employee responses to mergers and acquisitions, and HR Analytics. Martin has published in numerous international journals including the *Human Resource Management Journal, Human Relations, International Journal of Management Reviews, Economic and Social Democracy, European Journal of Work and Organisational Psychology*, and *Personnel Review*. Martin has also published books in the area of HRM, for example, co-author for *Predictive HR Analytics: Mastering the HR Metric* and co-editor of *Managing Human Resources; Human Resource Management in Transition*.

Vinit Ghosh is currently pursuing a Ph.D. at the Indian Institute of Technology Guwahati. He obtained his B.Tech in Information Technology and completed Masters in Human Resource and Organizational Management. Vinit has eight years of IT experience in several multinational IT firms. He worked as a senior BPM consultant in Service-Oriented-Architecture domain across USA, Europe, and the EMEA region. He has attended and presented papers in various international and national conferences, apart from publishing papers in peer-reviewed journals. His doctoral research focuses on how different levels of diversity interact with creativity and innovation in organizations.

Lars Haahr is an Assistant Professor at the Department of Management, Aarhus University. His research focuses on the management of digital transformation within organizational contexts. His recent publications deal with the issues of using social media in government managerial practices and the effect of social media on organizations in general. Lars is also engaged in the research on the use of artificial intelligence and robots in e-recruitment contexts. Prior to his academic career, Lars spent several years in industry as a company director and management advisor.

Christopher J. Hartwell is an Assistant Professor of management in the Jon M. Huntsman School of Business at Utah State University. He received his Ph.D. in Organizational Behavior and Human Resource Management from Purdue University. His research interests include social media in the workplace, employee selection, and transformational leadership. His work has been published in top journals such as the *Journal of Applied Psychology* and *Personnel Psychology*. Chris has years of professional work experience in the field of human resources and is a certified HR professional through both the Society for Human Resource Management (SHRM-CP) and the HR Certification Institute (PHR).

Anna B. Holm is an Associate Professor of Management at the School of Business and Social Sciences, Aarhus University. Her research interests span across various managerial disciplines, with the focus on competitive strategies and human resource (HR) management. Within the HR domain, Anna has conducted and published research on recruitment and selection with technology (i.e., e-recruitment and e-selection). She has also conducted research in distributed leadership, employment relations, and the crowdsourcing of work. Prior to her academic career, Anna worked in industry for over ten years as a consultant and managing project teams.

Cynthia A. Lengnick-Hall is Professor Emeritus in the College of Business at the University of Texas at San Antonio. Her recent research is in strategic management, strategic HR, and knowledge management. Her work has been published in such journals as the *Academy of Management Review, Academy of Management Journal, Strategic Management Journal, Journal of Management, Academy of Management Executive, Human Resource Management, Strategy and Leadership, Human Resource Management Review, European Journal of Operations Research*, and *Organization Studies*. She has co-authored three books and contributed numerous book chapters. Her work in strategic human resource management and in corporate entrepreneurship has received international awards. Dr. Lengnick-Hall has consulted in private industry and with government agencies and non-profit organizations. She has provided executive education in strategic management and decision making for managers in a variety of large and small organizations.

Mark L. Lengnick-Hall is Professor Emeritus of Management in the College of Business at the University of Texas at San Antonio. He earned a B.B.A. and an M.B.A from the University of Texas at Austin and a Ph.D. in Organizational Behavior and Human Resource Management from Purdue University. He has human resource management experience in both private industry and state government. Dr. Lengnick-Hall also has consulted with and provided training for numerous organizations. Dr. Lengnick-Hall's research has been published in journals such as the *Academy of Management Review*,

Academy of Management Executive, Personnel Psychology, Human Resource Management Review, Human Resource Management, International Journal of Human Resource Management, and the *Journal of Organizational Behavior*. His research interests include strategic human resource management, human resource management in non-profit organizations, volunteer motivation, overqualification, and the employment of people with disabilities.

Derrick McIver is an Assistant Professor at Western Michigan University, where he conducts research and teaches at the intersection among the domains examining people, strategy, and technology. Derrick consults with various companies, teaches executive education, and collaborates with students to explore critical elements of strategy, data analytics, knowledge management, technology, the digital transformation, and the future of work. He aims to learn and understand how science and workforce research informs these topics. He has published in leading journals such as the *Academy of Management Review, Journal of Knowledge Management, Human Resource Management Review*, and *Strategic Organization*.

Kent V. Rondeau is Associate Professor in the Faculty of Extension at the University of Alberta in Canada where he teaches a course in human resource analytics. He is presently conducting research exploring the contribution of high-involvement employee work practices to performance outcomes in healthcare organizations. Dr. Rondeau consults widely with business and government agencies.

S. Sampathkumar is a consultant with a rich experience of 37 years spanning design/delivery/project management/information security/strategy/competency development/CSR in public/private sector and multinational corporations. At TCS, India's largest software company, Sampathkumar was instrumental in taking many centers to coveted ISO 27001 certification in information security. Sampathkumar is a certified Assessor in Business Excellence, Baldrige, and EFQM models, and has guided many companies within and outside Tata group in their journey of excellence. He is an accredited facilitator in the REBT (Rational Emotive Behavior Technique) school of behavioral science and is a well-known trainer in leadership skills.

Tobias M. Scholz is an Assistant Professor of Human Resource Management and Organizational Behaviour at the University of Siegen, Germany. He has published articles on international management, human resource management, media management, and virtual teams. His research focuses on organizational technology studies, big data, gamification, eSports, algorithms, and Blockchain. He recently published the book "*Big Data in Organizations and the Role of Human Resource Management*" and is co-editor of the eSports Yearbook.

Shankar Subramaniyan has over 19 years of overall industry experience with wide exposure to various IT security requirements of global clients across industries. He has rich experience in IT risk management compliance audits, assurance, cloud security, privacy, security architecture, and disaster recovery solutions. He is trained and experienced in IT security regulations and has an extensive background in the formulation and implementation of enterprise security policies, procedures, standards, and awareness programs. With his extensive regulatory knowledge and technical process expertise, he has assisted clients with their audit issues, control frameworks, compliance requirements, and risk management processes.

Charissa Tan teaches Human Resources and Learning and Development at the Singapore University of Social Sciences. She has more than ten years' experience in the field having held senior manager positions in a multinational company and a non-profit organisation. She won two global awards for leading the training redesign in a multinational company across Asia-Pacific from traditional methods to mobile learning, and improved employees' time-to-productivity. Charissa has Masters degrees in Occupational Psychology and Creative Arts Therapies. She is now pursuing a PhD in Occupational Psychology and her research interest is performance at modern workplaces.

Nachiketa Tripathi received his doctorate in social psychology from the Indian Institute of Technology Kanpur and is presently working with the Indian Institute of Technology Guwahati as Professor of Psychology and Management. He has over 20 years of teaching and research experience. He has published his research work in reputed journals. Also, he has presented his research work in several international conferences, such as APA convention, ICP, ICAP, and ECP. He has supervised five doctoral dissertations. Professor Tripathi's areas of research are influence strategies, gender, organizational culture, and organizational learning.

Sharna Wiblen is a Lecturer (Assistant Professor) in the Sydney Business School at the University of Wollongong. Before earning a Ph.D. at the University of Sydney, Dr. Wiblen played a pivotal role in two competitively awarded government funded projects with colleagues at the University of Sydney Business School and amassed over 15 years of industry experience working as a management consultant and as a human resource, recruitment, and selection coordinator. Dr. Wiblen works at the boundaries of talent management and information technologies. More specifically, her research critically analyses the conceptualization of "talent" within organisational boundaries and the role of various information technologies in talent management practices.

Foreword and forward thinking on digital HR

Dave Ulrich

Rensis Likert Professor, Ross School of Business, University of Michigan
Partner, The RBL Group

HR is not about HR, but about delivering value to employees, organizations, customers, investors, and communities. To deliver value, HR professionals must appreciate the context in which they work and HR practices need to adapt to that context.

Today's business context has become technology obsessed with terms and concepts such as cloud/big data, social media, gamification, internet of things, robots/chatbots, virtual or augmented reality, blockchain, artificial intelligence, cognitive automation, machine learning, and so forth. When I present these ideas to business leaders or HR professionals, their eyes soon glaze over (as do mine) at the onslaught of technological innovation that shape a new digital reality.

No one doubts that this digital tsunami will fundamentally transform both business and HR, but how can we find simplicity on the other side of this complexity?

Mohan Thite has again done a masterful job in this volume at providing both breadth on the growing digital HR agenda and depth on specific topics. He has amassed an all-star team of digital HR thinkers who focus their insights by sharing how these new digital HR concepts can be taught to the next generation.

Let me offer an overall four-step logic about how to think about digital HR in the context of business performance and a few insights on moving forward, then comment in more detail on step 4 (Figure 0.1): How can HR impact both the business digital agenda and create an HR digital agenda?

Step 4: HR's impact on the business digital agenda

Every organization requires a digital agenda to use information to win in the financial, customer, and employee marketplaces. This digital business agenda enables the organization to source information that help the business win in their chosen financial and customer markets. I suggest that HR professionals play four roles in helping businesses create their business digital agenda:

1 Build a business case. A digital agenda requires awareness of and appreciation for the new digital world of work by employees throughout the organization. This means appropriately crafting and sharing technology trends that require new ways of working to compete.
2 Facilitate a digital business team. Turning technological literacy to digital success requires a multifunctional team effort, including experts from marketing, supply chain, operations, finance, information technology, and general management. HR professionals help form and facilitate these teams to bring many aspects to the creation of a digital business agenda.

Foreword and forward thinking on digital HR xvii

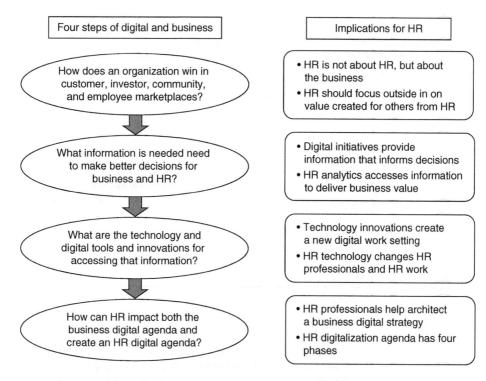

Figure 0.1 Overall logic for digital and business impact.

3   Articulate business digital outcomes. A digital business agenda has clear outcomes that need to be clearly articulated in terms of customer, financial, organization, and employee results. HR professionals who understand performance management know how to define and set goals.
4   Audit current business digital state. HR professionals who know how to audit organization and leader effectiveness can help create a digital business audit to define current and project future requirements.

As HR professionals fulfill these four roles for business digital agenda, they create enormous value.

Step 4: HR digital agenda

HR also must have a digital agenda to deliver increased value. The digital world of HR is a major theme for dozens of HR conferences and new applications and tools with great promise. Let me distill the divergence of HR technology work into four phases that can be the table of contents for an HR digital agenda (see Figure 0.2).

Phase 1: Use technology to streamline administrative HR work

Much of the HR technology work creates more efficiency in existing HR practices. e-HR efforts through shared services, computer-based design and delivery, and apps allows HR work to be done more efficiently.

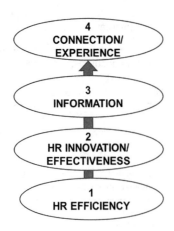

Figure 0.2 Phases of HR digital agenda.

Table 0.1 Use of technology to innovate HR practices

HR practice area	Examples of technology or digital innovations
People	• Recruiting: Interview by video, use of social media (e.g., LinkedIn) for sourcing, broadening the candidate pool including robotics • Employment contract: Employees working remotely, contingent employees • Training/development: Online education, pull training (vs. push), follow-up • Succession planning: Systems for career and succession planning
Performance	• Sharing everyone's goals and performance to create peer pressure for results • Managing performance and appraisal through automated evaluations or reporting interactions through online communication
Communication	• Sharing information with employees • Running online town hall meetings • Bringing customer expectations into the organization
Organization work	• Decision-making processes that involve more people • Creating policy manuals and applications through online information • Sharing best practices and creating learning communities

Phase 2: Use technology to innovate HR practices

Nearly every HR practice area is being upgraded through technology. These upgrades drive HR innovations as illustrated in Table 0.1. The list of these examples is growing exponentially.

Phase 3: Use technology to access information

We found in our research (*Victory Through Organization*) that information management is the most critical capability in delivering business results. Access to information traditionally gives leaders power because they have more information than their employees. Today, with open access of information through technology, information is less about power and more about the ability to make better business decisions. HR departments can influence information capability in a number of ways.

First, HR can help hire information experts. Sixty percent of occupations could have up to 30% of their activities automated, including radiologists, design engineers, market researchers, and HR professionals. They are being replaced by big data analysts, social media experts, cloud builders, app developers, and other types of information specialists. Software engineering jobs will grow at a rate of 18.8% by 2024, which is triple the rate of overall job growth. HR can help source and secure this talent.

Second, HR can ensure that external information comes into an organization to inform decisions. HR analytics is not just about using information to improve HR practices and more about accessing information to make better business decisions. In this regard, HR can be the architect of prioritizing key business decisions, then sourcing information both outside and inside the organization to improve those decisions.

Third, information that delivers business results may be structured information that is found on a spreadsheet and accessed through statistics or it may be unstructured information that is found in customer and employee experiences and accessed through thoughtful observation.

Phase 4: Use technology to create social experiences and connections

Recent research has found that social isolation increases mortality more than hypertension, obesity, or substance abuse. HR can use technology to build connections among people that create positive social experiences. Employees are often looking less for a job or even a career, and more for an experience that will increase their personal identity and well-being.

The concept of "belonging" becomes a critical factor for overcoming social isolation and for creating organizations that have a positive impact on people and performance. Belonging draws on attachment theory, which essentially states that when someone has strong emotional attachment to another (person or organization), personal well-being increases. This improved well-being in turn increases personal productivity and overall organizational performance. Organizations where we work, play, and worship should become settings for belonging.

Currently, in most firms, technology is used to deliver administrative efficiency (phase 1), upgrade and innovate HR practices (phase 2), and deliver information (phase 3). Increasingly, technology should encourage belonging through social and emotional connections among employees inside an organization and among employees and stakeholders outside an organization.

Conclusion

Let me end where I began: HR is not about HR, but about delivering value to employees, organizations, customers, investors, and communities. By understanding technology, HR professionals may help shape both a business and the HR digital agenda. This marvelous anthology offers insights that may further this agenda.

1 Electronic/digital HRM: A primer

Mohan Thite

> **Learning objectives**
> - Highlight how the digital world today dominates the technology landscape and its impact on the workforce
> - Provide an inclusive definition of digital HRM and resultant devolution of HR activities
> - Describe the changing roles of HR in the digital world
> - Explain the impact of technology on various HR functions, including unintended consequences
> - Understand the structure of the book and the key themes espoused in various chapters

Introduction

Gollub (2016) posted this blog on social media on 'how the future will look like':

> I just went to the Singularity University summit and here are the key learnings:
>
> In 1998, Kodak had 170,000 employees and sold 85% of all photo paper worldwide. Within just a few years, their business model disappeared and they (became) bankrupt. What happened to Kodak will happen in a lot of industries in the next 10 year(s) and most people don't see it coming . . . It will now happen with Artificial Intelligence, health, autonomous and electric cars, education, 3D printing, agriculture and jobs. Welcome to the 4th Industrial Revolution. Welcome to the Exponential Age.
>
> Software will disrupt most traditional industries in the next 5–10 years. Uber is just a software tool, they don't own any cars, and (yet, they) are now the biggest taxi company in the world. Airbnb is now the biggest hotel company in the world, although they don't own any properties.
>
> - Artificial Intelligence: Computers become exponentially better in understanding the world. This year, a computer beat the best Go player in the world, 10 years earlier than expected . . . Because of IBM Watson, you can get legal advice (so far for more or less basic stuff) within seconds, with 90% accuracy compared

with 70% accuracy when done by humans . . . Watson already helps nurses diagnosing cancer, 4 time[s] more accurate than human nurses. Facebook now has pattern recognition software that can recognize faces better than humans. (By) 2030, computers will become more intelligent than humans.
- Autonomous cars: In 2018, the first self driving cars will appear for the public. Around 2020, the complete industry will start to be disrupted. You don't want to own a car anymore . . . Traditional car companies try the evolutionary approach and just build a better car, while tech companies (Tesla, Apple, Google) will (take) the revolutionary approach and build a computer on wheels . . .
- Health: . . . There will be companies who will build a medical device (called the 'Tricorder' from Star Trek) that works with your phone, which takes your retina scan, your blood sample and you breath into it. It then analyses 54 biomarkers that will identify nearly any disease.
- 3D printing: The price of the cheapest 3D printer (has come) down from $18,000 to $400 within 10 years. In the same time, it became 100 times faster . . . In China they (have) already 3D printed a complete 6-storey office building. By 2027, 10% of everything that's being produced will be 3D printed.
- Business opportunities: If you think of a niche you want to go in, ask yourself: 'in the future, do you think we will have that?' and if the answer is yes, how can you make that happen sooner? If it doesn't work with your phone, forget the idea. And any idea designed for success in the 20th century is doomed to failure in the 21st century.

As you can see from the above (some of which are facts while some are just predictions), technology is all around us. It always has been. During the industrial revolutions of the last two centuries, the industrial economy ushered in transformational change. Mechanised mass production, the steam engine, electricity, the railway network and so on, had the same dramatic and disruptive effect that we see in newer technologies that have emerged since the start of the twenty-first century knowledge economy. One might argue that digital highways have simply replaced the railway networks. But the speed, intensity and uncertainty of disruptive change brought about by technology today has been unprecedented and is accelerating rapidly. It has been described as 'the fourth industrial revolution' (Industry 4.0), the 'new paradigm' and the 'big shift'.

Coupled with globalisation and demographic changes, digital technologies have radically altered the way we live, work, conduct business and communicate. In the process, they are dissolving the boundaries between personal and work life. The business management discipline has seen structural changes in terms of business strategies, research and development, product/service design, marketing, manufacturing, supply chain management, customer relationship management, human resource management (HRM) and other support services. It is now well established that traditional competitive advantages, such as market leadership, natural resources, financial resources and technology, cannot by themselves lead to 'sustainable competitive advantage' to any country or economy or business in the knowledge economy. It is the 'optimum leveraging of people, process and technology' (Thite, 2004) wherein technology acts as a catalyst with a multiplier effect provided the organisation has competent leadership along with a workforce and well defined work processes that are optimally aligned to business objectives.

From master craftsmen to standardised processes driven by mechanisation, to adaptable and then intelligent processes, the world of work has come a long way. Today, we live in the digital world. While digital technologies are generally used as an umbrella term for computer-based products and solutions, in the business context, they essentially refer to intelligent processes that use continuous real time feedback in order to make constant improvement in the efficiency and effectiveness of work design, processes and outcome (Thomas, Kass and Davarzani, 2013, p. 2). In the process, they directly influence and enhance customer value and organisational revenue.

What does the all-encompassing digital world mean for the HRM function? According to Stephen (2016, p. 97):

> For HR and business leaders, this digital transformation poses two fundamental challenges. First, HR can help business leaders and employees shift to a digital mind-set, a digital way of managing, organizing, and leading change. Second, HR has the opportunity to revolutionize the entire employee experience by transforming HR processes, systems, and the HR organization via new digital platforms, apps, and ways of delivering HR services.

Despite the enormous potential of digital technologies in transforming HRM and 72 percent of companies believing digital HR is an important priority, 'only 38 percent of companies are even thinking about it and only 9 percent are fully ready' (Stephen, 2016, p. 99). This shows that globally, the HR function is far from realising the potential of digital technologies.

This chapter is a primer on electronic/digital HRM. In that sense, this chapter is a kind of 'curtain-raiser' to the rest of the book. We will first look at the impact of the digital world on digital work and workforce. We will then critically examine what we mean by digital HRM and how it has influenced key HR functions and their outcomes. We will conclude with a preview of the key digital HR approaches, directions, applications and the related problems and prospects, as covered in the rest of the book.

Welcome to the digital world

There is no clear definition yet of what is 'digital'. As stated by Andersson, Lanvin and Van der Heyden (2016, p. 52):

> It is clear that the term *digital* currently defies definition. Each organisation's digital journey is individual, with no clear destination in sight. There is no one-size-fits-all way to 'do' digital, nor indeed any 'right way' to do digital ... The lack of a clear definition of the meaning of the term suggests that issues concerning the required competences, capabilities, talent, and resources (including human resources) are surrounded by a similar veil of ambiguity.

However, the business rationale for digitalisation, types of digital technologies and the impact of those technologies on the world of work provide important clues on what we generally mean by digital. The primary drivers for the digital initiatives undertaken by today's organisations are:

- Improve engagement with customers
- Increase efficiency
- Deliver on customer expectations

- Improve product and service offer
- Grow demand
- Customer acquisition

(Andersson, Lanvin and Van der Heyden, 2016, p. 53)

Digitalisation of the global economy is mainly powered by social, mobile, analytics and cloud (SMAC) technologies. To understand the impact of digital technologies on the business world in general and the world of work in particular, consider these developments:

- Illustrating the power of disruption brought in by new technologies, 'only 12 percent of the *Fortune* 500 companies from 1955 are still in business, and last year alone, 26 percent fell off the list' (Deloitte, 2017a, p. 3)
- We spend one-third of the time we are awake browsing the web and apps, surfing 1 billion websites online, playing with 4 million mobile apps and checking our smart devices 85 times a day
- There are more than a billion people on Facebook, over 100 million on Google+, over 450 million on LinkedIn and over 250 million on Twitter
- 42 percent of Americans play games online for at least three hours per week
- 'The Big Six social networks (Facebook, Twitter, LinkedIn, Instagram, Google+, and Pinterest) exceed 2.4 billion people' (Ulrich, 2017, p. 1)
- People in the USA look at their mobile phones 8 billion times a day (Deloitte, 2017a, p. 4)
- Thanks to automation and robotics, one in two jobs are at risk; however, due to new technologies powered by the internet of things (IoT), cloud computing and big data, nearly half a million new technology jobs will be created by 2024, many of which do not even exist today (Dehaze, 2016, pp. 36–37)

Digital work and the digital workforce

Traditionally, people expected to do the same work for the same employer as a full-time employee for most of their career. Loyalty and tenure were key determinants of career progression. Managers dictated what work was done, where, when and how. Career management, and training and development, were directed by the employer and employees were passive participants. Today in the gig economy that is characterised by a labour market consisting of freelance workers, more than a quarter of workers in Western countries are free agents without the constraints of where, when and how to work (Lanvin, Evans and Rodriguez-Montemayor, 2016, p. 11). Organisations are increasingly relying on the 'contingent workforce' of knowledge workers to be innovative, agile and flexible in order to address business uncertainty and unpredictability. In this section, we will explore how digital technologies have turned the world of work upside down.

As we get thrown into the whirlpool of the digital world, today's knowledge workers, whether employees or gig economy contractors, need to possess and continually fine-tune a new set of skills and competencies. With an ageing population that is living longer, people are expected to work well beyond 60 years. Rapid technological obsolescence means people need to continually upgrade their skills. As the global economy becomes more technology-intensive with innovation and creativity being key sources of competitive advantage, the demand for skilled talent, especially in science, technology, engineering and mathematics (STEM) has increased tremendously but the supply is yet to catch up.

Research shows that while 75 percent of the fastest growing occupations now require STEM skills (PWC, 2015: 12–14), there is an increasing shortage of numeracy and literacy skills across almost all Western countries (OECD, 2015). This has resulted in the shortage of technology professionals, so vital in an innovation-driven and technology-intensive global economy (WITSA, 2016), leading to an increasing global sourcing and 'global war for talent', with jobs going where talent is (via services offshoring) and talent going where jobs are (via skilled migration, both temporary and permanent). In the process, countries such as India and China have become key source countries for STEM talent (Craig et al., 2012: 2–7). At the same time, the global search for and sourcing of talent has become a hot political issue, with some commentators declaring that an increasing reliance on foreign talent may lead to a 'vicious cycle of off-shoring jobs, losing skills and competencies from the domestic economy and as a result moving more jobs off-shore could become institutionalized' (NIEIR, 2012: 1).

Further, developments in robotics and artificial intelligence (AI) are expected to result in 'technology-driven unemployment', with 40 percent of today's low- and medium-skilled jobs likely to disappear in the next 15 years. Today's millennials will be doing jobs that do not even exist today (PWC, 2015). However, it is not all doom and gloom. As a result of the combined effects of globalisation, automation and digitalisation, new business models are emerging creating new types of jobs, such as Uber drivers, just as it happened during the previous industrial revolutions (Lanvin, Evans and Rodriguez-Montemayor, 2016, p. 4).

Digital skills. In the age of dualities, there is a 'talent paradox' (Evans and Rodriguez-Montemayor, 2016, p. 70) in that employers today demand specific technical skills as well as generic soft skills because an innovation economy demands collaboration and co-creation of knowledge (Lanvin, Evans and Rodriguez-Montemayor, 2016, p. 12). Andersson, Lanvin and Van der Heyden (2016, p. 52) call them 'e-skills', a combination of advanced technical skills and high-level softer skills. Colbert, Yee and George (2016, p. 732) also highlight the importance of 'digital fluency' in the digital workforce, which refers to a level of proficiency that allows employees to 'manipulate information, construct ideas, and use technology to achieve strategic goals'. Table 1.1 lists some of the key skills and competencies that the digital workforce is expected to have.

Career management in the digital world. The career management process is caught in the whirlpool of environmental, organisational and HRM changes with far-reaching consequences for both organisations and individuals in managing careers. One of the major ironies of contemporary career management lies in the fact that the career-conscious employee is being asked to offer more and more, while the employer is in no position to offer the scale or the kinds of rewards that were available in the past. It is as if employers have adapted a 'help us but help yourself' attitude (Thite, 2001). Whymark and Ellis (1999) argue:

> Traditionally, (the) employment relationship was characterised by a clear psychological contract. Employers expected loyalty, respect for rules, and commitment in return for job security, steady career progression, and training and development. But today the relationship between the parties is viewed more as a short-term economic exchange arrangement instead of a long-term, mutually beneficial commitment.

Employers seem to be adopting a 'here-and-now' transactional attitude to career management rather than a long-term commitment.

Table 1.1 Competency portfolio of the digital workforce

- Future-focused
- Out of the box critical and innovative thinking
- Digital fluency (Colbert, Yee and George, 2016, p.732)
- Strategic thinkers (see Chapter 2)
- Systems-thinkers (see Chapter 3)
- Agile (see Chapter 4)
- Self-leadership
- Big data literate (see Chapter 5)
- Analytical (see Chapter 6)
- Social media-savvy (see Chapter 8)
- Organisationally ambidextrous (exploiting existing competencies while simultaneously exploring new opportunities; balance between alignment and adaptability, flexibility and efficiency, radical and incremental) (Nieto-Rodriguez, 2014)
- Interpersonal skills
- Communication skills, both in the virtual and real world
- Cross-cultural competency
- Emotional intelligence
- Multi-tasking
- Ability to work with multi-generational workforce
- Life-long learning
- Personal mastery (Senge, 1990)
- Team learning (Senge, 1990)

Source: Author.

Bereft of the life-support from employers, many individuals are clueless on how to manage their careers. Their predicament is aptly described by Gunz, Jalland and Evans (1998): 'it is hard for someone being swept downstream in a fast-moving river to make sense of where they are, let alone where they are going'.

As highlighted by Thite (2001), some of the fundamental changes that have influenced career management since the start of the twenty-first century are as follows:

- '*Networked*' and '*Cellular*' organisational structures wherein strategic business units (SBUs) function 'independently but by networking with others to share common knowledge and information, akin to human DNA, they learn, grow, and adapt to an uncertain environment. Within such cellular organisations, members take full charge of their careers and develop their careers around an agreed set of norms for self-governance and professional allegiance' (Brent, Snow and Miles, 1996).
- Staffing in organisations has moved from position-centred to *portfolio-centred*. Under portfolio-centred staffing, the contract output is identified, the matching portfolio of skills needed to complete the contract are specified, individuals with those skills are located in the HR information system and the contract is offered and then managed (Templer and Cawsey,1999).
- Handy (1996) suggests that organisations are taking on a '*shamrock*' configuration whose three levels comprise core, contract and temporary employees. Core employees are those central to the core competencies of the organisation. Contract employees are the new '*portfolio careerists*' – qualified, skills-oriented individuals with a portfolio of skills and clients. Temporary employees are those individuals needed for specific, lower-skilled tasks and are employed on a need basis.

The most important implication of the forms and features of the new economy on the career management process is that the individual is in full charge of his/her own career. Hall (1996) describes the career of the twenty-first century as '*protean*', a career that is driven by the person, not the organisation, and that will be reinvented by the person from time to time, as the person and the environment change. The second major implication is that an individual's career will be in *constant state of flux* and will change directions many times during the career span. Change in career directions also means change in skill components, skill levels, authority and responsibility levels, income levels and so on. Cianni and Wnuck (1997) predict that employees in the twenty-first century will periodically backtrack in their careers, moving from expert back to novice as they are required to have new competencies that may very well be in areas unconnected to their personal preferences. Similarly, noting that contemporary careers are more like '*spirals*', Gratton (2011) believes that individuals need to develop 'serial mastery' in being able to make lateral transitions from one career to another.

Studies also show that knowledge workers tend to have certain unique personality and occupational characteristics, such as craving for autonomy, challenging tasks, immediate and frequent feedback and rewards, ownership of ideas and enterprise, commitment to a profession more than an organisation, team work/community of practices and a liberal lifestyle (Thite, 2004, pp. 38–42). However, HRM in many organisations still tends to be practiced in the command and control management style and as such is out of sync with contemporary realities of the knowledge economy.

Unpacking digital HRM

Ever since computerisation was introduced in the HR function, many terms have been used to describe the 'nature, role and contribution of technology' in managing people. These terms include web-based HR, e-HRM, virtual HR, human resource information systems (HRIS) and recently, digital HRM and smart HRM.

e-HRM is the most commonly used and understood term in the HR discipline to denote the use of mainly web-based applications. According to Marler and Parry (2015, p. 2), e-HRM is a set of:

> configurations of computer hardware, software and electronic networking resources that enable intended or actual HRM activities (e.g. policies, practices and services) through coordinating and controlling individual and group-level data capture and information creation and communication within and across organizational boundaries.

HRIS became prominent and popular with the increasing emphasis on information systems and enterprise resource planning (ERP) (Thite, Kavanagh and Johnson, 2012). Hendrickson (2003, p. 381) defines HRIS as 'integrated systems used to gather, store and analyze information regarding an organization's human resources'. It highlights the critical importance of the systems development life cycle (SDLC) approach and pays attention to planning, analysis, design, implementation and maintenance aspects of technical project management (which is discussed at length in Chapter 3). Some of the important topics considered by HRIS are:

- Developing a business case for an HRIS
- Transformation of HR service delivery
- Determining the organisation's HRIS needs

- Planning process
- Design considerations
- Vendor selection
- Implementation of an HRIS
- Evaluation of the new system (SHRM, 2015)

Discussions of HRIS have mostly revolved around large, monolithic, inflexible ERP products. However, in recent times, with the rise of cloud computing, both large and small to medium enterprises (SMEs) need not make heavy upfront investment in ERP products and then struggle to implement and maintain them. Rather, they can rent HR and other enterprise applications from third-party service providers that are scalable, flexible and affordable. On the other hand, digital HRM includes the latest social, mobile, analytics, and cloud SMAC technologies. It aligns with the changing dynamics in the field that is rapidly moving away from traditional ERP to cloud-based software as a service (SAAS). Products and applications are evolving to a point in which the service provider takes care of the technology and the HR user is mostly concerned with the strategic use of the product as a whole rather than the processes in particular (see Chapter 7).

Considering the overall conceptual framework adopted in this book and the definitional expectations set by Bondarouk, Parry and Furtmueller (2017, p. 99) that 'it is important to acknowledge the significance of multiple elements that when integrated provide a direction for future e-HRM research, and help to understand the factors that influence its adoption and consequences', digital HRM can be defined as follows:

> *Digital HRM deals with the nature, role and contribution of technology in strategically managing talent in a digital world. It incorporates social, mobile, analytics, cloud (SMAC) and other emerging technologies for efficient and effective delivery of HR services. It covers related management trends in performing the operational, relational and transformational aspects of HR, such as the devolution of HR administration via self-service applications, shared services, and outsourcing as well as strategic aspects involving evidence based on big data, predictive analytics, artificial intelligence, and managerial insights. It is also conscious of and addresses unintended consequences of technology, including implications for information security and privacy.*

In this book, we use the terms e-HRM and digital HRM *interchangeably*. Some of the key aspects covered in the above definition are explained below.

HR activities covered by technology

Operational/transactional HR: All HR functions involve numerous and time-consuming 'administrative processes' that are routine and conducted on a day-to-day basis. Examples of operational HR activities include payroll, recordkeeping, updating policy and informational materials, generating and disseminating internal reports, complying with legislative reporting, benefits administration and administering labour contracts. In fact, 65 percent to 75 percent of HR activities can be classified as transactional (Wright et al., 1998). Because of their routine nature, they can be standardised and automated via electronic data processing (EDP) and in the process, save precious time of HR professionals. These activities can also be performed using self-service applications, shared services and outsourcing.

Relational HR: These activities include 'business processes' relating to HR functions, including HR planning, recruitment and selection, performance management, learning and development, and remuneration and reward management. These functions add value to an organisation only when they are strategically aligned to and fulfil business objectives. Through business process re-engineering (BPR) and management information systems (MIS), HR and IT can forge a strategic partnership to improve and enhance the efficiency and effectiveness of these functions.

Transformational HR: Being situated at the top end of strategic HRM (SHRM), these HR activities include strategic redirection and renewal, cultural change, learning organisation-driven knowledge management and leadership development. Through decision support systems (DSS) and executive information systems (EIS), HR can provide strategic support to top management to address what-if scenarios, using advanced big data mining, analytics and artificial intelligence.

Devolution of HR activities

Self-service applications: One of the implications of the computerisation of HR is the devolution or delegation of HR activities and processes to:

- Employees via self-services, such as accessing payslips, HR policies, leave balance and application, benefits administration, self-performance appraisal and self-nomination for training programmes.
- Managers via management information systems (MIS) such as performing recruitment and selection activities through the applicant tracking system (ATS), learning and development activities through the learning management system (LMS), performance management activities via an integrated talent management suite, compensation and benefits administration and other HR administration activities, including leave approval and accessing and submitting management reports.

Shared services centres (SSCs): The concept of shared services has been in practice since the mid-1980s with an aim to reduce costs, improve controls and enhancing customer service. According to Deloitte (2011, p. 4), 'an SSC operates as an internal customer service business. It typically charges the business units for services provided, and uses service level agreements as a contractual arrangement which specifies cost, time, and quality performance measures'. Transactional processes are the most predominant work performed by the SSCs, with finance, HR and IT being the most prolific users (Deloitte, 2017b, p. 8). While SSCs are a well-accepted model across the developed world, its implementation has been quite problematic and challenging as the optimistic proponents of the concept typically underestimate the costs and risks of customisation and implementation caused by behavioural factors, whereas the users fear loss of control (AIM, 2011, p. 2). Accordingly, experts recommend an 'integrated operating model which combines the benefits of central control, scale, and standardization with a flexible, service-centric approach' (PWC, 2010, p. viii).

HR outsourcing: Business process outsourcing has been one of the fastest growing trends in management, including in HR. Specialised third-party service providers are contracted to provide outsourcing services that are typically non-core to the organisation. The key drivers for outsourcing are access to greater expertise and process efficiencies, improvement in service quality and potential cost savings. The most outsourced HR activities are payroll, benefits administration, HR information technologies (HR-IT), expatriate relocation, staffing and training. The advantages and disadvantages of outsourcing and the best way to manage it are outlined in the debate section at the end of this chapter in the context of digital talent outsourcing. According to Reichel and Lazarova (2013), outsourcing non-core HR activities has a positive impact on HR's strategic position but outsourcing core HR has no impact. Similarly, a study by Glaister (2014) concluded that HR outsourcing stymies HR role transformation and that HR outsourcers experienced limited skill development and an increased focus on cost reduction at the expense of their strategic position.

Subsequent chapters in this book provide a detailed analysis of big data, analytics, cloud computing, social media and gamification in HR. You will also find a comprehensive account of the application of technology in different HR functions, followed by its strategic evaluation and implications for information security, privacy and future directions. Thus, the book incorporates, integrates and critically evaluates the key components of digital HRM as defined above. We now turn our attention to further understanding the present digital avatar of the HRM function.

Emergence of digital HRM

With the ever increasing innovation in and adoption of digital technologies and tools, digital HR is waking up to the possibility of creative design thinking in HR services. Table 1.2 lists some of the latest digital tools being adopted by leading companies in the HR space.

Table 1.2 Examples of digital tools in HR applications

Wade and Wendy	This chatbot service brings AI and chatbots to recruitment and career planning and helps candidates better understand career strategies and company culture
Mya	FirstJob's chatbot answers candidate questions during recruitment
Switch	This recruitment app gives Tinder-like experience for job search
Know Your Worth	This tool from Glassdoor provides compensation data for similar jobs by city, tenure, industry and company
Checkpoint	IBM's new performance management tool with new feedback process
CHIP	Powered by IBM Watson, CHIP (cognitive human interface personality) handles a wide range of HR-related queries
Embark	'Pre-boarding' application developed by Royal Bank of Canada
Brilliant U	An online learning platform by GE offering employee-driven learning opportunities where content is created and shared by employees
Recruiter Mobile	Dedicated app by LinkedIn for mobile recruitment
Gamified recruitment apps	– 'America's Army': a recruitment-oriented game developed by the US Army (see Chapter 9) – 'The Candidate': a recruitment campaign by Heineken (see Chapter 10)
Crowdsourcing	This is a cloud-based process of obtaining online information from a large set of people for completion of a particular project (see Chapter 7)
Virtual HRs	Enabled by 'Expert Cloud', V-HRs facilitate HR experts from around the world to collaborate to share knowledge, skills and expertise to quickly solve any business problem (see Chapter 7)
DataRobot	Automated machine-learning software program for HR data analysis (see Chapter 6)
Social Index	The company provides a digital footprint or online profiles for both candidates and recruiters (see Chapter 10)
MOOCs	Web-based Massive Open Online Courses through online learning platforms, such as Coursera and edX (see Chapter 13)
Experience API or Tin Can API	Learning technology that allows the tracking of e-learning activity (see Chapter 13)
SuccessFactors	Developed by SAP, it offers a complete, recruit-to-retire solution across all talent processes (see Chapter 10)

Source: The top 8 entries are adapted from Deloitte (2017a, p. 31, 90–91). The rest are drawn from different chapters in this book.

However, HR needs to go 'beyond digitizing HR platforms to developing digital workplaces and digital workforces, and to deploying technology that changes how people work and the way they relate to each other at work' (Deloitte, 2017a, p. 7). Thus, the focus of digital HR should be on

- a digital workforce (that is agile and innovation-minded);
- a digital workplace (an environment characterised by learning organisation mindset); and
- an inclusive culture (that is future-focused, global, culturally sensitive, ethical and sustainable).

HR is responding to these changing environmental demands. According to a 2017 Deloitte Global Human Capital Trends survey:

- Fifty-six percent of companies are redesigning their HR programs to leverage digital and mobile tools.
- Fifty-one percent of companies are currently in the process of redesigning their organisations for digital business models.
- Thirty-three percent of surveyed HR teams are using some form of artificial intelligence (AI) technology to deliver HR solutions, and 41 percent are actively building mobile apps to deliver HR services.

(Deloitte, 2017a, p. 87)

Technology-enabled HR roles

As explained before, for too long HR has been stuck in the industrial economy mentality and is yet to strategically align its role in the knowledge economy in a way that addresses the changing world of work and the needs and expectations of knowledge workers, both inside and outside organisational boundaries. Dave Ulrich's research on changing HR roles is highly regarded by HR scholars and practitioners for its breadth and depth. Let us briefly look at how he sees technology impacting the role of HRM.

Keeping in mind the strategic nature of HR in the new economy, Ulrich (1998) proposed four key roles of HR: strategic business partner, administrative expert, employee champion and change agent. Explaining the role of 'administrative expert', Ulrich (1998) emphasised that 'Within the HR function are dozens of processes that can be done better, faster, and cheaper. . . . Improving efficiency will build HR's credibility, which, in turn, will open the door for it to become a partner in executing strategy'. He gave the examples of shared services and centres of expertise to leverage technology. More recently, Ulrich et al. (2013) added the HR roles of 'Innovator & Integrator' (who builds integrated solutions with HR latest insights and practices that last in the long-run) and 'Technology proponent' (who differentiates between administrative and strategic work to improve efficiency and effectiveness).

In his latest work, Ulrich (2017, pp. 1–2) argues that:

> Digitisation is shaping HR through four *phases*: Phase 1 is performing HR practices more efficiently (e.g., insourcing HR service centers through automation); Phase 2 is the onslaught of HR innovations in all HR practice areas (people, performance, communication, work); Phase 3 is accessing and using information to deliver business results; and Phase 4 is forging connections among people . . . But the immediate

challenge of managing the tsunami of HR digitalization is to sort out which of these many new ideas HR should invest in.

He suggests five *criteria* for knowing which of these technology innovations deserve more attention (Ulrich, 2018):

- Focus outside-in (by connecting with external customers and investors)
- Build on previous practice and research (by relying on sound, time-tested principles and practices)
- Offer an integrated solution (that impacts and integrates many HR practice areas)
- Deliver on strategy and goals (by focusing on existing strategic agendas)
- Fit with values and culture (by not just buying a new app but forming a relationship with the creator of the app who will be a thought partner for future success)

See the Foreword by Dave Ulrich in this book where he explains further on his latest work on digital HR.

Technology-enabled HR functions

In line with digital trends, organisations need to overhaul the key HR functions, including recruitment and selection, performance and reward management, career management and learning and development. It is not just about re-skilling but creating a genuine transformational change to people management architecture and eco-systems, resulting in what Dehaze (2016, p. 39) calls '*Human Resources 4.0*'. In this new avatar, 'burdensome top-down HR processes are giving way to bottom-up digitally assisted systems to help people help themselves, shifting the onus for managing development from the company to the individual' (Evans and Rodriguez-Montemayor, 2016, p. 70).

Below is an illustrative, but not exhaustive account, of some of the radical changes that are needed in the HR function to succeed in the digital world.

Recruitment and selection. The fundamental role of HR is to find the right person for the right job at the right time. In the war for talent, every organisation aims for the best talent but what is best talent for one organisation need not be for another and as such, achieving the right *fit* between person, task, team and organisational culture is essential. This is where market intelligence, job analysis, competency mapping, cognitive tools and digital technologies, such as social media and analytics, play a crucial role in talent acquisition. To attract the best talent, the first step is to create a highly visible, compelling and enduring 'employer brand' using multi-media technologies across the intranet and internet. Third-party service providers, such as LinkedIn and job portals have become indispensable partners in spreading the recruitment net wide and far.

Gamification of recruitment tools is another innovation that is likely to appeal to millennials, the so-called digital natives. The next step is to design and develop a robust applicant tracking system (ATS) that creates well-defined and high quality business processes across the talent attraction spectrum. Leading high-technology firms, such as Google, have successfully harnessed the potential of analytics to design an optimum mix of talent acquisition and selection strategies. For example, Google did a 'study to find the optimal number of times a candidate should be interviewed' and after crunching the data settled on four rounds of interviews (Manjoo, 2013). Digital tools can dramatically reduce time and cost associated with talent acquisition and when strategically deployed, they can also improve the quality of hiring.

Performance and reward management. In recent times, companies are focusing more and more on providing continuous feedback rather than the traditional annual performance appraisal cycle, future-focused performance development over past-focused performance appraisal, improving if not abandoning the use of the forced distribution bell-curve and the bottom-up feedback process (Deloitte, 2017a, pp. 7, 67–68). Balanced score card and multi-source (360-degree) performance assessment tools are being used more often. Thus, new performance management methods are employee-centric and employee-driven. Some of the digital tools include mobile applications for teams to collaborate, set goals, update goals and track progress, productivity tools for continuous feedback and improvement, and big data tools for analytics. Analytics also help companies mine data to identify best suited performance metrics and measurement, especially for teams. However, digital technologies are yet to catch up with the renewed focus and change in direction of new performance management systems. It is still a work in progress. In this regard, an 'agile management approach' is being increasingly followed by leading organisations (see Chapter 4).

Learning and development. As outlined in the section on career management, today individuals are the chief executive officer (CEO) of their own career. They need to adopt a *self-leadership* approach and be pro-active in managing their own careers. Many leading companies, such as GE, have created learning platforms where employees themselves create and share content. However, it is the primary responsibility of organisations to show direction to their employees in terms of what skills and competencies are needed, valued and rewarded. Their role also includes role modelling, mentoring, coaching, providing on-the-job learning opportunities and facilitating workforce socialisation. New digital tools provide opportunities to companies to offer 'curated content, video and mobile learning solutions, micro-learning, and new ways to integrate and harness the exploding library of external MOOCs and video learning available on the Internet' (Deloitte, 2017a, p. 31) to create a state of the art learning management system (LMS). While digital technologies can be effective tools in this regard, they cannot substitute for the human touch essential in shaping employee careers.

Employee engagement. The motto of HCL Technologies, a premier information technology (IT) service provider from India is 'employee first, customer second'. While most organisations believe in customer-centric and shareholder-centric management, common sense and research evidence (e.g. Wright, Cropanzano and Bonett, 2007) dictate that happy employees make happy customers who in turn make happy investors. Therefore, there is a compelling logic to the argument that employees should be the primary focus of the organisation. Firms such as HCL aim for total employee engagement in order to harness employee potential and productivity. This can happen when there is optimal alignment between employee goals and organisational goals. Organisational culture plays a vital role in retaining talent. Trust, transparency, employee involvement and empowerment are some of the vital prerequisites for a happy, motivated, engaged and productive workforce.

Today, digital technologies, such as 'productivity and collaboration apps, engagement and feedback apps, performance management apps, well-being apps and employee service platforms', provide immense opportunities to engage employees and enhance the employee experience (Deloitte, 2017a, p. 56). HR can 'feel the pulse' of the workforce through digitised feedback tools, such as employee satisfaction and engagement surveys. Now people can work anywhere, anytime and make use of flexi-work options. Collaboration tools help better connect people across functional and geographic boundaries and thus, enhance workplace socialisation. Integrated employee self-service tools, such as performing administrative tasks, self-enrolment in training programmes and cafeteria employee benefits menu selection can streamline transactional tasks, provide more flexibility through self-selection and offer routine HR services faster, cheaper and better. Employee wellness and fitness apps can promote healthy living. Automated social recognition programmes (such as employee of the month programmes) promote non-financial rewards. Realising the importance of user involvement in HR design thinking, leading companies regularly conduct 'hackathons', inviting employee suggestions to offer programmes that best meet their needs and expectations.

Unintended consequences of technology

As can be seen below, the impact of technology has not been all positive.

- The digital world is dominated by two regions in the world, namely, the US West Coast and the East Coast of China, leading to a digital divide and 'tremendous spillover effects on wealth, value and power' (Candelon, Reeves and Wu, 2017, p. 2).
- The introduction of new technology has not really resulted in a noticeable increase in business productivity (Deloitte, 2017a, p. 3).
- 'Information overload and the always-connected 24/7 work environment are overwhelming workers, undermining productivity, and contributing to low employee engagement' (Schwartz et al., 2014, p. 1).
- 'Ever-increasing gap between technological sophistication and the amount of work actually performed (is resulting in) income inequality, wage stagnation, and social and political unrest around the world' (Deloitte, 2017a, p. 3).
- While technology is increasing at an exponential rate, human adaptability rises only at a slower, linear rate (Friedman, 2016) and this discrepancy is going to overpower people and fundamentally disrupt the world as we know it.
- According to Colbert, Yee and George (2016, p. 733), in a 24/7 digital world, we may not 'find the opportunity for reflection that increases our self-awareness' and in curating our social media profile, we may tend to aim for 'an aspirational image rather than presenting an authentic self'. They further argue that these developments affect inter-personal relationships leading to 'declining levels of empathy' and blur the lines between work and non-work domains (p. 734).
- Employees who spend a lot of time writing and answering emails tend to experience higher levels of work overload (Barley, Meyerson and Grodal, 2011).

HR needs to be conscious of and proactively address these negative consequences. You will find some proposed solutions to address these in the rest of the book.

Preview of what is ahead

The book is structured around four parts, namely, e-HRM approaches, directions, applications, and problems and prospects.

Part I: Key approaches to e-HRM

- *Chapter 2 (Strategic management approach to technology-enabled HRM)* highlights how an increasing number of organisations are recognising the importance of taking a strategic

approach to managing HR. It argues that organisations that manage human resources by smartly leveraging technology can create an advantage that is difficult for competitors to imitate.
- *Chapter 3 (Soft systems thinking approach to e-HRM project management)* highlights that the majority of IT projects fail to finish on time, within budget and satisfy users, primarily due to a lack of systems perspective and soft skills. It underscores the critical importance of systems thinking approach, systems development life cycle and quality management framework underpinned by a people capability maturity model.
- *Chapter 4 (Agile approach to e-HRM project management)* argues that in an uncertain business environment, agility is the key. This chapter introduces the philosophy and principles underpinning the agile way of working and specifically highlights the critical role played by HR that befits the overarching agile philosophy.

Part II: Key directions in e-HRM

- *Chapter 5 (Big data and e-HRM)* provides a critical perspective of big data, including the need for big data literacy. It introduces the tools to build knowledge from big data to lay the ground for a sense-making intersubjective communication of big data-based cognition, and to find an ethically sound approach to the use of big data in business.
- *Chapter 6 (HR metrics and analytics)* critically examines HR analytics as a way of helping encourage evidence-based decisions. It gives an overview of different analytics tools that can be used and then raises some challenges for the HR function that a focus on HR analytics may bring.
- *Chapter 7 (Cloud computing and e-HRM)* provides an in-depth understanding of cloud technology in the form of various cloud-features along with different cloud deployment models. It explains how cloud technology can increase the efficiency and effectiveness of various HR functions and provides a critical review of its advantages and limitations.
- *Chapter 8 (Social media and e-HRM)* outlines differences between personal and professional social media platforms, identifies challenges associated with the rapidly changing nature of social media and describes social media user patterns. It also identifies legal and ethical considerations of using social media in HR.
- *Chapter 9 (Gamification and e-HRM)* introduces the concept of gamification, explores the operational and strategic perspectives on gamification and highlights the implications of gamification for HRM in general.

Part III: e-HRM applications

- *Chapter 10 (e-Talent in talent management)* focuses on specific talent management practices – talent *acquisition*, talent identification, talent development and talent retention – to highlight the benefits and limitations associated with appropriating technology in strategic talent management.
- *Chapter 11 (e-Recruitment and selection)* presents an overview of e-recruitment and selection practices and discusses the use of technology throughout the hiring process.
- *Chapter 12 (e-Performance and reward management)* explores the nature and role of technology in automating *performance* and reward functions. It considers the critical

adoption factors, in terms of people, technology and organisation and highlights the critical success factors.
- *Chapter 13 (e-Learning and development)* addresses technology issues relating to and the advantages and disadvantages of *important* e-learning methods. Factors that impact the successful implementation of e-L&D systems in organisations are also discussed.

Part IV: Problems and prospects

- *Chapter 14 (Strategic evaluation of e-HRM)* shows that not only do many firms fail in *capitalising* on the advantages of e-HRM, in some cases, e-HRM may also lead to negative and unintended outcomes. It outlines ways in which the strategic value of e-HRM can be assessed.
- *Chapter 15 (Information security and privacy in e-HRM)* provides an overview of the basics of *information* security and privacy concepts and frameworks. It highlights the major roles HR can play in designing, applying and monitoring appropriate controls throughout the employment cycle.
- *Chapter 16 (Future directions in electronic/digital HRM)* draws the book to a logical *conclusion* by looking back and looking forward in terms of the evolution of the HR function. It examines the latest empirical trends in HR technology and presents a strategic framework of digital HR strategy.

Summary

Despite the claims made by HR technology vendors, the evidence so far suggests that the adoption of technology in HRM has not really led to strategic outcomes (Marler and Fisher, 2013). While technology has certainly been able to increase the efficiencies of most transactional and some relational HR activities in terms of cost reduction and speed, organisations today are more concerned about effectiveness of these activities in terms of strategic outcomes. Further, as further explained in the next chapter, strategic HRM is primarily most focused on transformational HR activities, such as culture change and leadership development, and here, technology has somewhat fallen short of expectations (Thite, 2013; Bondarouk, Parry and Furtmueller, 2017).

But as we will see in Chapter 3, technology is not the primary determinant of technical project management success. Instead, success is dependent upon organisational and social factors and actors, such as systems thinking, agility, user involvement and acceptance, managerial competency, communication, governance and stakeholder collaboration. Technology is only a tool and cannot fix broken processes and substitute managerial competence.

Today, disruptive digital technologies dominate the landscape and have already radically altered the way we work. It is too early to evaluate their effectiveness. The shape of the twenty-first century technology-intensive knowledge economy is still unclear. With lack of clarity on what is digital, what to do and how to do digital, 'most companies are still in a "digital fog" (and) most approaches are still in an exploratory phase' (Andersson, Lanvin & Van der Heyden, 2016, p. 56). With the digital world taking over the business and millennials who are born digital natives set to take over the workplace, time will tell whether going digital is a boon or a bane.

Case study: The workforce of the future – Employers' evolving relationship with workers

A chief human resources officer (CHRO) arrives at the office in a shiny town car, dropped off by a very polite Uber driver. The CHRO has returned from visiting corporate offices in three other countries where some work had been sent and where new business was developing. During the drive from the airport, the driver shared with the CHRO that he's an Uber driver when he's not working as an independent contractor in technology for multiple companies.

The driver explained that he'd learned that there was a lot of project work available – he just uses his phone to log into the available virtual talent marketplaces to bid on jobs that interest him and that meet his pay, location and schedule needs. He'd even done some work for the CHRO's company, and recently won a competition created by a software company to get the public to help it solve a tricky coding problem. While he didn't have health or other benefits, he proudly told the CHRO that he was making more money now than he had before being laid off in 2008 during the recession.

As the CHRO passes through the office lobby, she notes that the security officer is not actually an employee of the company, although he's wearing the company logo, and that the custodian going by with a cleaning cart has another company logo on her shirt. The CHRO is met upstairs by one of two administrative assistants; her assistants job share, with each working part-time, with a few hours of overlap for coordination of tasks. She sees that the hoteling office space is full; it's a seasonal business, and this is the season where extra employees are brought on board to help manage the workload. Now that many people are working from home, there is space available in the building.

As she sits in her office, the CHRO reflected on what she had just seen over the past 30 minutes. Traditional long-term, full-time, paid employment is being supplanted by other, newer, more flexible options. Everyone was now talking about the 'gig' economy. Companies didn't just have employees – they had people performing work in a variety of arrangements. These include part-time employment, temporary employment, independent contracting, franchisor-franchisee co-employment and customers performing work that was formerly performed by employees.

The CHRO knows some of the factors that are driving this development: global economic competition, de-regulation, rapid technological change, entrepreneurship and demographic changes. But she realised that she wanted to know more.

She has come to you, her newest addition to the HR team, and asked you to prepare a white paper answering one of the following questions.

Case study questions

- What are the implications of this 'gig' economy for current and future regulation of the 'employment' relationships, including such aspects as what constitutes an 'employee', discrimination, wages and hours, labour relations and health/safety?

- Considering all of the changes to the traditional long-term, full-time and paid employment relationship, what should be the role of the CHRO in leading and advising other senior executives and the board of directors? What should she be doing?

Source: National Academy of Human Resources. Ram Charan HR Essay Contest, 2016. Reproduced with permission.
Note: The winning essays of this competition can be accessed at www.nationalacademyhr.org/node/57

Debate: Digital HRM: Nirvana or nemesis?

Introduction

In the 'brave new world' of digital HRM, technology is often offered as a panacea to address all the issues and challenges associated with managing people. In order to do more with less and egged on by tall promises made by technology vendors, firms tend to invest heavily in social, mobile, analytics, and cloud (SMAC) technologies, often at the cost of human assets by taking a 'hard approach' to talent management. We need to critically examine whether technology is truly a transformational enabler for HR service delivery and, if so, how do we explain and address unintended consequences of technology implementation?

Arguments for digital HRM as nirvana

- When structurally and strategically aligned, technology can not only improve the efficiency of transactional and operational HR functions but also act as a catalyst to achieve transformational outcomes, such as change management.
- Everything and everybody are 'datafied'. Big data already transforms organizations and will have an impact on HRM by making it more objective and more precise than what it is currently.
- Data-driven HR metrics analytics help evidence based decision-making and can improve HR's credibility and influence with stakeholders.
- Digitisation provides tremendous opportunity to HR to revolutionize the entire 'employee experience' by transforming HR processes, systems and the function itself.

Arguments for digital HRM as nemesis

- Over reliance on technology in HRM may lead to unintended consequences, such as lack of human touch, digital divide, and short-term solutions turning into long-term problems.
- HR service delivery becomes more impersonal where employees and customers are often forced to rely on self- and shared service options. While this may

> lead to more efficient services in the short term, the 'effectiveness' of HR may get diluted from systems and long-term perspectives.
> - Big data are subjective and highly contextualized. Big data will not lead automatically to a new dawn of empiricism or rationalism. The aura of objectivity and the trust in numbers could lead to an often misguided data-driven HRM.
> - Increasing use of social media pose serious challenges, including the potential for discrimination and privacy concerns.
> - Robotics and artificial intelligence (AI) may lead to jobless growth and wage freeze.

Video learning resources

- What is 'digital'? www.youtube.com/watch?v=xsWbECkVqgI
- 2017 Global human capital trends: Rewriting the rules | Deloitte Insights: www.youtube.com/watch?v=dvTGfw4wWoE
- Digital HR: Using digital tools to unlock HR's true potential: www.youtube.com/watch?v=RyZRtolpmmw
- Digital transformation of HR: www.youtube.com/watch?v=2qkTjWJ2C-Y

Acknowledgements

The author gratefully acknowledges Professors Mark Lengnick-Hall and Cynthia Lengnick-Hall for their feedback on and suggestions for improvement of this chapter.

References

Australian Institute of Management (AIM). (2011). *Shared services in the public sector: A triumph of hope over experience?* Green Paper, September 2011, Australian Institute of Management, North Sydney.

Andersson, L., Lanvin, B. & Van der Heyden, L. (2016). Digitalisation initiatives and corporate strategies: A few implications for talent. In B. Lanvin & P. Evans (Eds.) *The global competitiveness index 2017: Talent and technology*. Fontainebleau: INSEAD, pp. 51–57.

Barley, S. R., Meyerson, D. E. & Grodal, S. (2011). Email as a source and symbol of stress. *Organisation Science*, 22: 887–906.

Bondarouk, T., Parry, E. & Furtmueller, E. (2017). Electronic HRM: Four decades of research on adoption and consequences. *International Journal of Human Resource Management*, 28(1): 98–131.

Brent, A., Snow, C. & Miles, R. (1996) Characteristics of managerial careers of the 21st century. *The Academy of Management Executive*, 10(4): 17–27.

Candelon, F., Reeves, M. & Wu, D. (2017). *The new digital world: Hegemony or harmony?* Boston Consulting Group. 14 November 2017. [Online] www.bcg.com/en-au/publications/2017/strategy-globalization-new-digital-world-hegemony-harmony.aspx (Accessed 24 January 2018).

Cianni, M. & Wnuck, D. (1997) Individual growth and team enhancement: Moving toward a new model of career development. *The Academy of Management Executive*, 11(1): 105–115.

Colbert, A., Yee, N. & George, G. (2016). The digital workforce and the workplace of the future. *Academy of Management Journal*, 59(3): 731–739.

Craig, E., Thomas, R. J., Hou, C. & Mathur, S. (2012). *Where will all the STEM talent come from? Research Report*. Accenture Institute for High Performance, May 2012.

Dehaze, A. (2016). The skills imperative: Shaping the future of work through talent and technology. In B. Lanvin & P. Evans (Eds.) *The global competitiveness index 2017: Talent and technology*. Fontainebleau: INSEAD, pp. 35–41.

Deloitte (2011). *Shared services handbook: Hit the road*. [Online] www2.deloitte.com/content/dam/Deloitte/dk/Documents/finance/SSC-Handbook-%20Hit-the-Road.pdf (Accessed 25 January 2018).

Deloitte (2017a). *Rewriting the rules for the digital age: 2017 Deloitte Global Human Capital Trends*. [Online] www2.deloitte.com/content/dam/Deloitte/us/Documents/human-capital/hc-2017-global-human-capital-trends-us.pdf (Accessed 19 March 2018).

Deloitte (2017b). *Global shared services. 2017 survey report*. [Online] file:///C:/Users/s254357/Downloads/us-global-shared-services-report.pdf (Accessed 25 January 2018).

Evans, P. & Rodriguez-Montemayor, E. (2016). Are we prepared for the talent overhaul induced by technology? A GTCI research commentary. In B. Lanvin & P. Evans (Eds.) *The global competitiveness index 2017: Talent and technology*. Fontainebleau: INSEAD, pp. 67–83.

Friedman, T. (2016). *Thank you for being Late: An Optimist's Guide to Thriving in the Age of Accelerations*. New York, NY: Farrar, Straus & Gioux.

Glaister, A. J. (2014). HR outsourcing: the impact on HR role, competency development and relationships, *Human Resource Management Journal*, 24(2): 211–226.

Gollub, U. (2016). *How the future will look like*. [Online] www.linkedin.com/pulse/how-future-look-like-udo-gollub/ (Accessed 28 January 2018).

Gratton, L. (2011). Workplace 2025 – What will it look like? *Organizational Dynamics*, 40: 246–254.

Gunz, H. P., Jalland, R. M. & Evans, M. G. (1998). New strategy, wrong managers? What you need to know about career streams. *The Academy of Management Executive*, 12(2): 21–37.

Hall, D. T. (1996) Protean careers of the 21st century. *The Academy of Management Executive*, 10(4): 8–16.

Handy, C. 1996. *Beyond Certainty*. Boston: Harvard Business School Press.

Hendrickson, A. R. (2003). Human resource information systems: Backbone technology of contemporary human resources. *Journal of Labor Research*, 24(3): 381–394.

Lanvin, B., Evans, P. & Rodriguez-Montemayor, E. (2016). Shifting gears: How to combine technology and talent to shape the future of work. In B. Lanvin & P. Evans (Eds.) *The global competitiveness index 2017: Talent and technology*. Fontainebleau: INSEAD, pp. 3–41.

Manjoo, F. (2013). *The happiness machine: How Google became such a great place to work*. [Online] www.slate.com/articles/technology/technology/2013/01/google_people_operations_the_secrets_of_the_world_s_most_scientific_human.html#! (Accessed 24 January 2018).

Marler, J. H. & Parry, E. (2015). Human resource management, strategic involvement and e-HRM technology. *The International Journal of Human Resource Management*, 27(19), 2233–2253.

Marler, J. & Fisher, S. (2013). An evidence-based review of e-HRM and strategic human resource management. *Human Resource Management Review*, 23: 18–36.

National Institute of Economic and Industry Research (Australia) & Australian Services Union & Finance Sector Union of Australia. (NIEIR). (2012). *Off-shore and Off work the Future of Australia's Service Industries in a Global Economy: An Update*. Clifton Hill, Victoria: National Institute of Economic and Industry Research.

Nieto-Rodriguez, A. (2014). *Organisational ambidexterity*. [Online]. www.london.edu/faculty-and-research/lbsr/organisational-ambidexterity#.WmPaKK6WaHs (Accessed 21 January 2018).

OECD. (2015). *OECD Skills Outlook 2015: Youth, skills & employability*. Paris: OECD Publishing. [Online] www.mecd.gob.es/dctm/inee/internacional/1-skillsoutlook2015.pdf?documentId=0901e72b81d77c93 (Accessed 24 January 2018).

Price Waterhouse Coopers (PWC). (2015). *A smart move: Future-proofing Australia's workforce*. [Online] www.pwc.com.au/pdf/a-smart-move-pwc-stem-report-april-2015.pdf (Accessed 24 January 2018).

PricewaterhouseCoopers (PWC). (2010). *Review of the shared services model for Queensland government*. Brisbane: Price water house Coopers, September 2010. [Online] www.hpw.qld.gov.au/SiteCollectionDocuments/SharedServicesReviewSep2010.pdf (Accessed 25 June 2018).

Reichel, A. & Lazarova, M. (2013). The effects of outsourcing and devolvement on the strategic position of HR departments. *Human Resource Management*, 52(6): 923–946.

Schwartz, J., Berkel, A., Hodson, T. & Otten, I. W. (2014). *The overwhelmed employee: Simplify the work environment*. New York, NY: Deloitte University Press, 7 March 2014. [Online] https://dupress.deloitte.com/dup-us-en/focus/human-capital-trends/2014/hc-trends-2014-overwhelmed-employee.html?id=gx:el:dc:dup682:cons:awa:hct14 (Accessed 19 January 2018).

Senge, P. M. (1990). *The fifth discipline*. London: Random House.

SHRM. (2015). *Designing and managing a human resource information system*. [Online] www.shrm.org/resourcesandtools/tools-and-samples/toolkits/pages/managingahumanresourceinformationsystem.aspx (Accessed 24 January 2018).

Stephen, M. (2016). Digital HR: Revolution, not evolution. In *Global human capital trends 2016. The new organization: Different by design*. New York, NY: Deloitte University Press. [online] www2.deloitte.com/content/dam/Deloitte/global/Documents/HumanCapital/gx-dup-global-human-capital-trends-2016.pdf (Accessed 19 January 2018).

Templer, A. J. & Cawsey, T. F. 1999. Rethinking career development in an era of portfolio careers. *Career Development International*, 4(2), 70–76.

Thite, M. R. (2000) *Career management in the new economy: Surfing the turbulent waves of change*. Proceedings of the 2nd Annual Conference of the International Association of Insight and Action. Brisbane: School of Management, Griffith University.

Thite, M. (2001). Help us but help yourself: The paradox of contemporary career management. *Career Development International*, 6(6): 312–317.

Thite, M. (2004). *Managing People in the New Economy*. New Delhi: Sage.

Thite, M. (2013). Problems and prospects of technology as an enabler of strategic HRM. *Journal of Human Resources Education*, 7(3/4): 22–30.

Thite, M., Kavanagh, M. & Johnson, R. D. (2012). Evolution of human resource management and human resource information systems. In M.J. Kavanagh, M. Thite & R.D. Johnson (Eds.) *Human resource information Systems: Basics, applications and future directions*. Thousand Oaks, CA: Sage, pp. 2–34.

Thomas, R. J., Kass, A. & Davarzani, L. (2013). *How digital technologies are changing the way we work*. Accenture. Outlook, No. 3. [Online] www.accenture.com/t00010101T000000Z__w__/au-en/_acnmedia/Accenture/Conversion-Assets/Outlook/Documents/1/Accenture-Outlook-How-Digital-Technologies-Are-Changing-The-Way-We-Work.ashx#zoom=50 (Accessed 28 January 2018).

Ulrich, D. (1998). A new mandate for Human Resources. *Harvard Business Review*, 76(1): 124–135.

Ulrich, D. (2017). *Do an HR technology audit to get the most out of digital HR*. [Online] www.linkedin.com/pulse/do-hr-technology-audit-get-most-digital-dave-ulrich/ (Accessed 25 January 2018).

Ulrich, D. (2018). *5 Things that will help you sort through endless HR technologies*. Melbourne: Australian HR Institute. [Online] www.hrmonline.com.au/section/featured/5-help-sort-endless-hr-technologies/ (Accessed 26 January 2018).

Ulrich, D., Younger, J., Brockbank, W. & Ulrich, M. D. (2013). The state of the HR profession. *Human Resource Management*, 52(3): 457–471.

Whymark, K. & Ellis, S. 1999. Whose career is it anyway? Options for career management in flatter organization structures. *Career Development International*, 4(2), 117–120.

WITSA. (2016). *The global skills gap and the changing nature of work and their impact on the digital age*. World Information Technology and Services Alliance, December, 2016.

Wright, T. A., Cropanzano, R. & Bonett, D. G. (2007). The moderating role of employee well being on the relationship between job satisfaction and job performance. *Journal of Occupational Health Psychology*. 12(2): 93–104.

Wright, P., McMahan, G., Snell, S. & Gerhart, B. (1998). *Strategic human resource management: Building human capital & organisational capacity*. Technical report. Itacha, NY: Cornell University.

Part I
Key approaches to e-HRM

2 Strategic management approach to technology-enabled HRM

Mark L. Lengnick-Hall, Cynthia A. Lengnick-Hall & Derrick McIver

> **Learning objectives**
> - Explain the concept of strategic human resource management and its importance to organizations.
> - Provide an overview of major theory lenses that underpin strategic human resource management.
> - Describe major trends in organizations, organizational work, and the role of human resources.
> - Understand the most significant threats and opportunities emerging technology creates for human resource management policies and practices.
> - Explain how e-HRM is influencing organizations.

Introduction

After a wildly successful run on Broadway, the producers of the musical "Hamilton" are expanding their productions to also include Chicago and Los Angeles in addition to New York (marketplace.org, 2017). They are currently conducting rehearsals for a London show. There are expectations that they will continue to expand and offer shows throughout the world. The show's business strategy is simple: continue to expand show locations, provide customers with a consistently great experience, and provide high financial returns to owners and investors. But, as with many business organizations experiencing rapid growth, they are confronting human resource management issues that must be managed strategically.

From a strategic human resource management perspective, staffing and training requirements for a single show in a single location are challenging enough. Now consider the challenges when the production opens up new locations around the world. Much like running a multinational business, the production of "Hamilton" faces the challenge of maintaining multiple shows each with their own casts. But what happens when one location has a key cast member out, and no backup locally? The producers need to manage their human resources in a way that supports the business strategy, maintains high quality productions, and enhances the well-being of their employees. Human resource practices have to be carefully crafted to create the organizational capability for them to deliver great shows one day after another. This is the essence of strategic human resource management.

In this chapter, we provide an overview of human resource management from a strategic perspective. We begin with a review of the concepts, theories, and research that forms the basis for managing human resources strategically. Next, we describe the changing technological environment, which poses both threats and opportunities for the management of human resources. Finally, we examine the role of e-HRM in this context.

Strategic human resource management

In this section, we first define strategic human resource management and distinguish it from traditional human resource management. Second, we identify the five different levels of strategic human resource management. Third, we explain the role of fit and flexibility in strategic human resource management. Fourth, we discuss how strategic human resource management is different in a global context. Fifth, we describe the three major theories that provide an underpinning for strategic human resource management. And sixth, we summarize the past and future of strategic human resource management research.

Strategic vs. traditional human resource management

Strategic human resource management has been defined as "the pattern of planned human resource deployments and activities intended to enable an organization to achieve its goals" (Wright & McMahan, 1992, p. 298). Two factors distinguish strategic human resource management from traditional HRM. One, human resource practices are specifically aligned with the organization's business strategy, and two, human resource practices are considered in concert with one another rather than as isolated activities.

As Wright and McMahan (1992, pp. 298–299) put it, strategic human resource management focuses on "the determinants of decisions about human resource practices, the composition of the human capital resource pool (skills and abilities), the specification of required human resource behaviors, and the effectiveness of these decisions given various business strategies and/or competitive situations." The focus is typically on creating strategic capabilities that can lead to competitive advantage because they are valuable, rare, inimitable, non-substitutable, and able to be exploited by the firm (Barney, 1995).

Corporate vs. business unit strategies

The strategy in strategic human resource management has different meanings depending upon the perspective taken. A large multi-unit organization may have both a corporate strategy and business unit strategies that it is pursuing. Corporate strategy generally refers to how an organization as a whole creates value across its different businesses (see Table 2.1).

A business unit strategy refers to how a particular business unit creates value within the context of the overall corporation. Strategic HR decisions at the business unit level involve such issues as which policies, programs, and practices best support and reinforce the organization's intended objectives, increase revenues and reduce costs, and create a sustainable competitive advantage.

Strategic human resource management levels

Strategic human resource management occurs at many levels in an organization (see Table 2.2).

Arthur and Boyles (2007) identify five levels of a strategic human resource management system: HR philosophy, HR policies, HR programs, HR practices, and HR climate. The

Table 2.1 Corporate vs. business unit strategies—strategic HRM issues

Level of strategy	Definition	Strategic HRM issues
Corporate strategy	How an organization as a whole creates value across its different businesses; this may involve such decisions as mergers and acquisitions of either related or unrelated businesses, the overall product and market scope of the organization, the organizational identity, and the basic value proposition for the firm	How much should HR policies, programs, and practices be the same across business units versus how much should each business unit be able to adapt HR policies, programs, and practices to its own unique conditions? What HR policies, programs, and practices are most crucial for value creation?
Business unit strategy	How a particular business unit creates value within the context of the overall corporation; this generally involves identifying specific sources of competitive advantage and understanding how each unit contributes to and complements the overall portfolio	Which HR policies, programs, and practices best support and reinforce the organization's intended objectives, increase revenues and reduce costs, and create a sustainable competitive advantage? How do employees contribute to organizational success and competitiveness?

Source: Authors.

Table 2.2 Strategic human resource management levels

Strategic human resource management level	Definition	Example
HR philosophy	Provides the overarching guidelines for how human resources will be managed within the organization	From Richardson & Company, LLP: "To create a friendly, dynamic work environment under a team concept while maintaining professionalism." "Provide an enjoyable and rewarding environment for all individuals to learn, grow and develop to their fullest potential."
HR policies	Organizational goals or objectives for managing human resources	Starbucks Base Pay Policy: "Determined by the competitive market pay rate for your job, your skills, experience and job performance."
HR programs	The set of formal HR activities used in the organization	From Zappos: "The Zappos Family New Hire program is four weeks of training designed to grow our culture, build a stronger team, and create lasting relationships throughout the entire company."
HR practices	The implementation and experience of an organization's HR programs by lower-level managers and employees	From an employee's Glassdoor Review: "The hours were long and maintaining a work-life balance became extremely difficult. It frequently felt like there was more to do than could possibly be done and it was all critical work."
HR climate	The shared employee perceptions and interpretations of the meaning of the HR principles, policies, programs, and practices in the firm	From an employee's Glassdoor Review: "ReveNew treats you well, looks out for each other and encourages each employee to take ownership of their success and rewards that success."

Source: Authors.

HR philosophy or principles provides the overarching guidelines for how human resources will be managed within the organization. It is defined as the stated values, beliefs, and norms regarding what drives employee performance and how organizational resources and rewards should be allocated. **HR policies** refer to organizational goals or objectives for managing human resources. This level reflects the relative emphasis among different HR functional areas such as staffing, training, rewards, and so on. **HR programs** are the set of formal HR activities used in the organization. This level is typically described as bundles of internally consistent HR initiatives and actions, such as those that comprise high performance work systems. **HR practices** are defined as the implementation and experience of an organization's HR programs by lower-level managers and employees. This definition captures the variation in employees' perceptions and experiences of a HR program based on the quality of the HR implementation. Merely having a HR program does not mean that employees are aware of it, use it, or are encouraged or discouraged from using it by managers. And lastly, **HR climate** is defined as the shared employee perceptions and interpretations of the meaning of the HR principles, policies, programs, and practices in the firm.

Fit vs. flexibility

Strategic human resource management focuses on fit and on flexibility (see Table 2.3). An underlying principle in strategic human resource management is that organizations should

Table 2.3 Key strategic HRM concepts

Concept	Definition	Example
External/ vertical fit	Organizations should strive for alignment or fit between their human resource practices and their competitive business strategy.	If an organization is pursuing a business strategy of cost leadership, it should emphasize human resource practices that focus employees on cost reduction, such as performance appraisals that assess efforts to reduce costs and create efficient operations with minimal errors.
Internal/ horizontal fit	The fit or alignment among the various human resource practices in a particular organization; whether messages (explicit or implied) sent by various HR practices are consistent.	If an organization emphasizes team performance, the reward system should not focus on individual contributions.
Resource flexibility	The breadth of different uses for employees' skills, employees' behaviors, and HR practices and the range of different outcomes that can be accomplished with a particular knowledge or skill set.	US Navy SEALs each have multiple qualifications such as Special Demolitions, Breeching, Loadmaster, Parachute Rigger, and Hazardous Cargo Certifier that can be used to achieve a variety of outcomes.
Coordination flexibility	The ability to quickly change and reconfigure employees' skills, employees' behaviors, and HR practices and to deploy and redeploy combinations of employee skill sets with agility.	IBM uses "agile" teams—self-managed, multi-disciplinary teams working together in physical spaces, armed with data and analytics and continually generating and refining ideas based on real-time feedback so they can quickly adapt to changing conditions and requirements.

Source: Authors.

strive for alignment or fit between their human resource practices and their business strategy. This is sometimes referred to as *external fit* or *vertical fit*. The underlying logic is that if an organization is pursuing a business strategy of cost leadership for example (in which it seeks to have the lowest cost of operations in its industry), then it makes sense to emphasize human resource practices that focus employees on cost reduction, such as performance appraisals that assess efforts to reduce costs and create efficient operations and rewards for actually doing so. Surprisingly, research has failed to provide overwhelming evidence for this proposition, although it may be a result of how past research has been conducted (Wright & Ulrich, 2017).

Equally important to external or vertical fit is *internal fit* or *horizontal fit*, which refers to the fit or alignment among the various human resource practices in a particular organization. Here the fit refers to whether messages (explicit or implied) sent by various HR practices are consistent. For example, if an organization emphasizes team performance, the reward system should not focus on individual contributions. Becker et al. (1997) refer to this distinction as "powerful connections" when HR practices are consistent and reinforcing and "deadly combinations" when they are inconsistent and send mixed messages. Research has been supportive of this notion of fit, but it does not apply in all situations.

Sometimes organizations need to focus more on flexibility and less on fit. This idea was first proposed by Lengnick-Hall and Lengnick-Hall (1988) and later elaborated by Wright and Snell (1998). **Flexibility** refers to an organization's ability to reconfigure resources quickly to meet new strategic challenges. This is particularly important for firms that operate in turbulent or unpredictable environments and markets. There are two types of flexibility: resource flexibility and coordination flexibility. **Resource flexibility** refers to the breath of different uses for employees' skills, employees' behaviors, and HR practices. **Coordination flexibility** refers to the ability to quickly change and reconfigure employees' skills, employees' behaviors, and HR practices. There is considerable research support for the benefits of human resource flexibility in dynamic environments.

Strategic international human resource management

Strategic human resource management becomes more complicated when conducted across national borders and by global organizations. Schuler, Dowling, and De Cieri (1993) provide a framework for viewing strategic international human resource management (SIHRM) that focuses on the **interunit linkages** (connections between subsidiaries of a parent organization that operate in different countries and contexts) and **internal operations** (focused primarily on how local units operate, independent of other sub-units). One of the greatest challenges of SIHRM is balancing the need to integrate operations across different countries to achieve organizational consistency while at the same time adapting appropriately to local conditions.

Taylor, Beechler, and Napier (1996) proposed that multinational organizations have a **SIHRM orientation** that takes one of three different forms: (1) *adaptive*: primarily adapting to local conditions without emphasizing integrating HR policies and practices across units in different countries; (2) *exportive*: primarily imposing corporate-level HR policies and practices on all international units, thereby de-emphasizing local adaptation; or (3) *integrative*: a combination of both adaptive and exportive in which best practices emerge from any of the international units and are adopted across all units.

Transferring knowledge effectively across units in a multinational organization is one means of gaining a competitive advantage; for example, the use of expatriates who are able to transfer knowledge developed in one unit to units in another country can have a positive effect on subunit performance (Wang et al., 2009). Minbaeva et al. (2003) have also shown that SIHRM policies can increase a subunit's *absorptive capacities* (a firm's ability to recognize the value of new information, assimilate it, and apply it to commercial ends; Cohen & Levinthal, 1990) by enhancing employees' motivation and ability to learn and share knowledge (Minbaeva et al., 2003).

Theoretical foundations of strategic human resource management

Three major theories have dominated the field of strategic human resource management: the resource-based view (RBV), human capital theory, and social exchange theory (SET) (Wright & Ulrich, 2017). The **resource-based view** is a strategic management theory that has been used to explain how human resources can be a source of competitive advantage. According to RBV, *competitive advantage* is superior performance relative to other competitors in the same industry or superior performance relative to the industry average (Barney, 1995). As implied by its name, RBV focuses on characteristics of resources that provide firms with a source of competitive advantage. Resources that are valuable, rare, difficult to imitate, and non-substitutable (VRIN) provide a source of sustained competitive advantage. In an influential article, Barney and Wright (1998) argued that human resources could lead to sustained competitive advantage if they were valuable, rare, difficult to imitate, and organizations had the systems and practices that allow the talents and capabilities that employees provide to create products and services that customers consider to be valuable (VRIO).

Sustainable competitive advantage stems from (1) *firm-specific skills* (those that provide value only to a particular firm, and are of no value to competing firms) more than general skills (those that provide value to a firm and are transferable across a variety of firms); (2) *teams* more than individuals (because how teams operate is causally ambiguous and often firm-specific, thus, making it difficult for competitors to imitate); and (3) **HR systems** more than single HR practices (because the interrelatedness of the HR system components make the advantage difficult, if not impossible for competitors to identify and copy).

Human capital theory was first proposed by Becker (1964) and as applied in strategic human resource management, focused on the general skills versus firm-specific skills distinction described previously. There is ongoing debate regarding whether general skills or firm-specific skills enable a firm to capture economic rents (the extra amount earned by a resource by virtue of its present use) more easily and consistently. Lepak and Snell (1999) provided a taxonomy of different labor pools within a firm that required different types of human resource management systems. Two factors were used to describe the different labor pools: the *value* of the human resources (how directly the human resources affect the firm's strategy) and the *uniqueness* of the human resources (how difficult it is to find or replace the human resources). These two factors (measured by high or low) yielded four labor pools labelled: (1) *strategic* (high value, high uniqueness); (2) *core* (high value, low uniqueness); (3) *support* (low value, low uniqueness); and (4) *collaborative* (low value, high uniqueness). Each of the labor pools benefits from being managed in specific ways that fit the context and conditions.

Social exchange theory (Emerson, 1976) proposes that when employees are treated well, they may respond by increasing their effort, thereby "paying back" the firm for their good treatment. When HR practices and systems are viewed from a social exchange theory perspective, the "deal" that employees perceive they are getting from the organization becomes paramount. As described later, relational psychological contracts create mutual expectations between employers and employees that are quite different from transactional psychological contracts.

In summary, a considerable amount of research has been published on strategic human resource management in the past 30 years. While progress has been made in understanding what factors are important in managing human resources strategically, much work is still needed to understand how human resource systems work to yield various outcomes (this is often referred to as the "black box" of strategic human resource management). As Wright and Ulrich (2017) implore, future research needs to become increasingly rigorous (methods and study designs that provide stronger evidence supporting or discounting hypothesized relationships), increasingly multilevel (considering the context within organizations), increasingly global (taking into account the broader organizational environment), increasingly focused on human capital (to better understand the "black box" described previously), and increasingly integrated with strategy research (to mutually enhance both disciplines).

The changing technological environment for human resource management

In this section, we describe several significant environmental trends that affect organizations and human resource management. We provide an overview of environmental trends, but focus primarily on (1) the increasing impact of automation, especially in the form of robots broadly defined; (2) the increasing impact of artificial intelligence; (3) the increasing use of alternative work arrangements, such as part-time and gig work; (4) how organizations are blending different work arrangements and leveraging technology to achieve objectives; and (5) the digital employee experience.

The world is becoming ever more interconnected through technology. Many of the characteristics of the workplace that evolved to adapt to the industrial revolution and the rise of large corporations in the 1900s no longer fit with the needs of a workplace that has radically changed as a result of new technologies. These new technologies present new possibilities for defining the nature of work and how work is accomplished, where work is accomplished, and how organizational activities are coordinated to produce goods and/ or services that consumers want and buy.

Ubiquitous computing

We are fast moving toward an environment of what Cascio and Montealegre (2016) describe as "ubiquitous computing." As they explain:

> [I]t reflects information and communication environments in which computer sensors (such as radio frequency identification tags, wearable technology, smart watches) and other equipment (tablets, mobile devices, etc.) are unified with various objects, people, information, and computers as well as the physical environment.

Ubiquitous computing has the following characteristics (Cascio & Montealegre, 2016): (1) context-aware technology that delivers the right information to the right person at the right place and time; (2) digitized inventories of talent; (3) individuals and companies exchanging continuous data through social media, mobile devices, electronic boards, and other means that create mutual awareness to transmit the right message to the right people at the right time; (4) access to instantly available knowledge, on-demand development of skills, and intellectual abilities through boundaryless delivery of instruction materials, virtual reality simulations, asynchronous training, educational games, chat rooms, and knowledge-management systems; (5) instant and on-demand appraisal, guidance, support and alerts enabled by digital traces of embedded and context-aware technologies tracking work and movements of goods as well as of roaming employees; and (6) employee-centric career arrangements in recognition that wants and needs vary over the span of an individual's career.

Automation and robots

Ubiquitous computing provides a fertile landscape for two important environmental trends: (1) the increasing infusion of automation into the workplace and (2) the increasing role of artificial intelligence in all aspects of our daily lives both at work and away from work. First, automation has always been a part of the changing workplace—however, the pace of automation infusion into the workplace is currently accelerating. For example, part of Amazon's disruption of the retail industry is dependent on finding ever more efficient ways to speed up operations and lower costs. This is most apparent in their warehouse locations where goods are inventoried, assembled for distribution, gathered for particular customers, picked from shelves, boxed, and then shipped.

Rather than lift, move, and place items—which are left to the robots—human workers "babysit" several robots at a time, and troubleshoot them when problems arise. "The robots make warehouse work less tedious and physically taxing, while also enabling the kinds of efficiency gains that let a customer order dental floss after breakfast and receive it before dinner" (Wingfield, 2017). Of the workers who used to do the manual labor now performed by the robots, some were retrained to become robot operators, others were transferred to receiving stations. And, contrary to many people's fears, Amazon continues to hire human workers. They plan on hiring up to 50,000 new employees when they open their second headquarters in North America.

Some employees, in particular people with disabilities, may benefit from augmentation afforded by robotics. For example, people with some physical disabilities may be able to use robotic exo-skeletons, allowing them not only to compensate for their disabilities, but even to perform with extra strength or stamina. In the same way that "cherry pickers" have reduced the need for workers to climb telephone poles to make repairs, these new robotic enhancements may create a more level playing field for employees and allow employers to take advantage of a larger talent pool.

Artificial intelligence

Artificial intelligence is playing an increasingly important role in the lives of employees. The focus of artificial intelligence is solving tasks that are easy for humans to do but hard for computers, such as planning, moving around in physical space, recognizing objects and sounds, speaking, translating, performing business or social transactions, and even doing creative work (Granville, 2017). Artificial intelligence is only beginning to diffuse into the workplace now that image classification by deep learning has achieved a 95%

human accuracy threshold, and speech and text processing has achieved about 99% accuracy (which accounts for the growing number of chatbots) (Vorhies, 2017). Machine learning, which is related to artificial intelligence, is a set of algorithms that are "trained" on a data set to make predictions or take actions, such as classify potential job applicants into good or bad prospects based upon historical data (Newitz, 2017). Machine learning involves analyzing large amounts of data and looking for patterns. And, similar to shopping sites such as Amazon or streaming services such as Netflix, these systems "learn" from experience and over time get a better understanding of what managers want and need for their operations.

Impact of technology on work

These new technologies have profound effects on how and where people work, communicate, collaborate, and interact. Employees no longer need to show up for work at a common location, work for a designated period (e.g., 8 am to 5 pm), and communicate and interact with other employees synchronously. Instead, most employees can work from anywhere, communicate both synchronously and asynchronously, and interact both in person and virtually—presenting new challenges and opportunities for managing human resources. "Computer networks allow employees to work from the office, their home, or anywhere. Employees are routinely collaborating with people they have never met, in places they have never visited, and staying connected with the office anywhere and anytime" (Cascio & Montealegre, 2016).

For employees, technology either can be enabling (improving efficiency/effectiveness) or oppressive (monitoring and invading privacy). For example, employees can have greater control over simple things like managing the temperatures in their own workplaces. Voice-activated assistants can reduce time spent on many tasks that require human-machine interactions. The Swedish company Biohax recently created small microchips that can be injected into an employee's skin (between the thumb and index finger) that can be programmed to communicate with other network devices. They claim it allows employees to, for example, wave their hand in front of a sensor to open a door rather than using a key. On the other hand, for example, Bluvision makes radio badges that allow companies to track the whereabouts of their employees, enabling them to see whether some employees are spending too much time at their desks, or perhaps too much time in the cafeteria, or even the restroom. There is obvious potential for abuse using these powerful technologies.

Flexible work arrangements

These new technologies also provide organizations with greater flexibility and a wider range of options for configuring and managing their human resources. The dominant form of employment during the twentieth century was the full-time job. A full-time job meant that work was performed on a fixed schedule at a firm's place of business and under the firm's control, and there was a mutual expectation of continued employment (Spreitzer, Cameron, & Garrett, 2017). A relational psychological contract (Rousseau, 1989) was created between the employer and the employee, raising mutual expectations: the employer would offer continuing employment, opportunities for training and advancement, and generous benefits such as health insurance and retirement pensions; in exchange, the employee would provide engaged and committed job performance over a long time period in which the employer could reap its investment in human capital.

In contrast, the twenty-first century is characterized by a growing use of alternative forms of work and the de-emphasis of the previously dominant full-time job. Increasingly, jobs are short-term, temporary, and not tied to a more traditional long-term relational psychological contract. New psychological contracts are more transactional in nature with fewer expectations between employers and employees beyond what is explicitly contracted. Employers do not provide incentives for these employees to remain, and employees do not provide outcomes beyond their negotiated role requirements.

Digital technology and mobile apps have given rise to new forms of work arrangements that have been informally described as a "gig" (i.e., part of the "gig economy"), and more formally described as "platform mediated contracting" (Spreitzer, Cameron, & Garrett, 2017). In this new work arrangement, workers contract for minutes, hours, or days for a job (or even a task, not a whole job) coordinated through a mobile app (Kuhn & Maleki, 2017). Not all online labor platforms are alike. They differ in terms of the workers' dependence on the firm (e.g., the platform is the primary source of income versus the worker has access to other sources of clients or income) and the amount of worker autonomy that is allowed (e.g., workers decide their own compensation rate versus the firm controls pay rates for defined tasks) (Kuhn & Maleki, 2017). Employers currently are wrestling with how best to manage workers in this type of highly transactional relationship.

In addition to gigs, which may be the shortest employment relationships, other more temporary forms of work that were once more peripheral in organizations, are now becoming more widespread in use (e.g., part-time work, on-call work, seasonal work, co-employment/agency work, and contract work) (Spreitzer, Cameron, & Garrett, 2017). Nowadays, organizations may have full-time employees working alongside part-time workers, co-employment agency workers, contract workers, and even robots or "cobots" (robots intended to physically interact with humans in a shared workspace). And, even the more traditional full-time regular employment model no longer fits the mold of the twentieth century. Today, nearly 50% of full-time workers do at least some of their work from remote locations (Mims, 2017).

The digital workplace

As a consequence of the changing environment, organizations are moving toward the "digital workplace" enabling employees to foster efficiency, innovation, and growth. The digital workplace is defined as all the technologies people use to get work done in today's workplace and ranges from human resource and business applications to email, instant messaging, social media, and virtual meeting tools (Deloitte, 2017). It is a virtual equivalent of the physical workplace that allows businesses to rethink traditional processes and increase efficiency and effectiveness. The digital workplace is the application of information and technology to raise human performance (McDonald, 2015). Organizations are embracing the digital workplace because it has the potential to increase revenue, reduce operational costs, accelerate time-to-market, enhance innovation, improve the customer experience, increase agility and flexibility, heighten staff satisfaction, raise productivity and efficiency, strengthen talent recruitment and retention, and improve employees' experience (Deloitte, 2017). For example, firms are adopting Microsoft's new Office Teams product and Walmart is using Facebook's internal social platform product to facilitate digital interactions among their employees.

Deloitte (2017) describes a four-part digital workplace framework that consists of (1) *use*: collaborate, communicate, and connect; (2) **technology**: the digital toolbox; (3) **control**: governance, risk, and compliance; and (4) **business drivers**: measurable business value. An important key to a successful digital workplace is enhancing employees' ability to do their jobs by collaborating, communicating, and connecting with others to enable knowledge sharing across the organization. The digital toolbox is a company's own tailored set of tools to fit their circumstances. Control is essential to ensuring that information flow complies with organization policies and industry regulations. And business needs guide the direction of the digital workplace.

To summarize, the changing environment poses both threats and opportunities for organizations. How organizations respond to the threats and how they capitalize on the opportunities will largely determine whether they survive and thrive. Human resources, once thought to be merely an expense to be minimized are becoming increasingly important as companies strive to gain competitive advantage in the marketplace. How to manage human resources strategically will be discussed next.

e-HRM and SHRM: Which comes first?

Marler and Fisher (2013) defined e-HRM broadly as "intended and actual HRM policies, activities, services, and collaborations with individuals and organizations, which are delivered and enabled using configurations of computer hardware, software, and electronic networking capability." As discussed in this chapter, advances in technology, in particular automation and robots, along with artificial intelligence, are creating new opportunities for human resource contributions to organization success as well as new possibilities for transforming the HR function in organizations in ways that are only partially imaginable today. What will the HR function of the future look like? We can only speculate that it will require fewer people doing more high-level design and analytical work while the more administrative and clerical tasks that used to take up the bulk of HR resources and efforts become completely automated. Even tasks such as answering employee questions about benefits or adjusting staffing schedules will be (and in some cases are now) handled by chatbots and other technological advances. So what does this mean for strategic human resource management?

There has been an ongoing discussion and debate about whether human resource management can play more than simply an administrative role in organizations. This has led to academic researchers focusing on the potential strategic role of human resources in organizational performance over three decades of research. Books, articles, and countless conferences have been devoted to promoting the strategic role of human resources, with some limited impact on actually achieving their objective. Getting HR a "seat at the table," meaning playing a significant role in top management teams has become almost a mantra. While the strategic importance of human resources is now both better understood and more widely accepted, a question remains about why it is not embraced more universally. Some academic researchers have questioned the foundation of strategic human resource management research (c.f., Kaufman, 2012). Others have suggested that the research methods themselves have been less sophisticated and rigorous, thereby unable to provide the most compelling evidence (Wright & Ulrich, 2017).

Marler and Parry (2016) offer an insight into the future roles of e-HRM and strategic HRM in organizations. They frame the issue in the classic "which came first, the chicken or the egg?" dilemma. Two competing perspectives are proposed. In one perspective, we might call it the e-HRM came first perspective, the argument is that the greater automation of administrative tasks and increasingly distributed access to data has led to increasingly decentralized decision making, so that HR professionals can focus on more complex, judgment-oriented, and professionally demanding tasks and responsibilities. This, of course, leads to greater professionalization and enhanced reputation of HR professionals and the HR function. In a competing perspective, we might call the SHRM came first perspective, managerial choice plays the primary role and decisions are made concerning technology that best facilitates the organization's ability to achieve its strategic objectives. In other words, e-HRM is adopted as an outcome or consequence of strategic decision making and managerial intent.

Using a large data set of companies located in North America, Europe, Australia, and New Zealand, Marler and Parry (2016) examined the competing perspectives. Their results showed support for both perspectives. In their words, "Managers involved in making strategic decision can determine the extent of an organization's e-HRM capabilities but in addition the deployment of e-HRM can have significant effects on the strategic role of HRM in organizations." Much like the strategy versus structure debate in strategic management (Chandler, 1962), the choices are interactive and iterative. Furthermore, the outcomes of combining e-HRM and strategic HRM are affected by external stakeholders such as vendors, political institutions, and market competitors.

Summary

A strategic approach to managing human resources differs from traditional human resource management. Organizations seek to align their human resource systems with their business strategies; additionally, they seek to ensure that their human resource practices themselves are internally consistent. However, in dynamic environments, organizations need to emphasize flexibility over fit; in particular resource flexibility and coordination flexibility. A strategic human resource system has multiple levels. Strategic human resource management becomes more complicated when conducted across national borders and by global organizations. Three major theoretical perspectives have influenced strategic human resource management, but the resource-based view has been the dominant one. And, over 30 years of research has provided insight on some important issues in the field, but we still do not have a complete understanding of strategic human resource management.

The landscape for managing human resources is changing rapidly. Several environmental trends are having a significant impact on the workplace, including: (1) the increasing impact of automation, especially in the form of robots broadly defined; (2) the increasing impact of artificial intelligence; (3) the increasing use of alternative work arrangements, such as part-time and gig work; (4) how organizations are blending different work arrangements and leveraging technology to achieve objectives; and (5) the digital employee experience.

For organizations, the HR challenges are clear. To be competitive in the future, investing in the creation of both e-HRM and strategic HRM capabilities will be imperative. What Murray (2015, p. 6) said regarding the impact of technological innovations seems to apply equally well to e-HRM and strategic HRM. "Together these innovations are hurtling us toward a new industrial revolution. Savvy corporate leaders know they have to either figure out how these technologies will transform their businesses or face disruption by others who figure it out first."

> **Case study: Design of an SHRM system**
>
> BlueGranite, a small boutique data and analytics consulting organization, became a solutions-provider partner with Microsoft. This increased business opportunities and meant BlueGranite had to operate under Satya Nadella's new "Hit Refresh" paradigm and adapt to Microsoft's employee "growth mindset." Microsoft expanded product lines and offerings quickly and frequently and updated products such as PowerBI multiple times a month, leading to quick market share and usability growth. This shift provided challenges and strategic opportunities.
>
> To continue to succeed, leaders at BlueGranite needed a deep understanding of the workforce and knowledge-in-practice to serve clients today, and to build the strategic human resource and knowledge management capabilities to be ready to meet future needs. CEO Matt Mace realized that the highly skilled workforce meant turnover was always a possibility as employees were poaching targets for other firms.
>
> Driven by the COO Eric Roll, BlueGranite applied its data, analytics, and IT capabilities to propel them forward along four objectives. (1) Career planning and strategic "fit" was increasingly important to develop a workforce that aligned personal fulfillment goals, company strategic plans, and business opportunities. (2) Learning plans needed to become much more transparent and efficient to ensure employees spent their time wisely, and to guarantee knowledge, skills, and abilities could be tracked and understood across the organization. (3) A combined buy and build knowledge management strategy meant employee satisfaction relied on finding and hiring the right employees and helping them grow and constantly update their skills. (4) Employee motivations, interests, and skills needed to be aligned with schedules, projects, and tasks from a growing client list.
>
> The leadership team believed success required BlueGranite to operate as a holacracy—decentralized management and distributing authority and decision making throughout a network of self-organizing teams. Employees are motivated by the right jobs and self-determination is a source of training and development motivation. Leaders need to understand knowledge, skills, and abilities across employees, teams, and the company, and also understand motivations and determine how to disperse crucial knowledge faster and more efficiently.
>
> **Case study questions**
>
> 1 What are the three most important outcome goals for BlueGranite's strategic HRM system design?
> 2 What is the most significant difficulty they are likely to face?
> 3 Why is there a link between employee satisfaction and skill development?
> 4 What are some of the most important characteristics BlueGranite should look for when hiring new employees?

Debate: Should human resources be managed as expenses to be minimized ("hard" HRM) or as assets to be developed ("soft" HRM)?

Introduction

A "hard" approach to HRM takes a more business/company-centric perspective. As Armstrong and Taylor (2014) note, this version of HRM views the worker as a commodity and focuses on the quantitative, calculative, and business-strategic aspects of managing human resources in a "rational" way similar to that for any other economic factor of production. A "soft" version of HRM, on the other hand, emphasizes the "human" part of HRM by focusing efforts on achieving competitive advantage by gaining commitment, adaptability, and high levels of performance of employees by using HR practices to create a high-trust, high-involvement organization. "Soft" HRM takes a more employee-centric perspective and emphasizes employee attitudes and relationships.

Arguments in favor of managing human resources as expenses to be minimized

- Human resources are a means to an end. They are like any other resource that is used to create products and services that customers want. They should be treated like any other resource; "exploited" to advance the interests of the company.
- Shareholder theory asserts that shareholders advance capital to a company's managers, who are supposed to spend corporate funds only in ways that have been authorized by the shareholders (Smith, 2003). As succinctly stated by Milton Friedman, "There is one and only one social responsibility of business — to use its resources and engage in activities designed to increase its profits so long as it . . . engages in open and free competition, without deception or fraud" (Friedman, 2007). Therefore, for example, shutting down plants that have been around for decades and moving operations to cheaper labor markets overseas is the "socially responsible" action to take because it increases profits and thereby shareholder value (despite its potentially devastating impact on employees and communities).
- Investments in human resources (e.g., improving morale) should only be made if they are the best investments of capital that are available.
- Organizations have an at-will relationship with their employees, which means that either party (employer or employee) can terminate their relationship with the other at any time. These relationships are often described as transactional, emphasizing a focus on the explicit aspects of the employment contract without accounting for the other needs of employees not addressed in the contract.

Arguments in favor of managing human resources as assets to be developed

- Human resources are an end into themselves and should not be treated solely as a means to advancing the interests of an organization.

- Stakeholder theory asserts that managers have a duty to both the corporation's shareholders and "individuals and constituencies that contribute, either voluntarily or involuntarily, to [a company's] wealth-creating capacity and activities, and who are therefore its potential beneficiaries and/or risk bearers" (Smith, 2003). According to the stakeholder theory, managers are agents of all stakeholders and have two responsibilities: to ensure that the ethical rights of no stakeholder are violated and to balance the legitimate interests of the stakeholders when making decisions. The objective is to balance profit maximization with the long-term ability of the corporation to remain a going concern.
- Organizations have relational psychological contracts with employees that are longer term, reflecting a social exchange that may require short-term sacrifices by one party for the other in order to sustain the organization in the long-run. For example, employees may be asked to take a pay cut during tough economic times with the understanding that when the economy improves, they will be restored financially. Likewise, an employer may continue to employ workers (to conserve human resources) during an economic recession rather than laying them off to reduce short-term expenses.
- "Being a socially responsible business ought to encompass the effect of management practices on employee physical and psychological well-being" (Pfeffer, 2010).
- "There is no reason why building sustainable companies should focus just on the physical and not the social environment. It is not just the natural world that is at risk from harmful business practices. We should care as much about people as we do about polar bears or the environmental savings from using better milk jugs and also understand the causes and consequences of how we focus our research and policy attention" (Pfeffer, 2010).

Video learning resources

- HR in alignment at Sysco: www.youtube.com/watch?v=0QmZDHDGvGY
- HR role models: www.youtube.com/watch?v=X_bKYXwTUrI
- How to build a strategy for "the long game": http://knowledge.wharton.upenn.edu/article/how-to-build-a-strategy-for-the-long-game/
- Life at Google. Inside Google's lair—How google employees work: www.youtube.com/watch?v=PA54HWLZ2e4
- Inside Facebook HQ—Mark Zuckerberg—Inside Facebook—BBC www.youtube.com/watch?v=cGEb-q5JMU0

References

Armstrong, M. & Taylor, S. (2014). *Armstrong's Handbook of Human Resource Management Practice.* London: Kogan Page Publishers.

Arthur, J. B. & Boyles, T. (2007). Validating the human resource system structure: A levels-based strategic HRM approach. *Human Resource Management Review*, 17(1), 77–92.

Barney, B. J. (1995). Looking inside for competitive advantage. *Academy of Management Executive*, 9(4), 49–61.

Barney, J. B. & Wright, P. M. (1998). On becoming a strategic partner: The role of human resources in gaining competitive advantage. *Human Resource Management*, 37(1), 31.

Becker, B. E., Huselid, M. A., Pickus, P. S. & Spratt, M. F. (1997). HR as a source of shareholder value: Research and recommendations. *Human Resource Management*, 36(1), 39–47.

Becker, G. (1964) *Human Capital*. New York, NY: Columbia University Press.

Cascio, W. F. & Montealegre, R. (2016). How technology is changing work and organizations. *Annual Review of Organizational Psychology and Organizational Behavior*, 3, 349–375.

Chandler, A. D. Jr. (1962). *Strategy and Structure: Chapters in the History of the American Industrial Enterprise*. Cambridge, MA: MIT Press.

Cohen, W. M. & Levinthal, D. A. (1990). Absorptive capacity: A new perspective on learning and innovation. *Administrative Science Quarterly*, 35, 128–152.

Deloitte (2017, October 2). The digital workplace: think, share, do transform your employee experience. Retrieved from www2.deloitte.com/content/dam/Deloitte/mx/Documents/human-capital/The_digital_workplace.pdf

Emerson, R. M. (1976). Social exchange theory. *Annual Review of Sociology*, 2(1), 335–362.

Friedman, M. (2007) The social responsibility of business is to increase its Profits. In: Zimmerli W. C., Holzinger M. & Richter K. (Eds.), *Corporate Ethics and Corporate Governance* (pp. 173–178). Berlin, Heidelberg: Springer.

Granville, V. (2017, January 2). Difference between machine learning, data science, AI, deep learning, and statistics. Retrieved from www.datasciencecentral.com/profiles/blogs/difference-between-machine-learning-data-science-ai-deep-learning

Kaufman, B. E. (2012). Strategic human management research in the United States: A failing grade after 30 years? *Academy of Management Perspectives*, 26, 12–36.

Kuhn, K. M. & Maleki, A. (2017). Micro-entrepreneurs, dependent contractors, and instaserfs: Understanding online labor platform workforces. *The Academy of Management Perspectives*, 31(3), 183–200.

Lengnick-Hall, C. A. & Lengnick-Hall, M. L. (1988). Strategic human resources management: A review of the literature and a proposed typology. *Academy of Management Review*, 13(3), 454–470.

Lepak, D. P. & Snell, S. A. (1999). The human resource architecture: Toward a theory of human capital allocation and development. *Academy of Management Review*, 24(1), 31–48.

Marler, J. H. & Fisher, S. L. (2013). An evidence-based review of e-HRM and strategic human resource management. *Human Resource Management Review*, 23(1), 18–36.

Marler, J. H. & Parry, E. (2016). Human resource management, strategic involvement and e-HRM technology. *The International Journal of Human Resource Management*, 27(19), 2233–2253.

McDonald, M. (March 3, 2015). What is a digital strategy? Retrieved from www.accenture.com/us-en/blogs/blogs-digital-what-is-digital-strategy

Mims, C. (2017, June 4). Why remote work can't be stopped. *The Wall Street Journal*. Retrieved from www.wsj.com/articles/why-remote-work-cant-be-stopped-1496577602

Minbaeva, D., Pedersen, T., Björkman, I., Fey, C. F. & Park, H. J. (2003). MNC knowledge transfer, subsidiary absorptive capacity, and HRM. *Journal of International Business Studies*, 34(6), 586–599.

Murray, A. (April 22, 2015) Fortune's tech coverage: Your guide for tumultuous times, p. 6. *Fortune*. Retrieved from http://fortune.com/2015/04/22/fortune-new-gigaom-writers

Newitz, A. (2017, May 19). An AI invented a bunch of new paint colors that are hilariously wrong. Retrieved from www.arstechnica.com/information-technology/2017/05/an-ai-invented-a-bunch-of-new-paint-colors-that-are-hilariously-wrong/

Pfeffer, J. (2010). Building sustainable organizations: The human factor. *The Academy of Management Perspectives*, 24(1), 34–45.

Rousseau, D. M. (1989). Psychological and implied contracts in organizations. *Employee Responsibilities and Rights Journal*, 2(2), 121–139.

Schuler, R. S., Dowling, P. J. & De Cieri, H. (1993). An integrative framework of strategic international human resource management. *Journal of Management*, 19(2), 419–459.

Smith, H. J. (2003). The shareholders vs. stakeholders debate. *MIT Sloan Management Review*, 44(4), 85–91.

Spreitzer, G. M., Cameron, L. & Garrett, L. (2017). Alternative work arrangements: Two images of the new world of work. *Annual Review of Organizational Psychology and Organizational Behavior*, 4(1), 471–499.

Taylor, S., Beechler, S. & Napier, N. (1996). Toward an integrative model of strategic international human resource management. *Academy of Management Review*, 21(4), 959–985.

Vorhies, W. (2017, April 10). A robot took my job—was it a robot or AI? Retrieved from www.datasciencecentral.com/profiles/blogs/a-robots-took-my-job-was-it-a-robot-or-ai

Wang, S., Tong, T. W., Chen, G. & Kim, H. (2009). Expatriate utilization and foreign direct investment performance: The mediating role of knowledge transfer. *Journal of Management*, 35(5), 1181–1206.

Wingfield, N. (September 10, 2017). As Amazon pushes forward with robots, workers find new roles. *New York Times*. Retrieved from www.nytimes.com/2017/09/10/technology/amazon-robots-workers.html

Wright, P. M. & McMahan, G. C. (1992). Theoretical perspectives for strategic human resource management. *Journal of Management*, 18(2), 295–320.

Wright, P. M. & Snell, S. A. (1998). Toward a unifying framework for exploring fit and flexibility in strategic human resource management. *Academy of Management Review*, 23(4), 756–772.

Wright, P. M. & Ulrich, M. D. (2017). A road well traveled: the past, present, and future journey of strategic human resource management. *Annual Review of Organizational Psychology and Organizational Behavior*, 4, 45–65.

3 Soft systems thinking approach to e-HRM project management

Mohan Thite & NMK Bhatta

Learning objectives

- Explain why the failure rate for technology projects is very high and how success factors are mainly around people and process rather than technology
- Describe the key principles behind systems thinking and the soft skills needed to adopt systems perspective
- Explain the phases of the system development life cycle (SDLC)
- Discuss the different levels of the people capability maturity model (P-CMM) and the human resource aspects to be considered at each level

Introduction

The Standish Group produces the CHAOS reports every year, judging the success of around 50,000 software development projects world-wide, based on six success criteria, namely, on time, on budget, on target, on goal, value and satisfaction. According to the 2015 report, only 29% of the projects were considered 'successful', 52% were considered 'challenged' (over budget and over time) and 19% ended in 'failure'. For 'grand' projects (costing over $100 million in labour costs), the success rate was only 2%; however, small projects reported a success rate of 62%. (Hastie & Wojewoda, 2015).

The report also concluded that for those projects that were successful, the following were the key success factors, in the order of importance:

1. *Executive support*. Financial and emotional backing from top management
2. *Emotional maturity*. Soft skills, including overcoming the 'five deadly sins' of project management (as referred to in Table 3.1), managing expectations, consensus building and collaboration
3. *User involvement*. Involvement of the users in project decision making and information-gathering process
4. *Optimisation*. A structured means of improving business effectiveness
5. *Skilled staff*. People who understand both the business and the technology
6. *Standard architecture*. Integrated practices, services and products for developing, implementing and operating software applications
7. *Agile proficiency*. The ability of the project team in following the agile process (see next chapter for a detailed explanation of the agile methodology)

8 *Modest execution.* Having a process with few moving parts, and those parts are automated and streamlined
9 *Project management expertise.* Application of knowledge, skills and techniques to project activities in order to meet or exceed stakeholder expectations
10 *Clear business objectives.* The understanding of all stakeholders and participants and project alignment with the organisation's goals and strategy

There are two key lessons from the above report: one, despite the enormous amount of money, time and efforts spent on planning, designing, implementing and maintaining technology projects, the failure rate is alarmingly high. This is particularly so with large-scale projects due to their extreme complexity, interdependencies and communication challenges (Brock, Saleh & Iyer, 2015). Two, technology is secondary in the success of a technology project management. It is the non-technical factors, including the soft skills as mentioned in Table 3.1 that are crucial in the success or failure of technology projects (Martinsons & Chong, 1999).

Accordingly, organisations need to adopt a long-term, holistic, systems thinking approach to designing and delivering technology projects. Technical projects are primarily resource intensive and the resources involved are knowledge workers with unique characteristics and difficult to handle attitudes. An in-depth knowledge of how technology projects are managed and what factors lead to their success or failure would help human resource (HR) professionals to provide appropriate customised support to the technical teams throughout the project phases.

In this chapter, we will explain the basics of systems thinking, the systems development life cycle (SDLC) that underpins systems thinking and role of HR in each phase of the SDLC. We will then introduce the people capability maturity model (P-CMM), a quality management framework widely used in the IT projects with associated HR aspects. Finally, using a Case Study, we will summarise the key managerial lessons to be learnt to increase the chances of success in e-HRM projects.

Table 3.1 Emotional maturity and five deadly sins of project management

Definition of emotional maturity

'"Emotional maturity" is the ability and capacity to perceive, assess, manage, and direct the emotions and actions of the project stakeholders. It is the ability to identify and remove unnecessary requirements, as well as the aptitude to deliver bad news and accept critical feedback. It is the skill to recognize and deal with the Five Deadly Sins of project management, which are overambition, arrogance, ignorance, abstinence, and fraudulence'.

'Five Deadly Sins' of project management:

- **Overambition:** a strong desire to execute a significant project to gain fame, fortune or power through the impact of overreaching goals.
- **Arrogance**: the unwarranted, overbearing pride evidenced by a superior manner towards superiors, peers and inferiors.
- **Ignorance**: the condition of being unaware, uninformed, uneducated and/or unsuspecting about the project and stakeholder goals, directions, details, issues and opportunities. This condition is often coupled with apathy.
- **Abstinence**: the act or practice of refraining from participation in and contribution to the project.
- **Fraudulence**: an action intended to deceive; it is deliberate trickery intended to gain an advantage or to avoid confrontation.

Source: Adapted from Standish Group (2014).

Systems thinking

A popular adage attributed to Aristotle says, 'the whole is more than a sum of its parts'. It refers to the capability of individuals coming together to achieve more than what they could do on their own, 'provided' they act together as a unified system. It is also reflected in another popular phrase, 'united we stand, divided we fall'. When we apply this thinking to complex organisational systems, such as technology projects, we can surmise that if the individuals involved in the system focus only on themselves or the tasks they are performing without seeing the 'big picture', they fail to recognise what others are doing or thinking and tend to blame each other when things start falling apart.

A system is 'any group of interacting, interrelated, or interdependent parts that form a complex and unified whole that has a specific purpose' (Kim, 1999, p. 2). According to Arnold and Wade (2015, p. 675):

> [S]ystems thinking is a set of synergistic analytic skills used to improve the capability of identifying and understanding systems, predicting their behaviors, and devising modifications to them in order to produce desired effects. These skills work together as a system.

Squires, Wade, Dominick and Gelosh (2011) explain further that 'systems thinking is the ability to think abstractly in order to

– incorporate multiple perspectives;
– work within a space where the boundary or scope of problem or system may be "fuzzy";
– understand diverse operational contexts of the system;
– identify inter- and intrarelationships and dependencies;
– understand complex system behavior; and most important of all
– reliably predict the impact of change to the system'.

These skills are however hard to acquire. As Senge (1990, p. 7) explains, human endeavours are also systems bound by invisible interrelated actions and people inside the system tend to focus on 'snapshots of isolated parts of the system' and find it 'hard to see the whole pattern of change'.

The project management discipline incorporated 'systems engineering' thinking in the 1990s. Sankaran, Haslett and Sheffield (2010) note:

> As project management spread its wings, 'softer' or more people-centric issues, such as personnel management, motivation, team performance, team structure, stakeholder management, negotiation, communications management, and leadership, were added to the list of Best Practices (McConnell, 1996). Systems thinking approaches also started to move away from 'hard systems' (product and technology-centric) to 'soft systems' (people and process) approaches
>
> (McConnell, 1996, p. 11)

The critical importance of people and process over product and technology in project management places HR managers as a key driver to ensure e-HRM project success. Any job advertisement for human resource information systems (HRIS) manager underscores the fundamental role of the position as a bridge between HR and IT professionals to ensure they understand each other's role and work together as a team. Green (2017) explains that as part of the job description of an HRIS manager:

> Strong analytical, troubleshooting and problem-solving skills are integral to the competence of HRIS managers. When employee management software crashes, for example, the manager uses these skills to troubleshoot the software and implement appropriate solutions, as well as uses operating systems and programming tools effectively. HRIS managers also need strong leadership skills to guide and supervise the HRIS team, which may include database administrators and data analysts. Good communication skills are also important to these managers, because they need to write clear and concise reports and communicate effectively with vendors of information systems.

If there is no proper understanding between the users, business analysts and software programmers of the project goals and requirements, the final product may fail to meet the user expectations and result in a terrible loss of time, efforts and money.

Systems development life cycle using waterfall methodology

Traditionally, Software projects followed a development approach called 'Waterfall Methodology'. This approach was originally promoted by the US Department of Defense in the 1950s and because of rugged delivery capability its prominence continues even today. Waterfall emphasises the concept of serially phased development philosophy in which various project phases are carried out in a serial manner. Every phase is completed with a proper verification and validation process and detailed documentation. Once completed, a phase is considered frozen and never revisited except under extraordinary circumstances. The phases of the waterfall model formed the SDLC for IT Projects. Figure 3.1 depicts various phases of the SDLC.

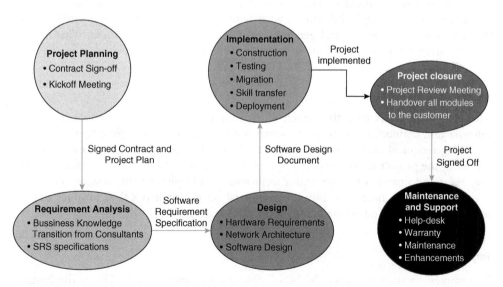

Figure 3.1 IT system development life cycle.
Source: Prepared by NMK Bhatta.

We explain below each phase of the SDLC:

Project planning

The SDLC starts with the objective to align the project as close to the strategic business goals of the organisation as possible. Clear priorities need to be established on how best to leverage technology to meet organisational goals and derive competitive advantage. This requires clear alignment between organisational strategy, information technology (IT) strategy and HR strategy. For instance, if the organisational strategy is to be a global technology leader, the IT strategy would be to deploy and harness state of the art, future-focused technologies. Similarly, the HR strategy would be to acquire a best of breed applicant tracking system (ATS) to attract the best talent and learning management system (LMS) to train the workforce.

The planning phase includes both long-term strategic planning and short-term operational planning. During this phase, HR needs to prioritise which HR technology projects are critical and how best to implement them.

Requirement analysis

The next phase of the SDLC deals with detailed requirement gathering to prepare a project scope document (typically called software requirement specification or SRS). It collects information about the current and proposed system in order to answer the three crucial questions, namely, where are we, where we want to go and how do we get there. To answer these critical questions, the organisation needs to document its current capabilities and future needs in order to clearly define the scope of an e-HRM project.

For example, for a e-recruitment project, the analysis team, consisting of HRIS manager, key users from concerned departments and external consultants, needs to determine which parts of the recruitment system need be automated, how does it interface with other HR and management systems, what information should be included, how does the information flow through the system, what types of reports would be generated, would the system be cost effective and generate reasonable return on investment, what impact it would have on staffing and how it would ensure information security and privacy.

Design

The next phase deals with the design of appropriate IT solution, including hardware, software and network infrastructure, which is essentially a technology intensive activity involving technical architects and designers. Once the blueprint of the new system is prepared, the project team prepares a request for proposal (RFP), which is used to identify, assess and finalise a vendor who can provide and implement the system. The most common approach here is to buy a commercial off the shelf (COTS) product from a reputed vendor with established credentials and a track record.

Implementation

The implementation phase of the SDLC follows the design phase. This is the longest phase of the entire SDLC and usually takes up to 60% of the project schedule. During this phase, the system is coded and tested before going 'live'. While the activity is essentially technical in nature, HR needs to be actively involved at every stage during the implementation phase. People's motivation levels are to be maintained at the highest level to surmount every challenge that comes their way during this phase. HR personnel need to integrate themselves with the project team and be present on a continuous basis to sense signals of stress and disengagement so that they can initiate necessary action before it snowballs into a major breakdown. Routine stress relief events such as outdoor fun activities that improve emotional bonding among people would be a major responsibility for HR in this phase. For these activities to be effective, HR teams must be co-located with the project teams to give them a feeling that HR is one among them.

During the implementation phase, managing employee attrition is another challenge that HR has to deal with. While attrition may not be completely avoidable as people with critical IT skills are always in high demand, strategic management of employee attrition is essential. For instance, every time a performance appraisal cycle is completed, there will be emotional stress among people whose performance rating does not match with their expectations, resulting in unexpected resignations. HR needs to handle each case sensitively and proactively.

Project closure

The next phase in the SDLC deals with the closure of the project. Project closure can sometimes be most frustrating as many of the so called less important activities postponed during various other phases become a serious bottleneck in project closure. Most of the technical personnel will be looking for their next assignment. The project manager finds it extremely challenging to wrap up all pending activities. A major responsibility of HR during this phase will be to keep the team together and make them work towards the project closure in a focussed manner.

Maintenance and support

Maintenance and support phase, often called the 'forgotten phase', follows the project closure. It includes corrective maintenance (where bugs in the system are fixed), adaptive maintenance (where modifications and enhancements are carried out), perfective maintenance aimed at continuous improvement and preventative maintenance to fine tune the hardware and software. As most of the maintenance projects are subject to a service level agreement (SLA) with outside third-party service providers, the promptness with which the vendor responds and resolves the maintenance issues is critical. Therefore, HR needs to acquire the capability for effective vendor management.

Figure 3.2 summarises the key technical and human resource aspects and success factors of each phase of the SDLC. As highlighted in Figure 3.2, there are two critical success factors that exert a major influence on all aspects of the SDLC, namely, user involvement throughout the process and ongoing and integrated communication with diverse stakeholders. Hsu, Liang, Wu, Klein and Jiang (2011, p. 514) emphasise that:

> active and fruitful participation of users in the development projects of information systems (IS) is a crucial factor in achieving success. However, difficulties such as conflict and apathy often plague IS development projects that do not rely on building effective partnerships between users and those responsible for the development.

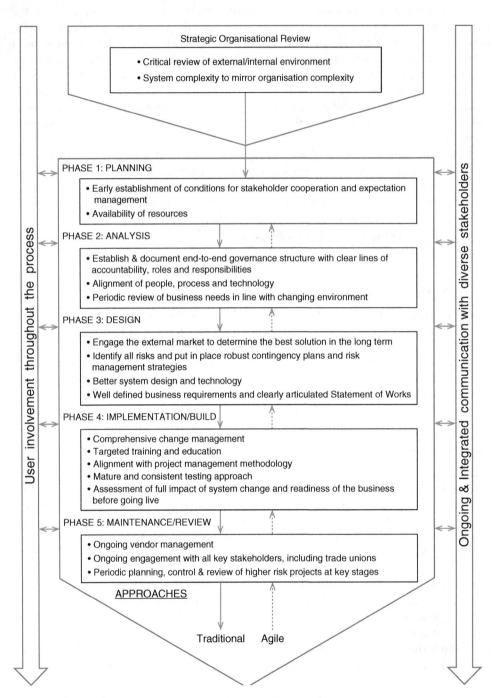

Figure 3.2 Key success factors in the systems development life cycle.
Source: Thite and Sandhu (2014).

Thus, most problems in software projects occur due to the neglect of social aspects, such as stakeholder resistance (Vrhoves, Hovelja, Vavpotic & Krisper, 2015).

Evaluation of the SDLC/waterfall model

As the analogy of waterfall suggests, it is a linear, structured and sequential model where each phase must be fully implemented before embarking on the next phase and unless exceptional circumstances warrant, the previous phases are not revisited.

The **advantages** of this model are:

- It adopts the systems thinking perspective where all phases from inception to completion are well thought out, planned and executed
- It is easier to understand and use
- As each phase is well defined and the project moves to the next stage only after ensuring successful completion of each phase as measured by clearly defined deliverables, tight project control and discipline are established
- It is suitable for well-defined large-scale projects with clear project goals, time lines, requirements and processes that are well communicated to all stakeholders

However, the **disadvantages** of the model are:

- There is no margin for error, leaving little scope to make major changes to project directions, requirements and deliverables, no matter how well justified the changes are
- Strict testing and sign-off of each phase before moving to the next stage may cause undue delays
- Once a phase is completed, there is no going back even though subsequent changes to the model incorporate iterative capability
- One cannot see the working version of the application until the end phase is reached
- Not suitable for fast changing and uncertain business environments where flexibility and adaptability are key

Quality management framework: people capability maturity model

Human resources are the backbone of any organisation in the 21st century knowledge economy. The knowledge workers are extremely critical to the success of high-technology firms in the information and communication technology (ICT) industry where an optimum combination of people, process and technology provide sustainable competitive advantage. However, the industry has traditionally suffered from serious people management issues, such as high turnover, burnout, stressful work environment and critical skill shortages. It took quite some time for the industry to realise that no matter how great the technology that was used, the key challenges were process and people related, as highlighted throughout this chapter.

To ensure sustainability, repeatability and scalability without compromising on quality, particularly while handling large-scale software projects and to address critical people issues, the Software Engineering Institute (SEI) at Carnegie Mellon University developed a process maturity framework called the people capability maturity model (P-CMM) as a model of best practices for managing and developing an organisation's workforce. Today, it is widely used by the most major ICT services firms and those that achieve P-CMM Level 5 maturity level are highly regarded.

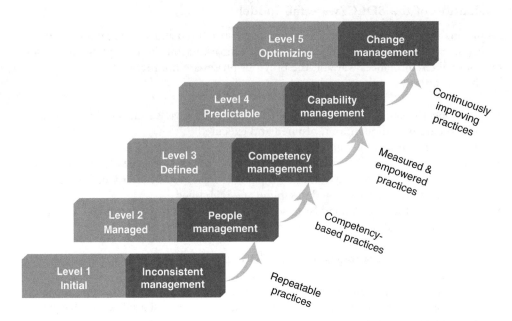

Figure 3.3 People capability maturity model.
Source: Curtis, Hefley & Miller (2009, p. 18). Reproduced with permission from Carnegie Mellon University.

According to Curtis, Hefley and Miller (2009), 'the People CMM helps organizations characterize the maturity of their workforce practices, establish a program of continuous workforce development, set priorities for improvement actions, integrate workforce development with process improvement, and establish a culture of excellence' (p. xiii). P-CMM consists of five maturity levels (as depicted in Figure 3.3) that establish successive foundations for continuously improving individual competencies.

As explained by Curtis, Hefley and Miller (2009, p. 12–13):

Level 1 (Initial: Inconsistent management). At this basic level, organisations are characterised by ad hoc and inconsistent work processes and the project personnel resort to cutting corners in a rush to meet deadlines resulting in poor quality, delays and cost blowout. 'A fundamental premise of the process maturity framework is that a practice cannot be improved if it cannot be repeated' (p. 12). Due to the immaturity of the organisation, people struggle to repeat successful work practices and meet delivery deadlines as goalposts keep changing. In this environment, people routinely deflect responsibility and become emotionally drained and detached. Managers either ignore or are ill-equipped to deal with HR issues leading to high employee turnover and low morale. The case study firm described at the end of this chapter typifies Level 1 organisations.

Level 2 (Managed: People management). In order to escape from inconsistent and unproductive work practices, organisations must first establish a stable work environment.

'The primary objective of a Maturity Level 2 environment is to enable people to repeat practices they have used successfully. To enable this repeatability, managers must get control of commitments and baselines' (p. 12). The top management needs to show firm commitment to learning and development activities in order to 'continuously improve the knowledge, skills, motivation, and performance of its workforce' (p. 21). As poor relations with an immediate supervisor is the primary cause of employee turnover, managers need to be held accountable for ensuring that HR practices are implemented effectively. By providing continuous performance feedback, they need to ensure that their team members have the necessary skills and resources to carry out their work and keep their knowledge up-to-date.

Level 3 (Defined: Competency management). At this level, organisations are able to identify competency-based best practices that most suit the organisational environment and incorporate them as everyday work practices. 'These practices are documented and integrated into a common process in which the entire organization is then trained' (p. 13), leading to a professional culture. The workforce capabilities should clearly align with business objectives leading to a distinct competitive advantage.

At this level, an organisation-wide framework of a strategic workforce plan and workforce competencies is established. This is further augmented by a learning and development plan to impart the knowledge, skills and process abilities related to each competency. However, employees will not be able to harness their competencies unless the organisational culture empowers the workforce to make decisions independently without managers with a command and control mindset breathing down their neck. 'When the organization achieves Maturity Level 3, the conditions required for empowerment—competent people, effective processes, and a participatory environment—are established' (p.26).

Level 4 (Predictable: Capability management). Once the work processes are standardised and institutionalised, the organisations acquire the necessary capability to predict and effectively manage its future performance. Where deviations occur, 'the cause needs to be determined and corrective action taken if necessary . . . When the organization can characterize the performance of its processes quantitatively, it has profound knowledge that can be used to improve them' (p. 13).

In order to further exploit the capability created by the organisational framework set up in Level 3, organisations need to institute formal mentoring programmes, establish an atmosphere of trust and increased levels of delegation. When competency-based processes have been institutionalised and teams start working autonomously, managers are free from operational issues and they are better able to focus on strategic issues. 'The quantitative management capabilities implemented at Maturity Level 4 provide management with better input for strategic decisions, while encouraging delegation of operational details to people close to the processes' (p. 27).

Level 5 (Optimising: Change management). At this highest level of maturity, the work processes and practices undergo continuous improvement to effectively meet the challenges of constantly changing environment. 'Managing technological and process change become standard organizational processes and process improvement throughout the organization becomes perpetual' (p. 13). People are empowered to engage in continuous improvement.

At this level, change management becomes an integral and routine part of organisational life. 'At Maturity Level 5, individuals are encouraged to make continuous improvements to their personal work processes by analyzing their work and making necessary process enhancements . . . Workforce practices are honed to support a culture of performance excellence' (p. 28). At the same time, organisations need to make sure that in an effort to constantly improve, there is no mis-alignment with organisational objectives. They also need to ensure that best practices are shared and implemented across the entire organisational network rather than being isolated to just some parts.

As Curtis, Hefley and Miller (2009, p. 13) conclude: 'the maturity framework builds an environment in which

- practices can be repeated,
- best practices can be transferred rapidly across groups,
- variations in performing best practices are reduced, and
- practices are continuously improved to enhance their capability'.

To ensure success, scalability and sustainability, organisations need to gradually scale up the maturity level built on sound foundation of practices.

Conclusion

Reiterating the critical importance of 'human agency perspective' in IT projects, Boudreau and Robey (2005, p. 3) observe that 'recent perspectives on organisational change have emphasised human agency, more than technology or structure, to explain empirical outcomes resulting from the use of information technologies in organisations'. Technology alone cannot result in organisational transformation. Strategic use, involvement and engagement of human resources are essential to convert the potential of technology into practice. Otherwise, technology adoption can lead to unintended and undesirable consequences, as illustrated by the case study organisation in this chapter.

Accordingly, the HR department needs to play a strategic role in realising the full potential of IT, particularly with respect to its role as a strategic business partner, change agent and employee champion (Haines & Lafleur, 2008; Voermans & Veldhoven, 2006). Further reinforcing this view, Dery and Wailes (2005) provide evidence suggesting that HR needs to be actively engaged in the introduction and ongoing functioning of IT systems in their organisations in order to realise their full benefits.

Case study: Queensland Health payroll crisis

Queensland (QLD) Health is the government health department in the state of Queensland, Australia and is entrusted with maintaining and promoting the health and well-being of over 4.5 million Queenslanders (see www.health.qld.gov.au/). It is one of the largest employers in Australia with over 75,000 full-time employees, spread over 300 worksites. The organisation has a complex system of employment terms and conditions governed by 12 awards and 6 industrial agreements which provide for over 200 different allowances and up to 24,000 different combinations of pay.

Due to the discontinuation of the old payroll system and to meet its growing needs, QLD Health decided to acquire a new payroll system through the government's IT shared services provider, CorpTech. The best available payroll product and technology vendor (IBM) were selected for the purpose in 2008. Few months later, it was revealed that 'the size, complexity and scope of this phase of the program had been severely underestimated' resulting in 47 change requests from IBM. Consequently, 'the system implementation was over 18 months after the scheduled Go-Live date and approximately 300% over the original cost budget'. When the new payroll system went live in March 2010, QLD Health experienced significant payroll errors resulting in staff being overpaid, underpaid, or not paid at all.

The Auditor-General of Queensland (AGQ, 2010), highlighted several key reasons for the failure of the new payroll system as below:

- Under-estimation of project scope and complexity that failed to recognise the organisational complexity leading to very little customisation
- Poor governance and conflict between key agencies (QLD Health, CorpTech and IBM) on roles and responsibilities
- Poor user involvement and buy-in
- Ill-defined project scope, resulting in 'project creep' (major changes in the middle of the project)
- Poor project management
- Mad rush to Go Live
- Poor risk management

An independent review identified ongoing people, process and technology issues and recommended the need for comprehensive support for subsequent projects in the form of 'change management, training planning and execution to support staff and minimize negative impacts, create consistent and broadly disseminated communication, and effective, targeted training and education'. The case study confirms the central message of the chapter that it is not technology per se but the underlying social and organisational processes that mainly derail the implementation and cause the failure to realise the intended benefits.

Case study questions

1. What are the key lessons to be learnt from this case study?
2. Using the SDLC framework, identify the key issues and challenges
3. Explain how the case study organisation can move from level 1 to level 5 as per the P-CMM.

(Source: Extracted from Thite & Sandhu, 2014)

Debate: Should organisations outsource talent?

Introduction

Outsourcing refers to letting an outside vendor/third party carry on the functions instead of doing it in-house. It can be on-site (on the company premises), off-site (away from company premises), near shore (near company premises) or off shore (in another country). With increasing globalisation and global competitiveness, organisations around the world are under constant pressure to produce 'more with less'. With disruptive technologies almost destroying old industries and skills and, in the process, creating new industries, the human resource management practitioners are similarly under pressure to constantly upgrade the skill profile of their workforce to make it most up-to-date, competent and cost-effective.

Arguments in favour

- The main drivers for outsourcing are operating efficiencies or cost reduction; access to specialist expertise; greater process control and risk reduction. Most importantly, for workforce management, it can be a key strategic enabler if planned and implemented strategically.
- Today, talent sourcing has become global with organisations scouting around the world for best talent and at the most competitive price. One can see doctors, nurses, IT managers, software developers, engineers and so on being recruited from a global pool of talent.
- An innovative economy demands state of the art skills that are rapidly changing. This is true particularly in science, technology, engineering and mathematics (STEM) areas. With booming demand for but declining supply of STEM talent due to the ageing population and so on, emerging economies, such as India and China have emerged as key source countries for STEM talent.
- Today, strategic partnerships and alliances with trustworthy and proven vendors/ suppliers across the globe are not only beneficial but imperative to compete.

Arguments against

- There are serious negative repercussions of outsourcing talent, such as long-term negative effects on costs, employee morale and loss of organisational knowledge. If not managed strategically, costs can spiral out of control, employee morale can sink and precious organisational knowledge lost.
- Talent management is indeed a core competency for most high-technology organisations and therefore, they need to adopt a long-term perspective on talent sourcing and make all out efforts, in collaboration with government and industry bodies, to develop local talent without unduly relying on outside talent. Otherwise, it may lead to contracting-out culture.
- Outsourcing vendors are committed to their own cause and not that of the organisation. Many companies outsource because of the hype and in the process lose both money and people (expertise).
- Therefore, outsourcing may not be an ideal solution for every industry, company and occupation every time.

Useful references

Lewin, A. Y., Massini, S. & Peeters, C. (2009). Why are companies offshoring innovation? The emerging global race for talent. *Journal of International Business Studies*, 40, 901–925.

Liew, S. (2006). Outsourcing: the poisoned chalice? *Risk Magazine*, 8 November 2006.
Stringfellow, A., Teagarden, M. B. & Nie, W. (2008). Invisible costs in offshoring services work. *Journal of Operations Management*, 26(2), 164–179.
Technology Councils of North America (TECNA) (2014). *Building software development talent: Steps for a sustainable future*. Santa Ana, CA: TECNA.
Woods, G. (2007). *The statistical evidence for offshore outsourcing and its impact on the Australian labour force. Parliamentary Library Information, analysis and advice for the Parliament*, 2 August, 3, 1–6. Canberra: Commonwealth of Australia.

Video learning resources

- What is project management? Training video: www.youtube.com/watch?v=9LSnINglkQA
- Software development life cycle (SDLC) – detailed explanation: www.youtube.com/watch?v=G-6qDY8UltU
- CIS 121 – System development life cycle: www.youtube.com/watch?v=mH-Nc5kvyQQ
- SDLC – Software development life cycle explained for beginners | Business analyst training: www.youtube.com/watch?v=eiXS9dyItnY
- Software development life cycle – simplified: www.youtube.com/watch?v=DRDD7UWX2y4
- Burning questions – Should we outsource our workforce? https://www.youtube.com/watch?v=Q3o4vp2OMKU&t=5s

References

AGQ (2010). *Report to Parliament No. 7 for 2010. Information systems governance and control, including the Queensland Health Implementation of Continuity Project*. Auditor-General of Queensland, Queensland Audit Office, Brisbane, Australia.

Arnold, R. D. & Wade, J. P. (2015). A definition of systems thinking: A systems approach. *Procedia Computer Science*, 44, 669–678.

Boudreau, M. & Robey, D. (2005). Enacting integrated information technology: A human agency perspective. *Organization Science*, 16(1), 3–18.

Brock, J., Saleh, T. & Iyer, S. (2015). *Large-scale IT projects: From nightmare to value creation. bcg. perspectives*. Boston, MA: Boston Consulting Group. www.bcgperspectives.com/content/articles/technology-business-transformation-technology-organization-large-scale-it-projects/.

Curtis, B., Hefley, B. & Miller, S. (2009). *People capability maturity model (P-CMM) version 2.0* (2nd edn). Pittsburgh, PA: Software Engineering Institute, Carnegie Mellon University. Technical Report CMU/SEI-2009-TR-003, ESC-TR-2009-003. www.sei.cmu.edu/reports/09tr003.pdf.

Dery, K. & Wailes, W. (2005). Necessary but not sufficient: ERPs and strategic HRM. *Strategic Change*, 14, 265–272.

Green, A. (2017). Job description of an HRIS manager. https://careertrend.com/about-6711738-job-description-hris-manager.html.

Haines, V. Y. & Lafleur, G. (2008). Information technology usage and human resource roles and effectiveness. *Human Resource Management*, 47(3), 525–540.

Hastie, S. & Wojewoda, S. (2015). Standish Group 2015 Chaos report: Q&A with Jennifer Lynch. *InfoQ*. www.infoq.com/articles/standish-chaos-2015.

Hsu, J. S., Liang, T. P., Wu, S. P. J., Klein, G. & Jiang, J. J. (2011). Promoting the integration of users and developers to achieve a collective mind through the screening of information systems projects. *International Journal of Project Management*, 29, 514–524.

Kim, D. H. (1999). *Introduction to systems thinking.* Innovations in Management Series. Waltham, MA: Pegasus Communications.

Martinsons, M. G. & Chong, P. K. C. (1999). The influence of human factors and specialist involvement on information systems success. *Human Relations*, 52(1), 123–152.

McConnell, S. (1996). *Rapid development: Taming wild software schedules.* Redmond, WA: Microsoft Press.

Sankaran, S., Haslett, T. & Sheffield, J. (2010). Systems thinking approaches to address complex issues in project management. Paper presented at PMI® Global Congress 2010—Asia Pacific, Melbourne, Victoria, Australia. Newtown Square, PA: Project Management Institute. www.pmi.org/learning/library/systems-thinking-soft-methodology-issues-6912.

Senge, P. (1990). *The fifth discipline, the art and practice of the learning organization.* New York, NY: Doubleday/Currency.

Squires, A., Wade, J., Dominick, P. & Gelosh, D. (2011). *Building a competency taxonomy to guide experience acceleration of lead program systems engineers.* In 9th Annual Conference on Systems Engineering Research (CSER) (pp. 1–10). CSER: Redondo Beach, CA.

Standish Group (2014). Law of the five deadly sins. The Standish Group International Inc. https://res.infoq.com/articles/standish-chaos-015/en/resources/5Deadly%20sins_2014-5.pdf.

Thite, M. & Sandhu, K. (2014). Where is my pay? Critical success factors of a payroll system— A system life cycle approach. *Australasian Journal of Information Systems*, 18(2), 149–164.

Voermans, M. & Veldhoven, M. (2006). Attitude towards E-HRM: An empirical study at Philips. *Personnel Review*, 36(6), 887–902.

Vrhoves, S. L. R., Hovelja, T., Vavpotic, D. & Krisper, M. (2015). Diagnosing organisational risks in software projects: Stakeholder resistance. *International Journal of Project Management*, 33, 1262–1273.

4 Agile approach to e-HRM project management

NMK Bhatta & Mohan Thite

> **Learning objectives**
> - Explain the Agile Manifesto and its key characteristics and principles
> - Present the process map of and the key terms used in the Agile Scrum Method
> - Discuss how HR can play a transformative role in implementing Agile with specific reference to organisational culture, recruitment and selection and performance and reward management.
> - Highlight the key components of the HR->T Talent Management Model
> - Critically present the major implementation challenges in implementing Agile

Introduction

In the previous chapter, we introduced the soft systems thinking approach and systems development life cycle (SDLC) framework as critical starting points for e-HRM project management. The waterfall methodology in the SDLC is a sequential approach where the project team goes to the next phase only after completely satisfied with the previous phase. The development work is broken down into small parts and distributed to teams based on their skills. The customer gets involved only later at the testing stage and further guides the process to completion.

The waterfall approach is particularly suitable for well-defined and well-scoped projects with pre-determined processes and comprehensive documentation. The rigidity in the system is supposed to keep the scope, costs and schedule well under control. However, in a business environment that is rapidly and radically changing, due to globalisation and disruptive technologies resulting in hyper-competitive market conditions, technology project teams require agility not rigidity in the way the project is executed.

The alarmingly high failure rate of technology projects as detailed in the previous chapter caused software engineers across the world to pause and rethink if the traditional methods of project management were suitable for all types of projects and all business situations. Their analysis revealed that the project management approach that they were hitherto following would work only when all the requirements of the customer are very clearly known and frozen upfront at the very beginning of the project. In an ever changing and dynamic business scenario where competitive pressures and technological advances compel businesses to continually reassess their requirements, the traditional approaches may not be suitable.

The analysis also found that the methodologies that they were following were too process oriented with little scope for creativity or out of the box thinking. Customers' perceived value addition was also low because with the conventional methods of IT project management, they had very little opportunity to preview the system until the end, by which time it was too late to make major changes. While the traditional waterfall methods can be continued for projects having absolute clarity of requirements with no changes expected, for other projects with stringent Go To Market constraints or with vague/unclear requirements, we need a completely new thinking of IT project management based on the principles of agility, transparency and adaptation and more active customer involvement. Thus, began a new philosophy called Agile Project Management with the release of an Agile Manifesto in 2001.

The Agile philosophy has been rapidly gaining prominence in recent times and 'has had a huge impact on how software is developed worldwide' (Dyba & Dingsoyr, 2008, p. 834) and in the process, 'revolutionised information technology' (Rigby, Sutherland & Takeuchi, 2016). In this methodology, the developmental life cycle is divided into smaller parts, called 'increments' or 'iterations' wherein the phases within the life cycle are visited repeatedly in order to incrementally and iteratively improve the project outcomes. According to Leau, Loo, Tham and Tan (2012, pp. 163–164):

> Agile methods emphasize on teams, working software, customer collaboration, and responding to change; while the conventional methods stress on contracts, plans, processes, documents, and tools . . . Taking the fact that customers' requirements are acquired iteratively as context, agile development is able to deliver an end-product that better meets customer needs.

According to the 10th Annual State of Agile Report (VersionOne, 2016), increasingly larger organisations around the world are embracing Agile, which is helping them to drive business success with continued positive impact. The Standish Group 2015 Chaos Report (Hastie & Wojewoda, 2015) also confirms that 'across all project sizes agile approaches resulted in more successful projects and less outright failures'.

In this chapter, we will introduce the philosophy, principles and characteristics of the Agile approach, with specific reference to scrum process. We will then highlight the critical role played by HR as a change agent and facilitator of the Agile journey and how it can reengineer the talent management tools and techniques to attract, assess, develop and reward talent. We will conclude with the implementation challenges and success factors.

The Agile Manifesto and principles

Agile software development methods took birth with the release of the Agile Manifesto in 2001 (Agilemanifesto.org), which states as below:

> We are uncovering better ways of developing software by doing it and helping others do it. Through this work, we have come to value
>
> **Individuals and interactions** over processes and tools
> **Working software** over comprehensive documentation
> **Customer collaboration** over contract negotiation
> **Responding to change** over following a plan
>
> That is, while there is value in the items on the right, we value the items on the left more.

Table 4.1 Principles of Agile methodology

1. 'Our highest priority is to satisfy the customer through early and continuous delivery of valuable software.
2. Welcome changing requirements, even late in development. Agile processes harness change for the customer's competitive advantage.
3. Deliver working software frequently, from a couple of weeks to a couple of months, with a preference to the shorter timescale.
4. Business people and developers must work together daily throughout the project.
5. Build projects around motivated individuals. Give them the environment and support they need, and trust them to get the job done.
6. The most efficient and effective method of conveying information to and within a development team is face-to-face conversation.
7. Working software is the primary measure of progress.
8. Agile processes promote sustainable development. The sponsors, developers, and users should be able to maintain a constant pace indefinitely.
9. Continuous attention to technical excellence and good design enhances agility.
10. Simplicity – the art of maximizing the amount of work not done – is essential.
11. The best architectures, requirements, and designs emerge from self-organizing teams.
12. At regular intervals, the team reflects on how to become more effective, then tunes and adjusts its behaviour accordingly'.

Source: http://agilemanifesto.org/principles.html

The Agile Manifesto puts self-organisation and team dynamics above a pre-determined and rigid set of processes or tools. A code that works is more useful than extensive documentation presented to the customer. As requirements can never be fully finalised up front for many projects, continuous customer participation in the software development is vital. A typical software project requirement can never be frozen and therefore, the ability of the project team to accept the changes at all stages will be critical for expected customer value creation.

Conventional methods may still be used where there is complete clarity on project requirements and they are fully stable. A vast number of companies still use conventional methods. But if there is any vagueness or incomplete requirements, Agile methods provide an answer. Many companies in fact combine conventional and Agile methods in a new series of methods called Hybrid Agile (which is out of scope for this chapter).

While several versions of Agile have been introduced after the release of the Agile Manifesto in 2001, all of them are built on the basic premise that people contribute their best when they have autonomy in decision making. Group dynamics and human psychology take centre stage in Agile. This calls for more focussed and innovative HR support for Agile projects with the HR ecosystem conforming to the Agile principles and manifesto.

The Agile Manifesto is underpinned by 12 Agile principles as outlined in Table 4.1.

Key characteristics of Agile methods

The following characteristics define the fabric of all Agile methods

- **Self-organising and cross functional teams:** In Agile, the project team is completely empowered and assumes authority over all technical and managerial matters. Each team features cross functional members so that they can meet the project objectives without any external help.
- **Time-boxed iterations:** All Agile methods stipulate that at the end of every fixed time interval (called a time-boxed iteration) some tangible pre-determined, potentially shippable delivery is made to the customer conforming to some shared definition.

- **Fully participating customer:** Agile methods argue that the customer should have the final say on what work should be carried out by the team and the team should have the final say on how that work will be carried out. It also insists on full-time availability of the customer for the team to seek any clarifications and to finally inspect the team's output at the end of each time-boxed iteration.
- **Minimal documentation:** In Agile, emphasis is more on working software and documentation is reduced to bare minimum as agreed between the customer and the team.
- **Collective/multiple ownership:** In Agile, the entire team takes the ownership of the deliverables collectively. This also gives a chance to every member of the team to review or improve the work done by any other team member. This helps in making full use of the team capabilities and competencies.
- **Rapid feedback and action:** Agile facilitates inspect output at the end of every iteration by the customer and the same is considered closed if it conforms to a pre-decided definition. Any further changes or improvements are handled as new requirements in subsequent iterations.
- **Servant leadership:** While teams in Agile are entirely self-organised and cross functional, it still has scope for one person to act as the servant leader of the team. Such a member is called a *Scrum Master* in the Scrum method of Agile. The Scrum Master has a role of protecting the team members from external interferences, resolving various problems (technical or otherwise) faced by the team members and to ensure that the team follows all Agile practices meticulously. However, he/she is not expected to manage the day-to-day working of the team. It is also possible that one of the team members assumes an additional charge of Scrum Master.
- **Retrospection and openness to criticism:** Agile believes that at the end of each iteration, the team and the customer retrospect on what went well during the iteration, what did not go well and how the subsequent iterations can be improved. Here, every stakeholder will be open to criticism by the other stakeholders on his/her performance during the iteration. While the entire retrospection is carried out with an objective of avoiding similar issues in future iterations, it still calls for tremendous maturity on the part of the members to have an open mind to constructive criticism.
- **Complete transparency:** The teams in Agile work in an environment of complete transparency. All team members and the customers are always aware of what each member has done, is doing and will be doing. Added to this, every team member is required to explain what he/she has done, will be doing and the impediments/challenges faced every day in a meeting called the daily stand-up meeting. This increases accountability and ownership on the part of team members.

Agile Scrum methodology

There are several Agile methods in use. According to the 10th Annual State of Agile Report (VersionOne, 2016), 58% of Agile users are using pure Scrum and 17% are using a combination of Scrum with other methods. The rest of the users adopt other Agile methods, including Kanban, Feature Driven Development, Lean and Extreme Programming. However, the core principles underlying all the methods are the same and are derived from the Agile Manifesto. As Burchardi et al. (2016, p. 2) emphasise, 'many forms of Agile have been developed, but at its heart, Agile is a set of beliefs. It is *iterative, empirical, cross-functional, focused, and continually improving*'.

Scrum process

Scrum is an Agile method with three major stakeholders, namely, Product Owner (PO), Scrum Master (SM) and the development team. Work is done in a series of time-boxed iterations called Sprints (which typically lasts for 1 to 4 weeks). The PO owns a prioritised list of requirements called Product Backlog and decides what work should be carried out. The development team decides how much can be done in each sprint and how it will be done. The SM helps both the PO and the team in following the scrum process and removing any obstacles on the way.

Figure 4.1 presents the Agile Scrum process diagram.

Before every sprint, a sprint planning meeting is conducted, where the work is broken down into tasks and the team distributes these tasks among themselves. A list of all these tasks is called sprint backlog. During each sprint, the team conducts a daily stand-up meeting every day to explain to each other on what has been done, what will be done and what are the obstacles. At the end of the sprint, the team presents its output (which is called a potentially shippable product) to all stakeholders including some business users. After the sprint review, the PO, the SM and the development team conduct a sprint retrospective meeting to retrospect on what went well in the sprint, what did not go well and what can be improved in the upcoming sprints. The process is continued sprint after sprint until the final product is released to the customer.

Table 4.2 summarises the key terms used in Agile Scrum.

Role of HR in Agile

Traditionally, HR has generally played a support role in e-HRM project management, mostly facilitating recruitment and resource allocation. In Agile however, HR plays a central role. Agile is completely based on people skills and team dynamics. The success of Agile depends on the proactive and strategic role of HR. Before joining an Agile project environment, HR professionals themselves must become agile. Kreissl (2012) argues that 'incorporating (the four values of agile development, namely) adaptability, transparency, simplicity and unity can help improve HR service delivery'.

A stated in the Agile Manifesto, the first and foremost principle of Agile is that we must value individuals and group interactions over processes and tools, which means that any processes introduced should facilitate empowerment and encourage social interactions. HR needs to focus on building an organisational climate and culture that explicitly encourages creative thinking and autonomous work groups. In Agile, HR's role starts with working on transforming the organisational culture to ensure a change of mindset from conventional project management to Agile. As all the HR functions are interrelated, the entire people management system, from recruitment to on-boarding to performance and reward management, needs to be aligned to the new work culture.

Underscoring the critical role of HR in the implementation of Agile, Gieles and van der Meer (2017, p. 2) state that:

> The role of HR in an Agile world is to facilitate and improve organizational agility and increase talent motivation. This implies: effectively changing the HR's mission and role to the more coaching and serving role of talent-specialists. This (is) in contrast to the traditional way, where the job of HR is mostly seen as implementing controls and standards to drive execution.

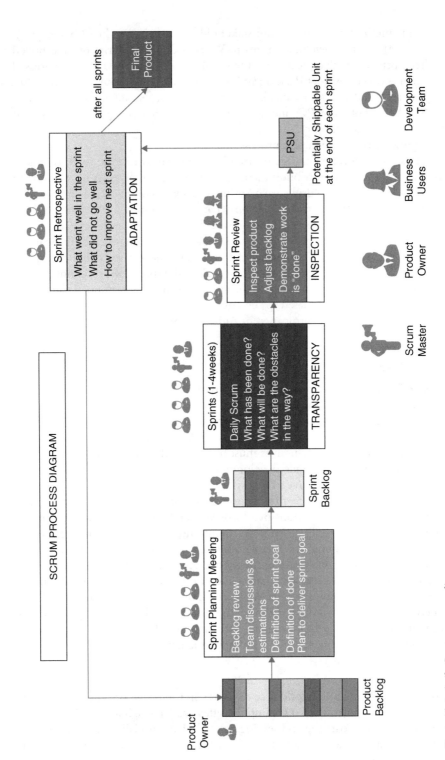

Figure 4.1 Agile Scrum process diagram.
Source: First author.

Table 4.2 Key terms in Agile Scrum

1. **Product backlog.** A prioritised list of all features that are required to be developed to achieve the business objective. It is highly dynamic and open to any changes as per the business needs.
2. **Product owner.** Product owner is the customer or their representative with complete business vision and goals of the project. The customer owns the product backlog and decides the prioritisation of goals and activities.
3. **Sprint.** This is a time-boxed period, at the end of which the team delivers a potentially shippable feature. The sprint periods may vary anywhere between one week to six weeks.
4. **Scrum Master.** He/she is the servant leader for the team and has three specific roles:
    a. To protect the team from external disturbances
    b. To resolve any problems/challenges that the team may be facing
    c. To ensure scrum processes and ceremonies are meticulously followed
5. **Development team.** This is the group of people who actually deliver the output to customers. In Agile, development teams are self-organised and cross functional.
6. **User stories.** They are a customer's way of explaining their requirements.
7. **Definition of done.** A shared understanding among all stakeholders about what 'done' means.
8. **Scrum ceremonies.** To make a scrum process effective and to ensure inspection, transparency and adaptation throughout, some essential ceremonies are introduced. These ceremonies include a sprint planning meeting, a daily stand-up meeting, a sprint review meeting and a sprint retrospective meeting.
9. **Scrum of Scrums.** When several scrum teams scale up to work together on the same project, it is called a Scrum of Scrums arrangement. One member of each team participates in an additional meeting called a Scrum of Scrums meeting, where they discuss interdependencies among various teams and brief each other on work completed and work planned for the future.
10. **Information radiators.** To ensure transparency, all information about product backlog, sprint backlog, work completed, work in progress and so on is displayed along the Agile rooms. These boards are normally called information Radiators as they give complete information on the project.

Source: Authors

Organisational culture: The most essential prerequisite for success of Agile in an organisation is conducive organisational culture. It is not easy for an organisation that was hitherto working on traditional methods to transform itself to Agile processes without radically altering the culture prevailing in the organisation. This transformation process is relatively slow and HR plays a critical role in making this happen. As change agents, HR professionals need to have a personal interaction with every member moving into Agile mode and ensure that they are attitudinally fit to take up the new roles. The learning and development function needs to take a major responsibility to familiarise everybody in the organisation with Agile principles, starting from top management right down up to the team member level through appropriate training programmes. These training programmes must include both behavioural training and training on Agile methods and principles. They should systematically work to build a culture of openness, trust and honesty in the organisation through continuous engagement of all stakeholders.

Talent management: HR plays a key role in proactively staffing and managing the entire talent ecosystem in an Agile organisation. Considering that Agile teams are self-organised and cross functional, there is no need for micromanaging them and, in fact, micromanagement could be counter-productive. Having recruited talent with the right mindset and competencies for Agile, HR should promote motivation and higher morale among the staff by offering them a chance to challenge themselves through complex projects, creating platforms that provide continuous learning opportunities by ensuring proper work life balance and creating ownership. Growth of employees will be the key to retention and this can be ensured only through transparent and flexible career graphs.

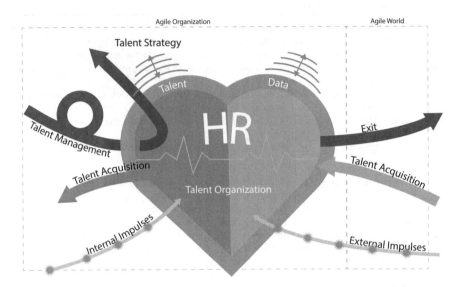

Figure 4.2 Gieles and van der Meer's HR->T Talent Management Model under Agile.
Source: Gieles and van der Meer (2017, p. 26): Reproduced with permission.

A well-oiled HR analytics model can help HR managers predict likely changes and help them handle the same proactively. A clear understanding of the skills requirement (both behavioural and technical) would help HR to contribute towards improving agility. A good on-boarding process, allocation on challenging projects and continuous evaluation on how they feel makes the employees feel important and engaged in an Agile system.

Gieles & van der Meer (2017, p. 23) believe that 'talent management is the beating heart of an agile organisation' and to visualise this analogy, developed the HR->T Model (see Figure 4.2) consisting of the following five components:

1 Talent organisation (planning and organisation)
2 Talent acquisition (recruitment and selection)
3 Talent management (compensation, performance, training and development)
4 Talent data (collection and analysis of data)
5 Talent strategy (proactive changes and innovative ideas)

As stated by Gieles and van der Meer:

> Like the heart, the talent team beats in a steady rhythm (Agile way of working). It receives impulses from the outside world and from different parts of the organization, so it can react and speed up or slow down as needed ... Any agile way of working is a short-cyclic, iterative and feedback-driven way of working.
>
> (2017, p. 7, 10)

HR must try and create an innovative and people focussed talent ecosystem driven by the power of data analytics which continuously works towards improving its service levels on the basis of feedback received from the operations team.

Recruitment and selection of Agile teams: HR's role in building an Agile organisation begins with attracting the right talent with the right attitude and mindset (Mahajan, 2013). The internal and external impulses in the T Model indicate demand and availability of talent. HR teams need to plan talent acquisition strategies appropriately with more emphasis on attitudinal aspects. Along with intelligence quotient (IQ) and technical skills, the talent acquisition team needs to look at emotional quotient (EQ) and adversity quotient (AQ). It should also assess the candidate's ability to collaborate and turn obstacles into opportunities. It is crucial to find alignment between vision, mission and values of the candidate, with that of the organisation before a candidate is on-boarded.

Each role in an Agile team is customised and as such needs specific skills (technical, behavioural and managerial) to successfully deliver the project on time, within budget and to customer specifications. The product owner should have astute business skills with overarching knowledge of business goals and vision of the customer's organisation. He/she should be able to clearly articulate the vision to the team and provide a clear roadmap on how best to achieve this and effectively address all the impediments on the way. The SM should essentially be a servant leader. Attitudinally, he/she should be a go-getter and should be adept in relationship building and diplomatic skills. The development team members should be good in interactive skills, collaboration and should be able to put team success above their individual success.

HR teams supporting Agile projects must maintain a detailed record of both technical skills and behavioural skills of employees observed through various team building and other group activities so that they can provide the right person for the right role at the right time. As reiterated by Gothelf (2014), '(in an agile organisation) HR teams need to start hiring for creativity, collaboration and curiosity. They need to seek out the non-conformists – the candidates that don't easily fit into a box. These are the generalists with an entrepreneurial spirit'.

Table 4.3 summarises the key skills and competencies required in Agile personnel.

Competency development: In an Agile environment, HR teams must focus towards continuously reskilling and reorienting the workforce to suite dynamically changing business needs. The learning and development system should be redesigned to promote design

Table 4.3 Key skills and competencies of Agile personnel

- Adaptability to fast changing organisational and project requirements
- Alignment/fit between individual and organisational goals (shared commitment)
- Ability to work effectively in an autonomous, self-managing team environment
- Self-leadership and servant leadership
- Lifelong learning attitude and with an open mind
- Innovative and creative mindset (out of the box thinking)
- Entrepreneurial spirit
- Professional and customer-centric work ethic
- Spirit of cooperation and collaboration
- Personal mastery (desire to excel)
- Emotional intelligence
- Cross-cultural and cross-functional competence in a diverse environment
- Ability and motivation to work on challenging projects in a volatile, uncertain, complex and ambiguous (VUCA) global business environment

Source: Authors.

Table 4.4 Design thinking principles of learning organisations

Senge (1990)	Morgan (1997)	Marsick and Watkins (2003)
– Systems thinking – Personal mastery – Mental models – Shared vision – Team learning	– Build whole into parts – Importance of redundancy – Requisite variety – Minimum specs – Learn to learn	– Create continuous learning opportunities – Promote enquiry and dialogue – Encourage collaboration and team learning – Create (IT) systems to capture and share learning – Empower people towards a collective vision

Source: Authors.

thinking and innovation. Continuous learning and development must be integrated into day-to-day working of the teams. The effort should be towards building a 'learning organisation'. Table 4.4 provides the design thinking principles of learning organisations as proposed by three leading thinkers in the field, namely, Senge (1990), Morgan (1997) and Marsick and Watkins (2003).

In Distributed Scrum, some of the stakeholders of the project are geographically separated from the other members. In many cases, the separated team members belong to different cultures, and speak different languages. As trust and communication are the backbone for the success of Agile, HR needs to work on ways and means of developing trust among disparate team members through appropriate policies and practices. Bridging cultural gaps is a critical requirement in distributed Agile and HR must leave no stone unturned to ensure this happens.

Performance management: Considering that Agile teams are self-managed, traditional methods of performance management by the managers will not be effective. Several organisations have customised their own performance management models with a 360 degrees feedback loop befitting their organisational priorities, environment and culture. We explain below how this can be done.

The *performance appraisal of team members* may be done at four levels as below:

Level 1:
Appraisal by self (S)

Level 2:
Appraisal by peers (average value) (P)
If P–S < 1, consider S
If P–S > 1, ignore S

Level 3:
Appraisal by SM/coach (M1)

Level 4:
Appraisal by PO (M2)

Final Rating:

Case 1: if P–S < 1,
(S + P + M1 + M2)/4

Case 2: if P–S ≥ 1
(P + M1+ M2)/3

The *performance appraisal of a Scrum Master* may be done as below:

Level 1:
Self-appraisal (S)

Level 2:
Average of appraisal by team members (T)

Level 3:
Appraisal by PO (P)

Initial Rating:

(S + T + P) / 3, if T − S < 1;
(T + P)/2, if T − S > 1

Rewards and recognitions (R&R): As Agile wants to bind its employees emotionally, a properly designed and transparent rewards and recognition (R&R) system is essential. An incorrectly designed R&R system could be counterproductive in an Agile environment. Unlike in traditional systems, where managers decide R&R for the people, in Agile, the teams are self-organised in deciding who amongst them should be rewarded. The usual process followed is that at the end of each sprint retrospective, the team members are asked to give preferential votes for a star of the team award and the final decision is made on the basis of the team's preference. All other recognitions should be team based on the basis of the entire team performance rather than any individual's contribution. Apart from financial rewards, social recognition rewards are equally valued in an Agile project environment.

According to Gothelf (2014), while the technology teams may embrace Agile way of working,

> they often find that the pace of work they desire is substantially hindered by the lack of agility in HR ... In an agile organisation, HR needs to provide the same services it's always provided – hiring, professional development, performance management – but in ways that are responsive to the ongoing changes in the culture and work style of the organisation.

While reiterating how HR drives the Agile organisation, Silverstone, Tambe and Cantrell (2015, p. 12) conclude:

> As agility becomes the new mantra of business, organizations will reshape themselves so that they can fluidly pull resources when and where they're needed to rapidly respond to changing business conditions. HR organizations of the future will have to reinvent themselves—and the HR and talent management practices they support— to drive agility in their organization. Those that fail to do so may put their organizations at risk of obsolescence.

Implementation challenges to Agile project management

While Agile way of working has been offered as a solution to the inertia and rigidity inherent in traditional IT projects, such as waterfall methodology, leading to their inability to address volatile business environments, the implementation challenges to Agile projects remain the same as they require the project team members 'to drastically change their work habits and acquire new skills' (Chan & Thong, 2009, p. 803). Overcoming employee resistance to change is the biggest challenge to organisations that attempt to radically change their organisational culture. According to Burchardi et al. (2016, p. 1), 'companies across many industries are struggling with the transition to Agile . . . (because, primarily) it is not easy to integrate self-directed, cross-functional Agile teams into the existing hierarchy of large companies'.

Research studies that examine technology adoption perspective, such as the Technology Acceptance Model (TAM), typically focus on technology characteristics (for example, perceived usefulness and ease of use) and overlook non-technology factors relating to employee ability, motivation and opportunity (AMO). In implementing Agile philosophy, organisations need to pay special attention to 'ability-related factors (e.g., self-efficacy), motivation-related factors (e.g., voluntariness) and opportunity-related factors (e.g., shared understanding)' (Chan & Thong, 2009, p. 812).

Dyba and Dingsoyr (2008, p. 850) conducted a systematic review of empirical studies of Agile software development and identified several benefits and limitations. They found that Agile development practices thrive in radically different environments, are easily adoptable and yield better code quality, customer and employee satisfaction. The limitations are that they

- are more suitable for small teams than for larger projects;
- work best with experienced development teams;
- do not pay enough attention to design and architectural issues; and
- require high levels of individual and team autonomy, interpersonal skills and trust.

Organisational transformation starts from the top and that is where the problem with Agile implementation often begins. According to Rigby, Sutherland and Takeuchi (2016),

> (untrained) executives launch countless initiatives with urgent deadlines rather than assign the highest priority to two or three. They spread themselves and their best people across too many projects . . . They talk more than listen . . . They routinely overturn team decisions. With the best of intentions, they erode the benefits that agile innovation can deliver.

Another difficulty with the Agile method is that it underplays the importance of 'documentation', causing junior development team members to raise too many questions to senior developers, delaying the delivery of iteration and potentially increasing the development cost. Further, the 'short time frame allocated to each iteration' makes it difficult for developers to meet tight deadlines. Agile requires excellent social and interpersonal skills from team members, most of whom are technical specialists with a poor understanding of the dynamics of informal workplace socialisation (Leau, Loo, Tham & Tan, 2012, p. 164–166).

According to Misra, Kumar and Kumar (2009), some of the key success factors in adopting Agile software development practices are: customer collaboration; customer commitment; decision time; corporate culture; personal characteristics; societal culture; and training and learning. As these factors require enterprise-wide culture change, many firms will struggle to meet the transformational expectations.

Summary

While IT projects are technology intensive, most projects fail due to non-technical reasons, including lack of agility in requirement handling and absence of customer involvement. Agile methods came into being to overcome these challenges and to exploit the power of empowerment, motivation, self-management, team dynamics and the fully participating customer. However, all these special characteristics of Agile require successful adoption of 'learning organisation' (Senge, 1990) with sweeping change in organisational culture, elimination of command and control managerial mindset, servant leadership and self-managing teams, which is a tall order to say the least. It also requires HR to strategise the Agile ecosystem and play a central role in making Agile successful.

That said, the Agile way of working is a must for any organisation operating in a fast changing, volatile, uncertain, complex and ambiguous (VUCA) global business environment with rising customer expectations to do more with less (time and money). Even though Agile thinking originated in software development, organisations can leverage its immense potential across all the core business units, including HR (Sherman, Edison, Rehberg & Danoesastro, 2017). As 'Agile development is an exercise in continuous improvement (and) not a one-off exercise' (Burchardi et al., 2016, p. 5), it is all about mindset, not methodology and it is a journey, not a destination.

Case study: The manager's role in sustaining Agile team performance

A 300 million USD, two-year IT project at John Neilson Software Limited, Australia, was to be delivered in Agile Scrum. Jessica, HR Director, had trained the team to be truly self-organising. Moses, the Scrum Master and originally a micro-manager, was coached, with the help of an external counsellor, to be more of a mentor and coach for the team.

After the third sprint, when team motivation and ownership picked up, Jessica went away on maternity leave for six months after suggesting to the management to put in a replacement. But the management felt that since things had stabilised and under control, they will be able to manage without an HR member until Jessica returned. In the ninth sprint round, the team ran into unexpected difficulties. Two critical members got into a big verbal duel and stopped collaborating. One of the key members resigned unexpectedly, which had a telling impact on the output and it went significantly behind plan. Moses was unable to resolve the situation and he particularly missed Jessica's guidance. His first instinct was to withhold the bad news from the customer.

One day, the vice president of the business group, Mr Raymond, ventured into the team's work area and by looking at the information radiators realised that the team was significantly behind plan. He asked for an explanation. Moses responded that the team encountered some challenges and was trying hard to get on track. Raymond retorted, 'Moses you are aware that this project is highly critical. We can't let it fall behind. As a manager, you have to ensure that the team delivers and fully obeys your instructions. From now on, I want you to take charge of every aspect of the project and make sure that we remain on track'.

Confused, Moses responded, 'Raymond, we had decided to deliver the project the Agile way and let the team be self-organised. Our frequent interference could only be counter-productive'. Raymond had been too busy to attend in-house Agile training. The HR team had mailed him a slide deck on Agile principles, self-organising teams and the new role for managers. But he didn't seem to have gone through the information pack. He said, 'Well, while the team may be responsible, I will hold you accountable if anything goes wrong. It's YOUR job to make it happen'.

In response, Moses got back to his micromanagement style and demanded to know from the team who had done what, what is left out and why. As the sprint progressed, Moses got more and more involved. Daily stand-ups got converted to update meetings. The team members who were earlier excellent performers became disengaged. Team motivation and morale suffered. No one seemed to be interested in any original thinking. The team changed itself into a submissive mode. At the sprint review, Raymond personally turned up and was quite happy to see that somehow the team met the sprint objective and generously complimented Moses.

Upon hearing this, everyone in the team decided not to stick their neck out in the subsequent sprints. As the sprints progressed, Moses got more and more involved in micromanaging the team, self-organisation was conspicuous by its absence, team morale and motivation took a dip and the productivity fell to an all-time low. Team communication broke down and those amazing initial sprints where the team was bubbling with motivation and performing beyond expectations had become more of a distant memory. The project went deep into the red and Raymond was puzzled what went wrong.

Case study questions

1 Identify the key implementation challenges faced by the team in the case study, using the 12 Agile principles.
2 Using the case study, explain the critical role played by HR in the Agile way of working.
3 Based on the lessons learnt from the case study, identify the key success factors in an Agile environment.

Debate: What is the key to project management success – agility or stability?

Introduction

One of the continuing challenges in the management discipline is how to achieve the right balance between managerial control and creative freedom. The industrial economy was dominated by the command and control management style that somewhat suited the relatively stable business environment. However, the present knowledge economy, which is characterised by rapid change and uncertainty demands employee agility, autonomy and empowerment so that knowledge workers are free from stifling bureaucratic controls. In the IT project management domain, waterfall or structured methodologies dominated for many decades. However, market dynamics and competition and ever evolving new technologies led to the emergence of Agile methods. It is still hotly debated as to whether Agile can be considered as a 'cure all' to the challenges in technology project management.

Arguments in favour of stability

- Stability helps maturity of development processes guaranteeing sustainability, repeatability and replicability of results, project after project.
- Stability provides ease of controlling and monitoring budgets and schedules that are critical for technology projects.
- Stability offered by structured methods provides ample scope for skilling of new resources.
- Stable methods are very apt for fixed price/budget projects.
- Large projects spanning a long duration are best delivered using the structured models.
- Detailed documentation helps project managers in overcoming challenges created by employee attrition. It also helps in easier maintenance after a project goes live.

Arguments in favour of agility

- All requirements can never be frozen at the beginning of any project in a dynamic business environment. Agility is the only answer under such conditions.
- Empowerment and flexibility offered by agility promotes innovative spirit in the team members, leading to better project outcomes.
- Continuous delivery of potentially shippable software, iteration after iteration helps business in deriving market advantage of frequent releases.
- Agility makes pre-closure of projects (if required due to business imperatives) easy, which is not possible with structured models.
- Sizable reduction in documentation promoted by Agile methods helps the teams to concentrate more on working software.

Useful references

Aghina, W., De Smet, A. & Weerda, K. (2015). *Agility: It rhymes with stability*. McKinsey Quarterly, December. www.mckinsey.com/business-functions/organization/our-insights/agility-it-rhymes-with-stability

Austin, R. D. (2007). CMM vs Agile: Methodology wars in software development –*Harvard Business Review* case study. PRODUCT #: 607084-PDF-ENG.

Boehm, B. & Turner, R. (2004). *Balancing agility & discipline: A guide for the perplexed*. Boston, MA: Pearson Education.

Orr, K. (2011). *CMM versus Agile development: Religious wars and software development*. Executive Report, Vol. 3, No. 7. Topeka, KS: The Ken Orr Institute. https://issuu.com/kenorr/docs/apm0702

> **Video learning resources**
>
> - Agile project management: Scrum and sprint demystified www.youtube.com/watch?v=DvBKevrItcc
> - Agile simulation – Meet the Agile team: www.youtube.com/watch?v=hgn_oNmfTqg
> - Agile simulation - The daily standup: www.youtube.com/watch?v=q_R9wQY4G5I
> - Kotter's 8 step change model: www.youtube.com/watch?v=jKXuTMfcO5c
> - What is change management? www.youtube.com/watch?v=__IlYNMdV9E

References

Burchardi, K., Hildebrandt, P., Lenhard, E., Moreau, J. & Rehberg, B. (2016). *Five secrets to scaling up agile*. Bcg.perspectives. Boston, MA: Boston Consulting Group. http://img-stg.bcg.com/BCG-Five-Secrets-to-Scaling-Up-Agile-Feb-2016_tcm9-87077.pdf

Chan, F. K. Y. & Thong, J. Y. L. (2009). Acceptance of agile methodologies: A critical review and conceptual framework. *Decision Support Systems*, 46: 803–814.

Dyba, T. & Dingsoyr, T. (2008). Empirical studies of agile software development: A systematic review. *Information and Software Technology*, 50: 833–859.

Gieles, H. & van der Meer, W. (2017). *Talent management as the beating heart of an Agile organisation*. www.scrum.de/wp-content/uploads/2017/11/prowareness-whitepaper-agile-talent-hannekegieles.pdf

Gothelf, J. (2014). Bring agile to the whole organisation. *Harvard Business Review*, 92(11): November 14.

Hastie, S. & Wojewoda, S. (2015). Standish group 2015 Chaos report: Q&A with Jennifer Lynch. *InfoQ*. www.infoq.com/articles/standish-chaos-2015

Kreissl, B. (2012). What is agile human resources? *Canadian HR Reporter*. www.hrreporter.com/columnist/hr-policies-practices/archive/2012/04/24/what-is-agile-human-resources/

Leau, Y. B., Loo, W. K., Tham, W. Y. & Tan, S. F. (2012). *Software development life cycle AGILE vs traditional approaches*. In: 2012 International Conference on Information and Network Technology (ICINT 2012), IPCSIT, Vol. 37, pp. 162–167.

Mahajan, A. (2013). *The importance of HR in agile adoption*. Westminster, CO: Scrum Alliance. www.scrumalliance.org/community/articles/2013/january/the-importance-of-hr-in-agile-adoption

Marsick, V. J. & Watkins, K. E. (2003). Dimensions of learning organisation questionnaire. *Advances in Developing Human Resources*, 5(2): 132–151.

Misra, S.C., Kumar, V. & Kumar, U. (2009). Identifying some important success factors in adopting agile software development practices. *Journal of Systems and Software*, 82(11): 1869–1890.

Morgan, G. (1997). *Images of Organisation*. Thousand Oaks, CA: Sage.

Rigby, D. K., Sutherland, J. & Takeuchi, H. (2016). Embracing agile. *Harvard Business Review*, May, 50: 40–48.

Senge, P. (1990). *The fifth discipline, the art and practice of the learning organization*. New York, NY: Doubleday/Currency.

Sherman, M., Edison, S., Rehberg, B. & Danoesastro (2017). *Taking agile way beyond software*. Boston, MA: Boston Consulting Group. www.bcg.com/en-au/publications/2017/technology-digital-organization-taking-agile-way-beyond-software.aspx

Silverstone, Y., Tambe, H. & Cantrell, S. M. (2015). *HR drives the agile organisation*. Accenture Strategy. www.accenture.com/t20160913T220140__w__/us-en/_acnmedia/Accenture/Conversion-Assets/DotCom/Documents/Global/PDF/Strategy_3/Accenture-Future-of-HR-Trends-Agile-Organizations.pdf

VersionOne (2016). *10th annual state of Agile report*. www.versionone.com/about/press-releases/versionone-releases-10th-annual-state-of-agile-report/

Part II
Key directions in e-HRM

5 Big data and e-HRM

Tobias M. Scholz

Learning objectives

- Gain a critical understanding of the concept of big data
- Explain the critical need for big data literacy and describe computational, statistical, and skeptical thinking
- Understand the evolution of big data in the management discipline
- Discuss the nature and role of big data in e-HRM, with specific reference to recruitment and selection, performance management, and human capital management

Introduction

Recently, a Wisconsin, USA, based organization gained attention for implementing microchips into their employees in order to replace their employee card (Astor, 2017). Although this sounds like science fiction, they are not the first organization to do so. The goal is to make the work environment more adaptable to the needs of their employees. The company claims that the information of the employees will not be used for tracking purposes (Kessler, 2017). This example highlights the kind of situations we will face in future workplaces. We are surrounded by data and that data can be repurposed for different uses. This development leads to interesting and important questions in human resource management (HRM). What are the ways to utilize the existing data for a variety of HR functions? What are the ethical boundaries of what to do with all that data? And what does that mean for the HR department? The concept of big data permeates every aspect of today's world and organizations need to decide how best to use them in a constructive way.

One crucial challenge for HRM will be the development of suitable personnel with the appropriate skillset to be able to harness the true potential of big data and to define its own positioning in this context. There is a critical shortage of capable personnel in terms of big data competencies. While there are numerous specialized data scientists, the social perspective on big data is normally not part of their expertise (Scholz, 2017). HRM requires its own set of relevant competencies in order to fulfill its new role and train employees adequately. This is where big data literacy is of utmost importance. People require training in computational, statistical, and, most importantly, skeptical thinking. Big data are complex and subjective, and it will become increasingly difficult to find meaningful data and to gain insights that provide a competitive advantage. It is, therefore, crucial that the employees have the competence to be data literate and be able to challenge algorithms (Mainzer, 2015).

This chapter will give a brief introduction of big data and critically reflect on the challenges in the usage of big data. It will then describe the impact of big data in e-HRM on the basis of the evolution of data within management in general and HRM in particular. Big data may not be superior to human decision making, but big data will enable the organizations to answer new questions. The implications of big data for workforce development will be discussed and a case study will be presented.

Big data: A critical perspective

Big data is everywhere and impacts all aspects of society. Its meaning, however, is still quite vague. The notion big data goes beyond the mere idea of collecting huge amounts of data. In order to get a better understanding it is important to define the term *data* first.

> English *data* is derived from Latin, where it is the plural of *datum*, which is in turn the past participle of the verb *dare*, "to give," generally translated into English as "something given." Sanskrit *dadāmi* and ancient Greek δίδωμι are related forms. While *data* (piece of information) and *datum* (calendar date) are separate lexemes in contemporary English, their association is not accidental; medieval manuscripts frequently closed with the phrase *datum die* (given on . . .), effectively time-stamping the preceding text.
>
> (Puschmann and Burgess, 2014, p. 1691)

Understanding the term data will help us to understand the usage of big data in modern society. There are several aspects that are linked with big data and interestingly there is a debate about the incompleteness of big data. Although several practitioners and researchers describe big data as a situation where we suddenly have enough data to gain knowledge, many highlight the fact that data are always just a selection of more data (e.g., Kitchin, 2014). As Kitchin notes, "data are never simply just data; how data are conceived and used varies between those who capture, analyze and draw conclusions from them" (2014, p. 4). This leads to a dilemma: on the one hand, data are often linked with objectivity and preciseness, but on the other hand, data are also subjective and selective.

Several academics, therefore, raise the question whether to view "big data as merely a shift in scale, reach, and intensity (a quantitative shift) or as a more profound, truly qualitative shift – implying both a shift in being [. . .] and meaning [. . .]" (Bolin and Schwarz, 2015, p. 2). There is more to just crunching the numbers, as "the world grows in complexity, overwhelming us with the data it generates" (Chakrabarti, 2009, p. 32) and this "demands a systematic response" (Bowker, 2014, p. 1797).

Data by themselves are abstract and are essential but not sufficient for any purpose as they require to be transformed into information and then knowledge. As stated in the knowledge management literature, data are part of the hierarchical view of knowledge (Alavi and Leidner, 2001). In order to utilize data, it is necessary to put data into context and understand the potential relations. By that, data will be transformed into information. Information can be transformed into knowledge by a combination of user experiences and understanding of patterns.

As described by Thite (2004, p. 8), it is generally understood that information technology provides the necessary structure to convert data into information but more importantly, it is the people who provide meaning to convert information into knowledge. And it is the actionable knowledge that enables organizations to provide faster, cheaper, and better products and services.

$$\text{Data} \xrightarrow[\text{(Structure)}]{\text{IT}} \text{Information} \xrightarrow[\text{(Meaning)}]{\text{People}} \text{Knowledge}$$

Source: Thite (2004, p. 8)

Big data may supply new data and lead to the discovery of new relations; however, without putting it into context, understanding the relations and discovering the patterns, the managers will not be able take efficient and effective decisions. Thus, big data are not going to automatically create better solutions or provide better answers. They only support people to make better decisions. This means that in the hands of incapable and incompetent managers, big data can actually be harmful to the decision-making capability of the organizations.

There is a fierce debate among analysts and scholars about the precise contribution of big data. On the one hand, big data have been placed on a pedestal for being something unique and precious (Mayer-Schönberger and Cukier, 2013). Today's discourse of big data makes them appear to be the solution to all problems of society (Steadman, 2013), and assumes that they are capable of making the world a safer and smarter place. Inherent to this discourse is the belief that making something more data-based or data-driven leads to more objective and deliberate decisions (McAfee and Brynjolfsson, 2012). On the other hand, generating and using big data is a process that is not as simple and straightforward as some suggest. Many believe in "objective quantification" (van Dijck, 2014, p. 198). But big data are "messy" (Harford, 2014, p. 14) and even just their collection causes a manipulation or "preconfiguration of data" (van Dijck and Poell, 2013, p, 10). For that reason, ascribing an "aura of truth, objectivity, and accuracy" to big data would be a fallacy (Boyd and Crawford, 2012, p. 664).

Critical need for big data literacy

With the advent of the information and knowledge economy, underpinned by big data and disruptive technologies, there is a drastic change in the roles performed by people in organizations. Increasing automation and artificial intelligence are freeing up people's capabilities hitherto locked in. People are no longer required to perform operational or transactional tasks as they are often repetitive. Such tasks can be automated by means of machines and algorithms. Big data can mimic artificial intelligence, but in the end, they excel at performing repetitive tasks. Employees gain space to focus on creative tasks and get to handle complex problems. This change is evident in the World Economic Forum's list of the top ten skills required in 2020 according to which complex problem solving, critical thinking, creativity, people management, coordinating with others, emotional intelligence, judgment and decision making, service orientation, negotiation, and cognitive flexibility are the capabilities most employers will be looking for in the near future (Gray, 2016). Today's world of work requires people to collaborate. Everything else is done by robots.

Nevertheless, the aforementioned move toward data driven decisions alongside the belief in their superiority remains prevalent. This development collides with a certain big data phobia. People tend to view big data as something intrusive that they have no control over. This is understandable in the face of the many cases of data abuse committed by governments, companies, or hackers. For that reason, the first goal of HRM is to demystify big data. The HR department is required to counteract phobia and to improve the acceptance of big data among employees. Oftentimes they do so by making the process more transparent and ethical. Another approach is to train people and close the big data gap. The big data gap describes the divide between people who have the knowledge about big data and the people who are ignorant. It is in the organization's best interest for employees to acquire big data knowledge.

Consequently, HRM needs to improve big data literacy within organizations (Christozov and Toleva-Stoimenova, 2015). D'Ignazio and Bhargava (2015, p. 2) describe the concept of big data literacy as follows:

- "Identifying when and where data is being collected
- Understanding the algorithmic manipulations
- Weighing the real and potential ethical impacts."

This can be translated into the three competencies, namely, computational thinking, statistical thinking, and skeptical thinking.

Computational thinking: Numerous scholars and practitioners in all fields (e.g., Lee et al., 2011) already demand teaching computational thinking. Wing (2006, p. 33) emphasizes that "computational thinking is a fundamental skill for everyone, not just for computer scientists." The goal is to teach students the logic behind programming (Shein, 2014). But this does not necessarily require them to learn programming (Conti, 2006). "Thinking like a computer scientist means more than being able to program a computer. It requires thinking at multiple levels of abstraction" (Wing, 2006, p. 34).

Statistical thinking: As the name suggests, it refers to an individual's ability to understand and conduct statistical analyses (Wild, 1994).

> [It] involves an understanding of why and how statistical investigations are conducted and the 'big ideas' that underlie statistical investigations. These ideas include the omnipresent nature of variation and when and how to use appropriate methods of data analysis such as numerical summaries and visual displays of data.
> (Ben-Zvi and Garfield, 2005, p. 7)

In the era of big data, these skills are more sought after than ever before. Every student will need to acquire a solid foundation of statistical competence in the future (Wild and Pfannkuch, 1999). Big data will be driven by statistics and, although there is some complexity involved (Greer, 2000), without extensive knowledge of statistics, people will find themselves controlled by a data-driven algorithm. The above aspects are often neglected in employee training and development.

Skeptical thinking: Finally, people require skeptical thinking as suggested by Sagan (1996), which is akin to critical thinking (Ennis, 1962). Big data are complex, subjective, and influential, and their impact may be difficult to understand. People require a skillset to ask the right questions and request alternatives. Skeptical thinking does not mean constantly questioning big data but refers to the ability to come up with new methods and to think outside the box. This creative thinking seems to be learnable by applying methods of complex problem solving, combining cognitive, motivational, and ethical components. Especially as the main shift in using data ethically and socially will be from collecting data to the secondary use of data, it will be essential to discover the flaws within this big data analysis and not to believe that big data is objective and ethical by magic.

Big data baloney detection kit

The use of big data in all aspects of life will increase exponentially in the coming years. The main argument in support of big data is that big data analyses are time-efficient and cost-efficient, especially as the data are just "lying around." Any opposition to big data may be seen as outdated thinking and resistance to change; however, a critical and holistic perspective on big data is a must because the wrong use of big data, intentionally or unintentionally, can be harmful. Big data are subjective and potentially inaccurate, therefore, relying on the data will increase the potential risks within an organization. Rather than providing a competitive advantage, the wrong use of big data may even endanger the future of an organization. In order to devise an efficient way of dealing with big data, the following rules can be very useful.

1. Seek for other data sources to validate your results.
2. Big data analyses are performed by a variety of different people and departments.
3. Even seemingly reliable sources (e.g., government agencies) can supply subjective data.
4. Correlations do not imply causation.
5. It is essential to search for the explanation behind correlations.
6. Quantifying data does not mean more data but rather better data.
7. Big data are always a selection of various sources of data and with potential different biases.
8. Big data analysis need to be tested and challenged by skeptical reasoning.
9. Big data will not replace knowledge and experience. The gut-feeling is still valid in some situations.
10. Think about the decision-making process—are the decisions purely based on data or is there a reasoning behind the data.

These ten rules highlight the importance of human oversight and insights within the big data analytical process. The underlying principle here is that people need to be always put ahead of the process because it is the intellectual capital that is a key sustainable competitive advantage in the knowledge economy, not technology or big data.

Evolution of big data in management

Using data in the business context for better management is not a new development. The concept of evidence-based management describes the general idea of turning data or evidence into management decisions. The goal is to decide more scientifically and be less influenced by personal preferences. Managers gather information and apply statistically rigorous principles and scientific methods in order to make sound decisions. There are, however, several obstacles to the practice of evidence-based management (e.g., Rousseau, 2006), but one aspect stands out, that is, managers do believe that they are unique and, therefore, their practices and problems are singular. Consequently, they believe that evidence-based management is not feasible for them. This can be traced back to the challenge of collecting data in the late 1990s and early 2000s. Managers were required to

Table 5.1 Moneyball: The art of winning an unfair game

A prominent example and probably the most commonly cited case study in big data is Moneyball (Lewis, 2003). In this book, the author talks about Billy Beane and his experience as the general manager of the baseball team Oakland Athletics. Facing a cut in their budget, the manager had to look for different ways to acquire talents. Using and analyzing data, he formed a highly successful team of quite unusual composition. Based on the data, he discovered a competitive advantage. However, two aspects strengthen the claim that, after all, it is people that make the difference. Firstly, the data expert he employed was the one who created the algorithm with a focus on different statistics, thus enabling the Oakland Athletics to perform better. The true difference was not made by the data collected, but by the person who used them, as well as Billy Beane himself who decided to take the risk. Secondly, the competitive advantage they found left them with only a short window of first mover advantage.

Source: Author.

collect their evidence on their own. Even if data was available, the gathering process was time-intensive as well as cost-intensive. Today, we are facing a novel situation, which is illustrated by the statement, "90 percent of the data in the world today has been created in the last two years alone" (IBM, 2017). There is a shift from data starvation to drowning in data (Puschmann and Burgess, 2014).

Big data will enable organizations to acquire more information as well as new sources of information. This new development will change the way of strategy making. It is possible to achieve a more bottom-up approach and, furthermore, a more heterogeneous way to derive strategies. Still, this process requires data practices that supports the strategy makers (Constantiou and Kallinikos, 2015). McAfee and Brynjolfsson (2012) highlight the impact of big data on the decision processes within organizations with major implications for leadership, talent management, technology, decision making, and organizational culture. They also emphasize that vision or human insight will not be replaced by big data.

Table 5.1 presents the well-known Moneyball case that highlights the competitive advantage gained by the smart use of big data that augments human insights.

Applications of big data in e-HRM

There are several examples in the HRM discipline that highlight the potential of big data. For example, Xerox wanted to increase the retention of their customer service employees. After crunching the numbers, the data showed that people who lived nearby or had a reliable transport to work were more committed to the organization. As a result, Xerox introduced a program to help the employees with their commuting situation and this resulted in a decrease in attrition by 20% (SelectGroup, 2013).

But there are also cases in which the usage of big data in HR has led to negative outcomes. Some organizations use hiring algorithms in order to shortlist job applicants and so it is not a surprise that 72% of the resumes are never seen by the managers (Accesswire, 2016). Without managerial oversight, these automated selection processes can lead to employment discrimination as the algorithm could discover that one ethnicity seems to perform better than another ethnicity. They may also discriminate against statistical outliers, as illustrated in Table 5.2.

The similarity in these cases is that some evidence was found in the data. So, why does the first example seem beneficial but the other not so? This leads to the conclusion that algorithms cannot decide on their own and require a managerial judgement call. Big data are incomplete and, therefore, produce imperfect solutions. Paired with competent and capable people, however, big data can create better solutions.

But how is it possible to give big data a human face and human context? One intersection of data and people in an organization is the human resource management (HRM) department. With the increasing popularity and use of electronic human resource management (e-HRM), the HRM department already has access to data, although this, at the most, qualifies as little data. There is scarce literature concerning big data in HRM and current studies are dominated by practitioners (e.g., Evolv, 2013). Table 5.3 presents a

Table 5.2 Disconnect between algorithms and automated applicant shortlisting

A significant number of organizations use automated Key Word Search and algorithms that screen resumes before any human person even looks at a resume. What will be the criteria to select? In a hypothetical case, we could say that the following correlations are deemed significant:

- Applicants with a degree from a top university will be more successful than applicants from community colleges
- Applicants past the age of 30 will be less adaptable to the changes through digitization
- Applicants with eccentric behavior would restrict the innovative capacity of an organization

These correlations sound reasonable at first sight and they can be backed up by data. Thus, people who are older or eccentric or have poor academic standing would be rejected by the algorithm. But what about statistical outliers? For instance, would organizations recruit Steve Jobs, Mark Zuckerberg, or Elon Musk?

Source: Author.

Table 5.3 Big data in HRM: Literature review

Authors	Key findings
Angrave et al. (2016)	The authors highlight that the HR profession is currently not capable of dealing with big data. Without new competences and the development of better methods, big data will not lead to the operational and strategic promises for HRM and caution that this may lead to the exclusion of HRM in strategic decision making.
Calvard (2016)	The emergence of big data will have an impact on the way people learn; consequently, big data will have an impact on organizational learning. The paper highlights the relevance of the understanding of interdisciplinarity in the analysis of big data as well as the responsible reflection on the data.
Galagan (2014)	The author describes the influence of big data on talent management. The article offers a balanced view highlighting the benefits of data by avoiding false assumptions, but also warns that badly designed algorithms can result in biases.
Miller (2013)	The author questions the need of big data within talent management and argues that there are already many technologies within talent management that are not used to the fullest potential. Rather than adding more complexity into talent management, it would be efficient to utilize existing tools first.
Scholz (2017)	The author describes the potential role of HRM in the new data-driven world. Especially as the human interface with data analysis makes all the difference, it will be essential to support people in the usage of data. Consequently, the role of the HR function will transform fundamentally to augment people's dealings with data.

Source: Author.

summary of some the studies on the use of big data in HRM. They highlight the critical importance of HR to facilitate optimum interface between human and data drive decisions, emphasize the need for HR to be data literate, and the importance of big data in organizational learning and talent management.

As we can see, big data in HRM can be utilized for a variety of purposes, though it may be debatable whether big data can be equally well utilized in human resources in small and medium-sized enterprises (Cappelli, 2017). It appears that there is an untapped well of data that potentially can lead to new insights and new ways of transforming HR service delivery. In recent years, the concept of HR or workforce analytics has gained momentum (Marler and Boudreau, 2017). The next chapter is devoted to examining this aspect in greater detail. Let us examine the use of big data in some specific HR functions.

Recruitment and selection: Many companies struggle to find the right talent for the right positions. When an organization advertises a position, it may receive too many or too few applications. Finding the right person can be time intensive and, consequently, is costly for any organization. Companies such as TripAdvisor try to find the perfect people for distinctive niche roles (Scholz, 2017). Other companies such as Fitbit try to identify the fit between an applicant and the task, the team, or organizational culture (www.fitbit.com/au/careers). With the use of social media, it is possible to scout for the right talent (see Chapter 8). It is also possible to utilize big data to find employees that do not fit the profile of current employees. For instance, Google and other Silicon Valley companies find that potential employees from Ivy League universities are not necessarily superior to graduates from other universities (Staley, 2017). Big data enable these companies to find new talents outside of the standard process of recruiting.

Performance management: Thanks to digitization and automation, today, organizations can collect enormous amount of data about their employees. In a recent report on the truck industry (Haubursin, 2017), it was shown that any truck driver could be constantly tracked and evaluated. Based on GPS-tracking, it is possible to see how long and how far the employee is driving. These so-called electronic logging devices are constantly monitoring the truck driver and evaluate the performance as well as the payment. There are many other examples, including in the call center industry (Thite and Russell, 2009), that show the move from a periodical evaluation toward a real-time evaluation. Furthermore, as it is data-driven, this evaluation is seemingly more objective. It is possible to transfer such key performance indicators into a dashboard or cockpit that allows the management to evaluate and manage their employees on an ongoing basis.

Human capital management: Talent management is already driven by data and information. Many examples utilizing big data for human capital are derived from sports. Besides the Moneyball example described in Table 5.1, there is another example of the football club FC Midtjylland. In this instance, the team wanted to be successful through an optimum combination of talent pool. This case shows that efficiency is not derived purely by data, but by the "synthesis of cold analysis and heart" (Biermann, 2015, p. 96). These cases illustrate how big data can help organizations to derive competitive advantage by leveraging human capital.

Employee retention: A lot has been written on the predictive potential of big data in analyzing employee turnover (which is also examined in the next chapter). The idea behind this is that if a person is starting to think about quitting a job, he/she will exhibit some behavioral patterns unconsciously. Observing those changes could help HR to take proactive and corrective actions to try to stop top talent leaving the organization before it is too late. It is important to highlight that in order to monitor the employee turnover, it is necessary to collect data on previous turnover and analyze that data.

These examples show the potential of big data in HRM. There are many other applications possible and should be considered. However, when it comes to managing people, big data needs to be handled in a sensitive, ethical way with due respect to privacy. These aspects are further explored in Chapter 15.

Summary

Big data can play a key role in shaping the future of HRM; however, it is up to HR professionals themselves on how best to use big data in transforming their function. "Big data does not create value . . . until it is put to use to solve important business challenges" (Schroeck et al., 2012, p. 11). Data and data analysis are useless without context, questions, hypotheses, and conclusions (Boyd and Crawford, 2012). We have to go beyond the monochromatic perspective on big data and substitute "either/or" with "both/and" (Morin, 2008, p. 33). Big data literacy will make all the difference for organizations as they increase the competency necessary to find hidden values. Big data are merely an enabler. The real difference is made by people.

It is for that reason that the HR department will inevitably gain significance in the future—if it takes over the role it is predestined for. People make the difference. If everyone has access to the same data, and the same technologies, consequently, the playing field is completely leveled, people make all the difference. In order to do so, however, they require the appropriate tools, which is why big data literacy is essential. HRM, yet again, has the chance to strategically transform the organization through workforce and managerial competency development. In the long run, big data will fortify the role of HRM. The question, however, is whether or not HR professionals will realize that before big data takes over HRM.

Case study: The digital organization

The organization you are working for has finally jumped on the big data bandwagon and implemented several tools and technologies for digitization and automation. As a result, it is able to collect more and more data about employees and has a granular picture of any person within the organization. The coffee machine sends information about the people using it, the robots in the company factory line identify the people surrounding them, and any project is tracked by elaborate project management tools. The working environment has become truly smart and everything is now connected. The employees have their own RFID chip and the data available to the organization can now truly be considered big data. Especially, in the HR department, the newly available data analytical capacities can now be applied to address strategic workforce challenges.

Your HR department is confronting a pressing challenge: How can we utilize the data floating within the organization in order to improve the productivity, capability, and engagement of our employees? Consequently, the IT department started to mine data and found several correlations and the newly introduced algorithms have presented several potential solutions as shown below.

Correlations	Proposed solutions
The longer people walk to get their coffee, the more productive they get.	Close down all coffee rooms except for a single one in a central location.
Users of the Chrome and Firefox browsers make better employees.	In the recruiting process, directly reject applicants using other browsers.
The more the people are motivated, the less accidents they have.	Utilize the number of accidents as a variable for motivation.
People with children are more empathetic in a conflict situation.	Prefer people with children for management positions.
The preference of eating curly fries correlates with the performance.	People eating curly fries are preferred in promotions.
People are more productive if they drink more coffee.	Install a coffee machine in every room.
Applicants who like the company page on Facebook less than ten days prior to the application are more motivated toward the company.	Include the Like-Page-Indicator into the recruitment process.

Case study questions

On the basis of these results, the top management wants to initiate change processes within the HR department. You as the head of the HR department are asked for a response toward these results:

- *Attention*: Discuss these correlations. Are there causal effects observable and do they make sense? What are the challenges and obstacles with these correlations?
- *Consciousness*: In which aspects are you skeptical about the results and why? Do you comprehend the reasoning behind the proposed solutions? What solutions are problematic?
- *Intention:* How are the data derived? What could be the problems in terms of context? Are there legal, ethical, social problems?
- *Stabilization:* How will you respond to the potential solutions offered by the algorithms? What would you propose to change this data-driven process?

Debate: Should management decisions be based on evidence or intuition?

Introduction

Some data analytics firms claim to eliminate the guesswork in HRM (Evolv, 2013) and eradicate the "touchy-feely" part of HRM (Walker, 2012). These claims imply that there is something inherently wrong about using intuition in HR related decisions. Data-driven concepts are grounded in the notion that the intuition is inferior to big data. As a result, HR often struggles to deal with the data-driven evidence-based decisions by IT, and IT in turn struggles to deal with the seemingly intuitive choices by HR. This barrier makes it difficult to utilize big data in HRM to its full potential.

Arguments in favor of "data-driven decisions"

- By eliminating the guesswork and utilizing the data, HRM becomes more analytical and, therefore, more precise.
- HR is not known for using their data smartly and strategically. Big data can help to improve every part of HRM.
- Personnel decisions are no longer subjective and based on instinct. HRM can now create transparency, objectivity, and accountability.
- Big data can find new correlations and build more understanding of people. These discoveries are far superior to any instinct.
- Big data in HRM will lead to a competitive advantage because the data is used to the fullest efficiency. The example of Google is quite striking. They use data to improve management decisions on hiring, performance, and reward management (Bock, 2016).

Arguments in favor of "intuition"

- Big data in HRM will dehumanize human resources (Cukier, 2013). Data-driven decisions could lead to a devaluation of HRM. The human touch is always paramount in people management.
- For big data, people will become only resources (Graham, 2013) and by that, the employees are treated like machines. That will have a negative impact on employee motivation, retention, and commitment.
- HR professionals do use intuition often. However, this gut-feeling is based on knowledge and insights gained from years of experience. Intuition is therefore "distilled wisdom," which may appear ad-hoc but is honed on the job over a long time.
- Data are subjective and contextual as well. It could be argued that big data are not more precise and they might as well be guesswork (Cappelli, 2017).
- Data-driven decisions are often used without reflection and discussion with stakeholders. There is an inherent trust in numbers, however, is there is no such thing as "evidence-based management" (Rousseau, 2006).

Useful references

Bock, L. (2016). *Work Rules! Insights from Inside Google That Will Transform How You Live and Lead*. London: Hodder and Stoughton.

Cappelli, P. (2017) *There is No Such Thing as Big Data in HR*. Available at: https://hbr.org/2017/06/theres-no-such-thing-as-big-data-in-hr (Accessed December 17, 2017).

Cukier, K. (2013). *Dehumanising Human Resources*. Available at: www.economist.com/blogs/schumpeter/2013/04/big-data-and-hiring (Accessed December 17, 2017).

Evolv (2013) Q3 2013 Workforce Performance Report. *Evolv White Paper*, pp. 1–20.

Graham, S. (2013). *It's Time to Rethink Human Resources, the Key to Employee Morale*. Available at: www.fastcompany.com/3002355/its-time-rethink-human-resources-key-employee-morale (Accessed December 17, 2017).

Rousseau, D. M. (2006) Is There Such a Thing As "Evidence-Based Management"? *Academy of Management Review*, vol. 26, no 2, pp. 256–269.

Walker, J. (2012). *Moneyball and the HR Department*. Available at: http://blogs.wsj.com/digits/2012/04/16/moneyball-and-the-hr-department (Accessed December 17, 2017).

Video learning resources

- What is Big Data and why does it matter? https://youtu.be/qXyzDd2heK8. Discusses critically the impact of big data on society.
- Big data is better data: https://youtu.be/8pHzROP1D-w. Discusses the potential of big data-driven technology as well as the promises of big data in the future.
- The era of blind faith in big data must end: https://youtu.be/_2u_eHHzRto. Discusses the obstacles and problems with using big data.
- How job surveillance is changing trucking in America: https://youtu.be/G_UHknhNbAQ. Describes the case how big data is transforming the trucking job due to permanent and real-time job surveillance.
- The beauty of data visualization: https://youtu.be/5Zg-C8AAIGg. Discusses the necessity of reflecting, preparing and visualizing big data in order to share and utilize information.

References

Accesswire (2016). *72% of Resumes are Never Seen by Employers*. Available at: www.accesswire.com/436847/72-of-Resumes-are-Never-Seen-by-Employers (Accessed December 17, 2017).

Alavi, M., and Leidner, D. E. (2001). Knowledge Management and Knowledge Management Systems: Conceptual Foundations and Research Issues. *MIS Quarterly*, vol. 25, no. 1, pp. 107–136.

Angrave, D., Charlwood, A., Kirkpatrick, I., Lawrence, M., and Stuart, M. (2016). HR and Analytics: Why HR is Set to Fail the Big Data Challenge. *Human Resource Management Journal*, vol. 26, no. 1, pp. 1–11.

Astor, M. (2017). *Microchip Implants for Employees? One Company Says Yes*. Available at: www.nytimes.com/2017/07/25/technology/microchips-wisconsin-company-employees.html (Accessed December 17, 2017).

Ben-Zvi, D., and Garfield, J. (2005). Statistical Literacy, Reasoning, and Thinking: Goals, Definitions, and Challenges. In Ben-Zvi, D., and Garfield, J. (eds.). *The Challenge of Developing Statistical Literacy, Reasoning and Thinking* (pp. 3–16). New York, NY: Kluwer.

Biermann, C. (2015). Moneyball im Niemandsland. *11 Freunde*, vol. 15, no. 6, pp. 90–96.

Bolin, G., and Schwarz, J. A. (2015). Heuristics of the Algorithm: Big Data, User Interpretation and Institutional Translation. *Big Data & Society*, vol. 2, no. 2, pp. 1–11.

Bowker, G. C. (2014). The Theory/Data Thing. *International Journal of Communication*, vol. 8, pp. 1795–1799.

Boyd, D., and Crawford, K. (2012). Critical Questions for Big Data. Provocations for a Cultural, Technological, and Scholarly Phenomenon. *Information, Communication & Society*, vol. 15, no. 5, pp. 662–679.

Calvard, T. S. (2016). Big Data, Organizational Learning, and Sensemaking: Theorizing Interpretive Challenges Under Conditions of Dynamic Complexity. *Management Learning*, vol. 47, no. 1, pp. 65–82.

Cappelli, P. (2017). *There is No Such Thing as Big Data in HR*. Available at: https://hbr.org/2017/06/theres-no-such-thing-as-big-data-in-hr (Accessed December 17, 2017).

Chakrabarti, S. (2009). *Data Mining: Know it All*. Burlington, MA: Morgan Kaufmann.

Christozov, D., and Toleva-Stoimenova, S. (2015). Big Data Literacy: A New Dimension of Digital. In J. Girard, D. Klein, and K. Berg (eds.). *Strategic Data-Based Wisdom in the Big Data Era* (pp. 156–171). Hershey, PA: Information Science Reference.

Constantiou, I. D., and Kallinikos, J. (2015). New Games, New Rules: Big Data and The Changing Context of Strategy. *Journal of Information Technology*, vol. 30, no. 1, pp. 44–57.
Conti, G. (2006). Introduction. *Communications of the ACM*, vol. 49, no. 6, pp. 33–36.
D'Ignazio, C., and Bhargava, R. (2015). *Approaches to Big Data Literacy*. Bloomberg Data for Good Exchange Conference, New York, NY, pp. 1–6.
Ennis, R. H. (1962). A Concept of Critical Thinking. *Harvard Educational Review*, vol. 32, no. 1, pp. 81–111.
Evolv (2013). Q3 2013 Workforce Performance Report. *Evolv White Paper*, pp. 1–20.
Galagan, P. (2014). HR Gets Analytical. *T+D*, vol. 68, no. 3, pp. 22–25.
Gray, A. (2016). *The 10 Skills You Need to Thrive in the Fourth Industrial Revolution*. Available at: www.weforum.org/agenda/2016/01/the-10-skills-you-need-to-thrive-in-the-fourth-industrial-revolution (Accessed December 17, 2017).
Greer, B. (2000). Statistical Thinking and Learning. *Mathematical Thinking and Learning*, vol. 2, no. 1–2, pp. 1–9.
Harford, T. (2014). Big Data: A Big Mistake? *Significance*, vol. 11, no. 5, pp. 14–19.
Haubursin, C. (2017). *Automation is Coming for Truckers. But First, They're Being Watched*. Available from: www.vox.com/videos/2017/11/20/16670266/trucking-eld-surveillance (Accessed November 23, 2017).
IBM (2017). *10 Key Marketing Trends for 2017*. Available at: https://public.dhe.ibm.com/common/ssi/ecm/wr/en/wrl12345usen/watson-customer-engagement-watson-marketing-wr-other-papers-and-reports-wrl12345usen-20170719.pdf (Accessed December 17, 2017).
Kessler, S. (2017). *A Company Implanting Microchips in its Employees Says it's not to Track Them*. Available at: https://qz.com/1038152/a-wisconsin-company-is-implanting-microchips-in-its-employees-fingers (Accessed July 30, 2017).
Kitchin, R. (2014). *The Data Revolution. Big Data, Open Data, Data Infrastructures & Their Consequences*. Los Angeles, CA: Sage.
Lee, I., Martin, F., Denner, J., Coulter, B., Allan, W., Erickson, J., Malyn-Smith, J., and Werner, L. (2011). Computational Thinking for Youth in Practice. *ACM Inroads*, vol. 2, no. 1, pp. 32–37.
Lewis, M. (2003). *Moneyball: The Art of Winning an Unfair Game*. New York, NY: W. W. Norton & Company.
Mainzer, K. (2015). Industrie 4.0, richtig gestaltet, eröffnet neue Freiheitsgrade für die Menschen. *G.I.B. Info*, vol. 4, pp. 54–65.
Marler, J. H., and Boudreau, J. W. (2017). An Evidence-based Review of HR Analytics. *International Journal of Human Resource Management*, vol. 28, no. 1, pp. 3–26.
Mayer-Schönberger, V., and Cukier, K. (2013). *Big Data: A Revolution That Will Transform How We Live, Work, and Think*. Boston, MA: Houghton Mifflin Harcourt.
McAfee, A., and Brynjolfsson, E. (2012). Big Data: The Management Revolution. *Harvard Business Review*, vol. 90, no. 10, pp. 60–68.
Miller, M. (2013). HR and Big Data: Not Yet, First Things First! *Workforce Solutions Review*, August/September, pp. 39–40.
Morin, E. (2008). *On Complexity*. Cresskill, NY: Hampton Press.
Puschmann, C., and Burgess, J. (2014). Metaphors of Big Data. *International Journal of Communication*, vol. 8, pp. 1690–1709.
Rousseau, D. M. (2006). Is There Such a Thing as "Evidence-Based Management"? *Academy of Management Review*, vol. 31, no. 2, pp. 256–269.
Sagan, C. (1996). *The Demon-Haunted World. Science as a Candle in the Dark*. New York, NY: Ballantine Books.
Scholz, T. M. (2017). *Big Data in Organizations and the Role of Human Resource Management. A Complex Systems Theory-Based Conceptualization*. Frankfurt am Main: Peter Lang.
Schroeck, M., Shockley, R., Smart, J., Romero-Morales, D., and Tufano, P. (2012). Analytics: The Real-World Use of Big Data—How Innovative Enterprises Extract Value from Uncertain Data. *IBM Global Business Services*, pp. 1–20.

SelectGroup (2013). *"Humanizing" Big Data to Extract Answers to Your Hiring Problems*. Available at: http://sg.com/2013/10/31/big-data-hiring-problems-solutions (Accessed December 17, 2017).

Shein, E. (2014). Should Everybody Learn to Code? *Communications of the ACM*, vol. 57, no. 2, pp. 16–18.

Staley, O. (2017). *Silicon Valley Hires the Most Alumni of These 10 Universities, and None of Them are in The Ivy League*. Available at: https://qz.com/967985/silicon-valley-companies-like-apple-aapl-hires-the-most-alumni-of-these-10-universities-and-none-of-them-are-in-the-ivy-league (Accessed December 17, 2017).

Steadman, I. (2013). *Big Data and the Death of the Theorist*. Available at: www.wired.co.uk/news/archive/2013-01/25/big-data-end-of-theory (Accessed December 17, 2017).

Thite, M. (2004). *Managing People in the New Economy*. New Delhi: Response Books (Sage).

Thite, M. & Russell, B. (2009). *The Next Available Operator: Managing Human Resources in Indian Business Process Outsourcing Industry*. New Delhi: Response Books (Sage).

van Dijck, J. (2014). Datafication, Dataism and Dataveillance: Big Data between Scientific Paradigm and Ideology. *Surveillance & Society*, vol. 12, no. 2, pp. 197–208.

van Dijck, J., and Poell, T. (2013). Understanding Social Media Logic. *Media and Communication*, vol. 1, no. 1, pp. 2–14.

Wild, C. J. (1994). Embracing the "wider view" of statistics. *The American Statistician*, vol. 48, no. 2, pp. 163–171.

Wild, C. J., and Pfannkuch, M. (1999). Statistical Thinking in Empirical Enquiry. *International Statistical Review*, vol. 67, no. 3, pp. 223–248.

Wing, J. M. (2006). Computational Thinking. *Communications of the ACM*, vol. 49, no. 3, pp. 33–35.

6 HR metrics and analytics

Martin R. Edwards

> **Learning objectives**
>
> - To gain insight into HR analytics as an HR specialism
> - Understand some of the key ideas and techniques behind some central HR analytics projects
> - Become familiar with a range of different HR metrics
> - Be able to provide an explanation of what HR analytics is and how it is different from a focus on HR metrics
> - Understand some of the challenges that are faced by the HR function with an increasing emphasis of HR analytics and metrics

Introduction

HR analytics as a specialism has, over the past decade, become a topic of considerable interest in the HR practitioner field, and more recently, academic circles. With numerous practitioner conferences now focusing on HR analytics and a multitude of books (e.g. Edwards and Edwards, 2016; Guenole, Ferrar and Feinzig, 2017) and blogs discussing how important HR analytics is, it is fast (seemingly) becoming a key HR offering. During the past five years, we have seen a rapid growth in practitioners (consultants and bloggers) arguing that organisations should be applying sophisticated statistical analyses in order to answer practical HR and business questions using people-related data (Marler and Boudreau 2017). Amongst notable practitioner books that argue the case include Smith (2013), Fitz-Enz (2010), Fitz-Enz and Mattox (2014) and Guenole et al. (2017).

Amongst the narrative of HR analytic discussion, some seemingly ambitious claims are being made as to the benefits of taking an analytics focus. Example claims include Fitz-Enz and Mattox (2014) who suggest that '*Arguably the most practical tool and greatest potential for organisational management is the emergence of predictive analytics*' and Huselid who argues, '*By identifying trends and patterns, HR professionals and management teams can make better strategic decisions about the workforce challenges that they may soon face*' (2014, see weblink).

In one sense, elements of HR analytics are not new. HR information and management information (MI) teams in large organisations have spent a considerable amount of time analysing certain types of data and producing descriptive reports (e.g. turnover reports) and data dashboards. This is analytics in one form and an HR analytics team may spend some time carrying out this analysis, however, it is important to distinguish between these kind of activities and more sophisticated analytic activities that many people are referring to when suggesting that HR analytics is on the rise. The kind of analytics that recent authors tend to be referring to as a 'new approach' involves the application of sophisticated statistical analyses to answer practical HR and business questions using people-related data (Marler and Boudreau 2017).

This approach is being referred to as a number of different labels, including 'HR analytics' (Fitz-Enz, 2010; Smith, 2013; Marler and Boudreau 2017), 'Talent analytics' (Davenport, Harris and Shapiro, 2010), 'Predictive HR analytics' (Edwards and Edwards, 2016), 'People analytics' (Isson and Harriott, 2016), 'Predictive analytics' (Fitz-Enz, 2010), 'Human capital analytics' (Minbaeva, 2017a) and 'Work-force analytics' (Kryscynski et al., 2017). A new element of the emerging trend involves discussions of HR analytics in a 'predictive' sense. As many pundits are suggesting, *predictive* HR analytics provides many opportunities for new insightful types of analysis. It is important to define what is meant by predictive HR analytics and the following is a useful definition:

> 'Predictive HR analytics' is: the systematic application of predictive modelling using inferential statistics to existing HR people related data in order to inform judgments about possible causal factors driving key HR-related performance indicators ... then apply these predictive models to make tangible predictions about particular results or outcomes (e.g. employee or organisational behaviour) that we might expect to find given certain conditions.
>
> (Edwards and Edwards, 2016, p. 2)

Whilst some are arguing for transformational benefits that the development of HR analytics has for HR functions (Fitz-Enz, 2010; Huselid, 2014; Bersin 2015), some argue that there is a risk that this is a passing fad (Rasmussen and Ulrich, 2015) and although Angrave et al. (2016) lack confidence that the HR profession can rise to the 'big data challenge', the increasing attention in the field of HR analytics and the ever-growing voices arguing for the importance of HR analytics seem to indicate otherwise.

In articles set out in recent journal special issues on HR analytics, authors such as Minbaeva (2017a, 2017b) discuss why there is a need to move towards analytics as a key element of what HR practitioners are involved in. Kryscynski et al. (2017) suggest that one of the reasons why HR struggles to position itself as a strategic partner in business is because of 'HR's lack of evidence-based rigor in decision making' (p. 1), and importantly, these authors then go on to demonstrate that where HR practitioners demonstrate 'analytical ability', they are not only rated as having higher performance than those who do not, but they also show that the HR functions with such abilities are more likely to be considered as creating value to external stakeholders. This finding has important implications for sceptics of HR's ability to 'rise to the analytic challenge' and for the HR profession as a whole, which has long been considered disempowered and in desperate desire to be considered an automatic component of 'the strategic engine room' of the organisation (Guest and King, 2004).

HR analytics in practice

As mentioned, some forms of HR analytics have been carried out by MI and HR information teams for many years, including, for example, basic update reporting of staff level and turnover rates (and changes) across a business and more sophisticated work-force planning. Workforce planning (see Liff, 2000) as a key activity has for many years been an important analytic project that organisations would undertake to ensure that the right people are in the right place at the right time. HR analytics will and can entail such activities, and as mentioned, an HR analytics team are likely to contribute to such activities, however, there are a number of key projects that a *new* HR analytics team might be involved in. One such example on turnover analysis is presented in Table 6.1 below.

Although theoretically HR analytics can involve a myriad of different projects, there are some key bread and butter analytics projects that all HR analytic teams will need proficiency. The emphasis here is on predictive element of analytic projects, sometime will be spent below setting out what these projects may involve and what their outcomes may be. Probably, the two main 'bread and butter' HR analytics projects will involve predictive analyses of staff turnover patterns and predictive analyses of employee performance. These two projects, turnover analyses and performance analysis are likely to be analytics projects that all HR analytics teams will be involved in on an on-going basis.

Table 6.1 HR analytics case study on turnover analyses

At a 2017 conference in Barcelona, the HR analytics lead at AstraZeneca presented a project that involved a turnover analysis using machine learning software (incorporating multiple years of global HR-related data). The analytics project was driven by two of the senior members of the analytics team and the aim was to run an analysis that helped identify predictors of voluntary turnover and to enable the identification of parts of the workforce who have a particularly high likelihood of leaving. The cost of turnover to the business was suggested as being over $20m PA and the analyst team needed to gain insight into predictors of voluntary turnover in order to be able to intervene and potentially reduce this turnover so the cost of replacement could be reduced. The analytics team partnered with specialists from IT in the organisation who were exploring the utility of a machine leaning software programme 'DataRobot'. This programme explores datasets that are uploaded into it in order to identify predictive models (in this case with logistic regression). The team created an Excel file with data on employees over a two-year period that involved 33 columns (and 100k rows); once uploaded, the software automatically ran numerous predictive models to identify the most effective combination of variables as predictors. The software then identified the best model and tested it on a larger part of the dataset.

Findings: The model presented a set of characteristics from the dataset along with statistics (%) of how likely it was that people with those characteristics were set to resign. The analyst could look at these likelihood figures associated with each characteristic and identify a profile of who would be most likely to leave or stay. In this case, the model identified that employees of one to three years in tenure in a particular region, who had worked in a particular job function and who had received a previous pay increase of less than 1.6% were the most likely to leave. It also identified employees who were older than 48 with long tenure (14+ years) based in a manufacturing function in particular European location were the least likely to leave. The profiles could help identify hot and cold spots of turnover and predict the risk of resignation against the workforce. There were four jobs in particular where the incumbent population were 30% more likely to leave. Interestingly, the analysis identified a potential job type hotspot that came as a surprise to HR (it was a relatively new role) and when investigated, they were able to identify it as problem area (from a turnover perspective).

Business impact and actions: The analyses helped inform retention strategies to better retain valuable employees and helped inform recruitment strategies to help recruit better fitting employees (people more likely to stay). When the results were communicated to the business, the findings supported and reinforced general perceptions of people in the business areas about what the hotspots were. This helped give more of a licence for HR to encourage investment in particular intervention strategies.

Source: Author.

More detail on the different examples of analytics projects will be set out below, however, because of the considerable monetary and disruption cost of staff turnover and the important pressure for HR to demonstrate that its investment will have an impact on employee performance (and the bottom line), turnover and performance projects will often feature as core analytics activities. What these projects require, however, is good quality, up-to-date, historical and current, readily available and reliable data across the organisation as well statistically savvy HR staff that can setup, run and interpret predictive statistical models. Importantly, these staff need to be given the time to explore and investigate different types of model setup. These contingencies, having the data, the staff competencies and the time to be able to undertake predictive analytic modelling are potentially key stumbling blocks to successful application of HR analytics.

Digital technologies and analyses systems

An HR function that decides to incorporate HR analytics as part of its HR offering to the business will be faced with a number of different choices; a key choice will be what technology or software to use to carry out the analytics. The decision here may be linked to how large the organisation is, how much data is stored and collected and its existing human resource information systems (HRIS) (see Kavanagh, Thite and Johnson, 2015, for an in-depth discussion of HRIS). Another key determinant of what an analytics system might be used by an HR function (or analytics team) is the statistical competency of the analyst team.

For example, conducting certain analytic models manually will require a good understanding of statistics; to be able to run these models manually, the analyst will clearly need to have some fairly sophisticated statistical competencies and knowledge. A good guide to running models manually can be found in '*Predictive HR Analytics*' Edwards and Edwards (2016). The book provides a 'how to' approach to run analysis with SPSS; it provides numerous case studies and datasets (see www.koganpage.com/phra). It is useful for students or analysts who have some experience of statistical analysis and access to SPSS. However, not all analysts will be familiar with SPSS; thus, set out below is a brief overview of the different statistical software programmes that analysts can use when manually undertaking statistical HR models.

'Hands-on' analytic statistical programmes

There are many different statistical software packages that can be used for HR analytics modelling; some have their advantages and disadvantages (Edwards and Edwards, 2016). Some of these packages are presented in Table 6.2.

Importantly, the use of these packages is only useful if the analyst has statistical capabilities. However, recent software tools have enabled the possibility of analysts conducting sophisticated analysis without choosing to test particular hypotheses and running the analyses manually. Although a review of machine learning as a statistical technique is beyond the scope of the current chapter, it is important to address this technique from an HR analytics standpoint as its use in the field is only likely to grow.

Automated analyses 'machine learning' software

Guenole et al. (2017) compare 'traditional statistics', meaning statistical analyses undertaken manually to test potential causal hypotheses, with machine learning. In short, machine

Table 6.2 Statistical analyses tools

- *SPSS*: SPSS is relatively simple to learn and its ability to run complex procedures using the menus and mouse makes it very popular. SPSS does cover 95% of the statistical analytic demands required by HR analytics teams.
- *Stata, often used by economists*: Stata mainly utilises a command-line interface; thus, taking longer to get to a good level of expertise.
- *SAS*: This has relatively few menu-interface procedures and is mostly a command-line package; again, taking longer to master.
- *Minitab* has been noted as another simple package to learn and involves a user-friendly menu-oriented interface without requiring users to have an understanding of syntax. Again, it covers what is required by 95% of users.
- *'R'*: As a package, R is free, thus making it increasingly popular. It is solely command-line syntax driven and its menu driven user interface is rather limited. R is more difficult to learn than SPSS or Minitab, thus, it is more daunting for a beginner. Its graphical output is, however, extremely good.
- *Python*: Another free data analysis software system is Python, often used by data scientists. Python is a syntax driven/programming system/language that has many statistical features and can be utilised and programmed to combine statistical analyses and data mining activities. This system requires syntax management capabilities to run analytics; Python is, however, a very versatile data analytic interface and can be used to programme sophisticated automated machine learning analytic programmes.
- *JASP*: A new software package to definitely look out for. At the moment, the JASP programme is in development stage and has a limited range of statistical analytical models in its menus; however, it shows potential and could be a useful starting point for an analyst who wants to quickly run some analytic models (e.g. regressions).

Source: Author.

learning involves conducting data analysis (sometimes using automated software) that explores datasets to get the best possible combinations of variables (potential independent variables) and identify the best possible predictive model that 'accounts' for the highest level of the variation on any particular dependent variable. Some examples of software programmes that utilise an automated machine-learning element include (for example) DataRobot and Watson Analytics. With both of these systems, the analyst will need to input datasets of potential predictors of any particular outcome that they want to account for (e.g. turnover, performance, engagement or sickness absence) an example case study where DataRobot was used is presented below.

A machine learning programme such as DataRobot will start testing different models on a randomly selected ('bootstrapped') small portion of the dataset (e.g. 15%); it uses a machine learning 'Random Forests' (Breiman, 2001) analysis as a model building strategy. Loosely, this involves the random selection of a subset of explanatory (predictor) variables and the comparison of alternative (potentially 'pruned') models (see Genuer, Poggi and Tuleau, 2008). With this approach, the software makes model choice decisions and provides indices of how good the model is at predicting the target variable.

As such an approach is not driven by theories, preconceived ideas or the testing of particular hypotheses, the process is purely data driven with the intention of identifying patterns and relationships in the whole dataset. Of course, with such an approach, there may be no real explanation for any key relationships found; or indeed, the explanations for the relationships may be completely obvious to an HR person in the organisation. The analysis may also uncover some hidden gems of (potentially predictive) knowledge that could make a real difference to the organisation. Although an HR analyst could feasibly load up datasets/HR data and run some very complex models with machine learning tools, there is of course a danger that the analyst may not fully understand the results or statistics behind the modelling; the analyst could then be left exposed if interrogated by any audience in which the findings were presented. Thus, it could be quite dangerous if an HR analyst was let loose on machine learning software without achieving the required level of capabilities.

Systems with analytics linked to HRIS

A number of HRIS providers have options to add to basic HRIS provision and include some aspects of predictive HR analytics. These would usually come at an additional cost of course. For example, IBM have interfaces that utilise SPSS as a statistical engine and Oracle have elements of their HRIS offering that can also run predictive models (e.g. predicting likelihood of leaving and expectations of predicted performance level for each employee). With such systems, the same problem exists that are present with machine learning, in that to fully understand what the systems are doing in their modelling, a high level of analytics capability would be required; without this, there would be a high risk that an HR member who used such systems without knowing what they were doing would expose themselves (and the function) to the likelihood of being embarrassed if interrogated on the underlying analysis when presenting results. This could well expose the function to credibility risks.

Evidence-based HR analytics and the utilisation of HR metrics

The growth in HR analytics as a key HR specialism can, to some extent, be seen as an extension of many calls that have been put forward by a number of HR experts over many decades that suggest HR needs to ensure that it is capable of utilising and deploying HR metrics as a way of measuring or auditing the effectiveness of HR practices and initiatives. One of the most influential texts in this regard is a book written by Becker, Huselid and Ulrich (2001) that actively puts forward a case for an HR metric-based framework and the development of an assessment system that helps demonstrate the contribution that HR can make on business performance. Becker et al. (2001) set out the importance of developing a measurement system that can track and demonstrate the potential impact and effectiveness of HR-related investments. Thus, many HR functions now ensure that they are able to carefully measure many aspects of the people management environment and many of these measures take the form of various HR-based metrics that can be utilised in an HR analytics team when conducting predictive analytics.

Key HR metrics often utilised by analytics teams

Whilst HR analytics does not necessarily have a set of standard measures or metrics that can be utilised in various projects, each project should really have measures and indicators specific to the needs of the project and there are a number of key metrics of which many HR analysts should be aware. Some examples of the focal measures are presented in Table 6.3. It is important note that this is not an exhaustive list as any particular focus might, for example, have many possible ways to measure a particular phenomenon. For example, whilst standard turnover rate (separation rate) is a key measure of employee flows, there are many different ways to measure employee flows (e.g. accession rate, separation rate, stability rate, instability rate, survival rate and wastage rate). The same will occur for most

Table 6.3 Example HR metrics

- *Recruitment oriented metrics*: Common metrics in the recruitment sphere include indices such as 'time to hire' (per job/average job – within any given business unit). Cost per hire – recruitment budget in a given period divided by the number of employees hired in a given period.
- *Turnover cost*: A number of assumptions will be made as to the actual cost of replacement that will include, for example, the cost per hire, also some calculation will be made as to the cost of induction and training. Further extensions of this calculation will include the cost of lower productivity of the new joiner (it may be easier to calculate this in organisations where employees produce specific output or they can have measures of revenue/income/sales). Each analytic team will want to come up with a formula that they are comfortable with in their organisation.
- *Diversity-oriented metrics*: Examples include: % of women per team/% women in senior roles/ % ethnic minorities per team/% ethnic minorities in senior roles/% pay gap for males vs. females. Other metrics comparing differing demographic groups, for example, % BAME (Black, Asian, Minority Ethnic).
- *Revenue-oriented metrics*: Metrics will depend on context and job; a key metric involves revenue/ income over time (per hour/per day/per week) relating to particular units (per employee/average per employee/total or average per team).
- *Performance-oriented metrics*: Most performance indicators linked to individuals can also be aggregated to other unit levels such as groups. Examples include appraisal rating, behavioural rating, peer feedback, sales performance figures, customer feedback, call rates, call load, engagement index, store/branch customer feedback, staff turnover, customer loyalty and customer reinvestment/ repeat business.
- *Productivity-oriented metrics*: Productivity measures require a measurable output for employees, the key here is that indices of output over time (per hour/per day/per week) relating to particular units (per employee/average per employee/total or average per team) will be constructed.
- *Employee flows*: The standard turnover measure used by organisations is: Separation rate = N of members who left during period divided by the average number of members during period (presented as a %: × 100). The organisation would need to be careful what sort of leaver (voluntary or forced) is included.
- *Talent/potential-oriented metrics*: Time (in months) until promotion (per employee/average per employee/total or average per team). *Performance 'potential'* (e.g. using the nine-box grid: places employees into three categories of performance (low/medium/high) and three categories of 'potential' (low/medium/high).
- *Engagement related*: See Edwards and Edwards (2016) for a discussion of different engagement measures. Engagement measure can provide an average mean score per unit (individual/work unit such as a team) or often presented is an average % of a work unit that agree or strongly agreed to engagement measures.
- *Sickness absence*: The number of days sick recorded over a given time (per hour/per day/per week/ per month) relating to particular units (per employee/average per employee/total or average per team). Organisational level: % of annual work days lost to sickness per employee/total working days lost to sickness (total days lost × average cost of a working day in the organisation).

Source: Author.

phenomena investigated; for example, performance metrics will vary massively on the basis of what kind of outputs are expected in a particular job. The list presented in Table 6.3 can stand as useful measures (there are simply too many to provide an exhaustive list).

HR analytics and utilisation of HR metrics for data-driven managerial decisions

Whilst the development of HR metrics as a preoccupation of HR is a particularly useful activity that an HR analytics team will be involved in, a focus on HR metrics as a HR activity tends to be oriented around showing the impact of HR initiatives. HR analytics goes beyond this as a key aim of HR analytics is to identify key strategic insights from people-related data (and HR metrics) that can lead to actionable recommendations and help make data-driven decisions. In addition to this, HR analytics experts can help interrogate and evaluate many aspects of the people management environment without necessarily attempting to evaluate HR activities; although this is something that an HR analytics team could get involved in. To some extent, a focus of HR analytics helps to answer a challenge that a number of critics of the HR function have put forward over the years, that as a function 'it has some way to go before it can be truly claim to be evidence based' (Briner, 2007, p.1) and that it needs to move away from 'copycat practices from other companies' and have a greater emphasis on 'Evidence Based HR' that involves 'promoting practices and advising the organisation's leadership' through a careful evaluation of research evidence available linked to the particular issue at hand, and accessing metrics and information available (Rousseau and Barends, 2011, pp. 222–223). Thus, HR analytics, which aims to uncover insights and help evaluate people-related data to help inform decisions, can help answer this call. Using data analyses to help ensure that management decisions being made are 'data-driven' is something that Scholz discusses in Chapter 5 of this book.

Examples of useful HR analytics projects

As mentioned previously, the two 'go-to' analytics projects that will be the bread and butter of HR analytics teams will be modelling and predicting turnover and employee performance; further detail of these are set out below, along with a short discussion on other types of projects involving diversity analysis, predicting engagement and the potential impact, recruitment and selection analysis.

Turnover analysis

Table 6.1 presented a case study on turnover analysis. The predicted cost of replacing an employee who leaves varies depending upon the level of employee and type of job; typically, the cost of replacing a senior manager might be between three and four times as much as non-managerial employees. As Griffeth and Hom (2001) argue, the projected total costs of replacing an employee can be substantial, which can range from 93% to 200% of employee salaries. Thus, the cost of replacing staff is not something to be ignored and any opportunity to understand and predict staff turnover patterns should put the organisation in a better position to manage future costs and understand issues that their staff face. Thus, with large organisations spending many thousands/hundreds of thousands and sometimes millions of £$€¥ replacing staff, being able to identify drivers of turnover and predict the likelihood of people leaving is something well worth while doing; especially if the team can identify interventions to reduce the likelihood of people leaving.

Many organisations start off this process by identifying the actual average recruitment, selection and onboarding costs in their own organisation; this gives greater precision in identifying what potential savings may occur by reducing turnover rates. Once the organisation identifies a cost of turnover in the first instance, they can model future costs, and importantly, present a business case for interrogating causes and potentially investing in interventions. Thus, if a 10% turnover rate is costing the organisation $1m (£€¥), an investment that reduces the turnover rate to 9% will provide a substantial notional potential saving that can justify targeted investment.

The turnover analytic project will, however, take two stages. First, an analysis needs to be carried out that identifies possible predictors of turnover, and second, applies the algorithmic models to the current employees to get a sense of the likelihood of each employee leaving. With this knowledge, the HR function can identify possible factors/areas to focus on and invest in, and importantly, identify possible individuals who would warrant more attention; this is in effect identifying possible hotspots of turnover risk.

Performance analysis

One of the top two bread and butter analytics projects involves analyses of employee performance. In the above metrics section, a number of possible performance indices are mentioned; however, there will often be job specific and context specific indices, which an analyst might want to focus on. In Edwards and Edwards (2016), a number of examples were presented where performance was an outcome to be predicted. Two example analytic models conducted were predictors of checkout scan rate for supermarket checkout operatives (using HR data/demographic data and information on training participation) and predicting performance of graduates (a year after they joined) using data collected at assessment centres (datasets are available from www.koganpage.co.uk/phra), the latter is presented in Table 6.4 below.

Diversity analysis projects

As discussed in Edwards and Edwards (2016), diversity can be explored both as a possible predictor of other metrics (e.g. turnover) and it can also be treated as a final measure that

Table 6.4 Predicting graduate performance simulation

In Edwards and Edwards (2016), a case study was presented where analysts collated data from a number of graduate assessment centres in previous years and used this data to predict graduate performance once hired (pp. 390–394). They developed a model to predict performance after one year with newly recruited graduates. The predictor variables (independent variables) in the dataset were gender, department, assessment centre scores (including competency ratings, aptitude scores and personality ratings), highest level of education reached and previous work experience. They also included indices of on boarding induction training. The analyses were conducted 'manually' (using windows and menus) using SPSS. The first regression model was conducted to identify what features/which independent variables predicted performance a year after hiring and a regression algorithm was then constructed to apply to assessment centre data for incoming graduates as a way of predicting the grades expected with these candidates.

Findings: The model identified that gender, certain personality traits (e.g. conscientiousness and extroversion), particular competency ratings and department joined predicted performance. The significant features in the data collected at assessment centre could then be used to create an algorithm to predict expected performance of incoming graduates.

Business impact: Whilst the regression presented was a simulation with organisational data rather than an actual project presented by an organisation; the analyses is the kind of project that would be very useful for an analytics team charged with helping validate and assist in assessment centre processes. The analysis would identify what aspects of the assessment centre were good discriminators of high performing candidates; importantly, once the regression algorithm is applied to new candidates, the predicted performance scores (predicted for one year in) that are produced with new candidates could potentially serve to help assist in job offer decisions (especially if other selection criteria left a panel undecided). Importantly, the predicted performance should not be considered as the main decision criteria but it could help predict performance levels of new comers.

Source: Author.

can be predicted. One of the key interests in diversity analysis is whether there is any evidence of any bias in various stages of the employee lifecycle starting with the recruitment process, through to selection, appraisal, promotion and ultimately exit or turnover. A key element of the analyses that teams will want to conduct is an exploration of the proportions of females (and other diversity demographics such as BAME and age) at the various levels of the organisation (e.g. senior management) that are as expected given the gender ratios in the entire company.

Also, for example, if women apply for promotion, do they have similar probabilities/likelihood of getting a successful result compared with males who apply for promotion. Interesting analyses that analytics teams can conduct is to see whether the relationship between performance ratings and pay elements such as bonus percentages are similar for males and females; ultimately, this is exploring whether gender moderates these relationships. Finally, an HR analytics team would want to explore many aspects of diversity across different characteristics, not just gender.

Employee engagement

HR analytics linked to employee engagement can take many forms and there are many ways to measure employee engagement. From an HR analytics perspective, Edwards and Edwards (2016) explain that there are a number of ways that a particular set of engagement scales can be interrogated for validity; in particular, measures should be subjected to factor analyses and reliability analysis. There are many ways that engagement data can be linked in with other people-related data to carry out analytic modelling.

A classic example is where performance measures over time are regressed/correlated onto engagement measures (either at individual or group/team level) to try and demonstrate the benefit of focusing on engagement. With this approach, one can present how much higher team performance tends to be when comparing highly engaged teams versus disengaged teams. This type of model is really a performance analytics model as performance is the dependent variable. Obviously, another form of model that an analytics team would tend to get involved in is identifying the drivers of engagement. These kinds of models are often provided by engagement survey providers, although the possible drivers are usually limited to other possible measures within the survey.

A more comprehensive analysis might involve taking all sorts of other HR information into account, for example, previous team bonuses, team performance, sickness absence rates, team member turnover and so on. When such HR information is combined with engagement survey data, the potential for identifying contributors/predictors of engagement beyond what a survey provider company could do is considerable.

Recruitment and selection analyses

Edwards and Edwards (2016) set out a number of case studies that demonstrate how one might want to analyse data from a recruitment and selection perspective. The performance analytics presented in Table 6.4 is an example of recruitment selection analysis; specifically looking at assessment centre selection data and whether it predicts performance. As mentioned previously with diversity analyses, a key activity that an analytic team might undertake is analyses of the probability of female versus male applicants going on to be offered interviews and subsequently job offers. Standard diversity checking will look at ratios of male and females who apply for particular jobs and whether these ratios flow through to the later stages of the recruitment process (e.g. shortlisting, invitation to interview and job offer).

Analytics competencies

HR, as a profession, has some work to do before HR analytics becomes the norm in most HR functions. At the moment, most HR functions lack the capability to fully exploit the available HR data to its full extent; they also lack the knowledge, experience or vision to understand or appreciate HR analytic modelling possibilities. As discussed by many who discuss HR analytics, a key gap in HR training is the presentation of statistical abilities and content as part of the training. Over ten years ago, Huselid and Becker (2005, p. 279) made a clear call for the HR profession to develop its analytics competencies: '*The development of HR's strategic role has been an evolution . . . The next step in the evolution is for HR professionals, and particularly senior HR professionals, to develop what we call analytic literacy*'.

It would be fairly safe to say that at the moment, the majority of HR functions are not likely to have the core capabilities to carry out predictive HR analytic activities. The vast majority of people who enter the HR profession in the UK for example are unlikely to have the requisite skills to conduct the majority of predictive HR analytics models. Many HR analytics jobs advertised tend to ask for graduates of numerical disciplines or data science graduates. They do not tend to ask for HR graduates. Although HR training tends to cover most of the core specialisms that an HR practitioner may enter, analytics is rarely one of them. This is something that needs addressing as a profession if the HR function wants to 'fulfil its potential' as Angrave et al. (2016) discuss.

Angrave et al. (2016), specifically reference the ability of HR to fulfil its potential to rise to the 'big data challenge'. Advances in technology mean that HR information systems now have the capability to collect and store vast amounts of wide ranging information linked to every employee, team and line manager. As such, this information is now being considered a particular form of so-called 'Big Data' (see Chapter 5). Whilst HR related 'Big Data' can be considered to have definitely arrived, what is not here yet is the capability for the HR function to fully utilise the available data or indeed to understand how to configure the data systems to get the most from HR analytics. A key point – of course – is that with additional data available for HR analysts to be able to model and analyse, the analysts need to have the competencies to handle the large amounts of data.

In many of the very recent articles written on HR analytics (Rasmussen and Ulrich, 2015; Angrave et al., 2016; Kryscynski et al., 2017; Minbaeva, 2017b), the discussion of the capability gap is a key point presented as a central limiter of the HR function's ability to realise its HR analytics potential. As Minbaeva (2017b) discusses, this lack of capability exists despite the fact that '75% of surveyed companies believed that using human capital analytics is important for business performance' (p.1); reportedly only 8% then argue that their organisation has strong capabilities in that area.

Models of HR analytic competencies

An understanding of statistical knowledge is not the only competency that is required for HR functions to excel on HR analytics, and recent authors have presented a number of competency frameworks with which to apply to the HR field as a way of understanding what is potentially needed for the HR function to improve in its strategic influence;

Table 6.5 HR analytic competency frameworks

Boudreau and Ramstad's LAMP framework (2007)	Becker, Huselid, and Ulrich's strategic HR competency framework (2001)	Kryscynski et al.'s (2017) HR professional's analytic competencies
1 **L**ogic – ensures causal logic between measures and business outcomes 2 **A**nalytics – ask valid questions, design analyses/models and present statistics as results 3 Ensures that the right **M**easures are built/and utilised and that data/measures are timely, reliable and available 4 the right **P**rocesses are in-place to ensure that business decision making can benefit from rigorous analytics	1 Able to display critical causal thinking 2 Understands the principles of good measurement 3 Able to estimate causal relationships 4 Able to communicate HR strategic performance results to senior line managers	1 Translates data into useful insights for [organisation name] 2 Identifies [organisation name]'s problems that can be solved with data 3 Uses data to influence decision making in [organisation name] 4 Effectively uses HR analytics to create value for [organisation name] 5 Identifies important questions about the organisation that can be answered with data 6 Accurately interprets statistics

Source: Author.

these frameworks obviously have particular relevance to reflecting on the HR analytic capability gap.

One of the competency models that certain authors (Kryscynski et al., 2017) are referring to is the Boudreau and Ramstad's (2007) LAMP framework; the argument presented is that in order to be as influential as other functions (finance and marketing), a 'paradigm shift' is required where the function focuses on developing its 'decision science' capabilities (see Table 6.5). It is very easy to see how this framework can be applied to the HR function, or specifically an HR analytics team within or linked to the HR function.

Another competency model that is being presented as a way to frame capabilities in HR analytics is a useful model set out by Huselid (2015), based on Becker, Huselid and Ulrich (2001), who outlines four key competencies that are required for HR analytics to help fulfil its strategic HR performance potential (see Table 1). There are some similarities between these competencies and those presented in the LAMP framework, as Kryscynski et al. (2017) discusses.

The big sell: Data visualisation and HR analytics

An extremely important competency that many authors refer to for HR analytics to be successful in an organisation is the analyst team's ability to communicate and explain the importance of any HR analytics findings (Huselid's key competency above). Many books and guides point to the importance of being able to sell the findings to a non-statistical savvy audience. As Boudreau (2017) says, 'HR must make people analytics more user friendly'. There is very little point in conducting some sophisticated statistical analyses and when trying to present the findings to the audience (usually someone that needs to be persuaded that they need to invest money in something), the presenter is met with blank stares and a lack of comprehension.

Guenole et al. (2017) discuss how important it is to translate statistical findings into stories that are inspired by insights from the data, these stories should then be simplified translated into visualisations that help a narrative lead into recommendations. The importance of visualisations as a tool to get a message across is well practiced in the market research space; often, graphic designers are employed as part of a team to help get messages across in presentations. As mentioned, a role of an HR analytics team is to garner understanding and persuade the audience to buy-in to the findings; thus, appropriate communication tools need to be employed. Guenole et al. (2017) set out some important steps that an analyst needs to consider when presenting a complex message. Key is the use of visualisations and they set out three key principles to consider when approaching the use of visualisations. The first is 1) clarify your visualisation message; then, 2) design your visualisation, selecting the appropriate medium and style for the message; and 3) test the visualisation with someone that has a similar background to the audience. Kennedy and Hill (2017) discuss the power and importance of visualisations as a method of garnering audience engagement; they discuss how visualisations can be key in stimulating emotional reactions in an audience when being presented numerical information. Numbers and statistics can turn many people off, thus, the use of imagery and visualisations to get a message across can be seen as a useful tool.

Challenges to HR analytics as a specialism

Having presented a positive case here for the application and development of HR analytics projects, it would be remiss not reflect upon some of the potential challenges that some of the recent authors have raised that could present barriers to the adoption of HR analytics as a regular arm of the HR profession. Those presenting critical arguments of the potential for success of the HR profession to utilise potential benefits of HR analytics projects argue that it risks being seen as a fad (Rasmussen and Ulrich, 2015). Many argue that HR as a function does not have the quantitative capabilities and that HR lacks the skills, knowledge or insight required to fulfil its potential.

Angrave et al. (2016) suggests that HR analytics will be viewed with scepticism because of the perspective that people cannot be reduced to metrics and that projects will be limited by the restricted interface often experienced with HR information systems that are predominantly designed to fulfil operational reporting requirements. There is also the danger that the more organisations start to build a culture of acceptance that analytics is an important everyday activity, a culture could be propagated where managers become overly focused on the achievement of particular performance targets on a range of metrics (that they may be judged against). This kind of culture, as Edwards and Edwards (2016) discuss, could foster a form of institutionalised metric-oriented behaviour (IMOB), which could have detrimental consequences for the organisation.

Edwards and Edwards (2016) also highlight some ethical concerns that may come to the surface with HR analytics projects, for example, they raise concerns about personal employee-linked data (that employees might consider to be private information) being used in analytic models; employees may not even know that data held on them is being incorporated into analytical models. A number of recent critiques have emerged of the automated use of algorithms (O'Neil, 2016; Canhoto, 2017) when making business decisions, some of this critique will be very important for an analytic team to consider. Predictive models are based on the identification of patterns and trends from historical data; if the data (e.g. performance ratings) analysed is linked to historical behaviour (ratings given by managers) and this historical behaviour is problematic or built on potentially bias or discriminatory decisions made by people in the organisation (e.g. managers may rate females as having lower performance due to a bias), then the application of an algorithm from this data may only serve to propagate the historical biases.

Thus, the potential for algorithms to reinforce and foster historical biases in their application is something an analyst must reflect upon. Such issues are a particularly important consideration if the HR function uses off-the-shelf predictive model products from existing providers without having knowledge of what algorithms are being used to make predictions.

Edwards and Edwards (2016) also raise the challenge that when modelling leads to the identification of a particular profile of employees, the organisation might then want to focus on current and/or potential employees with particular characteristics; this may lead to selective investments in particular groups of staff and this may raise equity concerns.

Summary

Recently, there has been a call for researchers to provide evidence of the benefit of HR analytics projects; Marler and Boudreau (2017), Angrave et al. (2016) and Rasmussen and Ulrich (2015) all suggest that there is a lack of strong evidence that analytics projects have the impact that is promised by practitioner literature. The 'field' of HR analytics is still in its infancy and there is some way to go before the field builds the evidence base needed for business (and academics) to be convinced that HR analytics should definitely be a key specialism that every HR function should have in place. Importantly, these challenges will need to be faced and overcome if the HR profession is to fully 'realise its potential' (Angrave et al., 2016) and achieve the 'next step in the evolution . . . for HR professionals'.

This chapter sets out arguments for HR analytics and outlines what sort of analytic activities are the key 'go to' projects for analytics teams, giving an overview of different analytics tools that can be used and then raises some challenges for the HR function that HR analytics as a specialism may bring.

Case study: Differing models of HR analytics offering

If one operates under the assumption that HR analytics is something that the HR profession is likely to develop as part of its offering to the business, there may be a number of models of implementation that it could take. For example, one possible model might be for organisations to buy-in HR analytics expertise by securing the services of analytics consultants. There are a number of firms who offer HR analytics consultancy and the market now exists for HR to effectively outsource its HR analytics activities. These consultancy firms would be able to enter the organisation with a suite of analytic projects that it may have explored in other organisations and ask which project the organisation would like to engage in. They would be likely to have a number of 'off the shelf' analytic techniques/products (e.g. turnover risk profile 'dashboards').

A different (second) model, would involve an organisation making rather than buying its own expertise; the HR function could systematically invest in training a number of its HR function in statistics and HR analytics and integrate this expertise into the strategic running of the HR function.

A third model may involve a channelling of investment into a general business analytics team in the organisation to ensure that there are people who could help focus on HR related business questions, this is in effect Rasmussen and Ulrich's (2015) model. In such a model, the analytics expertise would remain outside of HR, but the organisation's analytics team would itself be the service provider for the HR function.

Case study questions

1 Weigh up the advantages and disadvantages of each of the three models mentioned here of how to set up an HR analytics offering for an organisation.
2 Present a recommendation on a model to the HR director of an organisation of your choice, fully justifying which approach you recommend for your organisation.

Debate: Should HR functions invest in building HR analytics as a specific functional specialism?

Introduction

According to Angrave et al. (2016) and Rasmussen and Ulrich (2015), the HR function does not have the expertise to carry out HR analytics to its full potential. A half-hearted attempt to build such a specialism risks exposing the HR function's lack of capability in this area and runs the risk of leading to a failure of fulfilment of the potential that HR analytics as a specialism could bring to the organisation.

Arguments in favour

- Having a focus on HR analytics will add rigour to the HR function and help raise expectations around HR competencies required to face the big data challenges over the horizon (see Chapter 5).
- An increase in 'analytic capability' can help improve the function's actual and perceived performance; it will help ensure greater influence with internal stakeholders (Kryscynski et al., 2017).
- The HR team will be able to 'talk numbers' with other functional specialisms and operate on the same level from a technical standpoint.
- Becoming expert at analysing people-related data will help the HR function shed its 'touchy feely' image and demonstrate that it is a strategic force to be reckoned with.
- Being able to analyse and handle the growing amount of data that is collected and stored on employees will help to provide strategic insights that the HR function may have previously been ignorant of.
- It reinforces an evidence-based practice approach to management practice; thus, ensuring decisions are being made in a rational, scientific and thought through way, utilising the available sources of information and actively deploying HR metrics to their full extent.

Arguments against

- The HR teams are unlikely to have the requisite competency to be able to conduct HR analytics in a sophisticated form.
- There will be a cost associated with 1) buying in analytics skills or training internal individuals to be able to carry out predictive modelling and 2) investing in the HR information systems to ensure that the data contained is robust, consistent across the organisation and available to the HR analytics experts in the organisation.
- Focusing on analyses of employee data in all its forms will risking losing the people-oriented focus that may be important for the HR function.
- An overly focus on organisational metrics risks IMOB (Edwards and Edwards, 2016), where key managers become overly focussed on managing by metrics rather than proper people management; this could lead to a loss of a concern for the 'human' element of 'human resources'.
- Where statistical analyses, machine learning (and indeed AI) are used to identify possible drivers of and predictors of high performance/key talent, there is a danger that applying the resulting algorithms to help make business decisions may reinforce pre-existing biases that exist in the organisation.
- The 'big brother' concerns of an increased reliance on monitoring and analysing employee-related data can raise ethical and privacy concerns; this could lead to potential legal challenges and also undermine employee trust in the HR function.

Video learning resources

- People analytics: Interview with Laszlo Bock (SVP, People Operations, Google): www.youtube.com/watch?v=Cwlkxtp4TFs
- Can people analytics help firms manage people better? https://youtu.be/9Xyd2gnQaP8
- HR in alignment at Sysco: www.youtube.com/watch?v=0QmZDHDGvGY (start at 14 mins into the video)

References

Angrave, D., Charlwood, A., Kirkpatrick, I., Lawrence, M. and Stuart, M. (2016) HR and analytics: Why HR is set to fail the big data challenge. *Human Resource Management Journal*, 26, 1–11.

Becker, B.E., Huselid, M.A. and Ulrich, D. (2001) *The HR Scorecard: Linking People, Strategy and Performance*. Boston, MA: Harvard Business Press.

Bersin, J. (2015) The geeks arrive in HR: People analytics is here. *Forbes Magazine*. www.forbes.com/sites/joshbersin/2015/02/01/geeks-arrive-in-hr-people-analytics-is-here/.

Boudreau, J.W. (2017) HR must make people analytics more user friendly. *Harvard Business Review*, June, https://hbr.org/2017/06/hr-must-make-people-analytics-more-user-friendly.

Boudreau, J.W. and Ramstad, P.M. (2007) *Beyond HR: The New Science of Human Capital*. Boston, MA: Harvard Business Press.

Breiman, L. (2001) Random forests. *Machine Learning*, 45, 5–32.
Briner, R. (2007) Is HRM evidence based and does it matter? *IES opinion*. www.employment-studies.co.uk/system/files/resources/files/op6.pdf.
Canhoto, A. (2017) Ted Talk: Blind faith in big data must end. https://anacanhoto.com/2017/10/10/ted-talk-blind-faith-in-big-data-must-end/.
Davenport, T.H., Harris, J. and Shapiro, J. (2010) Competing on talent analytics. *Harvard Business Review*, 88(10), 52–58.
Edwards, M.R. and Edwards, K. (2016) *Predictive HR Analytics: Mastering the HR Metric*. London: Kogan Page. www.koganpage.com/PHRA.
Fitz-Enz, J. (2010) *The New HR Analytics*. New York, NY: AMACOM.
Fitz-Enz, J. and Mattox, J.R. II. (2014) *Predictive Analytics for Human Resources*. Hoboken, NJ: Wiley.
Genuer, R., Poggi, J.M. and Tuleau, C. (2008) Random forests: Some methodological insights. *Cornell University Library*. https://arxiv.org/abs/0811.3619.
Griffeth, R.W. and Hom, P.W. (2001) *Retaining Valued Employees*. London: Sage.
Guenole, N., Ferrar, J. and Feinzig, S. (2017) *The Power of People: Learn How Successful Organizations Use Workforce Analytics to Improve Business Performance*. London: Pearson FT Press.
Guest, D. and King, Z. (2004) Power, innovation and problem-solving: The personnel managers' three steps to heaven? *Journal of Management Studies*, 41(3), 401–423.
Huselid, M.A. and Becker, B.E. (2005) Improving human resources analytical literacy: Lessons from Moneyball. In L.M. Losey, S. Meisinger and D. Ulrich (Eds.) *The Future of Human Resource Management: 64 Thought Leaders Explore the Critical HR Issues of Today and Tomorrow*. Hoboken, NJ: Wiley.
Huselid, M.A. (2014) The corporate mirror. *D'Amore-McKim School of Business* [Online]. www.damoremckimleadersatworkblog.com/corporate-mirror-looking-big-data-analytics-workforce-management/#sthash.4qx5y7F3.dpuf.
Huselid M.A. (2015) Workforce analytics for strategy execution. In D.U. Ulrich, W.A. Schiemann and L. Sartain. (Eds.) *The Rise of HR: Wisdom from 73 Thought Leaders*. Alexandria, VA: HR Certification Institute.
Isson, J.P. and Harriott, J.S. (2016) *People Analytics in the Era of Big Data: Changing the Way You Attract, Acquire, Develop and Retain Talent*. Hoboken, NJ: Wiley.
Kavanagh, M.J., Thite, M. and Johnson, R.D. (Eds.) (2015) *Human Resource Information Systems: Basics, Applications & Future Directions*. (3rd Ed). Thousand Oaks, CA: Sage.
Kennedy, H. and Hill, R.L. (2017) The feeling of numbers: Emotions in everyday engagements with data and their visualisation. *Sociology*, DOI: 10.1177/0038038516674675.
Kryscynski, D., Reeves, C., Stice-Lusvardi, R., Ulrich, M. and Russell, G. (2017) Analytical abilities and the performance of HR professionals. *Human Resource Management*, DOI: 10.1002/hrm.21854.
Liff, S. (2000) Manpower or human resource planning—what's in a name? In S. Bach and K. Sisson (Eds.) *Personnel Management: A Comprehensive Guide to Theory and Practice*. (3rd Ed) Oxford: Blackwell Publishing, pp. 93–110.
Marler, J.H. and Boudreau, J.W. (2017) *International Journal of Human Resource Management*, DOI: 10.1080/09585192.2016.1244699.
Minbaeva, D.B. (2017a) Building credible human capital analytics for organizational competitive advantage. *Human Resource Management*, DOI: 10.1002/hrm.21848.
Minbaeva, D.B. (2017b) Human capital analytics: Why aren't we there? Introduction to the special issue. *Journal of Organizational Effectiveness: People and Performance*, 4(2), 110–118.
O'Neil, C. (2016) *Weapons of Mass Destruction*. New York, NY: Crown Publishing.
Rasmussen, T. and Ulrich, D. (2015) Learning from practice: How HR analytics avoids being a management fad. *Organizational Dynamics*, 44, 236–242.
Rousseau, D.M. and Barends, E.G.R. (2011) Becoming an evidence-based HR practitioner. *Human Resource Management Journal*, 21, 221–235.
Smith, T. (2013) HR analytics: The What, Why and How . . . CreateSpace Independent Publishing Platform.

7 Cloud computing and e-HRM

Vinit Ghosh & Nachiketa Tripathi

Learning objectives
- Explain the evolution of HR technologies from legacy technologies to digital and cloud technologies
- Describe the cloud architecture in the form of key cloud features
- Discuss different cloud service and deployment models
- Examine the applicability and importance of cloud computing in various HRM functions, including talent acquisition, goal setting, performance appraisal, and learning and development
- Critically evaluate the advantages and limitations of cloud technologies and the corrective measures to be undertaken before HR cloud implementation

Introduction

Not too long ago, when people sent a consignment by courier or wanted to check flight status, they had to call the courier company or the airport/airline to check the latest status. Now they can simply click on the online link provided by the courier company or simply 'Google' the flight number to see the status in real time. Similarly, today, people can track the status of their pizza order through the App on their mobile phone and can even set a time when they want their pizza to be delivered or picked up. The delivered pizza is like a 'managed cloud,' where we can specify what and when we want—all online, anytime, and anywhere.

Modern organizations are fast realizing the need for agility and flexibility in their business operations to cater to the dynamic and ever-growing customer demands. The trickle-down effect of such need is also felt in the modern HRM functions. As described in Chapter 2, the role of HR has transformed from a mere administrative/support function to a strategic business partner. Traditional HR managers were often considered as 'policy police' because of their compliance-oriented outlook. However, in the due course of time, HR leaders have realized the long-term detrimental effect of 'enforcement' and 'compliance,' and started encouraging autonomy and innovation as part of regulated enterprise operations.

Modern businesses need HR policies to be dynamic and contingent on business strategy to attain maximum impact on effectiveness and higher competitiveness (Nigam, Nongmaithem, Sharma, and Tripathi, 2011). The support for HR's growing strategic focus is facilitated through the advancement of information and communication technologies (ICT). Technology has had tremendous impact on contemporary organizations' knowledge management and human resource processes and practices. The use of technology in various HR functions has taken HR management in a new direction, which is commonly termed as electronic human resource management (e-HRM) (Hertel and Schroer, 2008; Stone and Dulebohn, 2013).

The strategic goal to relieve traditional HR from the repetitive administrative tasks can be fulfilled by seamless adoption of electronic-based HR processes and practices. Through e-HRM, physical capabilities are substituted leveraging digital assets that lower the HR transaction costs and headcount to a large extent (Stone, Stone-Romero, and Lukaszewski, 2006). In today's business world, most organizations are using a large number of HR metrics to audit their HR activities. For instance, with the support of analytics, the fast food restaurant giant McDonalds identified how staff demographics, management behaviors and employee attitudes interact to predict restaurant performance (Sparrow, Hird, and Cooper, 2015).

With the advancement in data analytics, organizations are trying to capture every single piece of internal and external business-related information to create customer value that can lead to customer delight. This has led the companies to adopt new tools and techniques that can store and manage such enormous volume of data and transactions. The real challenge that most companies face is to deal with the high purchase and maintenance cost of these sophisticated software packages. This is more so in the case of small and medium enterprises (SMEs) where due to limited budgetary allocations for infrastructure and technology developments, they fail to gain a competitive advantage over big firms (Simon, 2013). However, as emphasised in Chapter 5, relying on metrics and analytics is simply not good enough. These activities can reap the benefits if managers are given adequate information and they possess the capability to make better and different decisions. Managers should have seamless, real-time access to the current or changing state of human capital data (Sullivan, 2014).

Cloud computing, which is a web-based platform (Low, Chen, and Wu, 2011), is equipped with capabilities to handle complex business scenarios and can provide unbound scope for scalability, flexibility, and cost reduction. Cloud computing is the current shift in the way of accessing distributed applications, platforms, and infrastructures globally through the internet. It gives e-HRM the capabilities to develop reusable systems and processes that can attract, develop, maintain, and retain high-performing talent. This cutting-edge technology has large implications on organizational sustainability and success in a globally competitive market.

By implementing cloud solutions, SMEs can also compete in an innovative ICT[1] environment (Assante, Castro, Hamburg, and Martin, 2016) as these solutions are relatively more affordable. SMEs can use enterprise resource planning (ERP)[2] and customer relationship management (CRM)[3] softwares without purchasing them but simply renting high computing data centers. Acumatica ERP and Zoho CRM represent two of the multiple cloud-based solutions widely used by SMEs (Baltatescu, 2014). 'Human capital management on cloud' is the need of the hour to enable business growth by developing innovative staffing models based on offshore talent, contingent workers and global talent mobility.

In this chapter, we provide an overall understanding of the relevance and importance of cloud computing in e-HRM. We start with some background information on legacy technologies, especially enterprise resource planning (ERP) that dominated the IT landscape until the arrival of the cloud technologies. The section on cloud computing illustrates the importance of cloud technologies in today's HRM. An in-depth understanding of cloud-advantages in the form of various cloud features along with different cloud deployment models have been described in the section on cloud architecture. How cloud computing increases the efficiency and effectiveness of various HRM functions is covered in the section on cloud-based HRM. The section on customized off-the shelf HRM products provides a comparative view of the latest cloud-based HRM products available in the market. Finally, the advantages of being in a cloud-based environment and their limitations are described.

Evolution of HR technologies

The HR-Information Technology (IT) partnership has always been an outcome of strategic business choice. The traditional operating principles of mass production of the 1970s and 1980s are no longer valid; instead, organizations are moving toward tailored production and highly consumer centric customized systems. Therefore, re-engineering or major changes have been made to organizational structures, systems, and processes to cater to the dynamic business needs (Hoogervorst, Koopman, and Flier, 2002). Over the years, IT has been playing a crucial role in the alignment of such business strategies with HR strategies (Hoogervorst, Koopman, and Flier, 2002). The use of IT has reshaped the traditional business models built around the perimeter of time, distance, and functionality. Nowadays, the business models rely on a modular, distributed, cross-functional, and agile business process that enables work to be executed across boundaries of time, distance, and function (Ettlie and Pavlou, 2006; Kohli and Grover, 2008; Rai, Pavlou, Im, and Du, 2012).

The embracement of technology in the HRM was first witnessed in early 1970s when software was used by HR for employees' record-keeping purposes (Fitz-enz and Davison, 2002). In the due course of time, HRM has adopted technologies that re-engineered HR processes by automating specific HR functions or activities using business process management[4] tools. In modern times, the HR department has become one of most technology dependent users (Ikhlap, Khan, Mujtaba, and Sadiq, 2012). As noted in Table 7.1, both the HR function and IT have evolved concurrently leading to the emergence of the e-HRM discipline.

During the 1990s, the need to reduce service delivery times led to the development and adoption of ERP products that relied on computer and internet technologies to integrate internal (organizational systems) as well as external systems (supplier side). In today's data driven market, the golden source of business data is not just restricted to customers' financial transactional information but also includes their non-transactional activities such as their tastes and preferences through various online surveys, posts, and advertisements

Table 7.1 Evolution of HR technologies

Decades	1980s	1990s	2000s	2010s
HR evolution	Personnel administration	Human resource management	Strategic human resource management	Digital/next generation smart HRM
HR technology	Mainframe	Client/server	Web-based	Cloud-based and mobile technology

Source: Authors.

in social networking sites. The information regarding future stakeholders/customers of the firm are equally important to take today's business decisions.

The birth of new smart technologies such as 'Big Data'[5] and the 'Internet of Things (IoT)'[6], have opened up opportunities to extract more information and insights from internal and external sources, allowing significantly better performance from the workforce. Today, managers proactively use social platforms (e.g., Facebook, LinkedIn, etc.) and mobile applications to improve employee engagement and collaborations across geographically dispersed projects. Organizations can judiciously use these technologies to capture the consumers' and employees' knowledge creation, sharing, and ideation for product and service innovation purposes. However, according to Triple-T[7], a technology adoption evaluation model proposed by Obeidat and Turgay (2013), technology adoption within an organization can only be successful if it highlights the benefits that include cost savings, time and space efficiency, flexibility, scalability, and improved performance.

The roles and functions of HRM have continued to evolve with the adoption of new technologies. A few years ago, an ERP solution having an integrated HRM module was sufficient to run an entire enterprise. It offered depth and breadth of HRM functionalities (payroll, performance appraisal, training and development, etc.). However, ERP technologies and products had several serious limitations (Azevedo, Romao, and Rebelo, 2012), including:

- High software procurement and upgradation cost
- High customization required to meet user as well as business actual needs
- Monolithic and inflexible
- Longer implementation time
- Costly to configure and reconfigure
- Hierarchical rigidity and centralizing control and management
- Huge dependency on IT infrastructure and IT support.

As HRM functions became more strategic, the need for an integrated fully functional human resource information system (HRIS) was deemed necessary. This required the HRM discipline to adopt more advanced and state of the art technologies for enhanced HRM performance (Karimidizboni, 2013). Today, HRM capabilities are not restricted within an enterprise, but transforming toward a global delivery system of services. HRM applications are no longer seen as standalone 'boxes' but as highly flexible, scalable and abstracted services that can be consumed by employees anytime and from anywhere. Cloud-based computing is the new paradigm shift in accessing web-based distributed systems, platforms, and infrastructures globally through any mobile device (Low, Chen, and Wu, 2011), and equips modern HR leaders to build elastic and scalable solutions. This allows for quick response to change and cost savings.

According to 2017's Tech Trend Report by Deloitte Insights, digital, analytics, and cloud technology have been constantly bringing disruption and transformation in the way of doing business. HR Systems Survey by Sierra-Cedar (2016) revealed that 47% of global top performing organizations, 27% of the talent-driven organizations, and 34% of the data driven organizations have adopted cloud-based solutions. However, there are still many organizations that manually handle their data and incur huge costs in building data storage capacities. In this context, a significant cost reduction is possible with cloud-based computing (Aljabre, 2012; Conway, Carcary, and Doherty, 2015; Geczy, Izumi, and Hasida, 2011).

Gibson, Rondeau, Eveleigh, and Tan (2012) argue that large companies must focus on moving key HR practices toward cloud-based computing while SMEs can take advantage of its low capital expenditure. It is to be noted that SMEs, where latest HR technology adoption has taken place, have witnessed almost double the revenue per employee with a 12% increase in their overall HR, talent, and business outcome metrics (Sierra-Cedar, 2016). Moreover, according to the Deloitte report (Deloitte Insights, 2017), cloud-based software-as-a-service (SaaS) offerings can now be procured and operated without any long-term involvement of IT professionals. This indicates a gradual lowering of IT implementation costs of cloud-enabled solutions.

Cloud architecture

In line with other management fields, such as customer relationship management (CRM), the HR department requires high computational capabilities to make employee-related processes more efficient (in terms of cost and time/speed) and effective (better quality). To facilitate this, organizations need to provide HR managers with a computing infrastructure that integrates computation, services, and application components together as a 'ready-to-use' shared service and help them in analyzing and modifying HR systems and processes in a better way.

The latest technological advancements in cloud technologies offer the benefits that are desirable in most organizations. The technical features include:

- variable pricing (different prices at different times to use cloud services based on the available demand of that service);
- auto-scaling (dynamic determination and expansion of the service capacity to handle the incoming data load); and
- monitoring dashboards (maps and graphs for monitoring the performance of systems).

Thus, the cloud promises reliable services delivered through the next-generation data centres that are built on virtualized compute and storage technologies.

The cloud users can access applications and data from a 'cloud' anywhere in the world on demand. The cloud users are assured of the fact that the services will be available all the time and can be accessed from anywhere. To achieve this level of service delivery, computing services need to be highly reliable, scalable, and autonomic to support dynamic access, dynamic discovery, and composability. This is supported through the distinct features that cloud architecture provides. In particular, as identified in Table 7.2, five essential elements of cloud computing need to be understood to appreciate cloud advantages (Chabrow, 2011).

Table 7.2 Key features of cloud computing

- On-demand self-service: Employees and HR can avail service anytime and from anywhere
- Multiple supporting platforms: Service requests can be made from any internet-enabled electronic devices
- Resource pooling: Due to plug and play technology features, the users need not be conversant about the underlying software or hardware used
- Rapid elasticity: Consumers can scale up and scale down resources on demand
- Measured service: Consumers can measure the usage of the resources availed and pay accordingly

On-demand self-service: Ad hoc requests of a customer can be served instantaneously without the intervention of any third person. Through the click of button from any electronic device, a consumer with an instantaneous need of a particular service (e.g., current year's employee performance) can avail computing resources (such as central processing unit [CPU] time, network storage, software use, and so forth) in an automatic self-serving fashion.

Multiple supporting platforms: The cloud architecture supports a broad range of heterogeneous platforms (such as mobile phones, laptops, and personal digital assistants [PDAs]). A consumer can have any one of such platforms to access the desired computing resources located remotely by using network service (e.g., internet).

Resource pooling: Consumers need not bother about the location, formation, and sources of the resources they are using through a cloud service as they are handled by the service provider. Multiple consumers can access the same software instance simultaneously without being concerned about the underlying software, data storage, and concurrent users. This is known as the cloud's multi-tenancy or the virtualization feature.

Rapid elasticity: Cloud provides unlimited resource provisioning, that is, the availability of resources. Consumers can scale up resources on demand at the time of peak requirement and can release them when they decide to scale down.

Measured service: Cloud technology comes with metering capabilities through which consumers can measure the usage of the resources availed. Although computing resources are pooled and shared by multiple consumers (i.e., multi-tenancy), measured services help the consumers to know how much resources they have used and the amount of money they need to pay for those cloud services. Therefore, cloud vendors can project a viable transparent pay-per-use business model to the potential customers.

Cloud service models

The cloud service models can further demonstrate the advantages of a cloud platform that are described below:

Software as a Service (SaaS): Cloud consumers can access various software hosted on a remote environment through networks using various clients (e.g., web browser, PDA, etc.). Although cloud consumers do not have any control over the cloud infrastructure, the different applications shared by multiple consumers are organized in a single logical environment on the SaaS cloud. Examples of SaaS include SalesForce.com, Google Mail, and Google Docs.

Platform as a Service (PaaS): Through this service layer, the cloud consumers can develop a customized cloud service for themselves. PaaS offers a development infrastructure including programming environment, tools, configuration management, and so forth. While SaaS provides consumers a hosting environment, PaaS is a developmental environment for them. An example of PaaS is GoogleAppEngine.

Infrastructure as a Service (IaaS): Apart from using the application software on the cloud, cloud consumers can directly use the IT infrastructures (processing, storage, networks, and other fundamental computing resources) provided in the IaaS cloud. Hardware level virtualization is done at this layer to provide consumers with unlimited computing capability. The basic strategy of virtualization is to set up independent virtual machines (VM), which are independent from both the underlying hardware and other VMs. This feature helps a cloud-enabled organization for disaster recovery preparedness as a running memory image of a server can be deployed on another VM at the time of hardware failures. An example of an IaaS is Amazon's EC2.

Cloud deployment models

More recently, four cloud deployment models have been defined in the cloud community. They basically represent the appropriate cloud environment in which the organization decides to make their services available. The decision to go for a specific environment depends on the organization's size, scope of accessibility, financial capability, and ownership.

Private cloud: This cloud infrastructure is owned solely by a single organization, and the cloud data center is managed by the organization or a third party regardless of whether it is located in-house or off-premise. The organizations with multiple existing in-house systems often set up a private cloud to increase their internal processing capabilities. The organizations that choose to operate in a private cloud often need data privacy and security and thus want to have full control over their mission-critical activities.

Public cloud: This is the most used cloud computing deployment model. The cloud service provider has the full ownership of the public cloud data centers and opens its applications and services to the general public. The consumers pay for their usage according to the charging policy set by the cloud provider. Most of the organizations prefer to choose this deployment model as this model is economical. Organizations, in this case, do not have to bear operational cost to maintain data centers and licensing fee for application software. Many popular cloud services are public clouds including Amazon EC2, S3, Google AppEngine, and salesforce.com.

Hybrid cloud: This cloud infrastructure is a combination of two or more clouds (private and public) connected by a standardized or proprietary technology that facilitates data and application portability between them. Organizations can transfer their non-core competencies on a public cloud while controlling core activities on-premise through a private cloud. For example, HR services as SaaS components could be provisioned on a public cloud or Private cloud. The inter-operability and security concerns over accessing an organization's private and public cloud can be mitigated through the use of virtual private cloud (VPC), which encapsulates the organization's existing IT services and the public cloud services. In fact, all corporate security policies still apply to resources on the cloud even though it is on the public cloud. VPC represents a perfect balance between control (private cloud) and flexibility (public cloud).

Cloud-based HRM

In the context of HR, cloud computing can leverage the effectiveness of HR services by making their processes transparent to employees and the general public. HR can provide employees with in-context direct access and collaboration services that they can access on demand and through any internet-enabled devices. The solution includes various self-service and social collaboration features, apart from provisioning on-the-go access to HR applications and tools. A wide range of reports and dashboards are also available in HR cloud-based applications. From the perspective of HR operations, Global HRs can access dedicated cloud hosted services (through SaaS) such as predictive analytics and workforce modelling and can develop customized cloud services (through PaaS). The various HRM functions where cloud computing can be beneficial are as follows.

Talent acquisition: This is a vital HR function aimed at finding the right people at the right time for the right job. Cloud-based HR recruitment enables organizations to source, assess, and hire the best available talent locally and globally. The cloud-based *Crowdsourcing*[8] enables organizations to shift from a captive based labor model to a more efficient, effective, and flexible web-based job outsource model. In this context, they can benefit from a combination of global labor rates, more specialized skills, and more specialized task-management processes. Leveraging the benefits of business process automation and big data tools, an intelligent recruitment strategy can be formulated. Cloud-based talent acquisition tools are designed for targeted recruiting campaigns and can automatically access multiple network-based channels such as candidate portals, referral networks, and job board forums.

This software is able to create new potential candidate profiles after matching them with the organization's internal high performer profiles. Using tools such as applicant tracking, interview management, and requisition management, recruiters and hiring managers can streamline their hiring process. A potential candidate gets engaged in the organization's process by availing on-demand recruitment services such as enquiry services, interview scheduling, and offer letter management, and thereby develops a positive brand image of the firm. Some cloud-based talent acquisition softwares (e.g., Oracle HCM) allow the incorporation of video and other rich media content to increase candidates' engagement and conversion during the hiring process.

Goal-setting: It is a part of performance appraisal process and involves development of some action plans for employees to motivate and direct them toward a specific goal, which is generally tied to an organizational goal. Managers generally set SMART (specific, measurable, achievable, relevant, time-bound) objectives, aligned with overall business goals. A cloud-enabled goal setting process equips a manager to set specific or cascading goals at individual, teams, and at departmental levels, which can be tracked throughout the year with real-time alerts and reporting. Authorized cloud users can set individual task milestones that they can track and modify on a real-time basis. Employees can receive reminders for their goals or task deadlines in their mobile devices integrated with the cloud. HR department and line managers can set one-to-one meeting plans, set agendas, and send diary invites to employees through cloud-based video, audio and other applications. Cloud-based HRM software (e.g., SuccessFactor's Perform and Reward) allow managers and senior leaders to get a full overview of all performance goals. The managers can also get an insight into whether goals are aligned with business priorities.

Performance appraisal: This is one of the important HR functions where employees get evaluated on the basis of their performance on the set goals. The result of the evaluation is closely linked with an employee's promotion and compensation. Cloud-based appraisal makes it easier for HR and line managers to analyze and enhance employee performance by providing continuous feedback. HR can set multiple appraisal plans according to the employee's competency, hierarchy, and career aspirations. Each plan can have a unique combination of workflow, reminder rules, forms, scoring rules, and visibility rules. Appraisal plans can be integrated with employee goal sheets.

A 360-degree feedback system as a SaaS component allows superiors, colleagues, and subordinates to provide feedback on an employee's goal completion. Email or mobile message reminders can be sent to appraisers to remind them of the due dates. This facilitates meaningful performance management conversations throughout the year through cloud enabled systems without restricting performance appraisal to a fixed time period. To make performance reviews effective and efficient, HR cloud software (e.g., Success Factor's Perform and Reward) provides a dashboard-style view of an employee's performance with up-to-the-minute data on job quality, skills assessment, and positive and negative feedback (Rist, 2017).

Rewards and recognition: A fair system of rewards and recognition goes a long way in creating a committed workforce. A visually appealing key performance indicator dashboard, commonly known as a competition leaderboard, can be set up and used as a visual aid to motivate staff, as well as to identify top performers for rewards and recognition. Similar to multiple appraisal plans, HR can design ready-to-go reward program plans integrating with the employee appraisal process. Employees can select from the list of reward plans available to them and can then manage, modify, and monitor their rewards program through any mobile devices.

Learning and development: Learning and development needs of employees are to be carefully handled to meet the organization's strategic development plans. HR analytical tools can assess the training needs of an individual, group, or department from the skills and competency gaps reported during interviews, performance appraisals, customer feedback, and self-development plans. Employees can avail the trainings and certification programs onsite or remotely in the cloud-based information system.

Enterprises can outsource their training programs to other training providers, which in turn deliver customized training materials, expert opinions, and techniques over the internet in cloud. Employees can access such programs at any time through electronic devices and earn credit points on successful completion. Through this internet-enabled training platform, working days loss over training programs can be avoided. On the other hand, continuing professional development (CPD) activities such as qualifications and certifications acquired by employees and effective evaluation of training programs can be tracked seamlessly using cloud-enabled HR systems.

For instance, Hyatt, one of the leading hotels, immensely benefitted by implementing cloud-based training programs. By embracing cloud-based training solutions, it trained its 10,000 employees spread over 54 countries in a very cost-effective manner (Taylor, 2016). Cloud technology helped their employees to access and watch training videos in their native language using their mobile phones.

Compensation management: It is one of the important outcomes of organizational development strategies. The presence of assistive cloud computing functions such as statistical analysis can help to design effective compensation plans for multinational firms operating in different locations around the world. Customized compensation plans can be easily deployed on a cloud platform and the system can immediately respond to it together with other existing compensation policies. Online self-services related to accessing compensation data and compensation policies can result in a paperless HR compensation system.

Virtual HR: Navimipour, Rahmani, Navin, and Hosseinzadeh (2015) have proposed a new class of HR in the era of cloud computing called virtual HRs (V-HRs). HR functionaries spread over geographic and organizational boundaries can collaborate together via the 'Expert Cloud' sharing knowledge, skill, expertise, and experiences to quickly solve any business problem. Through this expert cloud, employees can experience all time availability of V-HRs who can solve their immediate problems or queries through discovering, ranking, message sending, and knowledge sharing over the internet. These specialized HR services in cloud are called Expert as a Service (EaaS), which provide customers with transparent access to experts, knowledge, and skills remotely over the internet.

Customized off-the-shelf HRM cloud products

Enterprises generally choose customized HRMS cloud solutions from well-known software vendors such as Oracle (HCM Cloud), SAP (SuccessFactors), and Workday to name a few. If an organization is maintaining some HR applications (say payroll on PeopleSoft), Oracle fusion offers an advantage that the organization can choose to retain running the payroll application on premise while migrating other functions on Oracle Cloud. Oracle has acquired different company products for different purposes; for instance, its integrated HCM cloud relies on Taleo—a software product that Oracle has acquired for talent recruitment purposes. Thus, for some organizations, Oracle's product acquisition and product co-existence strategy has added complexity in the firm's software acquisition and deployment strategy.

SuccessFactors offers customizable HR solutions like performance and learning. However, for the employee payroll system, it relies heavily on traditional SAP's on-premise payroll functionalities. Workday is well known as a SaaS provider, but it is yet to enrich its product functionalities by offering complex time-driven scheduling features. It also needs to come up with more localized payroll systems to become a true global HRMS cloud solution provider.

Evaluation of a cloud-enabled enterprise

Advantages: Modern business demands a unified cloud solution to drive and maintain its growth. It has been found in research studies that cloud-based computing solutions for payroll, compensation, recruitment, and performance management increase efficiency of the HR department (Bose, 2011; Celaya, 2015). The move toward integration of enterprise business functionalities and offering shared-cloud services are closely associated with the overall business strategy. The common data model architecture of a cloud platform helps to explore new market opportunities by providing immediate access and information through the financial management, human capital management, and sales management services in the cloud. Revenue analysis through predictive analytics and budgeting tools can help an organization's top management to determine which region can be targeted for market expansion.

The *cloud embedded HR collaboration* services can help to allocate resources for the targeted expansion. Through the use of the *predictive modeling* feature of human capital management services, HR can draw up a list of star performers. Using *cloud collaboration services*, meetings and interviews with recruitment experts and business unit heads can be arranged for the final selection of candidates. Using *self-service procurement services*, unit heads can open requisitions for new human capital resources. The *integrated cloud-enabled work-flow engine* routes the request in a sequential or parallel fashion to the business integrated mail inboxes of appropriate authorities for approval.

As the cloud services are designed on a *distributed service-oriented architecture*, global enterprises can adhere to cross country specific rules and policies while delivering their services to the respective country users or employees. Through the *business activity monitoring dashboards*, top management can analyze the performance of a team vis-a-vis the goals set and can take appropriate actions on deviations.

Limitations: Despite the above advantages, it is widely acknowledged that organizations are still struggling to find the right HRMS cloud product that perfectly fits their business, HR, and IT strategy. Unless they find the right fit, it is not possible to avail and maximize the cloud advantages. Quoting CompTIA's Fifth Annual Trends in Cloud Computing, van Eijk (2015) highlighted the following challenges faced by organization in implementing Cloud:

- Up to 40% of firms identified the learning curve as a key challenge.
- 23% to 34% were challenged by vendor lock-in.

- 44% had moved their cloud infrastructure or applications since adopting cloud—an exercise they cited as being costly and more difficult than the initial migration itself.
- Companies were finding it difficult to shift their business practices along with their new cloud strategies.
- 56% of respondents cited developing cloud expertise as a major hurdle.

Data security and privacy is the foremost concern of all cloud users as the user loses physical control of the servers hosting all the sensitive information. This aspect is further examined in Chapter 15. There is always a possibility that sensitive information may be compromised on the public cloud due to a lack of security controls. Cloud vendors make prolific use of third-party services and infrastructure (Baltatescu, 2014) and it is quite possible that their data privacy and security policy are very different from that of client enterprises. The enterprise cloud users should ensure that the vendor can provide data protection and security in the event of any disaster in the form of disaster recovery procedures that may include hosting the data on different servers in different locations.

Another major concern for cloud services customers is the risk of *vendor lock-in*. In such cases, customers become dependent on a certain vendor and are unable to change the vendor without incurring substantial losses or without substantial switching costs (Baltatescu, 2014). This issue can be addressed if vendors use compatible operating systems or adhere to open source software. Otherwise, the licensing rules and use of proprietary software can *hinder the establishment of open standards and interoperability* between cloud services providers.

Major concerns over data security and privacy, as well as lack of standardization and interoperability between cloud platforms are the major reasons for slow cloud adoption in highly sensitive data handling industries. In a recent research study on the enablers and barriers to cloud adoption in organizations, Celaya (2015) found that leadership support acts as a contributing factor for successful cloud implementation, whereas *lack of subject knowledge* impedes its success.

Measures for successful cloud implementation: One of the biggest challenges in a successful cloud implementation is to create a *climate for cloud adoption* as this technology is still in its nascent stage and enterprises can ill-afford financial and operational risks. A rigorous *cloud readiness assessment* on the organization's needs, assets, and capabilities should be performed before migrating any system on a cloud environment. It is recommended that rather than going in for a big-bang, whole-of-enterprise cloud implementation approach, organizations should take an *incremental approach* and start cloud migration with small pilot projects. Further, cloud computing *training* should be imparted across all management levels to successfully embrace cloud as the next-gen business enabler.

As cloud computing is based on a distributed service-oriented architecture, a clear *cloud governance framework* comprising of the management of identified and deployed services, and ownership and authorization of cloud-based systems and services has to be in place. The existing control models should be redesigned to support cloud centric service management along with a revision of existing policies and procedures. A *cloud service delivery management group* should be set up to manage the contracts, operational-level agreements, and service-level agreements (SLAs) for cloud-based services (Open Data Center Alliance, 2014).

Summary

The e-HRM's goal to have standardized HR processes by designing a common system across the organization can be achieved through a cloud-based HR system. A cloud based

HRIS reduces the total cost of ownership and increases the system efficiency many folds. However, the implementation of a cloud-based HR system is tightly linked with the overall business strategy of a firm. The reasons for the failure of most of the cloud-based implementations are generally misdirected objectives, application of wrong implementation methods, and misalignment of organizational competencies with business goals.

In future, the scope for HR technologies will not be restricted within or across organizational boundaries but will seamlessly get integrated with the human capital life cycle to tap an individual's likes, dislikes, and aspirations. Organizational researchers have started realizing the importance of 'implicit motivation,' as subconscious goals are becoming important predictors of an employee's performance (Shantz and Latham, 2011). A cloud-based business intelligence, process automation, and human-centric analytics have the potential to unearth latent factors. It can help HR to design and allocate tasks well suited for an employee's personal and professional growth in organizations.

In conclusion, while cloud computing offers immense opportunities to deploy state of the art technologies to provide better, cheaper, and faster HR services at a global level without having to incur heavy upfront costs, organizations need to take a very cautious long-term approach to this nascent technology trend by adopting a comprehensive cloud readiness assessment and governance framework, underpinned by well-crafted service level agreements with the service providers.

Case study: ABC Corporation's cloud journey—A bumpy road to success

ABC Corporation, which operates in more than six countries across the globe with more than 15,000 employees, has been steadily increasing its market share in the retail business space. According to US trade analysts, big players such as Walmart and Sears could pose a serious threat to brick and mortar companies like ABC. The newly appointed Chief Information Officer (CIO), Mr. Vikrant Sen, had observed that the organization was still maintaining huge spreadsheets for its supply chain planning and procurement. Moreover, information silos resulted in lack of communication, collaboration, and consistency across organizational departments.

The CIO of the company had started the cloud initiative in early 2017 with a vision to develop a faster and a collaborative communication environment. Building a new private data center was ruled out due to its high implementation and maintenance cost. Migration of organizational data to cloud seemed to be a feasible cost-effective solution. Moreover, the organization had expansion plans in Southeast Asia, and therefore the need for a reliable, scalable, and flexible IT infrastructure and a platform for an easy business process management and deployment was urgent.

However, the cloud implementation team could not meet the deadlines and the final implementation date kept shifting. Mr. Sen arranged an internal stakeholder meeting and identified the following barriers for cloud implementation.

- Most of the departments were not ready to change their on-going process of handling data and services. The departments were not aware of non-value-added activities of their business processes. Lack of coordination between IT and business resulted in misidentified or unidentified to-be cloud services.

- Regional HR office was reluctant to expose their sensitive employee information to the cloud environment.
- Lack of a centralized data management policy and procedure hampered the process of planning, creating, managing, protecting, improving, and disposing of organizational data. Every department had their 'own way of doing things.'
- Selection of a specific cloud vendor was a big issue as the suppliers and distributors of the ABC Corporation had different cloud providers. Incompatibility and security issues regarding data exchange between different cloud providers created panic among ABC Corp's IT personnel.

Mr. Sen realized that his 'big-bang' approach toward cloud implementation was a hasty decision. A comprehensive cloud readiness assessment and a well-planned data migration strategy were required under such circumstances. The migration strategy should also be underpinned by a well-assessed cloud vendor selection mechanism. After critically analyzing the issues pertaining to data security, data quality, and governance, Mr. Sen decided to go for a pilot cloud migration project with a few selected departments. Positive results started emerging within months of cloud implementation. The time for preparing critical HR reports was reduced from weeks to a few hours. The process efficiency observed in some business operational areas astounded Mr. Sen, and according to him, 'We have regained our confidence on cloud and we are now confident that we can deliver service with much more agility and confidence.'

Case study questions

- What prompted the CIO to take the decision to make ABC a cloud-enabled enterprise?
- What were the challenges faced by ABC Corp's cloud implementation team?
- How did the company address cloud implementation challenges? What were the key success factors?

Debate: Is cloud computing a passing cloud?

Introduction

Cloud computing has been creating quite a buzz lately in the technology space. However, two different schools of thought exist regarding the hype versus reality of cloud computing in the business world. According to some techno-market analysts, the emerging cloud concept has given rise to 'inflated expectations' among business leaders. The hype has been predicted to fade away in the near future when businesses start encountering major cloud integration challenges and face diminishing returns of the technology adopted (Waschke, 2017). On the other hand, tech-trend reports say that the scalability, flexibility, and the cost benefits that are being realized by early adopters will create a stable market place for cloud among the major players in the field. The pay-offs of cloud adoption in different domains and applications can move this technology to the 'plateau of productivity,' and thus, cloud computing can remain in the technology landscape for years to come (Adamuthe, Tomke and Thampi, 2015; van Eijk, 2015).

Arguments in favor

1. As most of the cloud adopters perceive their organization's sensitive information might be compromised on the public cloud due to its lack of security and control on the data, they may prefer private clouds over other deployment models. Therefore, the value propositions of other cloud deployment architectures may not be fully realized by an organization.
2. Cloud service providers have their own proprietary software and SLAs with clients. Lack of an open standard of communication between different cloud providers often leads to the problem of 'vendor-lock in' (van Eijk, 2015).
3. The laws and regulations that are enforced by different countries on 'data sovereignty,' making it difficult for cloud providers to store other country's data in a digitized format (Leinwand, 2017).
4. Cloud adopters often face integration challenges while implementing cloud across the organizational business areas. Although cloud computing is supposed to reduce IT support cost, organizations often end up spending more on IT to resolve integration issues.
5. As cloud computing is an emerging technology, lack of knowledge on the cloud domain among the top management personnel impedes its success. Top management often does not want to disturb the status quo and is reluctant to change the way of doing business.

Arguments against

1. Cloud computing is the only effective solution to handle the 'data explosion' complexities. It enables businesses to take informed decisions by giving them a platform to access, store, consolidate, analyze, and expose business data and services (Baguley, 2013).
2. The inherent scalability and flexibility features of cloud computing architecture allows small to large businesses to build rapid product designs or service prototypes before moving into actual production or market.
3. Cloud implementation benefits include almost zero software license fees, low hardware implementation, and low maintenance costs. Pay-per-use facility allows companies to scale up and scale down their consumption level depending on the available market demand.
4. This emerging technology has just passed the 'early adoption' phase. It is well accepted that the longer the company has been working with cloud, the fewer concerns it will face regarding data securities and control issues (McKendrick, 2012).
5. The real essence of cloud computing can be reaped by any business through the alignment of its business strategy with the cloud implementation strategy.

Useful references

Adamuthe, A. C., Tomke, J. V. and Thampi, G. T. (2015), "An empirical analysis of hype-cycle: A case study of cloud computing technologies," *International Journal of Advanced Research in Computer and Communication Engineering*, Vol. 4, No. 10, pp. 316–323.

Baguley, J. (2013), *How cloud computing is changing the world . . . without you knowing*. The Guardian. Available from www.theguardian.com/media-network/media-network-blog/2013/sep/24/cloud-computing-changing-world-healthcare.

Leinwand, A. (2017), *3 Things companies must know about data sovereignty when moving to the cloud*. The Enterprisers Project. Available from https://enterprisersproject.com/article/2017/1/three-things-companies-must-know-about-data-sovereignty-when-moving-cloud.

McKendrick, J. (2012), *From annoyance to harmonizer: Cloud computing's maturity curve*. Forbes. Available from www.forbes.com/sites/joemckendrick/2012/06/28/from-annoyance-to-harmonizer-cloud-computings-maturity-curve/.

Waschke, M. (2017), *Cloud failures can occur anywhere on the hype cycle*. InfoWorld. Available from www.infoworld.com/article/3188044/cloud-computing/cloud-failures-can-occur-anywhere-on-the-hype-cycle.html.

van Eijk, P. (2015), *The cloud hype is over—Are your clients ready for reality?* ITprenures. Available from www.itpreneurs.com/blog/cloud-hype-over-ready-for-reality-cloud-certification/.

Video learning resources

- Cloud computing: Explains the benefits of cloud computing over traditional IT resources by emphasizing its flexibility, scalability, and lower total cost of ownership (TCO): www.youtube.com/watch?v=ae_DKNwK_ms
- Software as a Service (SaaS): Explains the three-tier cloud architecture along with few commercial software products used across these three-tiers: www.youtube.com/watch?v=36zducUX16w
- Cloud HR: Explains how HR can leverage employee training, learning, and development through cloud enabled business operations: www.youtube.com/watch?v=rTPHOGrFpz8
- HR as a shared service: Demonstrates how HR capabilities can be deployed as shared services in cloud to increase organizational efficiency by combining Salesforce capabilities: www.youtube.com/watch?v=7oU1omWcBrk
- HR cloud readiness: Demonstrates the requirements and challenges to be taken care of during the implementation of a HR cloud solution: www.youtube.com/watch?v=vOQ8dKQW95M

Notes

1 ICT or information communication technology uses information technology to integrate enterprise communication services (mail, chat, instant messaging, video conference, audio, etc.), which enable users to access, store, transmit, and manipulate information.
2 ERP or enterprise resource planning products are business process management software that uses its inbuilt, customizable, and integrated applications to manage business functions.
3 CRM or customer relationship management products manage and analyze customer centric data throughout the customer lifecycle to improve business relationships with customers.

4 Business process management is a systematic way of designing, executing, and controlling business processes linking people, business functions, and technology.
5 Big data represents very large data sets that are mainly used for predictive analysis purposes.
6 IoT is the acronym for 'Internet of Things,' which comprises smart devices embedded with electronics, software, sensors, and network connectivity to collect and exchange data.
7 Triple-T is known as technology trade theory, which evaluates any specific technology adoption intentions by outweighing the adoption disadvantages from adoption advantages.
8 Crowdsourcing is the process of obtaining information or input online from a large set of people for completion of a particular project or task.

References

Aljabre, A. (2012), "Cloud computing for increased business value," *International Journal of Business and Social Science*, Vol. 3, No. 1, pp. 234–239.
Assante, D., Castro, M., Hamburg, I. and Martin, S. (2016), "The use of cloud computing in SMEs," *Procedia Computer Science*, Vol. 83, pp. 1207–1212.
Azevedo, P. S., Romao, M. and Rebelo, E. (2012), "Adavantages, limitations and solutions in the use of ERP systems (Enterprise Resource Planning): A case study in the hospitality industry," *Procedia Technology*, Vol. 5, pp. 264–272.
Baltatescu, I. (2014), "Cloud computing services: benefits, risks and intellectual property issues," *Global Economic Observer*, Vol. 2, No. 1, pp. 234–237.
Bose, I. (2011), "Cloud computing and its impact on corporate HR practices," *Advances in Management*, Vol. 4, No. 12, pp. 57–58.
Celaya, T. A. (2015), "*Cloud-Based Computing and human resource management performance: A Delphi study*" (Doctoral dissertation, University of Phoenix).
Chabrow, E. (2011), *5 Essential characteristics of cloud computing*. InfoRisk. Available from www.inforisktoday.com/5-essential-characteristics-cloud-computing-a-4189 (Accessed 25 August 2017).
Conway, G., Carcary, M., and Doherty, E. (2015), "A conceptual framework to implement and manage a cloud computing environment," In: *Proceedings of the Sixth International Conference on Cloud Computing, GRIDs and Virtualization*, Nice, pp. 138–142.
Deloitte Insights (2017), *Tech trends 2017: The kinetic enterprise*. Deloitte University Press. Available from www2.deloitte.com/us/en/pages/technology/articles/technology-consulting-tech-trends-collection.html (Accessed 25 August 2017).
Ettlie, J. E. and Pavlou, P. A. (2006), "Technology based new product development partnerships," *Decision Sciences*, Vol. 37, No. 2, pp.117–147.
Fitz-enz, J. and Davison, B. (2002), *How to measure human resources management (3rd edition)*. New York, NY: McGraw-Hill.
Geczy, P., Izumi, N., and Hasida, K. (2011), "Cloudsourcing: Managing cloud adoption," *Global Journal of Business Research*, Vol. 6, No. 2, pp. 57–70.
Gibson, J., Rondeau, R., Eveleigh, D., and Tan, Q. (2012), "Benefits and challenges of three cloud computing service models," In: *Proceedings of Fourth International Conference Computational Aspects of Social Networks* (CASoN), Sao Carlos, pp. 198–205.
Hertel, G. and Schroer, J. (2008), "Electronic human resource management (E-HRM): Personalarbeit mitnetzbasierten Medien," In: Batinic, B. and Appel, M. (Eds.). *Medienpsychologie*. Berlin, Heidelberg: Springer, pp. 449–475.
Hoogervorst, J. A., Koopman, P. L., and Flier, H. V. D. (2002), "Human resource strategy for the new ICT-driven business context," *International Journal of Human Resource Management*, Vol. 13, No. 8, pp. 1245–1265.
Ikhlap, K., Khan, A. F., Mujtaba, B. G. and Sadiq, U. (2012), "The impact of information systems on the performance of human resources department," *The Journal of Business Studies Quarterly*, Vol. 3, No. 4, pp. 77–91.

Karimidizboni, R. (2013), "Human resources information system," *Interdisciplinary Journal of Contemporary Research in Business*, Vol. 4, No. 10, pp. 1004–1017.

Kohli, R. and Grover, V. (2008), "Business value of IT: An essay on expanding research directions to keep up with the times," *Journal of the Association for Information Systems*, Vol. 9, No. 1, pp. 23–39.

Low, C., Chen, Y. and Wu, M. (2011), "Understanding the determinants of cloud computing adoption," *Industrial Management & Data Systems*, Vol. 111, No. 7, pp. 1006–1023.

Navimipour, N. J., Rahmani, A. M., Navin, A. H. and Hosseinzadeh, M. (2015), "Expert Cloud: A cloud-based framework to share the knowledge and skills of human resources," *Computers in Human Behavior*, Vol. 46, pp. 57–74.

Nigam, A. K., Nongmaithem, S., Sharma, S. and Tripathi, N. (2011), "The impact of strategic human resource management on the performance of firms in India: A study of service sector firms," *Journal of Indian Business Research*, Vol. 3, No. 3, pp.148–167.

Obeidat, M. A. and Turgay, T. (2013), "Empirical analysis for the factors affecting the adoption of cloud computing initiatives by information technology executives," *Journal of Management Research*, Vol. 5, No. 1, pp. 152–178.

Open Data Center Alliance (2014), *Master usage model: Business strategy enabled by Cloud Rev 1.0*. Available from https://opendatacenteralliance.org/article/business-strategy-enabled-by-cloud-master-usage-model-rev-1-0/ (Accessed 27 July 2017).

Rai, A., Pavlou, P. A., Im, G. and Du, S. (2012), "Interfirm IT capability profiles and communications for cocreating relational value: Evidence from the logistics industry," *MIS Quarterly*, Vol. 36, No. 1, pp. 233–262.

Rist, O. (2017), *The best performance management software of 2017*. Available from http://in.pcmag.com/cloud-services/102377/guide/the-best-performance-management-software-of-2017 (Accessed 25 August 2017).

Shantz, A. and Latham, G. (2011), "The effect of primed goals on employee performance: Implications for human resource management," *Human Resource Management*, Vol. 50, No. 2, pp. 289–299.

Sierra-Cedar (2016), *2016-2017 HR systems survey white paper, 19th annual edition*. Available from www.sierra-cedar.com/white-papers/ (Accessed 25 August 2017).

Simon, P. (2013), *Even small companies can tap big data if they know where to look*. Available from https://hbr.org/2013/12/even-small-companies-can-tap-big-data-if-they-know-where-to-look (Accessed 25 August 2017).

Sparrow, P., Hird, M., and Cooper, C. L. (2015), "Strategic talent management," In: Sparrow, P., Hird, M., and Cooper, C. L. (Eds.). *Do We Need HR?* London: Palgrave Macmillan, pp. 177–212.

Stone, D. L. and Dulebohn, J. H. (2013), "Emerging issues in theory and research on electronic human resource management (eHRM)," *Human Resource Management Review*, Vol. 16, No. 2, pp. 229–244.

Stone, D. L., Stone-Romero, E. F., and Lukaszewski, K. (2006), "Factors affecting the acceptance and effectiveness of electronic human resource systems," *Human Resource Management Review*, Vol. 16 No. 02, pp. 229–244.

Sullivan, J. (2014), *Top 15 design principles for talent metrics and analytics*. Available from https://drjohnsullivan.com/articles/top-15-design-principles-talent-metrics-analytics/ (Accessed 25 August 2017).

Taylor, T. (2016), *Hyatt turns to cloud-based employee training solution*. Available from www.hrdive.com/news/hyatt-turns-to-cloud-based-employee-training-solution/427031/ (Accessed 25 August 2017).

van Eijk, P. (2015), *The cloud hype is over—Are your clients ready for reality?* ITprenures. Available from www.itpreneurs.com/blog/cloud-hype-over-ready-for-reality-cloud-certification/ (Accessed 28 March 2018).

8 Social media and e-HRM

Christopher J. Hartwell

Learning objectives

- Describe social media in an HR context
- Distinguish between social media platforms (specifically professional vs. personal social media)
- Understand the legal and ethical issues surrounding the use of social media in organizations
- Be able to draft a social media policy for an organization
- Recognize the opportunities and challenges that social media presents in specific HR functions

Introduction

Before boarding a flight from Florida to New Jersey, Peter Shankman took to Twitter to jokingly ask Morton's Steakhouse to meet him at his destination airport with a porterhouse steak. When his plane touched down, a tuxedo-clad Morton's employee greeted a genuinely surprised Shankman with a full steak dinner in response to his tweet (Haines, 2016).

Morton's Steakhouse was quick to provide matchless service to its customer and, while the specific example may be unique, service requests from customers are not. A recent survey from J.D. Power asserts that two-thirds of consumers have utilized a company's social media page for customer service purposes (Power, 2013). Social media has also affected other business functions. Companies bet heavily on social media marketing, such as Mondelez International, who went all-in by spending solely on social media marketing for its Nilla-brand wafer cookies – and saw staggering results, including a massive increase in their Facebook page audience (from 15,000 to 356,000) and a 9% increase in sales (Segal, 2013). However, the impact of social media on organizations is broader than just the evolving relationship between companies and their customers. There are also implications for how organizations attract and select employees, as well as for managing employees within the organization. In other words, social media has the potential to change the nature of human resources (HR) in organizations.

Social media consists of online digital platforms where users can create content and interact and exchange information with other users. Some of the most common social media sites include Facebook, Instagram, Pinterest, LinkedIn, and Twitter (Greenwood,

Perrin, & Duggan, 2016). Social media users are individual people, as well as other entities. For instance, an individual employee at your company may have a personal Facebook account, but your company itself might have a Facebook account that employees monitor on behalf of the company. Wendy's restaurant, for example, employs a sassy "challenger with charm" strategy to its Twitter account, wittily roasting individual Twitter users (Gallucci, 2017) and other fast food chains alike (May, 2016), while also being the impetus and inspiration for the most retweeted tweet (the content shared by the most users) in the history of Twitter (Roman, 2017). Social media information and interactions, whether person-to-person, person-to-company, company-to-person, or company-to-company, have the potential for influencing various facets of a company's HR.

This chapter first explores social media as it relates to the HR context. Then several considerations of how and when to use social media in HR are outlined, including differentiating between social media platforms, the evolution of social media platforms, incremental utility provided by social media, different patterns of social media use, and legal and ethical issues associated with using social media in an organizational context. Following these considerations, the chapter presents various opportunities and challenges associated with social media use in a variety of HR functions, specifically recruitment, selection, onboarding/socialization, employee development, and performance management/discipline. At the end of the chapter, you will find both an HR case study and debate topic focused on social media.

Considerations regarding social media in an HR context

Numerous considerations regarding the use of social media span across the HR functions, and should be reflected in HR's decisions about if, when, and how to use social media. Among these considerations are differentiating between social media platforms, the rapid evolution of social media platforms, the utility of social media, different patterns of social media use, and legal and ethical issues.

Differentiating between social media platforms

All social media platforms are not created equal, and it is important to recognize and factor in the varying purposes behind different social media platforms, as well as the functionality of each. For example, YouTube focuses on video sharing, Instagram focuses on images and videos, while Twitter users share quick, short ideas or messages that are limited to 280 characters.

There are numerous ways to categorize various social media sites, such as by how well their purposes align, similarity in functionality, or the audience(s) available. As an initial categorization, differentiating between professional and personal social media sites is useful in an HR context. While an organization can create a "professional" profile on any social media site, the personal/professional distinction referred to here is more a function of the identified purpose of the platform, the information typically shared, and the expectations of the platform's audience.

Professional social media platforms generally focus on a user's professional identity and network, and users generally share information that aligns with this focus, such as education, work experience, skills, and recommendations. The largest professional social media platform is LinkedIn, which boasts more than 500 million members worldwide. Many industries also have their own professional platforms, such as SHRMConnect (for HR professionals), ResearchGate (for academics), and ActiveRain (for real estate professionals). In addition, job-seeker platforms that allow users to share information about companies and jobs also fall under the umbrella of professional social media. The most common of these platforms include Indeed and Glassdoor.

In contrast, the focus of *personal social media platforms* is the user's personal identity and network, and the information shared by the users on these platforms can be as unique and diverse as the individual users themselves. Some may share relationship information, vacation photos, and humorous videos, while others may share political opinions, personal memories, and movie clips. Facebook is the most popular personal social media platform, with over 2 billion active users. Other popular personal social media platforms include Instagram, Twitter, YouTube, Reddit, and Pinterest.

The evolution of social media platforms

Remember MySpace? How about Friendster? These early social media hubs have since fallen off the radar. Even Google+, a platform backed by a technology powerhouse, has failed to find much of an engaged audience. Rapid technological advances and stiff competition make the social media industry one that moves very quickly. For example, Snapchat introduced Stories in 2013, which allowed user to share a continuous series of photos and videos, each available for only 24 hours. While initially a huge success, Facebook and Instagram have both introduced a similar feature, and use of the feature on Instagram surpassed Snapchat within a year of its release (Castillo, 2017). What impact these copycat features will have on Snapchat is unclear, but what is clear is that there is no guarantee that your preferred social media platforms of today will be as relevant (or even still functioning) in the future.

Not only is it important to assess the probable longevity and growth of a social media platform, it is essential to also keep abreast of the changes that occur within the platform itself. Facebook, which began as a way for college students to connect, has evolved immensely (and continues to do so). As new features become available – such as Facebook's recently introduced embedded GIF feature – organizations and HR should consider the challenges and opportunities that they create.

Incremental utility provided by social media

Another social media consideration is the value provided in relation to costs, as well as the incremental value provided in comparison with other current practices. This utility should be assessed before adopting social media practices in HR, using available information about monetary costs, the target audience, labor needed, probable outcomes, and so on. Such forecasting allows an educated prediction about whether using various platforms in different HR functions will be an effective endeavor. As social media strategies are implemented, it is important to measure their effectiveness in order to make accurate conclusions about whether or not the goals of these strategies are being met.

For example, if an organization wants to recruit through LinkedIn, a cost/benefits analysis might include the following questions: How does one go about posting jobs on LinkedIn? What are the costs associated? How many applicants are expected as a result? Are these different from applicants attracted through other methods (e.g., job boards, employee referrals, etc.)? Which employee(s) will be tasked with implementing the strategy? After implementation, some important follow-up questions to assess effectiveness could include: What were the actual costs involved? How many qualified applicants were attracted through LinkedIn?

How many were ultimately hired? How do these employees stack up to the employees hired from other sources? What was the cost per hire and how does this cost compare with other methods? The more that these questions yield positive results that are not redundant with other similar methods, the more incremental utility is displayed, and the more likely it is that your social media HR strategies are adding value to your organization.

Different patterns of social media use

When examining social media users, it is important to understand the profiles of different types of users. Some initial research conducted by First Direct Banking (2013) identified 12 social media user types. Some users, identified as *Ultras* are almost constantly on social media and post content multiple times per day. Other users may be on social media just as frequently, but as passive consumers of others' content, rather than active producers of content (*Lurkers*). Still others may be infrequent users of the social media platform (*Dippers*). Some pose frequent questions to their networks (*Quizzers*), while others provide their network with novel and unique information (*Informers*). You can find the full list of the 12 social media user types in Table 8.1.

Table 8.1 Twelve types of social media users

Social media type	Definition
Ultras	These users consistently check and engage on social media dozens of times per day, and gladly admit their fixation.
Deniers	Similar to "Ultras," but without admitting their fixation. These users claim social media is not prominent in their life, but experience withdrawal when unable to access social media.
Dippers	These users access social media infrequently and can go long stretches of time (weeks or even longer) without accessing or posting content on social media.
Lurkers/observers	These users regularly access social media to consume others' information, but rarely (if ever) contribute their own content.
Peacocks	For these users, social media is a popularity contest, where high numbers of friends/connections and being able to demonstrate superiority are paramount.
Ranters	These are users that are highly opinionated on social media (even though they may not be as bold face-to-face), sharing polarizing opinions, political views, and so on.
Quizzers	These users generate online conversations through the use of questions posed to their social media networks.
Informers	The users gain satisfaction by being able to expose their network to new and novel information, and by providing information in response to others' questions.
Approval seekers	These users seek a high number of friends/connections and get validation through the number of likes, comments, and shares that their content generates from other social media users.
Changelings	These users adopt an identity and/or personality that is different from who they are face-to-face, so that their true identity remains a mystery.
Ghosts	These users create anonymous social media profiles, void of any personal information, due to fears about revealing such personal information online to strangers.
Virgins	These are new users to social media (or a specific social media platform) and often post information or engage in other behaviors that a seasoned social media user would not (such as trying to use Facebook's status bar like a search engine, thus posting your search query to your Facebook page).

Source: Adapted from First Direct Banking (2013).

One's social media user type is not necessarily the same across social media platforms, as the different purposes across platforms may lead to different behaviors. For instance, a person may put forth a very professional persona and provide useful work-related information (e.g., sharing insights about how to effectively lead a business) on a professional platform such as LinkedIn, while presenting a completely different persona (e.g., political rants, amorous comments) on a personal platform such as Facebook.

One particular challenge related to patterns of social media use are generational differences. The workforce consists of both *digital immigrants* – who grew up without the internet, mobile devices, and social media (i.e., Generation X and older) – and *digital natives* – for whom these technologies have always been a part of life, and who learn to use them in much the same way that they learn to walk or speak their native language (i.e., Generation Y and younger) (Prensky, 2001). Digital natives are much more comfortable with social media technologies and how to use them, while digital immigrants tend to use social media less often and have more uncertainty and privacy-related concerns (Kontos et al., 2010).

Legal and ethical issues

Some of the biggest considerations of using social media are the legal and ethical implications. While this topic could fill an entire chapter (or even book) itself, this chapter focuses on a few of the most relevant legal and ethical considerations: discrimination, privacy concerns, and retaliation. Finally, one major way to reduce legal and ethical concerns is presented – developing a social media policy.

Discrimination. Discrimination is at the heart of many HR functions. For example, the purpose of a hiring system is to discriminate between potential high-performers and low-performers in order to hire those most likely to succeed in the job. However, the dark side of discrimination presents itself when it is based on non-job-related information (e.g., race, gender, age, etc.). Such discrimination can be intentional (disparate treatment), where the choice to discriminate is a conscious one (e.g., "I will not hire those Black employees"). In many countries, disparate treatment is illegal, at least for certain groups (e.g., racial/ethnic minorities). However, discrimination can also be unintentional (disparate impact), where discrimination does not occur consciously, but is the result of a seemingly neutral process. For example, if there is a height requirement for a certain job, some groups (e.g., females, certain races) will be disadvantaged simply because their average height is less than that of other groups. While fewer countries have laws preventing disparate impact, it is still within an organization's ethical and business interest to minimize disparate impact. If the job requirements are not directly tied to effective performance on the job, a company could select out a sizeable part of the population that could prove to be effective performers.

All humans have biases, both implicit and explicit, that can cloud effective decision making. Thus, when using social media to make employment decisions, both disparate treatment and disparate impact are major concerns. As an example, if a hiring manager searched for applicant social media profiles, he or she has the potential to uncover a wealth of demographic information about the applicant, even just from a picture (e.g., color, gender, age), and such information can consciously or unconsciously impact that hiring manager's decision of whether to retain that applicant in the applicant pool. In fact, research has shown that, while HR managers do not believe that the social media profile image contains information useful in making judgments about applicants, the profile image often has just as much (and sometimes more) influence on the HR managers' ratings as directly job-related information, such as prior work experience and educational attainment (Hartwell, 2015).

Privacy concerns. Most social media platforms provide privacy settings that allow users to determine how much information they share and who they share it with. However, many users are not aware of these settings or do not know how to use them. And regardless of how and if privacy settings are used, many users consider any use of social media in organizations (particularly personal social media) to be a violation of their privacy. Thus, even where it is legal for organizations to monitor employees' social media accounts or use social media information to make employment decisions, organizations should consider the ethical implications of doing so, including the reactions of job applicants who are negatively affected and the impact on the morale of the company's workforce.

The expectation of privacy and the right to keep personal and professional lives separate are protected in some US states and may be protected through common law in other countries, such as Australia (Thornthwaite, 2016). However, even where legal protections are not in place, this is an ethical area that companies need to consider. If employees or applicants feel their privacy rights are being violated, they may choose to leave the company or withdraw from the application process, sharing their negative impressions of the company with other employees and/or potential applicants.

Retaliation. Many countries provide legal protections to employees that are treated unjustly or subjected to a harsh working climate (such as bullying, sexual harassment, discrimination, physical abuse, etc.). The use of social media by employees may be protected by these laws. For example, Hernan Perez was an employee for Pier Sixty (a catering company in New York City) who was fired after posting a profanity-laced tirade on Facebook about his supervisor. However, because his post encouraged employees to vote "yes" to an upcoming union vote, Perez successfully won a lawsuit against his company for retaliation based on protected concerted activity (White, 2017). Thus, it is important to understand what local and national laws may be pertinent to employee activity on social media (whether occurring inside or outside of work).

Developing a social media policy. One major way to minimize legal challenges and ethical concerns is to develop a social media policy. A social media policy should include a definition of social media, general guidelines for appropriate social media behaviors, references to corresponding policies, specifics regarding appropriate and inappropriate social media behaviors, and procedures for violations of the policy (including consequences). Specific purposes and considerations for each of these sections is outlined in Table 8.2. The Society for Human Resource Management (SHRM) provides a social media policy template on their website as well ("Social Media Policy," n.d.). Legal consultation regarding the specifics of the policy is recommended.

Opportunities and challenges for social media use in HR functions

Considering the factors outlined previously, there are numerous opportunities and challenges associated with the use of social media in HR (Poba-Nzaou et al., 2016). Social media is a relatively new context in organizations and, with few exceptions, there are no far-reaching legal precedents or ethical standards. When making the decisions of if, when, and how to use social media in HR, it is important to consider the pros and the cons (and to consult with the legal team in your organization, where available). In this section, I outline specific opportunities and challenges associated with social media use in the

Table 8.2 Recommended social media policy sections

Policy section	Purpose	Considerations
Definition of social media	To ensure that all employees understand what the organization defines as "social media"	• Does the definition include *all* online sharing of information inside or outside of work (blogs, chat rooms, website comments, etc.)? • It there an enterprise (internal) social media network? If so, is that under the same guidelines as external social media?
General guidelines	To provide basic guidelines that employees can use in the absence of specific instructions (as not every individual circumstance can be covered individually)	• What are the values of the organization? How are those values exhibited through social media behaviors? • What personal risks are involved when sharing online information (lack of privacy, permanence of information, etc.)?
References to other organizational policies	To reinforce existing policies and limit redundancies	• Does the organization have other policies (bullying, harassment, ethics, confidentiality, etc.) that tie to social media behaviors? • What is the best way to reference or summarize information from other policies?
Specific social media policies	To specify what are appropriate and inappropriate social media behaviors	• What social media behaviors should all employees follow? For example, can employees access external social media sites while at work? On company-issued devices? • Is there an enterprise social media platform? If so, how is it to be used? • Should separate policies be specified for employees with decision-making responsibility (supervisors, those involved in hiring, etc.)? • Who is authorized to use the organization's official social media accounts?
Violation procedures	To inform employees regarding how to report a violation, what procedures will be followed to investigate a violation, and what consequences may occur.	• What should an employee do to report a violation of the social media policy? • Is there more than one alternative for reporting (supervisor, HR, intranet form, etc.)? • What steps will take place to investigate a violation? • What are the potential consequences of violations (e.g., "up to and including termination")? • Is there language confirming that retaliation against those reporting violations is prohibited?
Distribution of policy	To ensure that the social media policy is known and understood by all employees	• How is the policy going to be distributed? • How frequently should refresher training be given to ensure that the policy is reinforced?

Source: Author.

following HR functions: recruitment, selection, onboarding/socialization, employee development, and performance management/discipline.

Recruitment

Integrating social media into an organization's recruiting function makes intuitive sense. Many companies already use social media as a marketing tool to curate and disseminate a company brand (Kissel & Büttgen, 2015). In many ways, recruitment is simply taking those marketing ideas and using them in within HR – instead of targeting potential customers, you are targeting potential employees. A recent survey by Jobvite (2015) suggested that over 90% of recruiters use social media, with LinkedIn and Facebook being most common.

One opportunity afforded by social media is the ability to target specific audiences. Using some social media platforms, such targeting can be very direct, such as a Facebook ad that targets users working in a specific industry or that have a specific skillset (Edwards, 2016). In addition, social media allows you to engage with users, who can contact you directly or comment with questions about a job posting. When a company is attentive and personable in these interactions, it signals to those prospective applicants of the company's positive environment.

A second opportunity is the ability to seek out passive potential applicants. If you were looking for an employee with prior experience at a similar company or with a specific hard-to-find skill, a social media search (particularly professional social media) could result in a list of high-quality candidates that meet your needs. Such passive candidates may not be actively seeking new employment, but if you contact them with an opportunity that exceeds their present situation, they could easily change their mind.

Social media sites are beginning to recognize these opportunities. Facebook recently introduced a specific jobs site (www.facebook.jobs) and LinkedIn has introduced a YouTube channel specifically focusing on talent solutions (LinkedIn, n.d.). Yet, while these recruitment opportunities continue to grow, there are also major challenges to social media recruitment that organizations should understand.

The first challenge is the time and effort needed to maintain engagement with potential candidates. As one talent executive put it, the key to sourcing through social media is developing relationships (SHRM Online, 2016). Just posting a job on social media and not responding to further inquiries can leave a negative impression. Second, recruiting solely through social media may have an adverse impact on certain demographic groups, especially ethnic/racial minorities and older potential applicants, both of which are less likely to use or have access to the internet and social media (Kontos et al., 2010).

A final challenge is measuring results. How do you measure the effectiveness of a recruitment advertisement posted on social media? Does the number of comments, likes, or shares have value? How about the volume and/or quality of the applicants recruited? Understanding the goals of your recruitment strategy, how social media fits into that strategy, and whether your social media efforts are helping to achieve the goals are all essential for effective social media usage in recruitment.

Selection

Like recruitment, there is a lot of potential for how social media can be used in selection. The Society for Industrial and Organizational Psychology (SIOP, 2015) even listed using social media to make employment decision as one of the "Top 10 Workplace Trends for 2016." A decade of annual surveys from CareerBuilder corroborates this trend, showing that the use of social media in the hiring process has grown dramatically, from 12% of hiring managers in 2006 to 60% in 2016 (see Grasz 2006, 2016). As with recruiting, the most commonly used platforms among those that use social media in selection are LinkedIn and Facebook (Hartwell, 2015).

Some initial research suggested that information from social media is useful in measuring applicants' personality traits and intelligence, as well as predicting future job performance

Table 8.3 Comparison of two approaches to social media screens

Approach (purpose)	Information assessed	Comparable selection procedures	Relevant SM category
Screen-in	Job-related qualifications (e.g., experience, skills, abilities)	Application blank Résumé Biodata questionnaire	Professional (e.g., LinkedIn)
Screen-out	Lack of "fit" (e.g., personality, values) or other red flags (e.g., inappropriate behaviors)	Personality assessment Background check Drug/alcohol screen Honesty/integrity test	Personal (e.g., Facebook)

Source: Author.

(Kluemper & Rosen, 2009), but other research has not achieved positive results (Van Iddekinge et al., 2016). Another study indicated that judging more comprehensive characteristics of an individual (e.g., person-job fit, hireability) may be more valid than attempting to make more fine-grained judgements about specific personality traits or work-related abilities (Hartwell, 2015).

There are a couple of different approaches to social media screens in the hiring process, as laid out in Table 8.3. First is a *screen-in approach*, in which job qualifications (e.g., knowledge, skills, abilities, certifications, experience) are screened in order to ensure that the qualifications of the job are met. This approach is similar to the approach used in reviewing résumés or applications. Professional social media platforms such as LinkedIn are best suited for this approach, due to the depth of job-related information contained therein.

The second approach is a *screen-out approach*, in which applicants are screened for information that would disqualify them from consideration. Such may include a lack of person-organization fit (differing values, conflicting personality) or other information deemed to be a red flag (e.g., drug use, aggressive behavior, discriminatory comments). This approach is more comparable with drug screens, background checks, and other assessments that attempt to ensure that a candidate is not hiding something negative. Personal social media platforms such as Facebook are best suited for this type of screening, due to the breadth of personal information often shared on such platforms.

While the use of social media screening during the hiring process has promise, it also has considerable challenges. A social media screen is a *passive selection procedure* that requires no direct input from the applicant. Instead, the organization relies on assessing social media information previously posted by the candidate. As such, the information provided is not as standardized as the information gathered through direct interactions with the candidate (e.g., applications, interviews). One way to combat this challenge is to standardize the social media screen itself as much as possible by following the same procedure for all job candidates. Some ways to standardize the process may include screening the same social media platforms for all candidates, considering the same timeframe (e.g., the past year) when gathering and screening information, using anchored rating scales to rate candidates, and training assessors as to what information is important to focus on.

As noted in a previous section, there are also legal and ethical issues surrounding the use of social media in selection, particularly using a screen-out approach and the use of personal social media. Ethically, candidates generally consider the use of such information as an invasion of their privacy, given that the purpose of such social media sites is not typically directly work-related. Legally, viewing social media may make a hiring manager privy to the candidate's age, race, gender, sexual orientation, disability, and so on, which may impact the hiring manager's judgements about the candidate. An organization will find it difficult to argue that their process is legally justified without validating it first.

Onboarding and socialization

Social media may be a way to make the onboarding and socialization process more efficient and effective. Newly hired employees could be added to a company-specific social media network to aid in embedding the new employee into the organization. A company-specific social media network could also be used to accumulate information that might be useful to new hires (e.g., frequently asked questions). For example, some organizations utilize social media platforms to provide information and engage employee discussion surrounding medical insurance and other benefits (Miller, 2017). Social media may also be a means for providing mentoring in an organization, as long as interactions between the mentor and the new employee are frequent (DiRenzo et al., 2010). Connecting with coworkers on social media may also provide a smooth social transition for new employees. In fact, as soon as an employee is hired, current employees could reach out and connect to begin the socialization process even before the new employee's first day on the job.

One challenge of using social media in onboarding and socialization is that a social media context does not provide the same richness of communication as face-to-face interactions, and this may lead to superficial interactions and a lack of deep connections. Thus, it should certainly not be used in isolation for onboarding, socialization, and/or mentoring, but should be used to supplement more personal face-to-face interactions. A second challenge is that there are differing opinions and comfort levels when it comes to integrating one's personal and professional lives. Having coworkers (and especially supervisors) attempt to connect on personal social media may make a new employee uncomfortable. A recent poll showed that these concerns are more likely among senior managers and that the younger employees have more positive views about connecting with colleagues on social media (Wright, 2017).

Employee development

Social media could be a useful in training employees to better meet current job demands, as well as developing employees' skills and abilities, both to provide employees with personal growth opportunities and to increase their mobility and promotional potential. Many major organizations maintain a company-specific social media platform, where employees can connect and share work-related information, questions, and ideas. Such an internal network encourages employee discourse, both with each other and with the organization, while also facilitating the creation of communities of practice, where employees with similar job duties can share best practices and job crafting techniques that increase effectiveness and efficiency (Shepherd, 2011). In essence, social media can support a culture of informal learning in an organization.

Another way that social media (particularly company-specific social media) can facilitate training and development is through formal learning. Social media provides a platform where organization-wide training and development programs can be designed and implemented. Similarly, these platforms can house employee assessments that build talent inventories and help tailor a specific set of developmental training and experiences matched to each employee's needs. Such an employee development plan could be followed at the employee's desired pace (some employees will have a stronger desire for development and growth) or facilitated and managed by the employee's supervisor or other organizational leadership (such as being part of a succession plan).

Performance management/discipline

The final HR function where social media is most likely to be used is managing current employees. A company-specific social media platform might be used to facilitate information sharing, allowing employees to recognize each other for exceptional performance, to share advice on how to be successful, or to even share grievances and recommend improvements. If a company-specific social media platform is not available, employees can create and join groups of coworkers on external social media sites. This could be done to increase social ties among coworkers, but also has the potential to become a place where employees share job frustrations and negative information about the company.

News reports abound with examples of how employee social media behaviors have been the impetus for discipline and termination. Here are a few examples: (1) a Nordstrom employee fired for posting a Facebook comment that suggested killing police (Iboshi, 2014); (2) a realtor fired for comments during a Twitter feud with a celebrity (Schwartz, 2017); and (3) a social media specialist for an English-language learning center fired for blogging about homophones (Rolly, 2014). Even recent US federal judicial nominees faced interrogations from the US Senate Judiciary Committee regarding past politically charged blog posts (Totenberg, 2017). A segment from *ABC News* (2015) highlights how a video posted on social media cost Adam Smith his job as chief financial officer and continued to negatively impact his future job search.

Monitoring employees' social media behaviors or acting upon negative information when it is brought to the company's attention, can be beneficial to ensure that employees are consistently and positively conveying the company brand and values. This is especially true when the individual is a public face for your company (e.g., a company leader, public relations, customer service) or when employees identify their employer on social media. Social media monitoring can also alert the company to other red flags, such as harassment or illegal activity. However, keeping tabs on employees when they are not on the job may be considered an invasion of privacy into the employees' personal lives. An employer has to question whether employee behaviors outside of work have an impact on job performance or the company's business. For example, an employee ranting about how she despises watching other people's children is likely not a cause for disciplinary action, unless she works for a daycare provider. There are also other legal considerations that can vary across countries. Freedom of speech and whistleblowing statutes in the US, for example, might protect the employee from negative employment actions based on complaints between coworkers about an employer.

There is the potential for company-specific social media to be a form of employee voice – allowing employees to constructively articulate their workplace concerns and suggestions for improvement (Holland, Cooper, & Hecker, 2016). One major step that employers can take is to develop a social media use policy that covers all employees in the organization. This policy should cover such things as accessing social media at the workplace (on company devices and on personal devices), how to voice concerns using social media, acceptable social media and blogging behaviors, company monitoring of social media and internet sites, and disciplinary measures for policy violations (see Table 8.2).

Once this policy is developed and put into place, it needs to be explicitly communicated to employees on a regular basis.

Having a comprehensive policy that is effectively communicated increases the likelihood that the company will successfully avoid legal challenges to any negative employment action made as a consequence of social media behaviors. Such was the case when Samuel Crisp, an employee at Apple Retail in the United Kingdom posted negative information about the company and its products on Facebook. Crisp was suspended and eventually fired when a coworker notified his boss about the posts. In a subsequent legal battle, Apple's decision was upheld, largely because of the explicit policy it had in place (and had communicated to employees) that prohibited any such comments that undermined the reputation of the brand (Mr. Samuel Crisp vs. Apple Retail [UK] Limited, 2011).

Summary

This chapter examined social media use in an HR context, including important considerations when making decisions about if, when, and how to use social media. Differences between professional and personal social media were outlined, and various legal and ethical issues were highlighted. Suggestions for developing and implementing an organizational social media policy were set forth. Finally, the potential utility of social media in recruitment, selection, onboarding/socialization, employee development, and performance management/discipline were discussed.

The use of social media in an HR context is still a relatively new organizational development, and there are many questions that remain unanswered. Legal and ethical issues regarding the practice are far from resolved and HR professionals should be careful in how social media is used in their organization, both by HR staff and other company employees. HR departments might consider partnering with other departments or specific employees that better understand the power of social media. Marketing, public relations, and information technology are logical places to start. Finally, it is important to measure the results of any social media efforts undertaken by HR in order to understand whether such actions provide value to the organization.

Case study: Social media implications

Sharon is one of the few female instructional designers in a company that develops online training. Having returned to work after having her first child, she was surprised to learn that her department recently underwent restructuring. The number of instructional designers was in the process of doubling, and about one-third of her former colleagues had been promoted to management.

"I planned on reaching out to you once the expansion decision was made, but the changes have kept me busy non-stop, and I haven't had the time," explained Dave, her supervisor, as she met with him on her first day back. "But I'm sure glad you're back! We've got a lot of new employees that need your help to get up-to-speed, assuming that you're going to be around, and not home all the time with a sick baby!"

"I am happy to help," Sharon replied, slightly annoyed at Dave's condescending tone. "But arrangements have been made in the past that allow designers to work half of their time at home – like when Bill broke his leg playing softball. I was hoping to work out something similar."

"Those arrangements are made on a case-to-case basis, and unfortunately the need for training new employees is too great right now." replied Dave.

Visibly agitated, Sharon loudly spoke. "I can't believe that while I was gone, I received no information about this expansion, or opportunity for promotion like my coworkers, and now I'm being told that I can't even take advantage of [the] same telecommuting arrangements that have been provided to others!"

"Listen, Sharon," Dave said sternly. "I understand your frustration, and I should've kept you in the loop. I know you have a lot going on in your life – we all do. But don't get so emotional and angry – engineers are supposed to look at things rationally. Which is probably why there are a lot more men in the engineering field."

Dave saw that his attempt at humor was not being received well. He continued. "Listen – this workplace is growing, and we all have to roll with the changes that come along with that. Why don't you take a day or two to catch up on what you've missed and then we'll talk about your role in training the new employees."

At the end of the day, Sharon went home to decompress. Still frustrated, she went on Glassdoor and vented by posting an anonymous comment: "If you're a female even thinking of having kids, you won't fit in here. If you take extended leave, you quickly become an afterthought. Supervisors don't understand the concept of gender discrimination, or even attempt to care."

You are the HR manager and Dave bursts into your office the following day, with a printout of the comment. "I know Sharon wrote this. We had a bit of a heated exchange yesterday. I am trying to keep her happy, while managing the growth in my department. But I can't allow a negative attitude like this! I think Sharon should be fired!"

Case study questions

- What steps would you take to resolve this situation?
- What sources would you look to for additional information?
- What would you do to minimize the chances of a similar occurrence happening in the future?

[Note: This case is fictional but is based on a real-life experience detailed in Smith (2017)].

Debate: Does social media provide accurate information that is useable for making employment decisions?

Introduction

The use of social media to make employment decisions – hiring, promotion, termination, and so on – has a lot of promise, but substantial challenges as well. One could argue that using such information allows organizations a more well-rounded picture of who the applicant or employee really is, thus allowing for more informed and valid decisions. On the other hand, it could be argued that much of what is found on social media may not be relevant to on-the-job behavior, which may even cloud judgement and lead to poorer employment decisions.

Arguments in favor

- Social media provides an inside look at the "true" applicant or employee, including who they are outside of work. This offers unique information from what can typically be gathered during the hiring process or at work during the course of employment (Chambers & Winter, 2017).
- Social media information has been shown to be an accurate indicator of work-related attributes (e.g., personality, intelligence) (Davison et al., 2016).
- Social media is a relatively cost-effective way to screen applicants and/or monitor employees to ensure that they will not and/or do not blemish the organization's brand of reputation (*Wall Street Journal*, 2014).
- Not utilizing social media in employment decisions could lead to hiring, promoting, or retaining someone without paying attention to red flags that were readily available, and the organization could therefore be at fault for later actions by this individual that harms others or negatively impacts the business (e.g., stealing, assault, defamation) (*Wall Street Journal*, 2014).
- Employees are representatives of the organization for which they work, and it is well within the organization's right to ensure that those employees are positively representing the organization, both at work and outside of work (*Wall Street Journal*, 2014).

Arguments against

- What a person posts on social media is an idealized self, meant to engage his or her specific audience of followers or friends, and may not fully portray the real self (Ungar 2015).
- Social media has not consistently demonstrated usefulness in measuring work-related attributed or predicting work-related outcomes (Chambers & Winter, 2017).
- Screening social media prior to employment can lead to negative applicant reactions, and monitoring employee social media behavior can erode trust and stifle employee job satisfaction and creativity (Kumar 2015).
- Using social media to make employment decisions opens a company up to a host of legal and ethical issues, such as discrimination and privacy violations (SHRM, 2017).
- What an applicant or employee does outside of work is not relevant to the organization, as long as he or she consistently comes to work and effectively performs the job (*Wall Street Journal*, 2014).

Useful references

"Should companies monitor their employees' social media?" 22 October 2014. *Wall Street Journal*, retrieved from www.wsj.com/.

Chambers, R. & Winter, J. 2017. Social media and selection: A brief history and practical recommendations. *The Society for Industrial and Organizational Psychology (SIOP)*, retrieved from www.siop.org/.

Davison, H. K., Bing, M.H., Kluemper, D.H., & Roth, P. L. 2016. Social media as a personnel selection and hiring resource: Reservations and recommendations. In: Landers, R. N. & Schmidt, G. B. (eds.) *Using Social Media in Employee Selection: Theory, Practice, and Future Research*. New York, NY: Springer.

Kumar, S. 22 May 2015. Why monitoring employee social media is a bad idea. *Time*, retrieved from www.time.com/.

Maurer, R. 25 January 2017. Know before you hire: 2017 employment screening trends. *The Society for Human Resource Management [SHRM]*, retrieved from www.shrm.org/.

Ungar, L. 13 July 2015. Presentation of the self in social media. *World Well-Being Project [WWBP]*, retrieved from www.wwpb.org/.

Video learning resources

- Recruiting in the social media era: www.youtube.com/watch?v=QHPQ61b40ss
- Former CFO now unemployed, on food stamps after viral video (cited in the text): www.youtube.com/watch?v=8LqoLBQ68Uw
- Social media and HR analytics: https://www.youtube.com/watch?v=ccz5Y2urpfE
- Employee engagement, HR social media #140MTL @PamelaMaeRoss – Socializing HR: www.youtube.com/watch?v=S6hHKUDJxLc
- Great-West Life's company employee social media guidelines: www.youtube.com/watch?v=sx7t5A00UsE
- LinkedIn talent solutions: www.youtube.com/user/LITalentSolutions

References

ABC News. 28 March 2015. Former CFO now unemployed, on food stamps after viral video. *ABC News*, retrieved from https://youtu.be/8LqoLBQ68Uw.

Castillo, M. 2017. Facebook's Instagram Stories crushes Snapchat with over 250 million daily active users. *CNBC*, 20 June, retrieved from www.cnbc.com/.

DiRenzo, M. S., Linnehan, F., Shao, P., & Rosenberg, W. L. 2010. A moderated mediation model of e-mentoring. *Journal of Vocational Behavior*, vol. 76, no. 2, pp. 292–305.

Edwards, J. 2016. How recruiters and stalking you on Facebook. *BBC*, 31 August, retrieved from www.bbc.com.

First Direct Banking. 13 May 2013. First Direct social experiment infographic. *First Direct Banking*, retrieved from www.newsroom.firstdirect.com/.

Gallucci, N. 2017. Behold the sass master behind Wendy's Twitter. *Mashable*, 5 January, retrieved from http://mashable.com/.

Grasz, J. 2006. One-in-four hiring managers have used Internet search engines to screen job candidates; one-in-ten have used social networking sites, CareerBuilder.com survey finds. *CareerBuilder*, 26 October, retrieved from www.careerbuilder.com.

Grasz, J. 2016. Number of employers using social media to screen candidates has increased 500 percent over the last decade. *CareerBuilder*, April 16, retrieved from www.careerbuilder.com.

Greenwood, S., Perrin, A., & Duggan, M. 2016. Social media update 2016. *Pew Research Center*, 11 November, retrieved from www.pewinternet.org/.

Haines, B. 2016. 14 Amazing social media customer service examples (and what you can learn from them). *Buffer*, 10 March, retrieved from http://blog.bufferapp.com/.

Hartwell, C. J. 2015. *The use of social media in employee selection: Prevalence, content, perceived usefulness, and influence on hiring decisions.* Doctoral dissertation, Purdue University, West Lafayette, IN.

Holland, P., Cooper, B. K., & Hecker, R. 2016. Use of social media at work: A new form of employee voice? *The International Journal of Human Resource Management*, vol. 27, no. 21, pp. 2621–2634.

Iboshi, K. 2014. Nordstrom fires employee, citing Facebook comments. *USA Today*, 16 December, retrieved from www.usatoday.com.

Jobvite. 2015. The Jobvite Recruiter Nation Survey 2015. *Jobvite*, retrieved from www.jobvite.com.

Kissel, P. & Büttgen, M. 2015. Using social media to communicate employer brand identity: The impact on corporate image and employer attractiveness. *Journal of Brand Management*, vol. 22, no. 9, pp. 755–777.

Kluemper, D. H. & Rosen, P. A. 2009. Future employment selection methods: Evaluating social networking web sites. *Journal of Managerial Psychology*, vol. 24, no. 6, pp. 567–580.

Kontos, E. Z., Emmons, K. M., Puleo, E., & Viswanath, K. 2010. Communication inequalities and public health implications of adult social networking site use in the United States. *Journal of Health Communication*, vol. 15, no. 3, pp. 216–235.

LinkedIn. n.d. "LinkedIn Talent Solutions." YouTube channel available at www.youtube.com/user/LITalentSolutions.

May, A. 2016. Sorry McDonald's, Wendy's Twitter account is winning the war on beef. *USA Today*, 31 March, retrieved from www.usatoday.com/.

Miller, S. 2017. Open enrollment: Using social media and decision-support tools. *SHRM*, 13 September, retrieved from www.shrm/org.

Mr. Samuel Crisp vs. Apple Retail (UK) Limited. 2011. Case number: 1500258/2011.

Poba-Nzaou, P., Lemieux, N., Beaupré, D., & Uwizeyemungu, S. 2016. Critical challenges associated with the adoption of social media: A Delphi of a panel of Canadian human resources managers. *Journal of Business Research*, vol. 69, no. 10, p. 4011.

Power, J. D. 2013. Poor social media practices can negatively impact a businesses' bottom line and brand image. 14 February, retrieved from www.jdpower.com/.

Prensky, M. 2001. Digital natives, digital immigrants. *On the Horizon*, vol. 9, no. 5, pp. 1–6.

Rolly, P. 2014. Blogger fired from language school over "homophonia." *The Salt Lake Tribune*, 30 July, retrieved from http://archive.sltrib.com.

Roman, L. 2017. Quest for free chicken nuggets inspires Twitter's most retweeted tweet. *National Public Radio (NPR)*, 9 May, retrieved from www.npr.com/.

Schwartz, T. 2017. Illinois real estate agent out of a job after sparring with Patton Oswalt on Twitter. *Chicago Tribune*, 2 February, retrieved from www.chicagotribune.com.

Segal, D. 2013. Riding the hashtag in social media marketing. *The New York Times*, 2 November.

Shepherd, C. 2011. Does social media have a place in workplace learning? *Strategic Direction*, vol. 27, no. 2, pp. 3–4.

SHRM. 30 September 2017. "Social media policy," viewed at www.shrm.org/resourcesandtools/tools-and-samples/policies/pages/socialmediapolicy.aspx.

SHRM Online. 20 May 2016 "The brave new world of social media sourcing," retrieved from www.shrm.org.

Smith, A. 2017. Discrimination claims on Glassdoor result in firing, EEOC lawsuit. *SHRM*, 15 June, retrieved from www.shrm.org/.

Society for Industrial and Organizational Psychology (SIOP). 6 December 2015. "SIOP announces top 10 workplace trends for 2016," retrieved from www.siop.org.

Thornthwaite, L., 2016. Chilling times: Social media policies, labour law and employment relations. *Asia Pacific Journal of Human Resources*, vol. 54, no. 3, pp. 332–351.

Totenberg, N. 2017. Senators grill Trump judicial nominees on provocative blog posts. *NPR*, 15 June, retrieved from www.npr.org.
Van Iddekinge, C. H., Lanivich, S. E., Roth, P. L., & Junco, E. 2016. Social media for selection? Validity and adverse impact potential of a Facebook-based assessment. *Journal of Management*, vol. 42, no. 7, pp. 1811–1835.
White, L. A., 2017. Using profanity on social media can be protected union-related speech. *SHRM*, 7 June, retrieved from www.shrm.org.
Wright, A. D. 2017. Friending colleagues on social media sites now less taboo. *SHRM*, 18 September, retrieved from www.shrm.org.

9 Gamification and e-HRM

Tobias M. Scholz

Learning objectives
- Understand the impact of gamification on organizations and human resource management
- Explain the concept of gamification and identify its benefits and shortcomings
- Discuss the usage of gamification in an operational and strategic context
- Understand the implications of gamification on HR service delivery in the context of the case study presented

Introduction

The US Army has a long history of adapting to new technology. In 2002, they published the video game *America's Army* for recruitment purposes by "using computer game technology to provide the public a virtual soldier experience that was engaging, informative and entertaining" (Wardynski in McLeroy, 2008, p. 7). *America's Army* was the first successful utilization of video games in the recruitment context. The Army recruited more people through that game than any other method at a fraction of the cost (Singer, 2010) and this has led to several sequels. It is important to highlight though that the game came under heavy fire (pun intended!) for being highly unethical and exploiting the minds of vulnerable young men by glorifying violence. However, the game helped to introduce the idea of linking games with business in the mainstream media. Today, organizations are utilizing gamification in various ways. People are the primary audience for gamification; therefore, gamification in the human resource management context has become increasingly popular.

Digitization is radically transforming the world of work. With the ongoing adoption and diffusion of technologies such as laptops, tablets, smartphones, smartwatches, and wearables, everybody is continuously connected. These technologies have an extensive impact not only on peoples' daily lives but also on their work. The astonishing number of more than 3.7 billion people having access to the internet (InternetWorldStats, 2017) is a constant reminder of the importance of digitization and the connectedness of any organization. In conjunction with the increased interconnectivity enabled by technological advancements, the public's interest in video games has surged. That interest can be traced back to the fundamental precondition of people to look for a playful approach.

Playing games has been part of human society for a long time and it is used to transfer knowledge in a safe environment. Huizinga (1949) considers play to be an essential aspect of being human, coining the label Homo Ludens. Today, technological developments seem to enable new forms of play that attract large audiences, as there are nearly 2 billion people who play video games at least casually (Intel, 2015). It is estimated that the gamification industry will be worth $11 billion by 2020 (Ireland, 2016). It seems that these days "everybody" plays video games. This widespread use of video games and the inherent preference of a playful environment are bound to influence the working life as well. Dewey (1916) found the idea of linking play to work quite innovative. The concept of play and the concept of work are compatible (Hamari, Koivisto, and Sarsa, 2014). This link lays the foundation for incorporating gamification in electronic human resource management (e-HRM).

The concept of gamification is not precisely defined and there is an ongoing debate about what exactly constitutes gamification. This chapter introduces the concept of gamification and highlights the difficulties of defining, designing, and implementing gamification. Several examples will be presented to illustrate both its potential and the risks involved. Finally, gamification will be discussed as a potentially powerful HRM tool for any organization.

What is gamification?

The term gamification first became popular in business and research in 2010 (Deterding et al., 2011), and since then, its popularity has been increasing in marketing (Hamari and Lehdonvirta, 2010; Bailey, Pritchard and Kernohan, 2015), organizational studies (Vesa et al., 2017), business intelligence (Burke and Hiltbrand, 2011), business data governance (Hay, 2014), and in the realm of academia (Hamari, Koivisto, and Sarsa, 2014). Gamification has outgrown its niche to become an extensive multi-disciplinary field (Nacke and Deterding, 2017). There is, however, still no common or unified understanding of gamification.

Researchers have defined gamification in various ways:

- "Gamification is the use of game design elements in non-game contexts" (Deterding et al., 2011, p. 1)
- "The process of game-thinking and game mechanics to engage users and solve problems" (Zichermann and Cunningham, 2011, p. XIV)
- "A process of enhancing a service with affordances for gameful experiences in order to support users' overall value creation" (Huotari and Hamari, 2012, p. 19)

These definitions are often used as a starting point to understand the concept of gamification.

Based on this understanding, the idea of gamification is highly linked with game design and, consequently, the principles of gamification mimic the rules of game design. The focus is on the mechanics, the dynamics, and the emotions. It is often called the MDE framework, which is adapted from traditional game design literature. Robson et al. (2015) describe them as follows: dynamics deal with the player behavior and how the player reacts to the gamification; emotions describe the player's state of mind; and mechanics are the building blocks of gamification and tackle the setup, rules, and progression. All of these three principles are linked with each other and the mechanics will influence the dynamics as well as the emotions of the participants.

Furthermore, it is essential to understand that the design of gamification follows certain *rules*. First of all, it is crucial to focus on the journey of the player in the gamification system. How is the onboarding for the new player, will the player be motivated to learn more in order to finally master the gamification? Consequently, balancing is critical, it should not be too easy or too difficult, so that there is a flow-experience. This can be designed and several building blocks can be used.

Some of the essential *building blocks of gamification* are as below:

- *Points*: This is the typical building block in many gamification systems. Players can collect points by following the rules of the gamification system. They are a way to keep score and give the player feedback about their progress.
- *Badges*: Similar to the points, badges are a different way for rewarding the players. However, they are also prestigious. People collect them to gather credentials. This is also a way to show the standing of a player in the social environment as it is possible to display the badges.
- *Leaderboards*: Based on the rules in the gamification system, the leaderboard is a way to rank the players and give feedback on the competition. The player can see the position compared with the competition.
- *Levels and titles*: Another way to achieve a sense of progress and make the path to the mastery transparent is introducing levels. Players learn and gain points over time, and this can be compared with progress. The player will rise in levels and also get a new title with time. This is linked with the status of the player in the gamification.
- *Achievements*: This building block can be part of the player journey or motivate players to spend time and effort to do difficult tasks. Collecting achievements is also a way to show dedication and progress in the gamification system as they are often time consuming or difficult.
- *Challenges/quests*: These elements are used to give the player tasks and assignments they have to master. This is often rewarded with points or other incentives. They give the player purpose and help them navigate through the gamification system. This is also a way to design a focus to certain tasks.
- *Progress bar*: Especially in the beginning, players are often overwhelmed by the new input, so progress bars give the player a sense of progress and advancement. The progress bar is often linked with the level progression.

These building blocks are all trying to focus on the aspect that gamification gives the player real-time feedback as well as ongoing feedback. Every action will lead to a direct reaction and players can evaluate their behavior. It is essential to design the gamification in that way so that the player is not underwhelmed or overwhelmed by the bar that keeps rising. This should include space for trial and error as well. However, there is a strong focus on rewards, and it is necessary to achieve a balance between enforcing competition and allowing collaboration.

Surrounding gamification is an ongoing terminological discourse (Deterding, 2014a). Many refer to gamification as a mere marketing concept (Zichermann and Linder, 2010) that results in the development of exploitationware (Bogost, 2014). They criticize gamification as being relatively narrow and focusing on the one-sided implementation of game elements such as points, badges, leaderboards, and rewards (Walz and Deterding, 2014). Some analysts call for "rethinking gamification" (Fuchs et al., 2014a) and that "gamification needs to either disappear or be rethought" (Fuchs et al., 2014b, p. 10). The rationale is to reposition gamification more toward "designing contexts as interventions, informed by game design" (Deterding, 2014b, p. 325). This means that gamification per se can be positioned on a spectrum between intensity and impact. Gamification can either be relatively operational and superficial or be extensive and initiate strategic change.

Gamification is often heuristically defined as being "something with games," without any reference to its underlying functionality. The question of the impact of gamification on an organization can be answered by its tendency of triggering behavioristic responses in the user. People are nudged (Thaler and Sunstein, 2008) into a certain direction without always being intrinsically motivated. Game design is, therefore, unique in its beneficial impact on non-gaming contexts.

Gamification and HRM

As technological developments unfold rapidly, employees need to be updated on new products continuously. SAP, the enterprise resource management firm, designed the game *RoadWarrior* to keep their sales team up to date. In *RoadWarrior*, sales professionals were challenged to close deals, challenge each other and collect points to be the best sales professional. While competing and playing, employees learn about new products and methods to close deals (SAP, 2012; Datagame, 2016).

Similarly, at Google, in order to save travel expenses, employees are challenged to be cost-effective travelers by using a gamified application; the travel expense game. Employees are incentivized to spend less by being promised that they can keep half of their savings for themselves (Datagame, 2016; Rocketrip, n.d.).

These examples highlight the connection between games and HRM. Motivation and training are vital aspects of HRM and gamification can augment their outcomes. In order to get a better understanding of this link, the concept of game and game design need to be defined. The gameplay follows specific game mechanics, a defined set of rules and elements for playing a particular game. As humans are receptive to play games, and given a large number of people currently playing games, it seems reasonable to state that we are susceptible to game mechanics. We do not only play for fun, and humans learn through play. Huizinga mentioned the example of children learning playfully (Huizinga, 1949). This playful environment can be translated into a gameful environment. Learning through games may, therefore, be a natural predisposition (Gee, 2003). The knowledge economy places a strong emphasis on learning by doing and the success of any organization, as well as the career of an individual, are linked to their ability to learn continuously (Wang and Ahmed, 2003). Due to the importance of continuous learning and our natural preposition to learn through play, the value of using game elements in an organizational setting is mandated. Utilizing gaming or game mechanics will potentially help increase organizational learning capacity, improving the working environment as a whole.

Playing is linked to learning and learning is intertwined with work. Approaches such as playful work (Hamari, Koivisto, and Sarsa, 2014) or playbour (Kücklich, 2005) increasingly address this combination of work and play. All of them include the importance of learning. The emergent trend of gamification (Oprescu, Jones, and Katsikitis, 2014) propagates the use of serious games, game mechanics, and similar tools in the business context. As games potentially motivate, stimulate, and enable people to learn even further than with traditional methods, the potential of using gamification in a work environment seems limitless. More specifically, implementing gamification in HRM will have potentially positive effects on employees such as increased motivation (Deterding, 2012) and learning (Landers, 2014). Gamification-based HRM aims to tap every employee's full potential.

The opening vignette on the US Army's war game illustrated the potential of gamification in recruitment and selection. There are several successful examples of high-technology companies using gamification to pre-screen candidates. They include:

- Uber's "Code on the Road": A coding game consisting of a series of coding challenges leading to a suggestion to work for the company.
- Google has also used coding challenges to hire people.
- In 2004, a company presented a mathematical problem on a billboard and directed people to its website for further challenges leading to an invitation to apply for positions.
- The French postal service, Formaposte, created a game to boost recruitment and employee retention.
- Other notable examples of computer games used as recruitment tools are the chance to run a Siemens factory or a Marriot hotel.

Ireland (2016, p. 2) points out that "what these games have in common is that they give players a taste of what working for those organizations might be like, and if they enjoy it in a game, they might enjoy it in real life."

Gamification: Strategic and operational approaches

A majority of commercial gamification products are geared toward supporting businesses. However, most gamification tools in the business context focus on the operational level by fixing stand-alone issues and, therefore, the strategic dimension is often neglected. Additionally, most gamification tools use only a few game design elements and game mechanics (Dorling and McCaffery, 2012). In contrast to the current evolution of video games, many gamification tools are still quite narrow and straightforward, and consequently, not useful for the strategic implementation of gamification. However, modern video games are highly complex, immersive, and create a massive world for the player (Mandal, 2014). This discrepancy between gamification tools and video games seems to be an ongoing trend in gamification and could be one cause of gamification not living up to its potential. We are currently merely scratching the surface of gamification and have yet to discover how to use it more profoundly, comprehensively, and strategically.

There is tremendous scope to transform operational gamification into strategic gamification. While at an operative level, simple gamification may suffice, at the strategic level, gamification can teach, activate, innovate, and transform organizations (Warmelink, 2014). Gamification can contribute to the realization of an organization's business strategy by focusing on stakeholder analysis, core competencies, and organizational capabilities. By supporting employees in an immersive gamification system throughout the entire HR process, gamification can be intertwined with the strategical development of an organization. Such gamification is more than a quick fix or an isolated solution, as it transforms every facet of the working environment. By doing so, gamification can increase motivation and learning, resulting in enhanced employee performance.

One can argue that strategic gamification is somewhat intrusive, but there is always a need for embeddedness within the organization. Gamification is, therefore, about the utilization of game design and the idea focuses on designing a separate "world." Furthermore, this means that gamification also includes a plan for the end-game or for the sustainability of gamification itself within the organization. Gamification is, consequently, linked to the organization and becomes an essential part of it. That is why gamification needs to be linked to an organization's vision and strategy. Strategic gamification done right is highly intertwined with every process within the organization. Every facet of the organization is somewhat influenced by the strategy behind the gamification transformation.

Consequently, strategic gamification is also a technology integration process. This process brings about a holistic digitization of the HR function. Strategic gamification, therefore, draws from the existing human resource information systems and e-HRM literature and enables a stronger integration of HRM into the organization.

> This new form of radically gamified HRM exploits the potential of understanding an organization in a modern way. The company no longer *has* an HRM – it *is* an HRM. Every employee and every manager is seen as an individual at a granular level, while still being an integral part of the overall way of shaping the people's development and fate in the organization.
> (T. M. Scholz and V. Stein, *Making playful dynamics work: The gamification of human resource management*. Unpublished manuscript.)

Some fundamental questions need to be answered before organizations start using gamification. The answers to these questions will affect the design and implications of gamification on HRM and the organization at large. Some key considerations in this regard include:

- *Strategic vs. operational*: Is there a stand-alone issue that needs to be solved by using game mechanics or do we truly want to reap the all-encompassing benefits of gamification?
- *Gamification is more than just a quick fix*: Using points, badges, and leaderboards to quickly fix an operational level challenge is too simplistic. Even if gamification is used for operational level challenges, game design and implementation is a delicate process and one that needs to be thoroughly examined.
- *Forces HR to think strategically*: Strategic gamification forces the HR function to consider the strategic orientation of an organization. The strategy needs to be considered when designing an effective gamified HRM system.
- *Long-term investment (lock-in)*: Gamification is a long-term investment. Even if used for operational level challenges, employees regularly face game mechanics in a work setting. In order for the gamification system to stay immersive, long-term considerations such as end-game and variety in game mechanics are important. Using gamification will eventually lead to a discussion about the strategic implication of gamification.

The strategic implementation of a gamification system precisely designed for the needs of the organization is, therefore, highly beneficial for HRM. Several aspects of gamification are relevant for HRM. First of all, gamification aims at complex problems for which the existing solutions are insufficient. Gamification can be helpful in gathering data about people and monitor them in real-time. However, it is still difficult to measure them in an ethical and fair way (e.g., motivation or performance). Second, gamification serves as a catalyst for professionalization (Stein, 2010): Designing HRM processes under the principles of gamification forces HRM experts to anticipate and overcome barriers, which can be considered "professionalization through the back door." They have to reevaluate their complete HR function, modernize it for the digitization, and transform their strategy accordingly.

Summary

While gamification may prove useful for a variety of purposes in HRM, it may also have unintended negative consequences. Rather than being used a quick-fix, gamification should always be approached from a long-term perspective. Gamification is a tool used to transform the HR department, but this transformation has to be planned and implemented by the HR department itself by acting as the gamification designer who makes the "game endless." In doing so, strategic gamification approaches the actual depth and complexity of game design and becomes a truly powerful tool for the HR department.

Case study: Gamification and employee productivity

John has been working as a manager for a medium sized recruitment firm for over six years. During the first two years of his tenure, the firm flourished. The firm was performing so well that additional personnel was regularly hired. As a result, the team that John supervised became too large for one manager. Hence, after a lengthy discussion with the CEO, John decided to split up the workforce into three separate teams. John hoped this would ensure efficient management by limiting the span of control. Additionally, he hoped this would increase team commitment.

During the first evaluation concerning these new teams, John noticed that the employees were satisfied with the smaller teams. Nevertheless, market share and revenue did not increase on an annual basis for the first time since John started working for the firm. While some employees attributed this lack of performance to general economic difficulties, John noticed other firms' performance increase. Searching for the causes of declining performance, John started reading into employee motivation and quickly became interested in gamification. He met with three gamification consultancy firms and decided to sign a three-year deal with the firm OptiGame. OptiGame provides a gamified system designed to increase employee performance.

OptiGame completely transformed the current work system at the recruitment firm. Now, the three teams were no longer named according to their geographical focus but were given the names "dominators," "raptors," and "conquerors." In this new game setting, the teams competed for the team of the week, month, and year awards. Additionally, competition within individual teams was added by awarding the best dominator, raptor, and conqueror of the week, month, and year respectively. Teams competed based on points that they collected by contacting a potential new customer (1 point), high weekly customer satisfaction scores (1 to 10 points), successful placements (10 points), and a range of other scoring opportunities. The leaderboards keeping track of the scores were put up in the office for everyone to see. Additionally, teams and employees could earn badges for completing special challenges such as managing a specific candidate placement within a certain time frame.

Initially, John was satisfied with OptiGame. Productivity increased tremendously. People seemed to be motivated by the system and eager to perform well. The teams seemed immersed in the competition and revenue and profit were back on track. After the first year, however, John noticed another decline in revenue, which reached a historic low by the end of the year. John noticed that severe rivalry had developed between certain members of different teams. While some employees were performing very well, others were struggling. In a later conversation with a colleague, John was surprised to hear that he did not want to increase the scores of the competitors.

Case study questions

- Why did employee motivation decline?
- What elements of game design spurred and stifled employee productivity?
- How would you deal with the situation differently?

Debate: Is gamification just a fad?

Introduction

The link between gamification and HRM seems logical, especially in the ever-increasing world of digitization. Everybody has access to a digital device and that has led to an increase in people playing video games. Using these game design concepts in the working environment should be a useful way to motivate people. At the same time, gamification is seen as a hype with little, if any, strategic value to an organization.

Arguments in favor

- Gamification is exploitationware (Bogost, 2014) and is just a way to exploit the employees to do their best. It can be compared with an electronic whip or Taylorism 2.0.
- It is still unclear as to what gamification really is. Gamification is still not precisely defined (Nacke and Deterding, 2017).
- Gamification is linked to the extrinsic motivation and may have a harmful effect on intrinsic motivation. Gamification may also lead to a crowding-out effect.
- A game usually has a natural end. Consequently, gamification has an end as well. Managing people is not a game and gamification, while may tickle employee interest for some time, will not offer long lasting solutions to structural aspects of employee motivation, engagement, and productivity.

Arguments against

- It is in the nature of humans to play and the playful approach is always more motivational than the just doing a task. Gamifying work is, therefore, beneficial for any person and could lead to an increase in motivation, creativity, and engagement (Deterding, 2012).
- Gamification is necessary as society is becoming more and more gamified. Everybody plays games and everybody is already targeted by gamification

elements. Gathering points is ubiquitous and, therefore, HRM is required to gamify work as well.
- Gamification is an efficient way to train employees and make a customized training experience by constantly raising the bar. As the learning curve in game design increases, the accumulated knowledge will help to improve HR development significantly (Landers, 2014).
- Strategic gamification could transform the organization by augmenting learning, engagement, and innovation (Warmelink, 2014) and make the organization more flexible, dynamic, and agile.
- Gamification is a way to utilize the collected data within an organization and transform them into information and solutions for HR issues and challenges (Cardador et al., 2017).

Useful references

Bogost, I. (2014) Why gamification is bullshit. In: Walz, S. P., and Deterding, S. (eds.) *The gameful world: Approaches, issues, applications*. Cambridge: MIT Press, pp. 65–79.

Cardador, M. T., Northcraft, G. B., and Whicker, J. (2017) A theory of work gamification: Something old, something new, something borrowed, something cool? *Human Resource Management Review*. 27(2), pp. 353–365.

Millet, J. (2017) The 2018 Human Resources trends to keep on your radar. *Forbes* [online]. Available from: www.forbes.com/sites/forbeshumanresourcescouncil/2017/10/26/the-2018-human-resources-trends-to-keep-on-your-radar/#786f1b2a21b3 (Accessed 17 December 2017).

Nacke, L. E., and Deterding, S. (2017) The maturing of gamification research. *Computers in Human Behavior*. 71, pp. 450–454.

Perkbox (2017) 6 trends shaping the future of HR in 2017. Available from: www.perkbox.com/uk/2016/12/30/6-trends-shaping-future-hr-2017 (Accessed 17 December 2017).

Warmelink, H. (2014) *Online gaming and playful organization*. New York, NY: Routledge.

Video learning resources

- Meaningful play: Getting gamification right: Discusses potential challenges in gamification and a meaningful design process. https://youtu.be/7ZGCPap7GkY
- Gamification – How the principles of play apply to real life: Critically discusses the principles of gamification and a world without distinction between play and work: https://youtu.be/1dLK9MW-9sY
- Gamification: The motivating spark: Discusses the motivating power of gamification: https://youtu.be/UyyDsQzwlvQ
- Gamification at work: Discusses the ways gamification can be utilized at work: https://youtu.be/6wk4dkY-rV0
- Gaming can make a better world: Discusses the potential of video games in different contexts: https://youtu.be/dE1DuBesGYM

References

Bailey, P., Pritchard, G., and Kernohan, H. (2015) Gamification in market research. *International Journal of Market Research.* **57**(1), pp. 17–28.

Bogost, I. (2014) Why gamification is bullshit. In: Walz, S. P., and Deterding, S. (eds.) *The gameful world: Approaches, issues, applications.* Cambridge: MIT Press, pp. 65–79.

Burke, M., and Hiltbrand, T. (2011) How gamification will change business intelligence. *Business Intelligence Journal.* **16**, pp. 8–16.

Datagame (2016) Examples of gamification in the workplace. Available from: https://datagame.io/examples-of-gamification-in-the-workplace (Accessed 10 November 2017).

Deterding, S. (2012) Gamification: Designing for motivation. *Interactions.* 19(4), pp. 14–17.

Deterding, S. (2014a) The ambiguity of games: Histories and discourses of a gameful world. In: Walz, S. P., and Deterding, S. (eds.) *The gameful world: Approaches, issues, applications.* Cambridge: MIT Press, pp. 24–64.

Deterding, S. (2014b) Eudaimonic design, or: Six invitations to rethink gamification. In: Fuchs, M., Fizek, S., Ruffino, P., and Schrape, N. (eds.) *Rethinking gamification.* Lüneburg: Meson Press, pp. 305–331.

Deterding, S, Sicart, M., Nacke, L., O'Hara, K., and Dixon, D. (2011) Gamification. Using game-design elements in non-gaming contexts. In: *Proceedings of the Conference on Human-Computer Interaction,* Vancouver, Canada, pp. 2425–2428.

Dewey, J. (1916) *Democracy and education. An introduction to the philosophy of education.* New York, NY: Macmillan.

Dorling, A., and McCaffery, F. (2012) The gamification of SPICE. In: Mas, A., Mesquida, A., Rout, T., O'Connor, R. V., and Dorling, A. (eds.) *Software process improvement and capability determination. SPICE 2012. Communications in computer and information science.* Berlin and Heidelberg: Springer, pp. 295–301.

Fuchs, M., Fizek, S., Ruffino, P., and Schrape, N. (2014b) Introduction. In: Fuchs, M., Fizek, S., Ruffino, P., and Schrape, N. (eds.) *Rethinking gamification.* Lüneburg: Meson Press, pp. 7–17.

Fuchs, M., Fizek, S., Ruffino, P., and Schrape, N. (eds.) (2014a) *Rethinking gamification.* Lüneburg: Meson Press.

Gee, J. P. (2003) What video games have to teach us about learning and literacy. *Computers in Entertainment (CIE).* **1**(1), p. 20.

Hamari, J., and Lehdonvirta, V. (2010) Game design as marketing: How game mechanics Create demand for virtual goods. *International Journal of Business Science and Applied Management.* **5**(1), pp. 14–29.

Hamari, J., Koivisto, J., and Sarsa, H. (2014) Does gamification work – A literature review of empirical studies on gamification. In: *Proceedings of the 47th Hawaii International Conference on Systems Sciences,* Hawaii.

Hay, J. (2014). Data governance gamification. *Business Intelligence Journal.* **19**(1), pp. 30–35.

Huizinga, J. (1949) *Homo ludens. A study of the play-element in culture.* London: Routledge.

Huotari, K., and Hamari, J. (2012) Defining gamification – A service marketing perspective. In: *Proceedings of the 16th International Academic Mindtrek Conference,* Tampere, Finland.

Intel (2015) The game change. *Intel* [online]. Available from: https://blogs.intel.com/technology/2015/08/the-game-changer (Accessed 10 November 2017).

InternetWorldStats (2017) Usage and population stats. *InternetWorldStats* [online]. Available from: www.internetworldstats.com/stats.htm (Accessed 10 November 2017).

Ireland, T. (2016) 'Code on the road', 'America's Army' and the gamification of recruitment. Available from: www.linkedin.com/pulse/code-road-americas-army-gamification-recruitment-tom-ireland/ (Accessed 29 December 2017).

Kücklich, J. (2005) Precarious playbour: Modders and the digital games industry. *Fibreculture* [online]. **3**. Available from: http://five.fibreculturejournal.org/fcj-025-precarious-playbour-modders-and-the-digital-games-industry (Accessed 10 November 2017).

Landers, R. N. (2014) Developing a theory of gamified learning: Linking serious games and gamification of learning. *Simulation & Gaming.* **45**(6), pp. 752–768.

Mandal, D. (2014) 10 of the biggest open-world video games released in terms of map size. *Hexapolis* [online]. Available from: www.hexapolis.com/2014/11/05/10-biggest-open-world-video-games-terms-map-size (Accessed 10 November 2017).

McLeroy, C. (2008) Improving "America's Army." *Soldiers.* **63**(9), pp. 7–9.

Nacke, L. E., and Deterding, S. (2017) The maturing of gamification research. *Computers in Human Behavior.* **71**, pp. 450–454.

Oprescu, F., Jones, C., and Katsikitis, M. (2014) I play at work – Ten principles for transforming work processes trough gamification. *Frontiers in Psychology.* **5**, pp. 1–5.

Robson, K., Plangger, K., Kietzmann, J. H., McCarthy, I., and Pitt, L. (2015) Is it all a game? Understanding the principles of gamification. *Business Horizons.* **58**(4), pp. 411–420.

Rocketrip (n.d.) More than a game. Gamification actually works. *Rocketrip* [online]. Available from: www.rocketrip.com/resources/gamification-thanks?submissionGuid=31d5d383-b202-4a7a-a9d3-8dd3d9f9312f (Accessed 10 November 2017).

SAP (2012) Game trailer RoadWarrior SAP. *Vimeo* [online]. Available from: https://vimeo.com/53538820 (Accessed 10 November 2017).

Singer, P. W. (2010) Meet the Sims . . . and shoot them. *Foreign Policy* [online]. Available from: http://foreignpolicy.com/2010/02/11/meet-the-sims-and-shoot-them (Accessed 10 November 2017).

Stein, V. (2010) Professionalisierung des Personalmanagements: Selbstverpflichtung als Weg. *Zeitschrift für Management.* **5**(3), pp. 201–205.

Thaler, R., and Sunstein, C. (2008) *Nudge. Improving decisions about health, wealth, and happiness.* New Haven, CT: Yale University Press.

Vesa, M., Hamari, J., Harviainen, J. T., and Warmelink, H. (2017) Computer games and organization studies. *Organization Studies.* **38**(2), pp. 273–284.

Walz, S. P., and Deterding, S. (2014) An introduction to the gameful world. In: Walz, S. P., and Deterding, S. (eds.) *The gameful world: Approaches, issues, applications.* Cambridge: MIT Press, pp. 1–13.

Wang, C. L., and Ahmed, P. K. (2003) Organisational learning: A critical review. *The Learning Organization.* **10**(1), pp. 8–17.

Warmelink, H. (2014) *Online gaming and playful organization.* New York, NY: Routledge.

Zichermann, G., and Cunningham, C. (2011) *Gamification by design: Implementing game mechanics in web and mobile apps.* Sebastopol, CA: O'Reilly.

Zichermann, G., and Linder, J. (2010) *Game-based marketing: Inspire customer loyalty through rewards, challenges and contests.* Hoboken, NJ: John Wiley & Sons.

Part III
e-HRM applications

10 e-Talent in talent management

Sharna Wiblen

> **Learning objectives**
> - Critically examine how the concepts of talent and talent management can be attributed meaning within organisations
> - Summarise the core components and attributes of e-talent
> - Consider examples of how e-talent can be used by organisations to pursue strategic goals and ambitions
> - Discuss various avenues for e-talent applications in talent management practices, including talent attraction, talent identification, talent development and talent retention
> - Discuss the potential benefits and limitations of e-talent in talent management

Introduction

The critical importance of people in the knowledge economy is now well established. But what kind of people – only those in key positions? A study of pivotal roles and positions in Disneyland reported that street sweepers are Disney's most pivotal talent (Boudreau and Ramstad, 2007). It is not, as you might think, the people that dress up as Disney characters. Rather, individuals that interact mostly with park patrons have the biggest impact on customer experience. Street sweepers do more than just keep the park clean. Individuals in these roles provide information about the best vantage points to view the parades, share information about toilet facilities and directions to rides and other park amenities. These roles play a pivotal role in delivering Disneyland's strategy – The Happiest Place on Earth.

Talent management – it is a term frequently appropriated in the corporate lexicon. According to management literature, 'talent' and 'talent management' contribute positively to organisational and financial performance (Capelli, 2008; Collings and Mellahi, 2009; Wiblen, 2016) and increase an organisation's competitive advantage (Lewis and Heckman, 2006; Stahl et al., 2007; Collings and Mellahi, 2013). People-based resources, it is argued, are an organisation's greatest and most valuable assets. These claims, when combined with arguments about a 'war for talent' (Michaels et al., 2001), skills shortages and an ageing population, create powerful battle-like imagery encouraging organisations to fight for the 'best people'.

Surveys frequently conclude that talent management presents both opportunities and challenges for organisations, senior executives and human resources (HR) and that there is a role for information technologies (IT) in talent management. For example, a recent survey of 1,379 Chief executive officers (CEOs) from 79 countries reports that talent and technology are primary sources of innovations for organisations worldwide (PwC, 2017). The deliberate and efficient management of both human and technical assets is required to capitalise on new opportunities and innovations in this interconnected world (PwC, 2017). CEOs however, simultaneously report that technological change is also a major threat. Notwithstanding somewhat contradictory survey results, the heightened competition for talent compels organisations to take action and pursue talent management.

Given these salient and broader contextual factors, there is a need to highlight the various definitions of talent and talent management, the processes and practices employed to manage this valuable cohort of employees before examining the interrelationship between e-HRM and talent management – 'e-talent' – and how e-talent enables and constrains talent management policies and practices.

There is no single definition and understanding of 'talent management'. While there is some debate about whether talent management is any different from traditional HR practices or the establishment of talent pools to facilitate succession planning, talent management is the attraction, identification, development, appraisal, deployment and retention of individuals formally recognised as 'talent' within the boundaries of an organisation. Advocates argue that talent management encompasses more than traditional HR because the former prioritises future-orientated practices that are informed by and aligned to strategic ambitions and goals. Strategic ambitions are the starting point for all talent management activities. Workforce differentiation is also a key attribute (Beechler and Woodward, 2009) because talent management policies and practices are premised on the assertion that some individuals are of greater value than others. Talented individuals are afforded more resources and opportunities than their non-talented counterparts.

In this chapter, we reflect critically upon the rhetoric, the research and the reality of talent management. More specifically, the chapter highlights how the use of information technology in four salient practices – talent acquisition, identification, development and retention – both enables and constrains effective and strategically aligned talent management practices.

Defining talent management

A foundational way to frame what talent management 'is', is to reflect that talent management is: 'a judgement-orientated activity, where humans make judgements about other humans. These judgements, while mediated by various contextual factors and variables (such as technology), should be informed by and aligned to, current and future strategic ambitions and goals'.

Regardless of the specific definition, the vast majority of practitioners and scholars encourage organisations to transition away from individualistic and intuitive talent management frameworks where decisions based on gut-instincts and personal beliefs are less effective than 'systems' approaches that prioritise integration. Consistent and standardised processes are essential to realising positive operational, financial and strategic outcomes (Aguinis and O'Boyle, 2014; Collings, 2014).

Current and future organisational strategies underpin talent management strategies, which are then used to articulate the 'talent' required to pursue and realise these goals. Therefore, organisations are inherently required to address talent and devise a definition

Table 10.1 Talent conceptualisations

Conceptualisation	Description
Individuals as talent	This approach refers to specific individuals as talent that an organisation should recruit and retain. These individuals are considered to be talent because they are of greater value than other employees and they contribute to the organisation's business activities and overall success. We commonly refer to these individuals as 'high performers', 'high potentials', 'stars', 'A players' and 'top talent'.
Valued skills and capabilities	This approach views talent in the context of particular skills and capabilities identified and evaluated as critical to operations, strategic directions and organisational performance. These skills and capabilities may be required to drive future growth or because they are hard to replace. Knowledge workers, professional services employees and technical experts are common examples.
Pivotal roles and positions	This approach considers talent as particular functions, roles and/or positions. Organisations are encouraged to identify and allocate appropriate employees to these roles, with the role and position remaining valuable and of strategic importance regardless of the individual in the position.
Everybody is talent	This approach asserts that all employees are valuable and indicative of talent. This is known as an inclusive approach where all employees are given access to talent management practices.

Source: Author

of 'talent' to enact both organisational and talent management strategies. Within Western societies, 'talent' is used as a generic term to describe an individual's ability, accomplishments, aptitudes, brilliance, capacity, expertise, facility, flair, genius, gift, ingenuity, knack, prowess, skill, strength or as per the Oxford Dictionary, a 'natural ability or skill' (926). There are, however, a wide spectrum of definitions of talent operating within the world of work (for an overview see Tansley, 2011; Gallardo-Gallardo et al., 2013; Thunnissen et al., 2013).

This chapter adopts Wiblen's (2016) four talent conceptualisations as presented in Table 10.1 to facilitate an understanding of how talent can be defined within organisations: individuals; valued skills and capabilities; pivotal roles and positions; and everybody.

The most valuable individuals, skills and capabilities or roles, however, are not always what may be thought of in the first instance, as pointed out in the Disneyland case. Rather than aiming for a unanimous agreement, definitions should be informed by, and aligned to, an organisation's business strategy and strategic goals. If organisations operate in different industries and seek to achieve different goals, then one should expect different understandings of 'who' or 'what' talent is. The definition can change in accordance with changes and updates in strategic ambitions and goals. Therefore, understandings of which individuals, skills and capabilities, roles and positions are pivotal can change. There is also the potential for various definitions of talent to be operating within the context of a single organisation. Despite the potential for differing opinions, organisations need to be aware of 'who' (individuals or an entire workforce) or 'what' (skills and capabilities or specific roles) is deemed 'talent' to practice talent management effectively.

Technology-enabled talent management systems and products

Talent management benefits from e-talent and the array of associated technologies including enterprise resource planning systems (ERP), human resource information systems (HRIS), social media, cloud computing and electronic human resource management (e-HRM). At a general level, e-talent enables the creation of centralised systems enabling employees and managers to

- collect, store and process HRM and talent information (Ceriello and Freeman, 1991; Marler and Dulebohn, 2005; Stone and Dulebohn, 2013);
- increase process and cost efficiencies (Bussler and Davis, 2001; Gueutal and Stone, 2005; Farndale et al., 2009);
- promote consistency in the way in which processes are enacted through automation (Benders et al., 2006; Grant et al., 2006); and
- provide stakeholders, not just HR professionals, with access to data about talent (Wiblen, 2016).

Of particular importance to the study of talent management is the implicit assumption that the systematic and strategic talent management approaches are facilitated through technologies (this is discussed further in the next section).

e-Talent technology vendors have benefitted from an expanding HR technology market driven by the growth and availability of cloud-based information technology. As explained in Chapter 7, Cloud computing allows organisations to acquire and deploy vendor-designed technologies at a significantly lower cost. This is because organisations can transition away from expensive proprietary (designed and owned by an organisation) or on-premises technology, towards a model of ubiquitous, convenient and shared pool of configurable resources available on-demand (Mell and Grance, 2011). Organisations can outsource software design, configuration and management to technology vendors in exchange for a licencing fee. Improvements and innovations, such as amendments to codes, algorithms and workflow processes, are updated and upgraded automatically by the vendor. In most situations, however, ownership and control of IT remain with the vendor, not the organisation. While this allows organisations to acquire and deploy specialised talent management software in a timelier manner than ever before without the need to invest significantly in IT expertise or resources (Wiblen et al., 2010), specific technology skills rather than organisational knowledge are deemed more valuable.

Talent management systems

The core value proposition of talent management modules of large enterprise resource planning systems, such as SAP and Oracle, is the ability to create a talent management 'system' (TMS), also referred to as human capital management (HCM) systems. This new generation of e-HRM can be structured as either part of an existing e-HRM or as a separate application. e-HRM software vendors market TMS as 'an integrated software suite' that provides technologically enabled functionality focused on the acquisition and growth of a talented and adaptable workforce and development of leadership capabilities (Johns and Kavanagh, 2012). Although earlier versions of TMS tended to be more functionally specialised and focused on a particular employee group such as applicants for recruiting and selection, and high potential employees for performance management and succession planning, more recent versions offer broader and integrated functionality and cover all employee groups. Nevertheless, a core differentiating factor of a TMS when contrasted with earlier e-HRM technology is TMS enabled workforce differentiation.

Organisations can now easily acquire specialised TMS capabilities to deploy for particular employee groups such as applicants or high potential employees.

It is important to recognise that e-HRM is only a tool. Various stakeholders influence the success and effectiveness of the technology. Technology is also part of larger organising systems, and further complexity arises when we consider that IT has both a physical and a procedural dimension (Orlikowski and Scott, 2008). The physical components include the hardware, software and communication network infrastructures. While these are separate from individuals, the physical aspect is nothing without individuals using it in organisational tasks (Marler and Parry, 2016). Therefore, when we think about the use of IT in talent management, we need to consider aspects of the computer (the desktop, laptop, monitor, keyboard, mouse, network connections, operating system, software, add-ons etc.) as well as the individuals that use the technology. Information technologies, while able to assist with the implementation of strategic decisions, can only complement the decision-making process. Information technology is only a tool. Human actors are essential in the design, implementation and appropriation of any technologically enabled software, platform or system.

e-Talent management products

Attesting to the appeal of functionality, flexibility, cost-effectiveness and workforce differentiation, the use of e-HRM in talent management is now big business. The global talent management software market is projected to grow from $5.3 billion in 2014 to $11.4 billion by 2019. North America is expected to be the largest market for spending and adoption of TMS (MarketsandMarkets, 2017). The landscape of e-talent vendors, however, is constantly evolving and complex as organisations seek to determine which e-talent is right for them.

Organisations today can choose from numerous cloud-based HR technology products from an array of providers including Oracle, SAP SuccessFactors, WorkDay, ADP, Ceridian, Meta4, and Ultimate Systems. Earlier versions of TMSs specialised in particular HR functions or on specific employee groups such as applicants for recruiting and selection, and high potential employees for performance management and succession planning. More recent versions offer broader functionality deployable across numerous functions and an entire workforce. Nevertheless, a core differentiating factor of a TMS, from earlier e-HRM platforms, is its ability to transition beyond automation, enable workforce differentiation and allow organisations to establish connections between human capital needs and strategic ambitions.

Today, organisations are also presented with an opportunity to adopt next-generation technologically enabled processes that go beyond the realised goal of automating transactional processes to instilling integrated approaches, therefore, permitting talent data to be shared. These capabilities highlight talent needs and assists in the accomplishment of strategic ambitions and goals.

For example, SAP SuccessFactors, one of the largest players, claims that their product provides a complete, recruit-to-retire solution across all talent processes. According to SAP, processes enacted via their products are seamless and comprehensive, and their united talent suite can help organisations build an unbeatable workforce (SAP SuccessFactors, 2017). Workday similarly highlights the ability to connect talent management with business strategy and invites clients to 'gain insight into your talent landscape, align top talent with key business objectives, and develop tomorrow's leaders' (Workday, 2017). By adding more functionality and relabelling products as integrated talent management suites, vendors have successfully repositioned their software products to show next-generation capabilities that can transform how HRM and TM work is performed.

While some organisations and technology vendors may profess that their TMS applies to all employees, others disagree on the basis that workforce differentiation and the disproportionate allocation of resources is key to talent management and therefore, should only apply to a select few. For instance, Collings and Mellahi (2009) argue that if a TMS applies to all employees, even lower performers, then differentiating between talent management and traditional HRM will be challenging.

e-HRM and talent acquisition

TMS and e-talent promises to provide organisations with IT-enabled frameworks to 'recruit and retain' star talent with technological innovations continually influencing recruitment and talent acquisition. Advances in technology mean organisations can encourage individuals to pursue a career with their organisation with a saving in both time and cost. Today, individuals can research a company via numerous mechanisms beyond the traditional organisational website, via platforms such as Twitter, Facebook, LinkedIn and YouTube to name a few. While technology has changed how organisations judge the value of potential talent, we must remain vigilant of the role afforded to technology because technology helps to make better decisions, it does not replace human decisions or judgments.

Use of social media to attract talent

In addition to discussions about e-recruitment and selection (see Chapter 11), changes in e-HRM have far-reaching implications for how organisations attract 'talent' with many organisations adapting their talent attraction practices to take advantage of new technologies and employ technologically mediated practices to circumvent skill shortages and win the widely promoted 'war for talent'. While traditional recruitment practices sought to recruit and select the best talent from the pool of individuals that applied for a formally advertised position, the advent of social media, and in particular LinkedIn, has fundamentally transformed the relationship between employers and potential employees. No longer are organisations required to engage intermediaries such as specialised executive search firms or head-hunters to find people because knowing who's who is now significantly easier.

The internet, when considered alongside with social media platforms, allows organisations to tap into formal and informal networks of employees to attract potential talent. Scholars have long advocated a greater scope for organisations to leverage the networks of their existing workforces to identify and attract talent. Today, organisations use technologically mediated capabilities to undertake numerous activities including asking existing employees to

- share information, via personal profiles in Facebook, LinkedIn and Twitter about job openings;
- share information about personal perceptions and experiences of working for the organisation, thereby providing a glimpse into daily activities and opportunities;

- ask colleagues, associates and friends for recommendations of individuals that may successfully fulfil open and future positions; and
- facilitate personal introductions between two previously unknown individuals.

Thus, e-talent makes it possible for all employees, not just HR managers or recruiters, to play a role in attracting and acquiring talent. Being able to draw upon and exploit the personal and professional relationships of existing employees increases cultural fit and minimises new starter shock because the organisation can garner tacit information and make initial judgements about the likelihood of success. Utilising these less formal mechanisms also potentially decreases advertising, process and time to hire costs. Some organisations are dictating that all employees establish and maintain LinkedIn profiles to promote the organisation and capitalise on personal and social networks, with others even offering referral bonuses if personal recommendations result in a successful conversion from suggested to attracted talent.

The deliberate transition towards the use of social media in talent attraction strategies (see Chapter 8) also influences perceptions about the role and strategic value of HR and recruiting managers. While recruitment and selection processes are enabled through e-HRM and HR functions, talent attraction is not considered the sole responsibility of internal HR functions. Rather, social media and its ability to effectively 'pull' individuals towards an organisation have elevated the role of marketing functions and managers. Talent acquisition involves promoting and 'selling' the organisation. Rather than directing resources to promote a product to a customer, talent attraction involves promoting the organisation to a potential candidate to encourage the individual to want and desire a job or career with them.

Consider Heineken's 'The Candidate' campaign as an example of the intersection between talent attraction and marketing. This campaign detailed a novel recruitment process to effectively promote the company as a 'fun' and 'youthful' place to work. The YouTube video (see 'Video learning resources' at the end of the chapter) went viral. Heineken's current attraction strategy includes a LinkedIn campaign encouraging individuals to 'follow' the company and 'Go places with Heineken' (see 'Video learning resources' at the end of the chapter).

The tension surrounding the extent to which social media should influence talent acquisition decisions is increasingly evident as debates rage over what is appropriate, normative or legitimate being played out in the public discussions, as well as in the courts and legislative environments (McDonald and Thompson, 2016). Much of this tension stems from social media's ability to blur the boundaries between public – your workplace and career identity – and private – such as sport, community and family – spheres as well as 'where' and 'when' to prioritise social media platforms and data.

Not all social media platforms are created equal. The value of social media data is influenced by 'where' (the platform) the data derives. LinkedIn currently dominates the talent acquisition market. Launched in 2003, LinkedIn in 2017 heralds a remarkable half a billion members in 200 countries. A core value of LinkedIn for talent management is the transparency of information about potential opportunities with over 10 million active jobs listed on the platform.

Social media data can negatively influence how recruiters and hiring managers judge and perceive potential talent. It is well established that interviewers' ratings of individuals and first impressions and handshakes influence the likelihood of selection success (see Chapter 11). Uneducated, untrained or ill-informed individuals can utilise publicly available data to make certain assertions about the 'value' and 'cultural fit' of an individual. This data, however, will be influenced by an array of selection biases including anchoring (locking into salient information too early in the process), confirmation (looking for confirming rather than refuting evidence) and illusory correlations (perceived associations).

The decision to use and apply this social media information and the stage in the process, is, however, usually made by the recruiter, not the potential talent. Therefore, it is imperative that individuals, both passive and active talent, deliberately manage their 'digital footprint' because 'Once you put something online, it's there forever' (The Social Index, 2016). Online profiles share both personal and professional pieces of information about individuals and the extent to which they are deemed talent within the context of the recruiting organisations operational and strategic requirements.

The Social Index is an example of an organisation that has arisen out of the transition towards a digital era, whereby senior executives, HR managers and recruiters judge individual's value both online and offline. This company offers both recruiters and candidates the opportunity to gather various information (Figure 10.1 is an example report) that provides insights about individuals above and beyond a superficial and uninformed 'Google' search.

e-HRM and internal talent identification

To manage internal talent, organisations need to identify the individuals, skills and capabilities or pivotal roles and positions, deemed valuable within its operational context. The processes of workforce differentiation, whereby certain employees come to be classified as talent and allocated to the internal talent pool is talent identification. Put another way; talent identification refers to the processes through which certain individuals come to be evaluated as greater value, categorised as talent and permitted membership of the internal talent pool. It is important to recognise that talent identification is not another term used to refer to succession planning.

Internal talent identification is a complex judgement orientated activity that involves stakeholders undertaking numerous judgements about an individual's ability to play a pivotal role in the pursuit and realisation of strategic goals and ambitions. Classification as 'talent' involves a two-step process. The first is largely experience-based technologically enabled processes that utilise performance management modules of traditional e-HRM systems. Performance management data attained via traditional annual performance review processes where individual and group 'performance' and 'potential' are the foundation for further analysis. Numerical evaluations of performance inform subsequent and complementary cognition-based (offline processes) decisions (Mäkelä et al., 2010) where senior stakeholders discuss and debate high-performing individuals and calibrate various interpretations of the extent to which a certain individual contributes to current and future operational and strategic needs. Identified talent subjects are allocated resources and invested in disproportionately via access to talent development to ensure that the organisation 'retains' these valuable individuals.

Justification for technology-enabled talent identification

There are some compelling reasons why organisations should use technology in talent identification. Table 10.2 illustrates the capacity of e-talent and the material properties embedded within technology to assist with identifying talent.

e-Talent in talent management   161

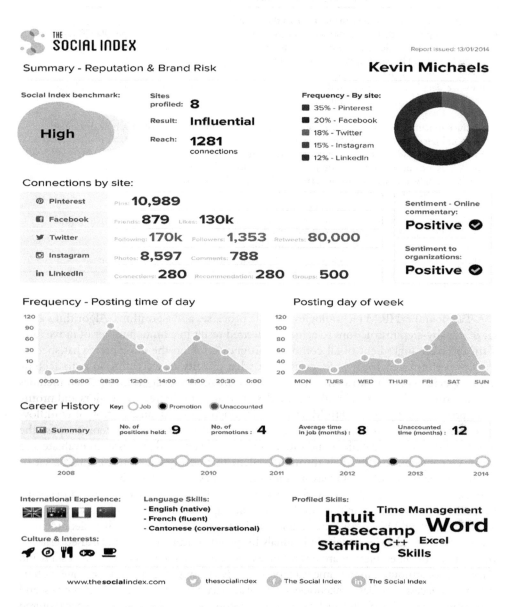

Figure 10.1 Example 'digital footprint' report.
Source: Reprinted with permission from The Social Index.

A core benefit of using software to evaluate a workforce is the perceived ability to create and enact a systematic and consistent approach to identify talent. Technology vendors provide organisations with the capabilities and workflow processes required to evaluate individual and group performance and potential. These workflows processes represent the 'how' and are built into the performance management modules, thus permitting the systematic and consistent evaluation of performance.

Table 10.2 Justification for technology-enabled talent identification

- Identify talent in a consistent manner across the organisation (Stahl et al., 2007)
- Identify employees that organisations want to develop and retain (Lah & Capperella, 2009)
- Forecast supply and demand from current and future talent pools (Hewitt's Human Capital Consulting and Human Capital Institute, 2008)
- Establish a unified and accessible talent database (Snell, 2008)
- Improve decision making by producing and providing information that can establish linkages between human capital assets and the performance of the organisation (Lengnick-Hall and Moritz, 2003)
- Produce dynamic, real-time metrics, analytics and data about an organisation's human capital assets and talent (Williams, 2009; Wiblen, 2016)
- Facilitate faster and more accurate decision making
- Allow HR practitioners to develop greater objectivity and balance in their decisions
- Forecast supply and demand from current and future talent pools (Hewitt's Human Capital Consulting and Human Capital Institute, 2008)
- Establish a unified and accessible talent database (Snell, 2008)
- Produce dynamic, real-time metrics, analytics and data about an organisation's human capital assets and talent (Williams, 2009, Wiblen, 2016)
- Facilitate faster and more accurate decision making
- Allow HR practitioners to develop greater objectivity and balance in their decisions

Source: Author.

e-Talent and e-HRM technologies provide processes and algorithms. Algorithms are a set of step-by-step instructions to achieve a desired result in a finite number of moves and form the basic ingredient of all computer programs, telling the computer what specific steps to perform in what specific order with what priority or weighting so as to accomplish a specific task (Orlikowski and Scott, 2015: 210). These algorithms (which includes coding, sorting, filtering and ranking) are designed and configured by vendors and promise to provide 'best practice' HRM processes founded upon a standardisation of workflow procedures. e-Talent is imperative in enacting a talent management 'system' because the software houses the capabilities and the technologically enabled processes to evaluate and identify talent consistently. It is through e-talent that an organisation can enact a set or system of practices. All employees are subjected to these 'best practices'.

e-Talent vendors, in addition to the provision of processes, provide structured dialogue, language and common definitions of the skills and capabilities required of individuals to be identified as talent. Due to software coding requirements, e-talent ensures that talent identification processes identify certain individuals by pre-determined and standardised criteria. In other words, all employees are evaluated against the same criteria (set of valued skills and capabilities or attributes) in the same way (process). By creating 'high performer', 'high potential' and 'success' profiles, stakeholders articulate factors such as the competencies and behaviours, personal attributes, technical and professional knowledge, and experience required of 'talent'. The result, many vendors proclaim, is a well-defined understanding of talent, or a one-size-fits-all definition, within the context of an organisation's operational needs and strategic ambitions. Some organisations may enact systematic processes based on 'hard' e-talent data because there is the belief that such processes are less politically charged (Dries, 2013).

Limitations of technology-enabled talent identification

While these capabilities, in theory, can be appealing, it can be argued that the technology may arbitrarily create externally defined boundaries around the definition of talent resulting in 'talent clones' and limit the ability to change the meaning of talent and pursue diversity. There is also the potential that the vendor, rather than the organisation, decides the criteria for talent evaluation and determination. A core premise of the use of e-talent and any reference to the use of data in talent management decision making is the assumption that an individual's 'value' is calculable, quantifiable and therefore, measurable. Line or HR managers evaluate an individual by allocating numerical scores (generally on a five-point Likert scale) to indicate their level of performance and/or potential. This is the foundation for talent management data and analytics. These scores are compiled and then analysed to generate talent 'rankings' that order the quantified value of a workforce. All of these processes are facilitated through the capabilities and algorithms embedded in the software.

There is, however, a fierce debate about the philosophy, policy and technology-enabled processes to measure talent. For example, Mellahi and Collings (2010: 147) acknowledge that 'Talent is often tacit, inherently complex and difficult to measure because it often deals with potential rather than performance'. Wiblen et al.'s (2012) study of the use of technology in talent management, further challenges the extent to which organisations will utilise technology to establish talent management systems and base talent determinations on technologically enabled data. Their study found that managers had differing opinions about whether talent was effectively identified via observations; think of the idea that 'I know talent when I see it', or via measurements and rankings generated by e-talent. This resulted in the role of e-talent differing within the context of the same organisation and highlights that technology and numerical data may not play a pivotal role in talent identification, despite its presence.

While the rhetoric about HR technologies, talent management and HR functions and the ability for organisations to enact talent identification systems that are strategically aligned and technologically enabled is glamorous and compelling, the reality is that many organisations struggle with identifying the talent they require (Collings, 2014). There is also limited empirically informed knowledge about how talent identification work is performed and the role of HR technologies (Wiblen et al., 2012 and Wiblen, 2016 are exceptions,) in seeking to automate processes and make predictive assertions about talent.

e-HRM and talent development

The vast majority of talent management definitions include reference to 'talent development' as part of a wider talent management system. Talent development occurs after talent identification processes because there is a propensity for organisations, via their HR functions, to use talent identification processes as the main mechanism to identify, and then nominate, certain individuals for a formalised development programme. Via a 'talent development programme', a cohort of talented employees is disproportionately allocated organisational resources, in the form of development activities. Talented individuals participate in a wider selection of educational and professional activities than those individuals that are not identified as talent. Talent development, therefore, is the provision of organisational resources, monetary and non-monetary, to individual talent subjects judged as of greater value to the pursuit and realisation of an organisation's strategic ambitions.

There is no doubt that organisations want to develop their high performing and high potential individuals. A key driver is that this cohort of employees are 'future leaders' of a firm. In addition to providing learning and development opportunities for all employees, specific individuals within an HR function may solely focus on creating and delivering specialised talent development programs. Many programs are tailored to the developmental needs of an individual rather than generic skills.

There are various technologies that organisations use to develop their identified talent. Traditional e-learning technologies are useful for developing talent as they can deliver just-in-time learning and education through technology. Online learning platforms where individuals can select what they want to learn, when and how are particularly useful and can act as the primary mechanism to develop skills, including leadership skills.

In addition to the value of e-learning and development tools (as detailed in Chapter 13), organisations can choose to provide additional e-talent resources to talented individuals only, or they can frame the value of the technology differently. For example, rather than promote the use of e-learning and development because of cost efficiencies, an organisation may want to provide additional resources as a way to illustrate investment rather than reduce the costs associated with the delivery and provision of learning through e-talent. The potential for significant costs is viewed positively. Access to e-talent is a way to illustrate to an individual that the organisation values them. It is a way to make them 'feel special'.

There are various e-talent development tools, including Lynda.com (owned by LinkedIn), Deloitte's Leadership Academy and Deloitte's Digital Centre for Immersive Learning, which enables organisations to teach leadership and other skills to talent. The latter of these platforms allows talent to participate in simulations that enable the individual to learn about particular techniques but also test these through guided simulations. This is considered valuable in much the same way that pilots learn and practice flying in simulations. A challenge for the organisation is determining whether participating in these technologically mediated development activities and programmes are structured as part of the normal undertaking of the job or completed on an individual's own time.

Many organisations believe that they can 'buy' an off-the-shelf solution to develop their talent. But the quality of these more generic and licensed tools can be fragmented and the content general in nature, rather than specific to industry, organisation or strategic ambitions. It is essential that this limitation is recognised because all talent management activities, including talent development, must be aligned to, and informed by, current and future strategic ambitions and goals.

e-HRM and talent retention

Organisations that identify, engage and develop their top talent require a talent retention strategy. This strategy details the resources allocated and activities conducted to ensure that identified talent subjects remain core to their workforce. Part of this resource allocation may include technological capabilities housed within e-talent or e-HRM software that provides organisations with an ability to capture and generate data and information about talent retention rates. Search parameters can be entered into the e-HRM to inquire about which employees have left the organisation and how many of these were 'talent'. Questions about causes and patterns of turnover can then be discussed between HR, line managers and senior managers (see Chapter 6). A core component is capturing and storing information about the employees, skills and capabilities or roles that were identified as talent. The absence of information about identified talent or about which employees are no longer employed can limit the ability to evaluate the effectiveness of talent retention activities.

Despite these challenges, numerous vendors state that their software product can assist with the retention of talent. Workday (2017), for example, states that it can use predictive and historical data to track retention risks, enabling organisations to act 'before it's too late'. Based on information about an individual's time between promotions, time at current job and some job functions, with publicly available information about the external demand for certain types of employees, the technology, via an embedded algorithm, calculates the perceived likelihood that the specific individual is leaving and replacement costs. It is assumed that if the individual in question is valuable, then there will be proactive efforts to retain the individual.

McKinsey's People Analytics is another example. McKinsey promotes the ability for the e-HRM to assist customers in retaining employees by determining the causes of attrition and those individuals most at risk. They then assist with the identification of actions 'to protect the workforce' (McKinsey, 2017). The practical value of the transition towards predictive analytics should be questioned, with information generated via a pre-determined algorithm that makes numerous assumptions about individual contexts and career trajectories. We need to be sure that these assumptions accurately reflect the work and experiences of all employees, not just talent.

Advances in technologies such as LinkedIn have also afforded the ability for external organisations to locate and subsequently 'poach' employees. It is now cheaper and easier for organisations to contact potential candidates and share information about other job-related opportunities. Technological innovations, therefore, can both enable and hinder talent retention.

Summary

The use of information technologies and the proliferation of e-talent software will only increase as we continue to transition towards new forms of work within the digital era. This chapter has illustrated how, within the current competitive environment whereby organisations must continually compete for the best talent, various types of IT can simultaneously enable and constrain the pursuit and realisation of operational and strategic goals.

The nature of the relationship between e-talent and organisational strategy was explained as being critical to firm performance. However, the proactive and deliberate management of talent is also complex because there are multiple meanings of 'talent' and 'talent management' operating within academia and industry. The various contributions of e-talent were also covered while also noting that technological innovations influence how organisations go about attracting, acquiring, identifying and developing talent. Despite promotional material produced by various vendors about the vast benefits of e-talent consuming much of the publicly available talk, the chapter also illustrated numerous challenges associated with implementing and enacting talent management systems that inherently privilege sameness and consistency. To what extent do organisations apply the same identification, development and retention practices to all employees or proactively differentiate between the workforce? Unfortunately, this means that the ability to deliberately and proactively manage talent, with or without IT, remains complex.

Case study: ProfessionalCo

A large multinational professional services firm – ProfessionalCo (an assumed name) – operates under a partnership model in 150 countries and employs approximately 245,000 employees worldwide. The firm publicly declares that talent and talent management are imperative to its operational and strategic ambitions. One of ProfessionalCo's Asia Pacific subsidiaries provides knowledge-based services to an array of clients via its Australian headquarters and six business units. Driven by a formalised talent management strategy, the subsidiary is proactively investing in talent management policies and practices to enhance the organisation's competitive positioning domestically and internationally.

The ability to effectively identify and manage the most valuable employees was, in practice, challenging. First, the organisation's talent management practices were not founded upon a pre-established definition of talent. There was no single agreed upon understanding of 'who' (individuals or everyone) and 'what' (skills and capabilities or pivotal roles and positions). Senior partners and HR managers were able to define talent in a way that they saw fit, without intervention from headquarters. This created a situation whereby there was potentially many, rather than a single definition of talent, operating throughout the organisation.

A second challenge was the absence of a 'talent management system'. The organisation did not have one e-talent tool to establish processes for how to identify their most valuable employees. Again, business units and senior partners were able to determine how they would identify a cohort of talented employees. These employees were invited to attend the organisation-wide talent development program.

Corporate HR executives tasked with providing talent development activities across the organisation would have liked to institute an organisation-wide approach that relied on technology to standardise the definition of talent. They thought that the implementation of a talent management 'system' would enable systematic and consistent processes whereby there would be greater potential for strategic alignment and synergism because all of ProfessionalCo's units 'would be doing the same thing'. The use of technology to identify talent would also permit 'objective' and 'fair' evaluations rather than subjective opinions. Corporate HR executives also viewed e-talent as a mechanism to insert the centralised HR function to the practice.

Certain business units agreed with this view. Despite the absence of a specific e-talent tool, senior executives in these units employed the functionality of a performance management module of the vendor-designed software-as-a-service e-talent platform (SAP SuccessFactors) to measure and evaluate individual and team performance. As part of the annual performance management practice, employees were measured and allocated performance scores out of five according to different criteria. Executives then called upon the algorithms embedded within the technology to rank individuals and identify 'top performers' and 'draw a line' under the percentage of employees that the unit wanted to focus on and identify as top talent.

However, other parts of ProfessionalCo did not prioritise e-talent and believed that there was limited need for technology because senior executives 'know talent when they see it'. There was an expectation that senior executives, rather than technology, possessed a set of competencies that enabled them to identify those individuals effectively who would be successful upon promotion.

Case study questions

- Evaluate whether the firm should establish an organisation-wide definition of talent. If you believe they should, what should this one definition be?
- Select which approach to talent identification is most effective. Defend your choice. What are the implications of these two different approaches to the role of HR? On HR skills and capabilities? Consider whether the use of e-talent enhances or minimises the role of HR in identifying talent.
- As the most senior HR manager in ProfessionalCo you have been asked by the CEO to devise a new talent identification process to be implemented organisation-wide. What would you recommend and why?

Debate: Is talent management only aimed at elite employees?

Introduction

Debate rages within both academia and industry about whether organisations should apply talent management policies and practices to all employees, or only a small proportion of their workforce. Much of the debate centres on the extent to which talent management differs from more traditional HRM and whether an inclusive (all of the workforce) or exclusive (a focus on elite employees) approach is more effective to realise the operational, strategic and financial benefits.

Arguments in favour

- Workforce differentiation and the disproportionate allocation of resources to more talented and valuable employees is a core differentiating factor between talent management and more traditional human resource management.
- While all employees are required for operational processes and outcomes, only some elite employees or those in pivotal positions facilitate the pursuit and realisation of strategic goals and ambitions. A focus on all employees, would not be either strategic or reflective of current demands (Lewis and Heckman, 2006; Collings and Mellahi, 2009; Daubner-Siva et al., 2017).
- Organisations should invest in resources that generate larger returns. Talent management concentrates on those employees who have exceptional, above-average abilities, and who can apply those abilities to achieve exceptional performance. Reflect on the saying 'biggest bang for your buck' within the context of investing in employees.
- Corporate discourses frequently note that organisations need to 'recruit and retain the best talent'. The focus on elite employees allows organisations to adopt numerous strategies to identify which valuable individuals are a source of competitive advantage and therefore, should be the subject of retention efforts. Elite employees are those individuals that the organisation would 'miss' if they left.

Arguments against

- The adoption of the 'everybody is talent' (Wiblen, 2016) recognises that all employees encompass talents deemed valuable to the organisation, and that is why they have been recruited in the first place. Consider the Disneyland example discussed previously.
- Every individual has the potential to contribute to an organisation's financial outcomes, inferring that all employees, not just elite employees, are valuable and worthy of investment (Thunnissen et al., 2013).
- The exclusion of the 'talent pool' may be demotivating for those employees not selected to participate in talent management programs. Potential negative outcomes include damage to morale and performance of 'non-talents' (Gallardo-Gallardo et al., 2013) and resentment among peers (Gladwell, 2002; Patel, 2002; Blass and April, 2008).
- There is no clear empirical evidence (yet) (Collings, 2014) that an exclusive approach is more effective as it is based on the flawed assumption that organisational performance is simply an aggregation of individual success (Pfeffer, 2001).
- The definition and conceptualisation of an 'elite employee' can differ between stakeholders each with their own views and interests potentially resulting in confusion between employees and managers.

Useful references

Blass, E. & April, K. 2008. Developing talent for tomorrow. *Develop*, 1, 48–58.
Daubner-Siva, D., Vinkenburg, C. J., & Jansen, P. G. W. 2017. Dovetailing talent management and diversity management: the exclusion-inclusion paradox. *Journal of Organizational Effectiveness: People and Performance*, 4, 315–331.
Gallardo-Gallardo, E., Dries, N., & González-Cruz, T. F. 2013. What is the meaning of 'talent' in the world of work? *Human Resource Management Review*, 23, 290–300.
Gladwell, M. 2002. The talent myth: Are smart people overrated? *The New Yorker*, July 22, 28–33. www.newyorker.com/magazine/2002/07/22 (Accessed 29 March 2018).
Patel, D. 2002. Managing talent. *HR Magazine*, 47, 112.
Pfeffer, J. 2001. Fighting the war for talent is hazardous to your organization's health. *Organizational Dynamics*, 29, 248–259.

Video learning resources

- Talent management, LinkedIn learning – What is a talent management strategy? Acknowledges that a talent management strategy needs to underpin all talent management practices: www.youtube.com/watch?v=snl7eC8LDLk
- Heineken – The candidate: Illustrates the relationship between social media and talent attraction, acquisition and marketing: www.youtube.com/watch?time_continue=4&v=hlvD4gPdbHQ
- Heineken – Go places: Example of a company that recognises the relationship between marketing, novelty and ability to attract (pull) talent towards the company: www.youtube.com/watch?v=0QoGzV72wR8

- Perspectives on performance management: An interview with Professor John Boudreau: Acknowledges and discusses the limitations associated with traditional performance management processes and what happens when you endeavour to allocate numerical values to individuals: www.youtube.com/watch?v=W0r9KCjzdGM
- Watson talent talks at HR Tech World: David Perring: The video interview discusses technological innovations in talent management and human capital software solutions and systems: www.youtube.com/watch?v=9XNWGu11unQ
- Talent analytics from IBM – The perfect balance: Example of a vendor designed talent management solution and illustrates the compelling rhetoric that underpins the use of technology generated data in making decisions about talent: www.youtube.com/watch?v=m7Z-G98b6bs

References

Aguinis, H. & O'Boyle, E. 2014. Star performers in twenty-first century organizations. *Personnel Psychology*, 67, 313–350.

Beechler, S. & Woodward, I. C. 2009. The global 'war for talent'. *Journal of International Management*, 15, 273–285.

Benders, J. G. J. M., Batenburg, R. S., Hoeken, P. P. W. M., & Schouteten, R. L. J. 2006. First organize, then automate: A modern socio-technical view on ERP systems and teamworking. *New Technology, Work and Employment*, 21, 242–251.

Blass, E. & April, K. 2008. Developing talent for tomorrow. *Develop*, 1, 48–58.

Boudreau, J. W. & Ramstad, P. M. 2007. *Beyond HR: The New Science of Human Capital*. Boston, MA: Harvard Business School Press.

Bussler, L. & Davis, E. 2001. Information systems: The quiet revolution in human resource management. *Journal of Computer Information Systems*, 42, 17–20.

Capelli, P. 2008. Talent management for the twenty-first century. *Harvard Business Review*, 86, 74–81.

Ceriello, V. R. & Freeman, C. 1991. *Human Resource Management Systems: Strategies, Tactics and Techniques*. Lanham, MD: Lexington Books.

Collings, D. G. 2014. The Contribution of Talent Management to Organization Success. In: Kraiger, K., Passmore, J., Dos Santos, N. R. & Malvezzi, S. (eds.) *The Wiley-Blackwell Handbook of the Psychology of Training, Development, and Performance Improvement*. Chichester: John Wiley & Sons, Ltd, pp. 247–260.

Collings, D. G. & Mellahi, K. 2009. Strategic talent management: A review and research agenda. *Human Resource Management Review*, 19, 304–313.

Collings, D. G. & Mellahi, K. 2013. Commentary on: 'Talent—innate or acquired? Theoretical considerations and their implications for talent management'. *Human Resource Management Review*, 23, 322–325.

Daubner-Siva, D., Vinkenburg, C. J. & Jansen, P. G. W. 2017. Dovetailing talent management and diversity management: The exclusion–inclusion paradox. *Journal of Organizational Effectiveness: People and Performance*, 4, 315–331.

Dries, N. 2013. The psychology of talent management: A review and research agenda. *Human Resource Management Review*, 23, 272–285.

Farndale, E., Paauwe, J. & Hoeksema, L. 2009. In-sourcing HR: Shared service centres in the Netherlands. *International Journal of Human Resource Management*, 20, 544–561.

Gallardo-Gallardo, E., Dries, N. & González-Cruz, T. F. 2013. What is the meaning of 'talent' in the world of work? *Human Resource Management Review*, 23, 290–300.

Gladwell, M. 2002. The talent myth: Are smart people overrated? [Online]. *The New Yorker*, July 22, 28–33. www.newyorker.com/magazine/2002/07/22 (Accessed 29 March 2018).

Grant, D., Hall, R., Wailes, N. & Wright, C. 2006. The false promise of technological determinism: The case of enterprise resource planning systems. *New Technology, Work & Employment*, 21, 2–15.

Gueutal, H. & Stone, D. L. 2005. *The Brave New World of eHR: Human Resources in the Digital Age*. San Francisco, CA: Jossey Bass.

Hewitt's Human Capital Consulting and Human Capital Institute. 2008. *The State of Talent Management: Today's Challenges, Tomorrow's Opportunities* [Online]. www.shrm.org/ResourcesAnd Tools/hr-topics/organizational-and-employee-development/Documents/hciLibraryPaper_79300.pdf (Accessed 29 March 2018).

Johns, K. M. & Kavanagh, M. J. 2012. Talent Management. In: Kavanagh, M. J., Thite, M. & Johnson, R. D. (eds.) *Human Resource Information Systems: Basics, Applications, and Future Directions*. Thousand Oaks, CA: Sage, pp. 536–556.

Lah, T. E. & Capperella, J. 2009. Using Talent Supply Chain Management to Overcome Challenges in the Professional Services Market. *Workforce Management*, 88(3).

Lengnick-Hall, M. & S. Moritz. 2003. The impact of e-HR on the human resource management function. *Journal of Labor Research*, 24, 365–379.

Lewis, R. E. & Heckman, R. J. 2006. Talent management: A critical review. *Human Resource Management Review*, 16, 139–154.

Mäkelä, K., Björkman, I. & Ehrnrooth, M. 2010. How do MNCs establish their talent pools? Influences on individuals' likelihood of being labeled as talent. *Journal of World Business*, 45, 134–142.

MarketsandMarkets. 2017. *Talent Management Software Market worth $11,367.0 Million by 2019* [Online]. www.marketsandmarkets.com/PressReleases/talent-management-software.asp (Accessed 20 July 2017).

Marler, J. H. & Dulebohn, J. H. 2005. A Model of Employee Self-Service Technology Acceptance. In: Martocchio, J. J. (ed.) *Research in Personnel and Human Resources Management* (Volume 24). Bingley: Emerald Group Publishing Limited, pp. 137–180.

Marler, J. H. & Parry, E. 2016. Human resource management, strategic involvement and e-HRM technology. *The International Journal of Human Resource Management*, 27, 2233–2253.

Mcdonald, P. & Thompson, P. 2016. Social media(tion) and the reshaping of public/private boundaries in employment relations. *International Journal of Management Reviews*, 18, 69–84.

McKinsey. 2017. *People Analytics* [Online]. www.mckinsey.com/solutions/orgsolutions/overview/people-analytics (Accessed 28 June 2017).

Mell, P. & Grance, T. 2011. *The NIST Definition of Cloud Computing. Recommendations of the National Institute of Standards and Technology. Special Publication 800-145*. Gaithersburg, MD: NIST.

Mellahi, K., & Collings, D. G. 2010. The barriers to effective global talent management: The example of corporate élites in MNEs. *Journal of World Business*, 45(2), 143–149.

Michaels, E., Handfield-Jones, H., & Axelrod, B. 2001. *The War for Talent*. Boston, MA: Harvard Business School Press.

Orlikowski, W. J. & Scott, S. V. 2008. Sociomateriality: challenging the separation of technology, work and organization. *The Academy of Management Annals*, 2, 433–474.

Orlikowski, W. & Scott, S. 2015. The algorithm and the crowd: Considering the materiality of service innovation. *MIS Quarterly*, 39, 201–216.

Patel, D. 2002. Managing talent. *HR Magazine*, 47, 112.

Pfeffer, J. 2001. Fighting the war for talent is hazardous to your organization's health. *Organizational Dynamics*, 29, 248–259.

PwC. 2017. *20th CEO Survey: 20 Years Inside the Mind of the CEO ... What's next?* [Online]. https://www.pwc.com/gx/en/ceo-survey/2017/industries/20th-ceo-survey-pharma.pdf (Accessed 29 March 2018).

SAP SuccessFactors. 2017. *Talent Management* [Online]. www.successfactors.com/en_gb/solutions/talent.html: SAP SuccessFactors (Accessed 11 July 2017).
Snell, A. 2008. The future of talent management. *Workforce Management*, 87(20).
Stahl, G., Björkman, I., Farndale, E., Morris, S., Paauwe, J., Stiles, P., Trevor, J., & Wright, P. 2007. Global talent management: How leading multinationals build and sustain their talent pipeline. Fontainebleau: *INSEAD Working Papers Collection*, 34, 1–36.
Stone, D. L. & Dulebohn, J. H. 2013. Emerging issues in theory and research on electronic human resource management (eHRM). *Human Resource Management Review*, 23, 1–5.
Tansley, C. 2011. What do we mean by the term 'talent' in talent management? *Industrial and Commercial Training*, 43, 266–274.
The Social Index. 2016. *What is your Digital Footprint & Why It Matters* [Online]. https://thesocialindex.com/why-use-the-social-index/ (Accessed 5 January 2018).
Thunnissen, M., Boselie, P. & Fruytier, B. 2013. A review of talent management: 'Infancy or adolescence?' *The International Journal of Human Resource Management*, 24, 1744–1761.
Wiblen, S. 2016. Framing the usefulness of eHRM in talent management: A case study of talent identification in a professional services firm. *Canadian Journal of Administrative Sciences*, 33, 95–107.
Wiblen, S., Dery, K. & Grant, D. 2012. Do you see what I see? The role of technology in talent identification. *Asia Pacific Journal of Human Resources*, 50, 421–438.
Wiblen, S., Grant, D. & Dery, K. 2010. Transitioning to a new HRIS: The reshaping of human resources and information technology talent. *Journal of Electronic Commerce Research*, 11, 251–267.
Williams, H. 2009. Job Analysis and HR Planning. In: M. Thite and M. J. Kavanagh (eds.) *Human Resource Information Systems: Basics, Applications, and Future Directions*. Thousand Oaks, CA: Sage, pp. 251–276.
Workday. 2017. *Talent Management: Make Talent Your Business* [Online]. www.workday.com/en-us/applications/human-capital-management/talent.html (Accessed 28 June 2017).

11 e-Recruitment and selection

Anna B. Holm & Lars Haahr

> **Learning objectives**
> - Describe the role of technology in the recruitment function, in terms of identification of applicants, sources of recruitment, recruitment message, processing applications and communication with applicants
> - Describe the role of technology in the selection function, in terms of screening methods, evaluative methods and selection of candidates
> - Critically evaluate the opportunities and challenges presented by digital technologies in e-recruitment and e-selection

Introduction

Rachel Bates is the vice president of sales at Workable. She recently wrote on her blog:

> My professional success depends on hiring the right people at the right time. But I constantly feel like I have no time at all. Then I realized I could hire people on my phone using a mobile applicant tracking system (ATS) app. It's been a total game changer for me ... With an iPhone or Android app, I can call candidates directly from the app, I can see my interview schedule at a glance, I get smart notifications and I don't have to wait for a free chunk of time to speed up the hiring process: I can do it on the go. As a busy executive with an ever-growing team, that's the only way I'll be able to hire the right people.
>
> (Bates 2017)

For many hiring managers like Rachel, recruitment and selection (hereafter referred to as R&S) of employees with the use of technology has become a natural part of work. For the recruitment profession, however, the transformation from traditional (i.e., paper-based) recruitment and selection to a highly digitalized process has been nothing less than revolutionary.

R&S plays a vital role for the development of human capital in organizations and is often viewed as part of strategic human resource management (Liviens and Chapman 2010, Millmore et al. 2007). The primary objective of recruitment is to identify and attract potential employees (Barber 1998: 10), while selection is about assessing and choosing the right candidates who will fit well into the organization, the vacant job and with their future co-workers, as well as other characteristics (Kristof-Brown et al. 2014, Ostroff and Zhan 2012). Thus, R&S can be defined as practices and activities carried out by an organization for the primary purpose of identifying, attracting, assessing, selecting and influencing the job choices of competent candidates who will fit the job environment.

Recruiting and selecting employees with information and communication technologies (ICTs), often referred to as e-recruitment and e-selection (e-R&S), has become a widespread practice across the globe, especially where organizations and labour markets have easy access to Internet-related technologies. Regardless of whether or not an organization chooses to execute a highly digitalized recruitment and selection process, it still goes through a series of tasks and subtasks that together constitute a business process (i.e., a set of logically related tasks performed to achieve a defined business outcome for internal or external recipients; Davenport and Short 1990).

In this chapter, we describe in detail technology-enabled R&S processes, including an evaluation of their effectiveness. We then analyse the challenges and opportunities associated with e-R&S.

Technology-enabled e-recruitment methods

The traditional R&S process can be described as a linear process with four recruitment and two selection tasks with subtasks. A graphical depiction of a typical R&S process is presented in Fig 11.1.

The first task in the process is to define hiring objectives, such as deciding on the positions to be filled, the necessary number of candidates required to fill the positions, job performance goals for new hires and their expected retention rate, the time frame available and the costs that the organization is prepared ready to bear for the entire process (Breaugh 2008, 2009). The next recruitment task is to identify the required applicants, which

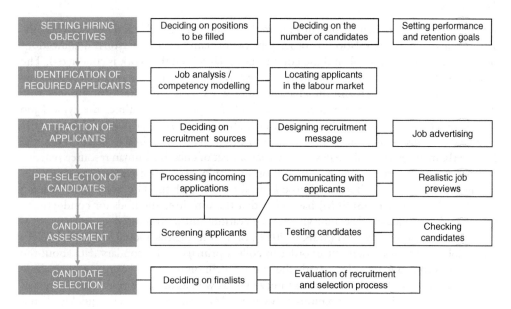

Figure 11.1 Recruitment and selection process: Tasks with subtasks.
Source: Authors.

includes conducting a job analysis and identifying the location and placement of the desired applicants in the labour market. The third task of recruitment is to attract and persuade qualified applicants to apply. This includes deciding on the recruitment sources and placing a job advertisement. Once recruiters receive the desired number of applications, they proceed with the fourth task of filing and sorting the applications and preparing them for initial screening. Here, R&S interweave as recruiters screen the applicants' curriculum vitae (CV) and other documentation to draw up a shortlist of the most qualified candidates. After communicating the pre-screening results to applicants, the selection part of the process commences. The tasks here are to first assess and then select the best-qualified candidates to make them a job offer.

The e-recruitment and selection (e-R&S) process consists of similar tasks and subtasks as the traditional R&S process, but the sequence and the timing of those tasks can change, as some of them can be performed concurrently. For example, the sorting of incoming applications and pre-screening of applicants can commence before the attraction activities are over. Communicating with applicants can also take place in parallel with other activities, as web technologies permit a time-unlimited and asynchronous communication process (Holm 2012). Moreover, a part of the assessment and selection can be performed even before candidates apply for a vacant position, as jobseekers are increasingly encouraged to take various online tests and use other evaluation tools to determine whether they fit the job and the hiring organization. Consequently, ICTs allow organizations to design a flexible R&S process that permits a ubiquitous candidate management.

Below, we discuss the major tasks, subtasks and activities of a recruitment and selection process that is performed with the use of various ICTs.

Identification of applicants

Job analysis

Job analysis is the systematic study of a job to determine which tasks, activities and responsibilities it contains, its relation to other jobs or job families, the personal qualifications necessary to perform the job and the conditions under which the work is conducted. The information obtained through job analysis allows the identification and description of the important aspects of a job and the characteristics workers need to perform the job well. The common outcome of a job analysis is a *job description* that outlines the typical job duties, functions and responsibilities of a position and a *person specification* that specifies knowledge, skills, abilities and other characteristics (KSAOs) required to perform the job. Many HR managers see job analysis as a pivotal aspect of effective human resource practice because an organization's success depends on its employees' performance (Guest 1997).

There are various methods to choose from for a job analysis. The Society for Human Resource Management (SHRM) has found that the top three methods for conducting a job analysis are face-to-face interviews, observation and a structured questionnaire of subject matter experts (SMEs) (SHRM 2014). Similar to the traditional job analysis, electronic job analysis is carried out in order to collect primary and secondary data about the job in question, but it is done with the use of technology. Data sources may include electronic surveys of SMEs and video interviews, as well as online discussions and panels with SMEs. The views and opinions of various SMEs can be easily and quickly shared electronically, thus streamlining the data-gathering process (Stone et al. 2013). The sources of information about the job may also include records from the *Occupational*

Information Network (O★Net), which contains information on hundreds of standardized and occupation-specific descriptors sponsored by the US Department of Labor's Employment and Training Administration. A study of the electronic job analysis in the US Navy found that the e-enabled job analysis resulted in more comprehensive descriptions of the job than the traditional method (Reiter-Palmon et al. 2006). Additionally, the electronic method also allowed the completion of the job analysis in a shorter period of time and was generally more flexible than the traditional method. SHRM estimated that, in 2014, around 25% of organizations in the USA used various online job analysis tools and around 13% used survey software (SHRM and ACT 2014).

Locating the appropriate pool of applicants

Once the hiring organizations have assessed what kind of potential applicants they want to attract, they need to locate them in the labour market. In this regard, it is vital to understand the overall *state of the labour market* and the supply of labour with the required qualifications. In some professions, unemployment can be quite low as the result of high demand from employing organizations. In this situation, it will be difficult to attract applicants for the vacant position, as most of the potential applicants are already employed. In this case, recruiters have to deal with *passive jobseekers*, who might not actively look for a new job but might consider changing employer if the job offer is good. Unlike active jobseekers, passive jobseekers do not scan job advertisements of career pages and need to be found and approached individually. Therefore, many organizations (e.g., in the USA) choose *employee referrals* as one of the main recruitment sources (SHRM 2016a). Also, advertising in professional media, networking, Internet data-mining and search agencies can be good recruitment sources for passive jobseekers (Phillips and Gully 2015: 179).

Applicant attraction

To attract applicants and persuade them to apply for a vacancy, organizations must choose recruitment sources that guarantee the maximum exposure of the suitable pool of individuals in the labour market to the recruitment message. The recruitment message can contain a simple job advertisement or it can be a multifaceted communication effort, transmitting not only the information about the vacancy but organizational attributes such as values, traditions, cultural norms, job locational advantages and even strategic objectives. The recruitment message will vary depending on the recruitment sources chosen and the recruitment objectives.

Recruitment sources

Traditionally, the most commonly used sources for external recruitment were newspaper advertisements, private and public employment agencies, employee referrals, colleges and universities, search companies, job fairs and so on (Ployhart et al. 2006). With the expansion and acceptance of general ICTs by organizations and labour markets, many of the traditional recruitment sources have lost their importance. According to a survey conducted by the UK-based Chartered Institute of Personnel and Development (CIPD) in 2017, HR professionals find the most effective methods for recruiting to be their own corporate websites (74%), followed by professional networking sites (60%) and Internet job boards (58%) (CIPD and HAYS 2017). In 2016, an SHRM survey of HR professionals in the

USA found that 83% of the respondents use employee referrals as their main recruitment source, followed by corporate websites (81%), social networking sites (67%) and Internet job boards (66%). Only 34% of the respondents used printed advertising and 18% placed job advertisements in trade publications (SHRM 2016a).

CORPORATE WEBSITES

Corporate websites play an important role for corporate communication in general and for R&S in particular, and, as mentioned earlier, they are often considered as one of the most important recruitment sources. Organizations typically have a special job and career section on their website where they post job advertisements, describe the recruitment and selection process and inform about the conditions of potential employment and possibilities for future development. Most organizations also provide an email address or a link to a page where applicants can apply for a job and submit their CV and other documentation. Many employers have integrated their e-recruitment systems, often referred to as applicant tracking systems (ATSs), with their websites – thus automatizing the application process and reducing the administrative burden for their recruiting staff.

Corporate websites are also an excellent medium for the employer to tell potential applicants about the organization and communicate organizational values by describing the organization's talent philosophy, its core values, mission and vision. This can be done using rich media, such as video interviews with current employees, photo and slide presentations of the organization's history and a virtual tour of the office. This promotion of the organization as an employer is called *employer branding* (Backhaus and Tikoo 2004) and is often considered to be the most important communication activity in the recruitment process (Lievens 2007).

Many organizations prioritize employer branding and candidate communication as a dominant activity on their corporate websites. Therefore, some employers even conduct employer branding and recruitment activities on the front page of their websites and have transformed these activities into an interactive involvement of potential applicants (Aggerholm and Andersen 2017). Due to this increasingly important function of corporate websites in the attraction of future employees, four important points are worth emphasizing.

First, hiring organizations have to make sure that jobseekers become aware of their websites. Therefore, *constant advertising of the website* may be necessary (Allen et al. 2007). The advertising of corporate career websites must be viewed positively and as an integrated part of recruitment practices in order to generate jobseeker attention and engagement in the offered employment opportunities (Cober et al. 2004).

Second, corporate websites can easily provide large amounts of information about job opportunities. Therefore, in order to attract and engage applicant interest, organizations should take the user experience seriously and design the website, which presents this information, in a coherent and easy-to-understand manner. *Navigability* or the overall ease for a candidate to browse a corporate website for information is therefore important in maintaining the interest from applicants (Allen et al. 2007).

Third, the *aesthetic features* of the website (e.g., colour scheme, pictures and animations) have an impact on the engagement of applicants. These features not only define the overall experience on the website but also signal the innovativeness of the organization and therefore play a considerable role in attracting applicants and even matching them with the organization (Cober et al. 2004).

Fourth, in several ways, corporate websites become the first critical source of recruitment contact and thus influence early attraction. If the corporate website succeeds in providing both accessible and effective information, the website might further motivate the applicant to engage in appropriate *self-selection* behaviour (Cober et al. 2004). If the website can sustain such a self-selection by providing feedback to candidates concerning person–organization (PO) or person–job (PJ) fit, it can help produce a more qualified applicant pool.

SOCIAL NETWORKING SITES

Social networking sites (SNSs), or social media (SM), are an increasingly important recruitment source for many organizations. The most popular SNSs in the western hemisphere to date include LinkedIn, Facebook, Twitter, Instagram and Snapchat. Whereas private users predominantly inhabited these SNSs in their early days, nowadays they increasingly serve as an arena for interactions between individuals and corporate actors (Roth et al. 2013). SNS technology is constantly evolving and SNS companies and third-party software providers offer diverse services to candidates, organizations and recruitment agencies. Consequently, they have also become the new digital platform where employers engage with users when recruiting and searching for candidates (Brown and Vaughn 2011).

Today, recruiters have taken advantage of the large activity on SNSs by searching, scanning and monitoring both passive and active candidates. They systematically crawl SNSs for information, data crunch this information, match candidates with vacant positions and eventually select and contact candidates of interest (Brown and Vaughn 2011, Van Iddekinge et al. 2016). However, the validity and use of information gathered on SNSs about potential candidates is greatly discussed (Roth et al. 2013), as detailed in Chapter 8.

Organizations also use their presence on SNSs to facilitate employees becoming active as brand ambassadors and making employee referrals. Employee referral activity is often sustained by a *content management software system* that encourages – and sometimes rewards – employees to take an active part in attracting candidates to vacant positions. However, not all employees feel immediately motivated to function as brand ambassadors and recommend potential candidates, and it can be challenging for employers to motivate employees to like and share company postings (Cervellon and Lirio 2017).

INTERNET JOB BOARDS

Most hiring organizations use Internet job boards for advertising their vacancies. *Paid job boards*, such as Monster and CareerBuilder, as well as free job boards function as some of the strongest tools in recruitment. Together with employee referrals, corporate websites and social media, they are among the most used recruitment sources of external candidates (SHRM 2016a). A distinctive characteristic of job boards is that they are primarily effective in reaching active jobseekers, whereas social media platforms also reach passive jobseekers (Phillips and Gully 2015: 179).

Aside from general job boards, *specialized job boards* that are formed around specific educational training or specific industries are also an effective recruitment source. For example, the portal www.nurse.com targets individuals from the nursing profession. This specialized platform also serves other purposes than pure job advertising and searching for candidates. In addition to posting jobs, it provides diverse learning opportunities on how to write a good CV and how to perform well at a job interview.

Job boards also offer valuable information on labour market and remuneration statistics, analyses and forecasts, information on education, training and certification. Today's job boards thus function as a service for both recruiters and jobseekers and represents a transformational recruitment service platform in terms of interactivity, automation and artificial intelligence.

EMPLOYEE REFERRAL

Employees can be very useful in locating suitable candidates in their networks, social circles and even on SNSs and can recommend them to their employers. They use their knowledge about the relevant individuals and the vacancies to make an initial judgement of fit. They can also provide insider information to the candidates about the employing organization and the job. Therefore, the candidates generated from employees' referrals often have realistic expectations of the potential employment and also develop an earlier commitment to the employing organizations. Research has found that these candidates require less transition time and demonstrate higher performance and retention rates (Breaugh 2008). Thus, employee referrals are considered to be one of the most effective recruitment sources for either passive or active jobseekers.

(A) Recruitment message

Recruitment messages or job advertisements can have a major impact on whether individuals will consider applying for the vacancy and eventually accept a job offer (Breaugh 2009). It serves as a means to *'psychological contract'* fulfilment wherein prospective employees are provided with a realistic view of the position advertised and not just a glossy, superficial and a feel-good picture. Therefore, the recruitment message that the hiring organization chooses to communicate must be well designed. It should contain information that is (1) important for the target group; (2) specific; and (3) realistic. The recruitment message can also build or reflect the organization's employer brand that truthfully and justly represents the organization as an employer. Studies suggest that when applicants have realistic expectations, hiring organizations experience lower turnover and better performing employees, with higher job satisfaction and greater trust of the organization (Breaugh 2009).

Typically, a job advertisement will contain essential information about the details of the job, duties, location and benefits. However, some other information can be important for certain groups of applicants. For example, applicants with long commute times might look for a job where they can work from home at least some days, senior applicants will often search employment with reduced working hours and individuals with small children might look for a part-time job.

With the intensifying competition for qualified applicants, employers find it increasingly important to stand out with their message on various digital platforms. However, the effectiveness of various online activities can be difficult to measure and analyse. Therefore, hiring organizations need to evaluate recruitment sources based on sound metrics, such as cost per application, time to hire, cost per interview or cost per hire, when evaluating source and message effectiveness. For example, the data analytics and online recruitment marketing company Ontame.io helps recruiters collect, merge and analyse data from corporate career websites and ATS. The service is able to track not just where applicant and referral traffic comes from but also how this correlates to the quality of an applicant and whether it leads to an eventual hire. The analysis permits optimization of the use of various recruitment sources and messages (O'Hear 2016).

(B) Processing applications

Digitalization has transformed the handling of incoming applications from a manually conducted paper-based process to an automated and digitalized process with the result that the sorting and registering of incoming applications happens automatically. The automatization further includes the sorting of applications according to the algorithms' or categorizations' set-up in the ATS. Further, a significant change is the implementation of a self-service procedure in which the applicant him- or herself does the registration work involved in the application process. In combination, this standardization and self-service results in an automated process in which the applicant fills out a standardized online form, including the contact information, attaches the CV and other supporting documentation, and may even add his or her notes on the expectations and motivations of applying for the job. With regard to the application form, some organizations have started drawing on third-party vendor software such as LinkedIn and therefore request applicants to feed their LinkedIn profile into the organization's ATS.

Besides application processing, an ATS often facilitates pre-screening, interviews and other tasks. Such systems also serve as a platform for collaboration and communication between recruitment stakeholders, who have instant access to the valuable information on the organization's staffing activities. A contemporary ATS also helps in the communication with applicants throughout the entire hiring process, which is no longer only a final step in the recruitment process but is an ongoing task (Holm 2012).

(C) Communication with applicants

Due to the automation features of the e-recruitment systems, candidates today are often notified immediately that their job application has been received. In some cases, the candidate can track his or her own status in the recruitment process online, which makes the whole process more transparent and adds to the perception of fairness by the applicants. Today, rejected candidates are also informed promptly about the result of the pre-screening, often even before the vacancies are formally filled. Applicants consider this immediate response practice to be very advantageous, as it means that recruiters do not have to keep them waiting unnecessarily to hear that they have not been selected for further assessment. Furthermore, in the contemporary labour market, this increased speed of operations and the practice of responding immediately functions as a positive signal of the professionalism of the hiring organizations, adding to its employer brand.

Table 11.1 summarizes the key steps, processes and considerations at each stage of the e-recruitment process as discussed above.

Technology-enabled assessment and selection

In practice, the selection process starts with the pre-screening of incoming applications, but formally it starts when shortlisted candidates are invited for a series of assessment procedures. When assisted with technology, it is commonly referred to as e-selection. Stone

Table 11.1 Key steps, processes and considerations in e-recruitment

Steps	Processes	Considerations
Identification of applicants	Job analysis	– Job description – Person specification (KSAs) – Data from subject matter experts – O★Net
	Locating appropriate pool of applicants	– Demand and supply of the labour market – Attracting passive job seekers
Applicant attraction		– Recruitment message
Recruitment sources	Corporate websites	– Employer branding – Rich media communication – Advertising career websites – Navigability/ Ease-of-use – Aesthetic features – Candidate self-selection
	Social media/social networking sites	– Evolving technology and providers – Data crawling to monitor users – Employees as brand ambassadors
	Internet job boards	– General job boards – Specialized job boards
	Employee referral	Employees' networks
Recruitment message	Communication	Targeted, specific and realistic
	Psychological contract	Realistic picture of the position
	Evaluating recruitment sources	Data analytics software
Processing applications	Enhancing efficiency	– Automation and digitization – Self-service registration – Linking with third-party vendor software (e.g., LinkedIn)
Communication with applicants	Projection of professionalism and courtesy	– Automatic receipt notification – Tracking – Application outcome notification

Source: Authors.

et al. (2013) define e-selection as the use of various forms of technology, such as online application screening earlier in the recruitment process, various web-based tests, videoconference interviews and so on, to assess individuals' KSAOs.

In nature, selection can be simple or complex depending on the qualification requirements of the vacancies and the desired personal characteristics. Shortlisted candidates might be required to undergo a series of cognitive, physical, psychometric and other tests that can reveal their ability to perform the tasks required by the job. Recruiters and hiring managers can also conduct a series of interviews to determine whether the candidates fit the organization's culture, values and traditions.

Hiring organizations can choose among many different selection methods depending on their validity, costs, usability, appropriateness and adverse impact on candidates. Selection methods should also be employed to work in synergy and be suitable for the organizational context. The most important criterion is the methods' validity or the ability of the selection system to predict work outcomes, such as job performance, turnover and absenteeism. A combination of selection methods should also make it possible to establish whether the candidate fits the organization, the job, the team and other criteria (Kristof-Brown and Guay 2011).

Research has shown that, similar to traditional paper-and-pencil tests, computerized assessment tests can be valid predictors of performance. However, employers cannot assume that paper- and computer-based tests are equivalent, and thus they must first validate each test before deployment (Johnson and Guetal 2013). Another issue that might prevent companies from deploying web-based candidate testing is the risk of cheating by candidates, as there is often no supervision. Cheating is rare though when speeded tests are used, and, where absolutely necessary, hiring organizations can administer follow-up or confirmatory tests in controlled settings (ITC 2005).

In some countries, organizations' assessment procedures can be subject to anti-discrimination laws and regulations. For example, in the USA, Title VII of the Civil Rights Act of 1964 (Title VII), the Americans with Disabilities Act of 1990 and the Age Discrimination in Employment Act of 1967 prohibit the use of discriminatory employment tests and selection procedures. The US Equal Employment Opportunity Commission (EEOC) takes remedial and enforcement actions against employers who use discriminative assessment and selection practices. To help relevant organizations to comply with the federal laws, the EEOC, along with three other government agencies, adopted Uniform Guidelines on Employee Selection Procedures (EEOC 2010).

(A) Screening methods

Application screening is most suitable early in the selection process and is mainly about screening CVs, application letters and other information about the jobseekers. A systematic approach to collecting and scoring background information from applicants is weighted application forms. In addition, many organizations perform telephone screenings before inviting potential candidates to further selection procedures.

Organizations can use *automated keyword searches* for CVs and applications to quickly sift through large volumes of applicants. The searches are effective when the choice of keywords or phrases are job-related. Therefore, it is best to base keywords and key phrases on the information from job analyses and competency models. Otherwise, screening may lead to hiring the candidates who tailored their CV for the most used keywords (Johnson and Guetal 2013).

Weighted application forms

When applying for a job online, applicants are often asked to complete an online application form (also referred to as a *blank*) with multiple fields. The fields typically represent individual characteristics relevant for the job, such as education, experience, knowledge and specific skills. Each field may be assigned a weight based on the predictive power for future performance and the application form is then scored like a test. In this way, the application form can be used as a weighted application form selection method. Scores can be calculated for the entire application or hiring managers can establish cut-off scores for items such as education and experience from similar occupations.

As a selection method, weighted application forms have a good validity. However, some administrative factors (e.g., the length of the application form or the complexity of the questions in the field) can affect its effectiveness. In particular, ease of use, efficiency and 'friendliness' of the application system affect individuals' willingness to apply (Cober et al. 2003).

Telephone screens

Some organizations develop sophisticated, multitiered interview screening processes that employ a variety of technologies. For the screening purposes, candidates can be asked to answer a series of questions over the phone or through an *interactive voice response* (IVR). When using IVR, applicants are asked to respond to pre-recorded application form questions that are read with a human or computer-generated voice. They respond to the questions verbally or use numbers on a telephone keypad and the system stores their answers (Stone et al. 2013). Passing candidates can then be scheduled for an online video interview (e.g., via Skype or another video interview platform).

Although being a time-saving solution when a large number of individuals apply for a job, IVR-based screens may produce responses different to those acquired through paper- or web-based weighted application forms. Unlike IVR, using web technology allows respondents to control the time, location and pace of their responses. Additionally, IVR systems do not provide a visual presentation of interview questions and response options. The IVR auditory mode places a time pressure on applicants and encourages rapid, top-of-mind responses and may thus result in a more frequent selection of the scale endpoints (Yang et al. 2011).

Realistic job previews

Organizations may also choose to provide potential candidates with realistic job previews (RJPs) as a part of the screening process. RJPs are about presenting both positive and potentially negative information about the job to the candidates. The objective of an RJP is to give an accurate picture of the future position and organization. RJPs permit candidates to conclude whether there are fits between them and the job, the organization, the future team and other parameters (Kristof-Brown et al. 2014). This allows candidates to opt out of the recruitment and selection process if the opportunity is not a match for them. Furthermore, RJPs may perform as a *'vaccination'* against unpleasant features of the job, allowing employees to develop coping mechanisms. In addition, employees who received RJPs may be more committed to the choice because they accepted the job despite its negative aspects (Wanous 1980). Research has shown that after receiving RJPs, fewer applicants accept job offers, but those who accept stay longer in the organization (Suszko and Breaugh 1986).

(B) Evaluative methods

Organizations have many options when choosing evaluative assessment methods. Research has shown that, among evaluative methods, structured interviews, cognitive ability tests, job knowledge tests and work samples have the highest validity and predict performance in most jobs (Ryan and Tippins 2004). Unstructured interviews, personality testing, integrity and situational judgement tests have lower validity but are still deployed because they may add additional information about the candidate and can help to establish a more objective perception of her or his fit with the job environment. Evaluative methods vary considerably on the cost of development and implementation, usability and the adverse impact (Phillips and Gully 2015: 267). If candidates do not believe that a specific test is fair, they may develop a negative perception of the hiring organization.

Applicant interviews

Interviews are one of the oldest and most used methods for employee selection. They permit measuring a variety of abilities and skills, particularly non-cognitive skills, such as leadership style, interpersonal skills and so on (Ryan and Tippins 2004). When well developed and executed, they can be a reliable technique for employee selection.

The most valid interview method is a *structured interview* in which candidates are asked a series of standardized, job-related questions, with different weights and predetermined scores for different answers. Structured interviews can include behavioural, situational and case-based questions. Well-executed structured interviews result in good identification of potentially high-performing employees. According to SHRM (2016b), over 50% of organizations use structured interviews as the main assessment method for any category of employee, and in 74% of the cases, structured interviews are deployed for selection at executive level.

When interviews are unstructured and not well prepared, questions vary from candidate to candidate and differ across interviewers. The interview questions in this situation are often casual and open-ended. Such a mode of interviewing has poor validity and may lead to poorer selection results. According to industry statistics, around 20% of organizations still rely on unstructured interviewing as the main selection technique (SHRM 2016b).

Today, face-to-face interviews are often replaced by *synchronous or asynchronous online interviews and video conferencing*. One of the popular methods of conducting asynchronous interviews is asking candidates to answer a set of questions and recording their individual answers in a video at a time and place that is convenient for them. The answers are then sent to the hiring organization for evaluation. Many companies found this method very useful as it permits them to make a candidate-by-candidate comparison based on individual questions.

Research has shown that online interviews are not equivalent to face-to-face interviews and can have substantial impacts on the candidates' perceptions of fairness and their behaviour (Johnson and Guetal 2013). Interviewers' perception of candidates can also vary across interview modes. Furthermore, a face-to-face interview is a richer and more interactive communication mode than other modes. Electronically interviewed candidates may not be able to fully communicate their skills and abilities online. Face-to-face interviews are also perceived as being more fair and personal and send the message that the hiring organization cares about the candidate, while telephone interviews, online interviews and video conferencing can be perceived as a cost-saving exercise (Johnson and Guetal 2013).

Moreover, research has shown that different interview modes can lead to different candidate ratings because of the candidates' appearance. The 'less attractive' candidate can receive higher evaluations in a phone interview than in a face-to-face interview. In addition, candidates who are first screened through an electronic interview and then face-to-face have an advantage over those who were not first interviewed electronically (Johnson and Guetal 2013). Therefore, in order to ensure the reliability of selection interviews, organizations need to ensure that the interview mode is the same for all candidates in the pool. This permits a fairer candidate-to-candidate comparison and increases the overall validity of the assessment.

Cognitive ability tests

General cognitive ability tests measure mental abilities such as logic, reading comprehension, verbal or mathematical reasoning and perceptual abilities, typically with paper-and-pencil or computer-based instruments (Ryan and Tippins 2004). These tests have good validity and are powerful predictors of job performance, which increases with job complexity (Bartram 2004). For example, in selection for management jobs, it has been found that mental ability measures, such as verbal reasoning, numerical ability, numerical reasoning and visual speed and accuracy, significantly distinguished the top from the middle manager group (Cascio and Aguinis 2011: 286).

Computer-based and online cognitive ability tests are often based on the *computer-adaptive testing* (CAT) principles. In this case, all candidates taking the test are first presented with a set of questions of average difficulty and, if the answers are correct, the system presents them with items with a higher level of difficulty. Similarly, if the answers are not correct, the system displays questions with a lower level of difficulty. This adaptive technology is clearly superior to the paper-and-pencil-based instruments in the assessment situation (Olson-Buchanan 2002). Potentially, there are other advantages of using digital cognitive ability tests. Primarily, the administration of testing can be easier, as there is little human bias in test proctoring – all candidates receive similar instructions on the screen. In addition, the results of testing are automatically recorded, thus reducing the burden of manual registration and the occurrence of data entry errors. Second, individuals can access the test from a remote location and thus represent a geographically wider pool of applicants. Third, computers can accommodate special needs of applicants with disabilities. Finally, evidence suggests that web-based testing does not aggravate adverse impact (ibid.).

On the other hand, paper- and computer-based tests may not be equivalent when it comes to results; however, the research on this is inconsistent. Many factors may play a role here (e.g., reading speed on computer can be slower than reading on paper, especially for senior candidates). Also, hardware and Internet technology affect the speed and accuracy of testing (Johnson and Guetal 2013).

Knowledge and skill tests

Job knowledge tests are used to measure candidates' knowledge, often technical, that is required by a job. They can be administered in various forms, such as an essay, questionnaire, test or assignment. In job simulations, candidates are measured on their abilities and skills through tasks similar to those performed on the job. In some *high-fidelity tests*, realistic scenarios and often expensive equipment are used. Candidates can also be required to perform work samples – observable work tasks or job-related behaviours – that can predict future job success. They are most useful for jobs and work tasks that can be completed in a short period of time.

Personality tests

Personality tests or personality inventories are used for the evaluation of candidates' behaviour, attitudes and beliefs. Research by Bartram et al. (1995) and Coyne and Bartram (2000) found that many employers, especially small organizations, put a greater emphasis on personal characteristics of the candidates. Honesty, integrity, interest in the job, conscientiousness and the 'right general personality' are often regarded as more important than qualifications, experience or training – skills and knowledge can be acquired on the job, but the employee's attitude, honesty and way of dealing with other people are viewed as characteristics that are difficult to change (Bartram 2004).

When testing personality, most often candidates are assessed on the 'Big Five' personality traits that are consistently related to job performance (Bartram 2004). These are *openness, agreeableness, extraversion, conscientiousness* and *neuroticism*. In particular, measures of agreeableness, conscientiousness and openness to experience appear to be related to performance in a wide range of jobs (Judge et al. 1999). For example, openness predicts creativity and expatriate performance, extraversion predicts salesperson performance and agreeableness predicts performance in jobs involving teamwork. Conscientiousness and neuroticism predict performance in most occupations.

When deploying an online personality test, it is important not to assume that it is always equivalent to its paper-and-pencil version. For example, there is evidence of differing response patterns between ethnic groups and differing patterns of socially desirable responses across methods (Johnson and Guetal 2013). A study by Ployhart et al. (2003) examined the equivalence of computerized and paper measures of conscientiousness, agreeableness and emotional stability (i.e., neuroticism). The results of their study indicated that the mean scores of applicants on all three variables were higher for the paper than the computerized measures. Likewise, the variances for conscientiousness and emotional stability were greater for the computerized than the paper measures. However, the internal consistency reliability estimates were greater for the computerized than the paper measures. Nonetheless, many other studies confirm the equivalence of measurements of paper- and computer-based personality inventories (Stone et al. 2013), which suggests that when used consistently, computerized personality tests are quite reliable.

Integrity and situational judgement tests

Integrity tests use multiple choice or true/false questions to measure candidates' attitudes about their trustworthiness, honesty, moral character and reliability. They are highly valid for predicting more generally counterproductive behaviours, including absenteeism and disciplinary problems. Integrity tests are relatively inexpensive and can be administered at any time during the hiring process.

Situational judgment tests (SJT) measure a variety of non-cognitive skills by presenting individuals with short scenarios that can be in written or video format and asking what their most likely response would be or what they see as the most effective response (Ryan and Tippins 2004). Research by Ployhart et al. (2003) found that there may be some advantages in using computerized SJTs, as the SJT in the study produced higher internal consistency reliability estimates, showed more variability and had higher relations with other measures compared with its paper-and-pencil equivalent. However, computer-based SJTs may have different response patterns between ethnic groups (Johnson and Guetal 2013).

Contingent methods

Contingent assessments are often the final step in the selection process. They are conducted for checking candidates on a number of criteria that are not directly related to their knowledge, skills and abilities. The most common contingent assessments include a reference check, drug test and medical exam.

Table 11.2 Key steps, processes and considerations in e-selection

Steps	Processes	Considerations
General: – Validity, costs, usability, appropriateness and adverse impact – Equivalency between paper-and-pencil and computer-based tests – Risk of cheating – Adherence to anti-discrimination laws and regulations		
A. Screening methods	Automated keyword searches	Keywords to be job-related
	Weighted application forms/online application forms	Administrative factors affecting effectiveness
	Telephone screens	Interactive voice response (IVR)
	Realistic job previews	– Facilitating self-selection – 'Vaccination' against unpleasant job features
B. Evaluation methods	Applicant interviews (Face-to-face vs. online/telephone/video interviews)	– High validity of structured interviews – Impact of interview modes on candidate ratings
	Cognitive ability tests	– Computer-adaptive testing (CAT) principles – Equivalency between paper-and-pencil and computer-based tests
	Knowledge and skill tests	– Job simulations – High-fidelity tests – Work samples
	Personality tests	– High validity of 'Big Five' personality traits – Impact of culture/ethnicity – Equivalency between paper- and computer-based tests
	Integrity and situational judgement tests (SJT)	Likely impact of ethnicity
	Contingent methods: Reference checks, drug tests, medical exams	Impact of social media/online information posted by applicants on selection
C. Selection	Decision support system (DSS)	– System design – Assessment results
D. Evaluation of e-R&S	Quality of hire	– On-the-job performance – Retention rate – Performance appraisal score
	Assessing validity of performance predictors	Relevant metrics
	Adverse impact analysis	Validation of selection procedures

Source: Authors.

Recruiters are increasingly using Internet data mining and SNSs for background checks and even the evaluation of candidates. According to a survey of more than 2,000 full-time, US hiring and human resources managers conducted by Harris Poll, 52% of employers use SNSs to research job candidates, and 35% of employers are less likely to interview applicants who they cannot find online (CareerBuilder 2015). Candidates' online information can either help or hurt their odds of being selected for a job. According to the responses, the most damaging content for candidates was provocative or inappropriate photographs (46%), information about candidates drinking or using drugs (40%), candidates bad-mouthing their previous company or fellow employee (34%), poor communication skills (30%) and discriminatory comments related to race, religion, gender and so on (29%). Therefore, one can assume that SNSs will be increasingly used in the future for background checks and the evaluation of candidates.

(C) Selection of candidates

Choosing the best candidates

The last step of the selection process is about making the crucial decision regarding which candidate should be hired, where recruiters or hiring managers combine candidates' scores on different assessments and make the final decision. An e-recruitment or e-selection decision support system can assist hiring decisions by accumulating information about each of the evaluation criteria and candidate performances in relation to them during the entire selection process. Moreover, decision makers have access to this information at any stage of the selection process. The use of e-selection-based decision support systems helps employers make more valid inferences about candidates (Stone et al. 2013).

(D) Evaluation of the recruitment and selection system

The last step in the selection process is about evaluating the effectiveness of the selection system, assessing the validity of predictors and conducting adverse impact analyses. A survey by SHRM (2016b) found that only approximately 23% of companies in the USA measure quality of hire when evaluating their recruitment and selection systems. The most used metrics include on-the-job performance, as measured by the hiring manager, retention rate and performance appraisal score.

Contemporary ATSs that also contain assessment and selection information can assist hiring managers to assess the validity of performance predictors and conduct adverse impact analyses. They can also be used to generate the necessary reports for governmental agencies and other stakeholders. Table 11.2 summarizes the key steps, processes and considerations at each stage of the e-selection process as discussed above.

Opportunities and challenges with e-recruitment and e-selection

A technology-enabled R&S process provides numerous *advantages*.

1. It enables the automation of a number of routine tasks that can reduce the administrative burden for HR professionals and can consequently reduce the costs of hiring.
2. It can improve the overall experience of the application process and assessment procedures when the process is tailored to and caters for the desired segment of potential applicants.
3. It can provide a broader geographical coverage, allowing highly qualified applicants from remote locations to apply for vacancies and offering these applicants an evaluation with the use of various online tools.
4. It allows time- and space-independent interaction and communication with applicants, candidates and between recruiters.

Thus, ICTs provide endless possibilities for designing and implementing various e-recruitment and e-selection practices, and new HR technological solutions appear on the market almost daily. Nevertheless, technology is only a tool to assist HR professionals and hiring managers in achieving their organization's staffing objectives. Most HR systems require human intervention and cannot substitute HRM competencies. Some of the *opportunities and challenges* in this regard are explained in the following sections.

New skill and competency demands on the digitized HR profession

In Chapter 5, we learnt the importance of 'big data literacy' to be able to strategically harness the big data potential. Similarly, Chapter 6 emphasized the critical need for 'analytic competencies' to be developed either in-house as a specialism or borrowed from outside the organization to undertake complex and pragmatic prescriptive analytics. HR professionals and hiring managers face a daunting task of mastering sophisticated e-HRM systems as well, often referred to as HR information systems (HRISs). e-HRM system facilitation ranges from simple advertisement text templates to advanced analytics concerning former candidate performance and predictions of future performance in the pool of potential candidates.

For example, while producing a standard job advertisement has become a routinized task facilitated by a text template and a set of commands for the further distribution of the advertisement, business intelligence modules give hiring organizations the opportunity to track and examine how many impressions the advertisement receives on the corporation's website, on specific job boards and in social networking sites such as LinkedIn. Additionally, a business intelligence module can provide an opportunity to encourage existing employees to share the advertisement or make a referral. These ample ICT-enabled choices and opportunities for fine-tuning digitalized recruitment and selection processes constantly require new skills from an HR professional.

Mobile and smart technologies

Smartphones provide a newer avenue for recruiting activities. The growing use of mobile phones has caught the attention of technology vendors and resulted in new mobile-enabled recruiter services, often referred to as m-recruitment. There are a number of ways in which organizations can integrate m-recruitment. First, mobile devices can be used for recruiting on social media and engaging with jobseekers. Second, employers can implement mobile-rendered career pages that change based on the type of screen and resolution of the device on which the website is viewed. Third, employers, job boards, social networking sites and other recruitment industry players can offer mobile apps for jobseekers (Miller-Merrell 2013). For example, in 2013, LinkedIn launched a dedicated app for mobile recruitment named Recruiter Mobile. Customers of the LinkedIn Recruiter package have the option of allowing LinkedIn users to apply for an open job position by clicking on an 'Apply' button in the smartphone app.

The pervasive use of smartphones has also created a new opportunity for recruiters to communicate with applicants through mobile apps. By utilizing a mobile platform, recruiters become able to reach and communicate with candidates not only faster but perhaps, more importantly, in a way that matches the candidate's expectation of an attractive future employer. For example, reports from tech vendors such as Google point to mobile devices as the preferred means of communication in generation Z (Google Inc. 2017).

From within the professional HRM industry institutions, recruiters are thus encouraged to use smartphone applications in order to streamline the recruitment and selection of candidates (SHRM 2016c).

Although m-recruitment is not entirely new, there are some indications that organizations do not utilize the full potential of m-recruitment technologies. According to some estimates, just 3% of Fortune 500 companies offer a way to apply for jobs from a smartphone and only 33% have optimized their career sites for viewing on the small screen of a phone (Weber 2013). Therefore, the full potential of m-recruitment technologies is yet to be utilized.

Equivalency of digital testing tools

One of the main challenges for using technology for candidate assessment is that organizations focus increasingly on identifying candidates with a set of desired general competencies rather than specific skills. This makes it more challenging to design and implement computerized assessment tools, as the desired competences can vary significantly across recruiting organizations. Also, various research contributions have shown that one cannot always assume equivalency between digital and analogue modes of assessing candidates. Therefore, organizations should always consider what technology to use when assessing candidates and designing assessment tools to minimize the potential negative aspects of digital approaches. However, as time passes, candidates are beginning to prefer online testing to the paper-and-pencil mode, mainly due to the flexibility, quicker feedback and perceived relevance (Johnson and Guetal 2013). In addition, candidates view online testing designed for specific jobs as being more relevant and valid because the tests resemble the tasks and assignments they might be completing if hired.

Gamification

As elaborated in Chapter 9, gamification within the human resource management field has been successfully applied to four major areas, namely recruitment, selection, training and performance management (Armstrong et al. 2016). In the recruitment context, potential applicants can learn about the hiring organization by engaging themselves in games online and can thereby decide whether to apply for a vacant position. Through employee referral schemes and programmes, existing employees can engage potential applicants in game-enabled competitions and thus motivate jobseekers to either apply or accept a job offer if they are selected. Additionally, gamification can also function as a tool for self-assessment (Laumer et al. 2012) and job-specific games can provide a realistic job preview. An example of the latter is the game 'America's Army', developed and used by the US Army for recruitment purposes, especially targeted at young Americans.

Within selection, gamification can likewise help to identify the best applicants by engaging them in situations in which they can demonstrate their competences for the position in question. Due to the mediating dimension, the gamification in itself may minimize negative reactions to assessment procedures and maximize the perception of assessment fairness (Armstrong 2006). The improvement of assessment by gamification may also be obtained because game-like situations elicit job-relevant behaviour more readily than it is possible with traditional questionnaires. The gamification of recruitment and selection is thus an opportunity to increase organizational attractiveness and achieve a better PE fit of the candidates.

Data protection issues

HR professionals also face the issue of cybersecurity and data protection in implementing and operating various HR systems in general and e-recruitment and e-selection systems in particular. In addition, significant implications for the overall practice of HR derive from the application of the European Community Data Protection Directive and regulation that applies from 25 May 2018. As stated by the European Commission, 'the objective of this new set of rules is to give citizens back control over their personal data, and to simplify the regulatory environment for business' (European Commission 2017). However logical this statement may sound, organizations find it to be an overwhelming task to adjust their data management practices to the new data protection rules. The EU's Data Protection Directive also foresees specific rules for the transfer of personal data outside the EU, which has direct implications for moving data to or from an EU-based system as well as when the data just passes through a server in one of the EU member states. As noted by Sale (2006), this is still an uncertain and developing area of practice with many regulatory and legal bumps ahead (Bu-Pasha 2017). You can find more information about information security and privacy issues in Chapter 15.

Summary

The recruitment and selection of employees is a vital organizational function and involves practices and activities carried out by an organization for the primary purpose of identifying, attracting, assessing, selecting and influencing the job choices of competent candidates who will fit the job environment. It is a business process that starts with the setting of hiring objectives and proceeds with the tasks of the identification and attraction of the required applicants, the pre-selection of candidates and then the assessment and selection of candidates to hire. When carried out with the use of ICTs, the tasks and their subtasks can be performed concurrently.

ICTs have eased, enriched and made the R&S process more complex. Recruiters must master new digital skills to operate e-recruitment systems and must be able to communicate the organizational characteristics through multiple digital channels. This is because corporate career websites, job portals and social networking sites have become the main recruitment sources for most professions. The screening of applicants is increasingly performed with the help of automation and artificial intelligence. Moreover, a lot of communication with applicants and candidates takes place in cyberspace, and smart phones are becoming the preferred channel of interaction by younger jobseekers. Furthermore, many assessment tools are computerized, allowing the time-and-space-independent assessment of candidates – although not being equivalent to paper-and-pencil testing.

ICTs are constantly evolving, providing additional opportunities and challenges for the recruitment profession. When adopting innovative technologies, however, the main objective should not be to attract as many applicants as possible but to identify the strongest applicants, attract them to the organization and convert them effectively to new hires – and doing it better and faster than competitors.

Case study: Hiring at XYZ

XYZ is a tech company engaged in the development of online IT solutions. The company was founded in 1998 by three IT developers who started their business by offering creative designs of corporate web pages. The business quickly became a success and grew significantly over the next ten years. Today, XYZ has approximately 200 employees. Most employees have a background in IT development, multimedia and graphic design. Typically, they were sourced by the founders through their professional networks without any job advertising. In the early days, interesting candidates would be invited for an interview with all three owners, who subsequently made a joint decision on who to hire.

With the current size of the company, the owners have realized that they can no longer use this attraction and assessment approach. They have furthermore become aware that there is a need to have broader employee profiles if they are to move forward with their growth strategy. One of the reasons is the fast pace of technology development that makes it necessary to hire IT engineers with the very best technical competencies that exist in the labour market. Another reason is the strong company culture, which is characterized by a flat management structure, good interdisciplinary and cross-organizational cooperation with considerable flexibility for the employees to perform their work. Moreover, employees are actively involved in the company's social activities and organize and participate in joint excursions, team-building events and staff parties. Many also actively participate and represent the company at various local sporting events.

Case study questions

As XYZ staffing manager, you have been asked to develop and present a new, technology-based recruitment and selection process at XYZ.

- Explain the key steps, processes and considerations in your proposed e-recruitment policy.
- Explain the key steps, processes and considerations in your proposed e-selection policy.

Debate: 'Is social media a good recruitment source?'

Introduction

The survey of hiring managers and human resource professionals conducted by Harris Poll in 2015 found that 52% of employers use social media (SM) to research job candidates (CareerBuilder 2015). Moreover, 32% of respondents indicated that the information found on SM caused them to hire a candidate. The main reasons listed were as follows:

- the candidate's background information supported job qualifications (42%);
- the candidate's personality came across as a good fit with the company culture (38%)
- the candidate's site conveyed a professional image (38%);
- the candidate had great communication skills (37%); and
- the candidate was creative (36%).

However, some research studies indicate that recruiter ratings of candidates based on SM profiles are generally unrelated to candidates' subsequent job performance, turnover intentions and turnover (Van Iddekinge et al. 2016). In addition, the study by Van Iddekinge et al. (2016) discovered that Facebook ratings tend to be higher for females than for males, and, in several instances, higher for White individuals than for Black and Hispanic individuals.

Arguments in favour

- SM allow the creation of a huge and inexpensive database of potential candidates, who can be sorted geographically, professionally and on the level of a specific competency.
- SM provide information about candidates that is readily available for evaluation without the physical presence of a candidate, which saves time and money for a hiring organization.
- With organizations increasingly struggling to find qualified candidates, SM can be an effective tool to find, screen and contact passive jobseekers (SHRM 2016c).
- SM can be used to screen applicants for substance abuse, arrests, poor morale and related problems at work, such as low conscientiousness or lack of integrity.
- SM information could be used to assess personality. For example, the number of 'friends' in a candidate's social network, and the comments these friends post about the candidate, may indicate traits such as agreeableness and extraversion. The creativity with which candidates arrange their SM profile, and the types of activities and quotes they post, may reflect their openness to experience (Van Iddekinge et al. 2016).
- Millennials account for around 35% of the workforce in the USA, according to the US Bureau of Labor Statistics. They will account for 75% of the global workforce by 2025. This group of employees communicates actively via SM sites and connected devices and will continue doing so in the future (Segal 2014).

Arguments against

- SM can give recruiters inaccurate information about individuals/applicants, as the SM content may be limited to specific interests, geography and professional or personal activities (Rao 2011).
- SM can give recruiters irrelevant information that can cloud their judgement (Rao 2011).
- SM may provide information that is either prohibited to use or must be limited in recruitment due to, for instance, equal opportunity employment laws. For example, recruiters may discover, and find difficult to ignore, information concerning candidates' demographic characteristics, physical disabilities, religious beliefs, marital status or sexual orientation (Van Iddekinge et al. 2016, Segal 2014).
- In the USA and some other countries, asking a candidate or employee SM passwords can violate international, federal or national laws. For this reason, recruiters are only allowed to look at content that is public and most likely not representative of the individual in question.

Video learning resources

- Understanding an applicant tracking system: www.youtube.com/watch?v=avvaecomss4
- Apple's employee recruiting video: www.youtube.com/watch?v=x9sk052cf3c
- Facebook recruiting video: www.youtube.com/watch?v=GBmHv84NM5o
- How corporate recruiters use Google to find candidates: www.youtube.com/watch?v=49XOAIqiHOc
- Online recruitment problems: www.youtube.com/watch?v=bvsqqxYwhaw
- Navigating the recruiter dashboard in SAP e-recruiting: www.youtube.com/watch?v=VXKW6erq0Gs

References

Aggerholm, H. K. and Andersen, S. E. (2017) *Social Media Recruitment 3.0: Creative Strategies and Beyond in Strategic Recruitment Communication*. Aarhus University.

Allen, D. G., Mahto, R. V. and Otondo, R. F. (2007) Web-based recruitment: Effects of information, organizational brand, and attitudes toward a web site on applicant attraction. *Journal of Applied Psychology*, 92(6), 1696–1708.

Armstrong, M. (2006) *A Handbook of Human Resource Management Practice*. London: Kogan Page.

Armstrong, M. B., Landers, R. N. and Collmus, A. B. (2016) Gamifying recruitment, selection, training, and performance management: Game-thinking in human resource management. In: Gangadharbatla, H. and Davis, D. Z. eds. *Emerging Research and Trends in Gamification*. Hershey, PA: IGI Global, 140–165.

Backhaus, K. and Tikoo, S. (2004) Conceptualizing and researching employer branding. *Career Development International*, 9(5), 501–517.

Barber, A. E. (1998) *Recruiting Employees*. Thousand Oaks, CA: Sage.

Bartram, D. (2004) Assessment in organisations. *Applied Psychology*, 53(2), 237–259.

Bartram, D., Lindley, P. A., Foster, J. and Marshall, L. (1995) The selection of young people by small businesses. *British Journal of Occupational and Organizational Psychology*, 68, 339–358.

Bates, R. (2017) Recruitment. I'm too busy to hire. My mobile ATS is my only solace [online]. https://resources.workable.com/blog/mobile-ATS (Accessed 23 December 2017).

Breaugh, J. A. (2008) Employee recruitment: Current knowledge and important areas for future research. *Human Resource Management Review*, 18(3), 103–118.

Breaugh, J. A. (2009) *Recruiting and Attracting Talent: A Guide to Understanding and Managing the Recruitment Process*. Alexandria, VA. Society for Human Resource Management.

Brown, V. R. and Vaughn, E. D. (2011) The writing on the (Facebook) wall: The use of social networking sites in hiring decisions. *Journal of Business and Psychology*, 26(2), 219–225.

Bu-Pasha, S. (2017) Cross-border issues under EU data protection law with regards to personal data protection. *Information & Communications Technology Law*, 26(3), 213–228.

CareerBuilder (2015) *35 percent of employers less likely to interview applicants they can't find online, according to annual CareerBuilder social media recruitment survey* [online]. www.careerbuilder.ca/share/aboutus/pressreleasesdetail.aspx?sd=5%2f14%2f2015&siteid=cbpr&sc_cmp1=cb_pr893_&id=pr893&ed=12%2f31%2f2015 (Accessed 22 December 2017).

Cascio, W. F. and Aguinis, H. (2011) *Applied Psychology in Human Resource Management*. 7th ed. Upper Saddle River, NJ: Pearson.

Cervellon, M. and Lirio, P. (2017) When employees don't 'like' their employers on social media. *MIT Sloan Management Review*, 58(2), 63–70.

CIPD and HAYS (2017) *Resourcing and Talent Planning: Survey Report 2017*. London: Chartered Institute of Personnel and Development.

Cober, R. T., Brown, D. J. and Levy, P. E. (2004) Form, content, and function: An evaluative methodology for corporate employment web sites. *Human Resource Management*, 43(2–3), 201–218.

Cober, R. T., Brown, D. J., Levy, P. E., Cober, A. B. and Keeping, L. M. (2003) Organizational web sites: Website content and style as determinants of organizational attraction. *International Journal of Selection and Assessment*, 11(2–3), 158–169.

Coyne, I. and Bartram, D. (2000) Personnel managers' perceptions of dishonesty in the workplace. *Human Resource Management Journal*, 10(3), 38–45.

Davenport, T. H. and Short, J. E. (1990) The new industrial engineering: Information technology and business process redesign. *Sloan Management Review*, 31(4), 11–27.

EEOC (2010) *Employment tests and selection procedures* [online]. Washington, DC: The US Equal Employment Opportunity Commission. www.eeoc.gov/policy/docs/factemployment_procedures.html (Accessed 12 November 2017).

European Commission (2017) *Protection of personal data* [online]. Brussels: DG Justice and Consumers. https://ec.europa.eu/info/law/law-topic/data-protection_en (Accessed 15 November 2017).

Google Inc. (2017) *Generation Z. New insights into the mobile-first mindset of teens* [online]. https://storage.googleapis.com/think/docs/GenZ_Insights_All_teens.pdf (Accessed 22 November 2017).

Guest, D. E. (1997) Human resource management and performance: a review and research agenda. *International Journal of Human Resource Management*, 8(3), 263–276.

Holm, A. B. (2012) E-recruitment: Towards an ubiquitous recruitment process and candidate relationship management. *Zeitschrift fuer Personalforschung*, 26(3), 241–259.

ITC (2005) *ITC Guidelines on Computer-Based and Internet Delivered Testing*. Brussels: International Test Commission.

Johnson, R. D. and Guetal, H. (2013) Research-based tips for increasing the effectiveness of e-selection: Part I. *Workforce Solutions Review*, 4(5), 4–7.

Judge, T. A., Higgins, C. A., Thoresen, C. J. and Barrick, M. R. (1999) The big five personality traits, general mental ability, and career success across the life span. *Personnel Psychology*, 52(3), 621–652.

Kristof-Brown, A. and Guay, R. P. (2011) Person–environment fit. In: Zedeck, S. ed. *APA Handbook of Industrial and Organizational Psychology*. Washington, DC: American Psychological Association, 3–50.

Kristof-Brown, A. L., Reeves, C. J. and Follmer, E. H. (2014) The goldilocks pursuit during organizational entry: Applicants' and recruiters' search for the 'perfect fit'. In: Yu, K. Y. T. and Cable, D. M. eds. *The Oxford Handbook of Recruitment*. New York, NY: Oxford University Press, 437–453.

Laumer, S., Eckhardt, A. and Weitzel, T. (2012) Online gaming to find a new job – examining job seekers' intention to use serious games as a self-assessment tool. *Zeitschrift für Personalforschung*, 26(3), 218–240.

Lievens, F. (2007) Employer branding in the Belgian Army: The importance of instrumental and symbolic beliefs for potential applicants, actual applicants, and military employees. *Human Resource Management*, 46(1), 51–69.

Liviens, F. and Chapman, D. (2010) Recruitment and selection. In: Bacon, N. A., et al. eds. *The Sage Handbook of Human Resource Management*. London: Sage, 133–154.

Miller-Merrell, J. (2013) *25 companies using mobile hiring apps to recruit* [online]. Available from: https://blog.shrm.org/blog/25-companies-using-mobile-hiring-apps-to-recruit (Accessed 25 April 2017).

Millmore, M., Lewis, P., Saunders, M., Thornhill, A. and Morrow, T. (2007) *Strategic Human Resource Management: Contemporary Issues*. Harlow: Pearson Education Ltd.

O'Hear, S. (2016) *Ontame.io wants to be 'Google Analytics' for recruiters* [online]. TechCrunch. https://techcrunch.com/2016/09/13/ontame-io/ (Accessed 2 November 2017).

Olson-Buchanan, J. B. (2002) Computer-based advancements in assessment. In: Drasgow, F. and Schmitt, N. eds. *Measuring and Analysing Behaviour in Organizations*. San Francisco, CA: Jossey-Bass, 44–87.

Ostroff, C. and Zhan, Y. (2012) Person-environment fit in the selection process. In: Schmitt, N. ed. *The Oxford Handbook of Personnel Assessment and Selection*. Oxford: Oxford University Press, 252–273.

Phillips, J. M. and Gully, S. M. (2015) *Strategic Staffing, Global Edition*. Harlow: Pearson Education Limited.

Ployhart, R. E., Schneider, B. and Schmitt, N. (2006) *Staffing Organizations: Contemporary Practice and Theory*. 3rd ed. Mahwah, NJ: Lawrence Erlbaum Associates, Publishers.

Ployhart, R. E., Weekley, J. A., Holtz, B. C. and Kemp, C. (2003) Web-based and paper-and-pencil testing of applicants in a proctored setting: Are personality, biodata, and situational judgment tests comparable? *Personnel Psychology*, 56, 733–752.

Rao, P. (2011) Are social networking sites good recruitment sources? In: Rao, P., *Taking Sides: Clashing Views in Human Resource Management*. New York, NY: McGraw Hill.

Reiter-Palmon, R., Brown, M. H., Sandall, D. L., Buboltz, C. and Nimps, T. (2006) Development of an O★NET web-based job analysis and its implementation in the U.S. Navy: Lessons learned. *Human Resource Management Review*, 16, 294–309.

Roth, P. L., Bobko, P., Van Iddekinge, C. H. and Thatcher, J. B. (2013) Social media in employee-selection-related decisions: A research agenda for uncharted territory. *Journal of Management*, 42(1), 269–298.

Ryan, A. M. and Tippins, N. T. (2004) Attracting and selecting: What psychological research tells us. *Human Resource Management*, 43(4), 305–318.

Sale, R. (2006) International guidelines on computer-based and internet-delivered testing: A practitioner's perspective. *International Journal of Testing*, 6(2), 181–188.

Segal, J. A. (2014) *LEGAL TRENDS Social media use in hiring: Assessing the risks* [online]. SHRM. www.shrm.org/hr-today/news/hr-magazine/pages/0914-social-media-hiring.aspx (Accessed 24 December 2017).

SHRM (2014) *Three-Fourths of HR Professionals Use Job Analysis Data for Recruitment, New SHRM Survey Finds*. Alexandria, VA: Society for Human Resource Management.

SHRM (2016a) *Talent Acquisition: Recruitment*. Alexandria, VA: Society for Human Resource Management.

SHRM (2016b) *Talent Acquisition: Selection*. Alexandria, VA: Society for Human Resource Management.

SHRM (2016c) *Using Social Media for Talent Acquisition – Recruitment and Screening*. Alexandria, VA: Society for Human Resource Management.

SHRM and ACT (2014) *SHRM Survey Findings: Job Analysis Activities*. Alexandria, VA: Society for Human Resource Management.

Stone, D. L., Lukaszewski, K. M., Stone-Romero, E. F. and Johnson, T. L. (2013) Factors affecting the effectiveness and acceptance of electronic selection systems. *Human Resource Management Review*, 23(1), 50–70.

Suszko, M. K. and Breaugh, J. A. (1986) The effects of realistic job previews on applicant self-selection and employee turnover, satisfaction, and coping ability. *Journal of Management*, 12(4), 513–523.

Van Iddekinge, C. H., Lanivich, S. E., Roth, P. L. and Junco, E. (2016) Social media for selection? Validity and adverse impact potential of a Facebook-based assessment. *Journal of Management*, 42(7), 1811–1835.

Wanous, J. P. (1980) *Organizational Entry: Recruitment, Selection, and Socialization of Newcomers*. Boston, MA: Addison-Wesley.

Weber, L. (2013) *McDonald's Caters to job-seekers on the go* [online]. https://blogs.wsj.com/atwork/2013/03/25/mcdonalds-caters-to-job-seekers-on-the-go/ (Accessed 1 December 2017).

Yang, Y., Callegaro, M., Bhola, D. and Dillman, D. (2011) IVR and web administration in structured interviews utilizing rating scales: Exploring the role of motivation as moderator to mode effects. *International Journal of Social Research Methodology*, 14, 1–15.

12 e-Performance and reward management

Kent V. Rondeau

> **Learning objectives**
> - Provide an overview of performance assessment and reward systems, particularly in terms of purposes, attributes, and design principles
> - Describe the general attributes of e-performance and reward management systems and their overall effectiveness
> - Outline the adoption factors for e-performance and reward management applications
> - Evaluate the critical success factors for e-performance and reward management

Introduction

Outlining the seven deadly sins of performance management, Melanie O'Connor, an HRM consultant from Australia says,

> Performance management is hugely challenging. I think of it as being a really powerful tool ... to my mind it's the lynchpin, the missing link that can transform the vision and mission statement into action - if it's done well. If it's done badly – and so many are – it's like any power tool and can rip off legs and arms and mangle bodies.
>
> (WorkplaceInfo, 2002)

O'Connor's views above resonate with academic scholars and practitioners and highlight the potential and pitfalls of performance management. Employees are a significant investment for organizations as they are a major contributor to organizational effectiveness (Pfeffer, 1998). In order to compete successfully in the market, organizations are investing in ways to improve employee performance. Human resource management (HRM) practices play a seminal role in enhancing employee performance (Pauwe, Guest, & Wright, 2013). Of all HRM practices, the employee appraisal and reward process is seen as essential for improving individual, team, and organizational performance, yet a poorly designed approach accounts for a large degree of employee dissatisfaction in terms of its perceived fairness and accuracy (Thurston & McNall, 2010). Dissatisfaction with the performance assessment process can be linked to a variety of adverse employee and group outcomes including lower job satisfaction, diminished morale, and organizational commitment, as well as increases in absenteeism, grievances, and turnover intentions (Harrington & Lee, 2015).

Traditional employee performance appraisal is the process by which the performance of individual employees is evaluated over time. Performance management goes beyond performance appraisal in that it is typically understood as "encompassing all the activities a firm undertakes to improve employee's performance, beginning with the evaluation of performance and subsequent feedback to the employee, and continuing through training and administration of rewards" (DeNisi & Smith, 2014, p. 131). Performance (and rewards) management can be seen as a complex system in which managers help their employees to set expectations, measure and review results, and reward performance with a view to improve organizational success. Performance management thus has consequences for individuals as well as organizations, but its overall success is heavily dependent on the way that it is designed and implemented.

In this chapter, students will get an overview of performance assessment and reward systems and learn about managing the complexity and contradictions in e-performance management and e-compensation design and implementation. They will be introduced to the general attributes of e-performance management and reward systems and will learn about their overall effectiveness, including their potential to motivate employees to improve their overall performance. Readers will be made aware of some of the problems and pitfalls associated with moving from traditional "pen-and-paper" forms of appraising and rewarding employee performance to automated self-service, web-based applications. Future directions, developments, and challenges for e-performance management and e-compensation will be elucidated.

An overview of performance and reward management

Employee performance appraisal is a long-standing ubiquitous *administrative practice* (Claus & Briscoe, 2009). The terms "performance management" and "performance appraisal" are often used interchangeably, yet appraisal is generally understood as more narrowly conceived (Furnham, 2004). Performance appraisal is that part of the performance management process in which an employee's contribution to the organization during a specified time period is assessed. Performance feedback lets employees know how well they have performed with respect to the standards of the organization and with respect to the performance of others (Mohrman, Resnick-West, & Lawler, 1989).

Performance assessment is a *mechanism to reinforce organizational values, norms, and culture*. It plays an important role in ensuring that employees pursue goals and strategies that the organization desires or requires. For instance, if the strategy is service excellence and this has been clearly defined in the performance assessments, employees are more likely to pursue actions that enhance service quality. Conversely, if the focus is on cost control, employees will seek ways to manage cost and may subsequently be recognized and rewarded when operational efficiencies are improved. Performance assessment becomes a means of establishing whether employee behavior is consistent with the overall strategy, yet it also makes visible any negative consequence in the strategy-behavior link. For instance, a single-minded approach to cost reduction may include potential negative consequences such as decreased quality and cooperation. Performance appraisal is thus an important mechanism by which organizations can review the strategy-behavior link (DeNisi & Pritchard, 2006).

Performance management is the integration of performance appraisal systems with broader HRM applications that effectively aligns employee work behaviors with organizational goals. It is a *dynamic and iterative process* that is designed to enhance employee capability and organizational productivity. Performance management serves many purposes, including *developmental uses* such as employee goal-setting and for identifying training needs, as well as *administrative uses* such as determining merit pay allocations and promotions, as well as for identifying performance laggards and for the documentation requirements that address potential future legal challenges. While some performance assessments are *"trait-based"* and focus on the personal characteristics of those being evaluated, a more appropriate focus is to make appraisals *"behavior-based"* that assesses the frequency and magnitude of performance-related behaviors or *"results-based"* that focuses on the attainment of desired outcomes (Latham & Wexley, 1982).

Purposes. While there is no one best way to assess and manage performance, most systems of performance management are designed to achieve four goals (Stone, Stone-Romero, & Lukaszewski, 2006, p. 237).

- First, performance needs to be defined in such a way that it *supports and advances the organization's strategic goals*. Setting clear and motivating goals for individual employees and groups of employees is a key component of performance management.
- Second, the appraisal process must be *clearly defined and consistently applied* across the organization. While there are many ways that employee performance can be appraised, the adopted system needs to work within the context of a particular organization and be aligned with its operating characteristics, including its culture and strategy.
- Third, performance measurement must bring together multiple types of performance assessments into a *unified framework*. In this way, performance can be measured often and the information obtained can be tracked over time.
- Finally, to improve performance, employees need *feedback* on their performance, along with *guidance* in helping them reach a higher level of performance. Without frequent feedback, employees are unlikely to know that their behavior is not leading to the attainment of organizational goals.

An effective performance management system should also *align with an organization's human resource management system* (Delery & Roumpi, 2017; Pauwe, Guest, & Wright, 2013). There is a large body of accumulating evidence that "bundles" or "systems" of high performance work practices have the potential to impact a number of key organizational performance outcomes (Delery & Doty, 1996), including financial performance (Huselid, 1995). In an examination of means by which HR work practices affect both individual as well as firm-level outcomes, Jiang et al. (2012) examine the mediating mechanisms by which the attitudes and behaviors of individuals may be affected by certain HR practices, characterized as high performance work practices (Kehoe & Wright, 2013). By fostering a "climate for performance," the skills of individual employees are amplified through the influence of these HRM work practices that can lead to performance benefits realizable at the organizational-level.

DeNisi and Smith (2014), drawing on this work, describe a model of a performance management system predicated on *"skill-enhancing," "motivation-enhancing," and "opportunity-enhancing"* HR practices, which, when aligned with an organization's culture and strategy, are "bundled together in a way that is visible, salient, legitimate, relevant, consistent, instrumental, and fair [that] will enable and motivate employees to transform their generic KSAs (knowledge, skills and abilities) that are relevant to the performance of a specific firm" (p. 156).

Skill-enhancing high performance work practices such as selective hiring, extensive training, and teamwork can have an important impact on the ability of individuals to achieve higher levels of organizational performance. Motivational-enhancing practices such as pay-for-performance that increases employee motivation toward the pursuit of valued organizational objectives have been found to be effective (Peterson & Luthans, 2006), while opportunity or empowerment-enhancing practices refer to those HR practices that employees have at their disposal that are needed to complete job-related tasks as well as the discretion and authority to decide how to perform tasks. Opportunity-enhancing practices refer to those high performance work practices such as the open sharing of information ("open-book" management), the use of self-managing teams, and the reduction of status differences for members of a work group.

Attributes. Of course, discussions about the means by which organizations leverage individual-level attitudes and behaviors to produce group-level and organizational-level outcomes, requires a preliminary discussion about how performance, at whatever level of analysis, is to be defined and evaluated. The question of which type of performance to assess and how to measure it is shaped by four fundamental attributes of any performance measure: validity, reliability, bias-free assessment, and user acceptance.

Validity. In order for a performance assessment to be *valid*, it must measure important and appropriate characteristics of a job and be free from extraneous influences that do not align with desired the performance behavior or outcome. Fisher, Schoenfeldt, and Shaw (2006) contend that for a performance measure to be valid, it must be relevant, non-deficient, and uncontaminated. A relevant measure of job performance assesses only those aspects of performance that are important for determining job effectiveness. A non-deficient measure assesses all important aspects of job performance, while a measure is uncontaminated if it avoids assessing constructs other than performance. In order for a performance management system to be valid, a thorough job analysis must be conducted before developing performance measures so that all relevant aspects of performance are covered and irrelevant factors do not contaminate the assessment measure.

Reliability. It refers to the degree of concurrence when two or more raters agree on job performance. Inter-rater reliability is usually highest when performance raters come from the same level in the organization as there is more often disagreement between raters at different levels due to differences in "line-of-sight." Reliability may also be poor when performance factors are fixed as highly subjective constructs when more objective criteria are available, or when the rater does not have a good view of all of the relevant aspects of performance. Nevertheless, reliability over time may not be a significant problem given that job performance tends to fluctuate with effort or when remediation is required through training or disciplinary actions (Hofmann, Jacobs, & Gerras, 1992).

Bias-free assessment. Freedom from rater bias has two fundamental components: legal issues that prevent discrimination based on certain characteristics of the job incumbent and rater biases that refer to the subjective biases associated with assessing performance. In the first instance, a performance assessment is free from bias if it is fair (and seen to be fair) to all employees and indifferent to non-relevant personal factors that include race, gender, age, national origin, and disability status, among other factors. A performance management system may identify specific performance characteristics as long as they are "bona fides" (related to successful performance) and do not have an unjustifiable adverse impact on any protected group. Because all assessment systems require raters to make judgments about the performance of others, ratings may be intentionally or unintentionally biased.

Examples of common (unintentional) rating biases include the degree to which raters are either too harsh or too lenient in their assessments (the *leniency/severity effect*); the inability of raters to distinguish higher or lower levels of job performance (the *central tendency effect*); the temporal order in which evaluations are being conducted (*contrast effect*); and the tendency of raters to rely on a single performance characteristic when assessing job performance (the *halo/horns effect*).

User acceptance. When designing a performance management system, it is critical that it be accepted by those whose performance is being assessed if it is to have any potential to motivate (Singh, 2012).

Many organizations integrate their employee performance assessment process with compensation as the way to identify and then reward their high performers. While research suggests that pay is not always the best way to motivate for high performance, it remains a popular one by which organizations recognize individuals and groups for performance goal accomplishment (Rynes, Gerhart, & Minette, 2004). When integrated with the employee compensation function, an effective performance management (and reward) system needs to achieve two things. First, it should motivate employees to higher levels of performance. Second, it should have the potential to unambiguously translate employee performance standards to clear reward structures so that when individuals (or groups) reach certain performance targets they receive the reward.

Design principles and guidelines. Of course, when constructing a performance management system, it is essential that the benefits of its implementation outweigh the costs. A good performance management system must be understandable, easy to use, and must have a high degree of acceptance by all stakeholders. When designing a performance management system to enhance employee motivation and reward behavior or outcomes, McAfee and Champagne (1993) advanced several key guidelines.

- First, management must identify the critical competency areas, and discuss and negotiate with the employee to establish a viable action plan.
- Second, employee performance goals must be mutually developed and need to be specific, measurable, attainable, relevant, time-based, and sufficiently challenging.
- Third, as a product of implementing any performance management system, an organization needs to establish specific follow-up procedures to help managers ensure that employees are achieving their goals and provide them with the required training when they are unable to do so due to a skill deficiency.
- Finally, managers should be provided with background training to help them explain performance goals as well as the specific methodology used in the performance management system. Employee "buy-in" is essential and is compromised when managers are unable to defend a system in those instances when employees question its validity.

Consistent with these guidelines, Nankervis and Compton (2006) in their study of 961 Australian companies reiterated similar principles for the effective design and implementation of a performance management (and reward) system, while identifying others. Their list of key performance management system features includes: user friendliness; consistency of treatment; equity; transparency; a clear and unambiguous link between appraisal and merit allocation; human resource development opportunities; and coaching and succession planning applications.

DeNisi and Pritchard (2006), in their discussion of the use of performance management systems to meaningfully impact employee motivation, identified several features of a performance management system that strengthens the behavior-reward motivation link. Performance standards should be visible, understandable, agreed upon, and easily communicated. In addition, performance feedback requiring remedial actions and performance assessment for allocating rewards should be separate and distinct activities that constitute performance assessment. Frequent employee feedback should be reinforced through the consistent application of pre-established reward or remediation protocols.

While instructive, the ideal design features that ensure the overall effectiveness of any performance management (and reward) system provides the starting point for the design and implementation of its electronic human resource management application (Bondarouk & Ruël, 2009; Lednick-Hall & Moritz, 2003; Ruël, Bondarouk, & Van der Velde, 2007). The need to strongly integrate the performance management system with other key human resource functions (such as e-recruitment and selection, e-training and e-organizational learning, and e-compensation) provides the rationale to more firmly embrace and leverage information technology to accomplish this task (Bondarouk, Parry, & Furtmueller, 2017; Johnson & Gueutal, 2011). Building on our earlier discussion, we turn now toward a review of the attributes and characteristics of an effective e-performance management (and reward) system.

Role of technology in performance and reward management

At the heart of it, performance and rewards management focus on the nature of the basic exchange between employers and employees: employees provide performance in exchange for organizational rewards. The primary goal of a performance management system is to direct and influence employee behavior, ensuring that it strongly aligns with organizational goals. It also allows for the identification of employee competencies and characteristics that either lead to, or detract from, the accomplishment of higher levels of performance.

Drawing on the need to match employee knowledge, skills and aptitudes (KSAs) that leads to the accomplishment of organizational goals, Al-Raisi, Amin, and Tahir (2011) suggest that "an e-performance management system is a competency-based system that measures people not only on goal attainment but on the very competencies that are required for their role" (p. 20). An effective performance management system enables the organization to assess an employee's fitness to achieve success. One can quickly see if an incumbent has the "right" qualities (competencies) for the job, and can identify those who require training, coaching, and the development needed to succeed.

People vary with respect to their abilities, talents, and aptitudes (Wright & McMahan, 2011). One of the most important goals of an organization's HR function is the effective management of employee performance that provides for the identification of high and low performers. An effective performance management system needs to identify those individual employees who may require additional assistance to improve their performance, as well as those higher performing employees suitable for extra assignment, merit-based compensation, promotion, or leadership development.

In order to meet the overall goal of shaping employee behavior to improve performance, many organizations are now using automated, self-service, and electronic (e-) human resources applications to facilitate the performance management process. Indeed, e-performance management systems are now becoming quite ubiquitous, especially for large organizations that employ in excess of 500 people. Stone et al. (2015, p. 223) reported that 93 percent of surveyed US organizations use some sort of an electronic performance management system. These integrated systems assist managers to measure performance, assemble and write performance reviews, and provide detailed feedback to employees (Cardy & Miller, 2005).

The performance management process is enabled through the use of information technology that provides detailed assessments of employee performance and provide for the construction of uniform reports for the provision of employee feedback. The *360-degree feedback* can be deployed when multiple raters receive email messages to complete an online evaluation of the performance of a particular employee (Antonioni, 1996). The resulting assessments are merged and feedback is provided to the employee. This allows for the effective comparison of the performance of certain employees at the workplace level with others working at different functions within the organization, or can be used for the purpose of more broadly benchmarking employee performance levels with other organizations or industries.

Computerized performance management systems have the capacity to provide *employee monitoring* by keeping counts, for instance, of variables such as the amount of time spent on certain tasks, the number of work units completed, the number of errors and mistakes committed, and the amount of idle time spent. By more closely monitoring employee performance using such systems, organizations are able to achieve greater supervisory spans of control, thus reducing the amount of time managers spend on observing (and documenting) the behavior and performance of certain employees.

Electronic performance management intranet systems can be used to efficiently assemble feedback from multiple raters. E-performance management systems enable the tracking and comparison of *group-level and unit-level performance analytics* with respect to criteria such as tardiness, attendance, grievances, satisfaction, and turnover. Data collected at the unit-level can be used to identify HR problems, uncover potential rating errors, or highlight exceptional performance. The use of HR analytics makes it easier to collect, document and retrieve a variety of performance data from various sources to provide managers with better information needed to observe and address employee performance issues in terms of both behavior and outcomes (Sharma & Sharma, 2017).

One of the most important objectives of a performance management system is to help organizations motivate and retain their most talented employees. This goal is critical if an organization is to achieve sustained excellence. Compensation is a powerful means by which employees are motivated and rewarded. Increasingly, organizations are using information technologies to support *compensation planning and administration*. A major impetus for doing so is that e-compensation systems are thought to reduce administrative costs and the amount of time needed for compensation planning. In general, organizations are using technology to assist the compensation process in three major ways:

- the automation of the payroll system;
- the design of compensation system and its relationship to employee performance assessment; and
- communication and administration of compensation and benefits through *employee self-servicing* systems (Dulebohn & Marler, 2005).

e-Compensation systems are used to communicate data about *benefits options* to employees and it provides them with an opportunity to select benefit plans online. Online systems facilitate the use of flexible benefits and benefit packages that, given their self-service feature, allow employees the opportunity to alter their benefit packages as their needs change (Gueutal & Falbe, 2005). When combined with decision support software, employees can use the e-compensation system to pose hypothetical questions about proposed changes to their benefits package or to actual changes in their work-life situation.

It allows managers to develop budgets and ensure the impact of incentive systems so that salary allocation decisions are seen as appropriate and fair.

For instance, such systems will provide managers access to salary data that, when combined with employee performance data, can be used for making decisions related to profit sharing, merit increases, the awarding of stock options, bonuses and commissions, and so forth. They are also enabled to ensure that an organization's compensation and reward system has achieved an acceptable degree of *"internal equity"* when comparing job compensation levels across the organization, as well as *"external equity"* when employee and job compensation levels are made comparable and consistent with those in other organizations.

Research suggests that employees have greater satisfaction and retention when pay systems are perceived as fair, where there is a clear and direct 'line-of-sight' between performance and reward, and when there is an unambiguous relationship between "cause" (the demonstration of a desired employee behavior or outcome) and "effect" (the administration of a desired reward). Sharma, Sharma, and Agarwal (2016, p. 228) state that a performance management (and reward) system:

> cannot be expected to be effective unless employees respond to these in ways intended. For effectiveness, such systems need to be perceived as fair in terms of [the] distribution of outcomes (distributive equity), processes followed to arrive at distributions (procedural justice) and clarity of communication mechanisms (interactional justice).

While it is usually necessary to fully involve affected individuals in the design of a pay-for-performance approach to compensation as a way of increasing perceived equity, organizational benefits derived from their engagement can be undermined quickly when they are allowed to "game the system" for their own benefit (Woolhandler, Ariely, & Himmelstein, 2012).

Adoption factors for e-performance and reward management applications

Like other functions of HRM, performance management and employee compensation have been extensively automated, a transformation that has the potential to effectively integrate a firm's HR functions in ways that is difficult to achieve without the aid of computing, automation and web-based technologies (Kavanagh, Thite, & Johnson, 2015). Indeed, over the past 40 years, organizations have increasingly adopted electronic human resources management (e-HRM) applications (including e-performance management and e-compensation systems) in the belief that doing so would achieve administrative and strategic benefits, including cost reductions and service improvements (Bondarouk, Parry, & Furtmueller, 2017).

e-HRM systems, which include e-performance management and e-compensation systems, are rarely crafted from "whole cloth," but rather are adapted from an organization's existing HRM practices and system. The decision to pursue e-HRM should always be preceded by a compelling rationale, a strategy and a detailed transfer (implementation) plan between an existing (or partially existing) HRM system and a targeted e-HRM system, with a goal to achieve total acceptance (uptake) by its targeted users. Bondarouk, Parry, and Furtmueller (2017) suggest that research on e-HRM applications and effectiveness have concentrated almost exclusively on adoption factors and on outcome (consequence) factors. In their extensive review of the academic literature on e-HRM, they state that "since the 1970s, 168 [discrete] factors have been found empirically for the e-HRM adoption and 95 factors for e-HRM factors for e-HRM consequences."

Bondarouk, Parry, and Furtmueller (2017) suggest that adoption factors for any particular application of e-HRM, including e-performance management and e-compensation systems, include three broad categories: *people factors, technology factors, and organizational factors*. While their review of these factors is appropriate for the adoption of all e-HRM applications in general, the factors identified remain particularly salient for e-performance management and e-compensation system adoptions. Successfully engaging those affected in the design, implementation, and use of any e-HRM system is essential for successful adoption.

People factors. These include top management support, user acceptance, effective communication between involved stakeholders and units, having the relevant expertise and skills in HR, and cultural factors. Top management support has been identified as a key people factor in several research studies that have looked at the successful adoption of an e-HRM system (Reddick, 2009). Visionary, supportive, and encouraging leaders that advocate strongly for adoption are found to contribute to the acceptance (and uptake) of new systems. User acceptance has also been well-cited as a crucial factor in e-HRM application adoptions, including e-performance management systems.

DeSanctis (1986) showed that involving users during systems development positively influenced employee and HR department satisfaction, thus increasing adoption success. In their study of employee resistance to e-HRM adoption, Olivas-Lujan, Ramirez, and Zapata-Cantu (2007) found that employees tend to resist new e-HRM systems when they believe it will increase their workload. The quality of communication and the relationship between HR individuals, IT staff, and unit-level managers is also considered critical for successful adoption (Panayotopoulou, Vakola, & Galanaki, 2007). Successful adoption requires exceptional and seamless cooperation between the HR and IT departments, so that operating units receive consistent messages. HR departments are often directly responsible for e-HRM adoption, but the contributions from IT are critical for successful adoption. Training typically plays a crucial role in achieving a more sophisticated use of systems. For instance, in-house training was found to be more effective than self-training with respect to user satisfaction. Many of the examined "people factors" focus on cultural and stakeholder psychological factors.

Technology factors. These are strong contributors to system adoption. Current information systems capability and capacity in an organization directly influences the extent to which human resources can be automated and brought online. The process of customizing existing Human Resources Information System (HRIS) software is critical to long-term success. Nevertheless, while a "plug-and-play" system is rarely available for easy installation, an extensive modification of an existing software package can lead to system errors. HR processes also require a high degree of standardization and a modicum of "manageable complexity" for e-HRM adoption to be successful. Bondarouk, Parry, and Furtmueller (2017) suggest that in the past, "several key technology factors were identified as influencing HRIS adoption: data integrity, system usefulness, system integration, and in-house development versus using external HRIS software" (p. 105).

Organizational factors. These consist of a wide array of factors that impact the successful uptake of e-HRM: organizational characteristics; existing constraints in terms of how human resources are being deployed; data access, security, and privacy issues; and capability and resource constraints. While larger organizations are more likely to adopt an e-HRM application in general, Strohmeier and Kabst (2009) describe larger companies as the most likely to be "earlier adopters," yet "successful adopters" are less size dependent and include many smaller organizations. Adoption may also depend on the nature of the enterprise and the way that it traditionally deploys its human resources or the nature of its enterprise.

For instance, companies that rely on employee telecommuting or possess geographically distributed business units adopt e-HRM approaches more frequently. Data access, security, and privacy issues also impact the adoption decision (see Chapter 15). For instance, employees often fear that the movement to a self-servicing, online performance management system will generate security and privacy issues when additional people are invited to provide performance-related data. These fears need to be resolved and assurances provided that the new system has sufficiently robust security protocols if employee and user confidence is to be attained. Organizations that do not have the sufficient designated resources and capabilities do not generally pursue e-HRM adoption. Organizations with modest budgets or with a shortage of qualified technical personnel are less interested in adopting e-HRM applications, yet organizations with a high concentration of such personnel are often more likely to pursue e-HRM, even when other enabling factors are absent. Organizations without a history of HR and IT working collaboratively are less likely to successfully adopt e-HRM applications.

Evaluation of e-performance and reward systems

A major reason that organizations use an e-performance management system is the belief that the technology will streamline the performance evaluation process, cut costs, and decrease the time and effort needed to manage employee performance. Research to date is limited and somewhat inconclusive on the general effectiveness of this e-HRM application. Where research has been done, there is some evidence for the effectiveness of e-performance management systems from the perspective of employees whose performance is being assessed. Payne et al. (2009), Earley (1988), and others have found that employees generally have a favorable impression about computerized feedback and often express feelings of being more involved in the performance assessment process (Cardy & Miller, 2005).

In addition, employees are more likely to trust feedback that is provided by a computer when it aligns strongly with the feedback communicated by the supervisor. However, when employees are more concerned with "image management," they are more likely to prefer supervisor-provided feedback to computerized feedback. The overall employee acceptance of an e-performance management system depends on the extent to which they view them as facilitating the achievement of their personal goals (Stone, Stone-Romero, & Lukaszewski, 2006).

Some employees whose performance is being monitored by computers may have lower levels of satisfaction and anxiety if they believe that the system has been designed to tightly monitor their behavior, impacting a belief that their privacy is being invaded by the e-performance system. Employee motivation is also potentially affected by the means by which feedback is provided. Computerized feedback may result in lower levels of employee motivation loss when compared with feedback conveyed by a supervisor (Kluger & Adler, 1993). This may be particularly salient when the feedback is harsh or negative. When negative feedback comes from a supervisor, as opposed to a computer, it may be more likely to be interpreted as more subjective and coming from someone with a personal agenda or bias, thus undermining their confidence and motivation.

An important consideration in evaluating e-performance management systems is the impact they have on *employee-supervisory relations*. One of the espoused advantages of e-performance management is that supervisors will spend less time assessing performance and more time managing performance, while engaging in more performance-related conversations. While there is limited empirical evidence that has addressed this question, Zuboff (1988) demonstrated that when performance data is captured using computerized systems, supervisors tend to rely more heavily on the data that is generated when evaluating their employees and engage less in "fact-finding" interactions. In this way, e-performance management systems have the potential to increase the *interpersonal distance* between supervisors and their subordinates by decreasing opportunities for face-to-face communication. When feedback is provided electronically and when supervisors do not meet with their employees to discuss their performance with employees, it may be less likely to capture their attention, alter their behaviors, and affect their performance.

e-Performance monitoring systems may also lead employees to behave in rigid ways where they are more motivated to "look good" vis-à-vis the performance characteristics that the system is assessing, while ignoring other performance-related behaviors that the system is not designed to assess.

A benefit of using an e-performance management system is the potential to incorporate the views and perspectives of multiple evaluators. Yet, researchers have long argued that 360° feedback may be subject to biases that have the potential to provide inaccurate performance data (Waldman, Atwater, & Antonioni, 1998). A possible reason for this bias is that performance assessors involved in providing assessments may not have had the opportunity to observe sufficient aspects of employee performance needed to gain a good understanding of that performance, nor be aware of the scope of job requirements, including an employee's job-related goals. This is of real consequence when performance data collected in this way is being used to allocate reward. In a merit based pay-for-performance system with a fixed amount of money to reward performance, employees could be more likely to provide negative assessments of their workmates because they are aware in doing so will result in higher payouts for themselves. It is now widely recommended that multiple evaluator assessments (360° evaluations) be used more for developmental purposes and not as a means to make reward allocation decisions (Antonioni, 1996).

One of the most important goals of the HRM process is to motivate and retain the most talented employees. It can be argued that e-compensation systems decrease overall payroll costs, errors, and the time it takes to implement compensation planning (Dulebohn & Marler, 2005). Brink and McDonnell (2003) reported that a company saved $850,000 per year in administrative costs when they automated their compensation planning system. In another instance, Stone et al. (2015, p. 225) cite a 2010 American Payroll Association report that suggested automating payroll can reduce mistakes by 80 percent.

Most e-compensation systems use an employee self-service interface. This internet-based technology permits employees' access to a centralized HR database that allows them to review their personnel data, including performance-related data, enroll in benefits, participate in open enrollment schemes, and self-nominate for additional training and development. Hawking, Stein, and Foster (2004) identify several benefits and drawbacks regarding the use of employee self-service systems. Naturally, the use of employee self-service systems is positively related to decreases in processing time, increased accuracy of decisions and improved productivity. While self-service systems are often initially resisted by employees, they are more likely to accept them when they have been provided sufficient training.

Employee and managerial acceptance of employee self-service systems depend upon a number of factors including the amount of organizational support and training that is provided. If these stakeholders view the implementation of self-service systems as a way that human resources have outsourced and off-loaded an activity they have traditionally performed, they may be less likely to view this development in a positive light. Nevertheless, potential savings by moving to an employee self-service e-benefits system may not provide the expected savings because of the continuing need for HR to explain the features of the benefit options provided. Employee self-service systems tend to be one-way communication that does not give employees an opportunity to pose questions and propose scenarios.

Summary

As highlighted throughout this book, in recent years, the forward march of technology has had a dramatic impact on the field of human resources, including performance management and reward. Despite widespread adoption of both e-performance management and e-compensation management systems there remain a number of questions about whether these systems will enable organizations to achieve their primary human resources goals. Stone et al. (2015), in their assessment of e-HR applications, provide a summary critique that is salient for our discussion: "the current systems have a number of limitations including the fact that they employ one-way communication systems, are impersonal, passive," and may preclude employees with low computer skills from gaining access to information about their performance and compensation, including benefits (p. 226).

While the growth of e-performance management and e-compensation systems are expected to increase in the future with the transition to cloud-based applications and with the inclusion of the vehicle of social media to collect performance-related data in real time, there will be the need to continually examine the primary goal of human resources. Is the "real" goal of moving traditional functions of performance management and reward to a technologically automated online system a search for "administrative efficiency" or a quest for "organizational effectiveness"? The jury is still out with respect to resolving this question. In the end, the application of technology can only be a decision support tool that is there to enhance, not replace, the role of HR professionals and managers in the performance assessment and reward process.

Case study: e-Performance management at Sontech Pharmaceuticals

Robert Savage, director of sales at Sontech Pharmaceuticals, was troubled and unsure about the impeding roll-out of the new e-performance management and reward system. A number of his sales staff had let him know that they had some trepidation about moving the performance management and compensation system to an employee self-service web-based platform.

Sales staff expressed grave doubts about the ability of the new system to accurately track sales performance at an informal meeting that he had with them a few weeks after the company announced its intention to replace its person-to-person performance appraisal process and manual entry sales reporting with an integrated electronic online tracking system. Several people indicated having some apprehension that the new electronic system would depersonalize interactions between people and change the organization's people-centered culture for the worse.

"*Sales are all about people,*" said one. "*These automated systems have the potential to decrease social interaction between people.*" Another stated that "*we should be wary of introducing a new technology that seeks to automate and regulate human performance.*" One lamented that "*performance evaluation is really more art than science. I think it is folly to try to translate human behavior into stiff quantifiable factors. Too much will be lost in the translation.*"

Two salespersons posited that the implementation of such a system would limit the freedom and autonomy of individuals. People will resist any performance management system that seeks to place firm controls on their behavior.

"*I heard that such a system has the potential to keep track of variables such as the number of keystrokes that I use when I communicate with my clients, what sites I visit on the internet, or the amount of time that I spend on certain tasks,*" declared a salesperson of long tenure. Another quipped, "*I can't see any benefit to micro-managing us and getting up close and personal in how we choose to spend our time!*"

One person questioned how the new system would affect his compensation.

"*I am wary that a new performance management system will translate into less compensation. After all, half my salary is commission, so I worry that this new performance management approach is being designed with the intent of trying to lower sales commission payouts around here!*"

One recently hired salesperson warned that moving to an automated system from a manual one creates a number of implementation challenges.

"*In the last place that I worked, they tried to automate the personnel functions and that created all kinds of confusion. One part of the system that was automated couldn't communicate with another part that wasn't automated. They had information, technology, and data spread out all over the place and nothing was compatible. As a consequence, people weren't getting paid what they were supposed to and they weren't getting paid on time.*"

Another openly worried that management might try to implement a new automated system without providing sufficient resources or try to do too much, too fast.

"*I heard that last year, they implemented an automated performance management system at Roby Industries with disastrous results. They tried to roll-out the new system at the same time they were cutting budgets and reducing their payroll, including IT support. When they reduced their expenses by 20 percent they let go a whole bunch of HR and IT staff. In the end, there wasn't enough expertise left in the organization to explain it or train others on how to properly use the new system!*"

As Savage thought about the impending implementation of the new online performance management system, he wondered how its particular design and implementation would address some of the concerns that he was hearing. He also knew the project to automate the pay-for-performance system at Sontech was now $275,000 over budget and that senior management was counting on a smooth roll-out over the next six months. He did not want to disappoint.

Case study questions

- Why do you think there is so much resistance among the sales staff to the new e-performance management and reward system?
- What does Savage need to know in order to make the design and roll-out of the new e-performance management and reward system acceptable to those who would use it?
- What should Savage do to get his staff "on-side" so they see this new system as a good way to improve their performance and compensation?

Debate: Does technology take away the human element in managing employee performance?

Introduction

Results from research on e-performance management and reward systems suggest that employees generally prefer a more interactive, interpersonal, and information-rich approach to the assessment of their performance. Although most e-performance management applications do not necessarily preclude this, the emphasis has been to emphasize human resource transactions at the expense of human relationships. Is the goal of automating the performance assessment process to streamline the process, reduce HR costs, and decrease the amount of time it takes supervisors to make employee performance assessments, or is it about the impact on employee perceptions of the organizational culture, climate, and strategy? If e-HR applications are perceived as being impersonal and data-intense, HR relevance will likely decline and with it, organizational effectiveness.

Arguments in favor

There is empirical research on e-performance management systems that show that:

- Employees are concerned that e-PM systems have the potential to violate their privacy and that such systems are not sufficiently secure.
- The use of e-PM systems has the potential to dramatically reduce interpersonal distance between supervisors and employees, reducing face-to-face communication between supervisor and employee, potentially leading to misunderstanding and distrust.
- Employees do not always understand or agree with the feedback from e-PM, especially if it is given to them without any additional human input.
- Some employees are wary of e-PM because they believe it reduces personal contact with their supervisor and thus undermines their ability to "manage the relationship" with their supervisor.
- e-PM has the potential to reduce employee motivation, especially if employees believe the system is not able to capture all relevant aspects of their performance.

Arguments against

There is empirical research on e-performance management systems that show that:

- Computerized employee performance assessments can closely replicate the design features of the traditional "pen-and-paper" employee appraisal system.
- Employees generally prefer computerized feedback to that provided by a supervisor because it is more "objective." Employees believe that feedback provided by supervisor is potentially more biased, subjective, and "political."
- Compared with supervisor provided feedback, computerized feedback results in less motivation loss and higher levels of performance than feedback conveyed by a supervisor.
- e-PM can produce "richer" assessments of employee performance because it has the potential to assemble performance assessments from multiple evaluators while providing detailed feedback in an articulate, standard format that employees can understand.
- Employee performance assessments can be collected in a more continuous fashion and be made available to employees in "real time," enabling them to know how well they are performing, potentially improving their overall job satisfaction and motivation.

Video learning resources

- PeopleSoft e-performance management 9.2 video: www.youtube.com/watch?v=MYIXabzSi_o
- Electronic performance appraisal – ePerformance Mercury: www.youtube.com/watch?v=I2eY95SM9fE
- Performance appraisal software: www.youtube.com/watch?v=_oonUupNXBw
- Software as a service providers of rewards management systems and what you should expect from them: www.youtube.com/watch?v=OrOg8_lYuFE
- Employee performance and compensation management – beqom: www.youtube.com/watch?v=9-ILd9w2vng

References

Al-Raisi, A., Amin, S. & Tahir, S. (2011). Evaluation of e-performance analysis and assessment in the United Arab Emirates (UAE) organizations. *Journal of Internet and Information Systems*, 2(2), 20–27.

Antonioni, D. (1996). Designing an effective 360-degree appraisal feedback process. *Organizational Dynamics*, 25(2), 24–38.

Bondarouk, T., Parry, E. & Furtmueller, E. (2017). Electronic HRM: four decades of research on adoption and consequences. *International Journal of Human Resources Management*, 28(1), 98–131.

Bondarouk, T. V. & Ruël, H. J. M. (2009). Electronic human resource management: challenges in the digital era. *International Journal of Human Resource Management*, 20(3), 505–514.

Brink, S. & McDonnell, S. (2003). *E-compensation*. Emerging Technologies Series, 18. Burington, MA: IHRIM Press, 1–4.

Cardy, R. L. & Miller, J. S. (2005). eHR and performance management: a consideration of positive potential and the dark side. In H. G. Gueutal and D. L. Stone (Eds.). *The brave new world of eHR: human resource management in the digital age* (pp. 138–165). San Francisco, CA: Jossey-Bass.

Claus, L. & Briscoe, D. (2009). Employee performance management across borders: a review of relevant academic literature. *International Journal of Management Reviews*, 11(2), 175–196.

Delery, J. E. & Doty, D. (1996). Modes of theorizing in strategic human resource management; tests of universalistic, contingency and configurational performance predictions. *Academy of Management Journal*, 39(4), 802–835.

Delery, J. E. & Roumpi, D. (2017). Strategic human resource management, human capital and competitive advantage: is the field going in circles? *Human Resource Management Journal*, 27(1), 1–21.

DeNisi, A. S. & Pritchard, R. D. (2006). Performance appraisal, performance management and improving individual performance. A motivational framework. *Management and Organization Review*, 2(2), 253–277.

DeNisi, A. & Smith, C. E. (2014). Performance appraisal, performance management, and firm-level performance. *Academy of Management Annals*, 8(1), 127–179.

DeSanctis, G. (1986). Human resource information systems: a current assessment. *MIS Quarterly*, 10(1), 15–27.

Dulebohn, J. H. & Marler, J. H. (2005). E-compensation: the potential to transform practice? In H. G. Gueutal and D. L. Stone (Eds.). *The brave new world of eHR: human resource management in the digital age* (pp. 166–189). San Francisco, CA: Jossey-Bass.

Earley, P. C. (1988). Computer-generated performance feedback in the magazine-subscription industry. *Organizational Behaviour and Human Decision Processes*, 41(1), 50–64.

Fisher, C. D., Schoenfeldt, L. F. & Shaw, J. B. (2006). *Human resource management*. 6th Edition. Boston, MA: Houghton Mifflin.

Furnham, A. (2004). Performance management systems. *European Business Journal*, 16(2), 83–94.

Gueutal, H. G. & Falbe, C. M. (2005). E-HR: trends in delivery methods. In H. G. Gueutal and D. L. Stone (Eds.). *The brave new world of eHR: human resource management in the digital age* (pp. 190–225). San Francisco, CA: Jossey-Bass.

Harrington, J. R. & Lee, J. H. (2015). What drives perceived fairness of performance appraisal? Exploring the effects of psychological contract fulfillment on employees' perceived fairness of performance appraisal in US federal agencies. *Public Personnel Management*, 44(2), 214–238.

Hawking, P., Stein, A. & Foster, S. (2004). E-HR and employee self service: a case study of a Victorian public sector organisation. *Journal of Issues in Informing Science and Information Technology*, 1, 1019–1026.

Hofmann, D. A., Jacobs, R. & Gerras, S. J. (1992). Mapping individual performance over time. *Journal of Applied Psychology*, 77(2), 185–195.

Huselid, M. A. (1995). The impact of human resource management practices on turnover, productivity, and corporate financial performance. *Academy of Management Journal*, 38(3), 635–675.

Jiang, K., Lepak, D. P., Jia, J. & Baer, J. C. (2012). How does human resource management influence organizational outcomes? A meta-analysis investigation of mediating mechanisms. *Academy of Management Journal*, 55(6), 1264–1294.

Johnson, R. D. & Gueutal, H. G. (2011). *Transforming HR through technology: the use of hER and human resource information systems in organizations*. Alexandria, VA: SHRM Effective Practice Guidelines Series.

Kavanagh, M. J., Thite, M. & Johnson, R. D. (Eds.). (2015). *Human resource information systems: basics, applications and future directions*. 3rd Edition. Thousand Oaks, CA: Sage.

Kehoe, R. R. & Wright, P. M. (2013). The impact of high-performance human resource practices on employees' attitudes and behaviors. *Journal of Management*, 39(2), 366–391.

Kluger, A. N. & Adler, S. (1993). Person versus computer-mediated feedback. *Computers in Human Behavior*, 9(1), 1–16.

Latham, G. P. & Wexley, K. N. (1982). *Increasing productivity through performance appraisal*. Reading, MA: Addison-Wesley.

Lednick-Hall, M. L. & Moritz, S. (2003). The impact of e-HR on the HRM function. *Journal of Labor Research*, 24(3), 365–379.

McAfee, B. R. & Champagne, P. J. (1993). Performance management: a strategy for improving employee performance and productivity. *Journal of Management Psychology*, 8(5), 24–33.

Mohrman, A. M., Resnick-West, S. M. & Lawler, E. E. (1989). *Designing performance appraisal systems: aligning appraisals and organizational realities*. San Francisco, CA: Jossey-Bass.

Nankervis, A. R. & Compton, R. L. (2006). Performance management: theory in practice. *Asia Pacific Journal of Human Resources*, 44(1), 83–101.

Olivas-Lujan, M. R., Ramirez, J. & Zapata-Cantu, L. (2007). E-HRM in Mexico: adapting innovations for global competition. *International Journal of Manpower*, 28(5), 418–434.

Panayotopoulou, L., Vakola, M. & Galanaki, E. (2007). E-HR adoption and the role of HRM: evidence from Greece. *Personnel Review*, 36, 277–294.

Pauwe, J., Guest, D. E. & Wright, P. (Eds.). (2013). *HRM and performance: achievements and challenges*. Chichester, UK: John Wiley & Sons.

Payne, S. C., Horner, M. T., Boswell, W. R., Schroeder, A. N. & Stine-Cheyne, K. J. (2009). Comparison of online and traditional performance appraisal systems. *Journal of Managerial Psychology*, 24(6), 526–544.

Peterson, S. J. & Luthans, F. (2006). The impact of financial and nonfinancial incentives on business-unit outcomes over time. *Journal of Applied Psychology*, 91(1), 156–165.

Pfeffer, J. (1998). *The human equation: building profits by putting people first*. Boston, MA: Harvard Business School Press.

Reddick, C. G. (2009). Human resources information systems in Texas city governments: scope and perception of its effectiveness. *Public Personnel Management*, 38(4), 19–34.

Ruël, H. J. M., Bondarouk, T. & Van der Velde, M. (2007). The contribution of e-HRM to HRM effectiveness. *Employee Relations*, 29(3), 280–291.

Rynes, S. L., Gerhart, B. & Minette, K. A. (2004). The importance of pay in employee motivation: discrepancies between what people say and what they do. *Human Resources Management*, 43(4), 381–394.

Sharma, A. & Sharma, T. (2017). HR analytics and performance appraisal system. A conceptual framework for employee performance improvement. *Management Research Review*, 40(6), 684–697.

Sharma, N. P., Sharma, T. & Agarwal, M. N. (2016). Measuring employee perception of performance measurement system effectiveness. Conceptualization and scale development. *Employee Relations*, 38(2), 224–247.

Singh, A. (2012). Performance management system design, implementation and outcomes in Indian software organizations: a perspective of HR managers. *South Asian Journal of Management*, 19(2), 99–120.

Stone, D. L., Deadrick, D. L., Lukaszewski, K. M. & Johnson, R. (2015). The influence of technology on the future of human resource management. *Human Resource Management Review*, 25(2), 216–231.

Stone, D. L., Stone-Romero, E. F. & Lukaszewski, K. (2006). Factors affecting the acceptance and effectiveness of electronic human resource systems. *Human Resource Management Review*, 16(2), 229–244.

Strohmeier, S. & Kabst, R. (2009). Organizational adoption of e-HRM in Europe. *Journal of Managerial Psychology*, 24(6), 482–501.

Thurston, P. W. & McNall, L. (2010). Justice perceptions of performance appraisal practices. *Journal of Managerial Psychology*, 25(3), 201–228.

Waldman, D. A., Atwater, L. E. & Antonioni, D. (1998). Has 360 degree feedback gone amok? *Academy of Management Executive*, 12(2), 86–94.

Woolhandler, S., Ariely, D. & Himmelstein, D. U. (2012). Why pay for performance may be incompatible with quality improvement. Motivation may decrease and gaming of the system is rife. *BMJ*, 345, e5015. DOI: 10.1136/bmj.e5015.

WorkplaceInfo. (2002). The 7 deadly sins of performance management [Online]. http://workplaceinfo.com.au/hr-management/performance-management/analysis/the-7-deadly-sins-of-performance-management#.WmBFDK6WaHs (Accessed 18 January, 2018).

Wright, P. M. & McMahan, G. C. (2011). Exploring human capital: putting "human" back into strategic human resource management. *Human Resource Management Journal*, 21(2), 93–104.

Zuboff, S. (1988). *In the age of smart machines: the future of work and power*. New York, NY: Basic Books.

13 e-Learning and development

Charissa Tan

> **Learning objectives**
>
> - Discuss the transformation of traditional training to e-L&D from a historical perspective
> - Discuss digital technology applications in the learning and development function as well as learning management systems to support business strategy
> - Explain key methods in e-L&D, including online learning, social media, MOOCs, e-mentoring, mobile learning and wearables
> - Explain the advantages and disadvantages of e-L&D methods
> - Identify key success factors in in e-L&D projects through a case discussion.

Introduction

Imagine your first day at work. You are full of hopes and enthusiasm, but at the same time nervous and not sure whether you will fit in. If you are directed to move to a traditional training room where you hardly interact with your future colleagues but get bombarded with boring talks from senior managers and PowerPoint presentations, you will most likely feel let down and go home disappointed. Now consider the new-hire orientation at Adobe Systems using Adobe Connect, which claims to transform 'new-hire orientation from locally facilitated events to a standard, shared virtual experience' giving the company more 'flexibility and creativity to continually evolve digital learning experiences' (Adobe, 2014, p. 2). It incorporates 'activities, games and other types of interactivity', so that new hires actually 'shape the content and experience itself, making sessions fully immersive' rather than being passive participants. Thus, Adobe Connect aims to achieve emotional connection, face-to-face interactions and 'virtually meet other people doing a similar job' in order to engage employees 'on the same platform at the same time' and deliver consistent messages about the company goals across its global network.

The landscape of learning and development in work organizations is evolving rapidly. Many prominent companies such as Microsoft and Cisco have incorporated technology, like the one described above, to seamlessly bring together different physical locations and time-zones. This is in line with the growing trend of 'teleworking' (Wright, 2017). It is projected that by 2020, more than three-quarters of the workforce will comprise a mobile workforce in the USA (SHRM, 2017). This new landscape creates new possibilities and challenges for learning professionals and learners.

Learning and development is a significant pillar in the organizational 'human resource system' responsible for adding value and delivering results. With the rise of disruptive technologies that have significantly disrupted work in organizations today, learning and development function has similarly changed from traditional forms of classroom-style training to modern forms of electronically aided learning approaches. A review of the literature spanning interdisciplinary domains of workplace learning, psychology and education reveals that there is currently no unanimously agreed upon definition of 'e-learning and development' (henceforth referred to as 'e-L&D'). The field of e-L&D is relatively new and cutting-edge, with relatively little published work on the topic. For the purposes of this chapter, e-L&D is defined as

> an approach to learning in organizations that integrates three elements: the philosophy that the individual is responsible for learning and that performance is the primary objective of learning with technology as a central enabler of learning.

Accordingly, this chapter presents an overview of the field of e-L&D by identifying its historical roots, present developments and future directions. With a focus on the value of electronic systems in enhancing learning effectiveness and driving performance, this chapter discusses the potential transformative power of e-L&D. It concludes with a case study and a debating topic that stimulate readers to think deeply over critical issues in leading change in e-L&D in any organization.

A fundamental shift from training to learning

Understanding the evolution of L&D will help us better understand the present and subsequent future (Szasz, 2006). A scan of historical developments in L&D reveals three significant transformative changes: (1) change from training to learning; (2) change of role from administration to learning and performance; and (3) transformation of tools used for learning.

Burbach (2015) explains that there are substantive differences between the traditional training and contemporary L&D: *training* refers to planned activities focusing on acquisition of knowledge, skills and abilities (KSA) to perform specific tasks or jobs; *learning* refers to the cognitive process of assimilation, whereby cognition and behaviours are changed through experience, practice and feedback; and *development* refers to advancement towards greater complexity and manifests as activities that prepare employees to take on future roles in or outside the organization. In other words, training focuses on skills to improve current performance, whereas L&D is future-focused, long-term oriented and aims to develop life-long competencies.

Sloman (2005) further explains the shift from training to learning as being a shift from top-down influence on individuals by organizations to continual processes of self-directed learning by individuals. This is reflected in the changes in related terminologies, for instance, the use of the term 'learners' to replace 'trainees', in line with the fundamental premise that only learners can learn and the ways they learn are changing. The responsibility of learning has also shifted from the organization to the individual.

Three developments in theory and practice have propelled this shift. The first development was the emergence of *new theories of learning*, for example, Kolb's (1984) experiential learning theory (ELT) and his study of learning styles, which subsequently led to the generation of more research on learner preferences. Experiential learning theory by Kolb and Fry from MIT first emerged in the early seventies (Kolb & Fry, 1975), culminating in a book '*Experiential Learning*' published in 1984 that focused on learning. This theory was influenced by Dewey's philosophical pragmatism, Lewin's social psychology and Piaget's cognitive developmental genetic epistemology (Kolb, 1984). ELT conceptualizes learning as 'the process whereby knowledge is created through the transformation of experience' (Kolb, 1984: 38). Kolb's research created fundamental shifts from passive to active learning. Following this, in the nineties, the American Psychological Association echoed the new thinking through the publication of the 14 *learner-centred psychological principles* (APA, 1997) (see Table 13.1) pertaining to learning and the learning process, which influenced the design of educational and training curricula.

Table 13.1 Learner-centred psychological principles

1	Nature of the learning process	The learning of complex subject matter is most effective when it is an intentional process of constructing meaning from information and experience
2	Goals of the learning process	The successful learner, over time and with support and instructional guidance, can create meaningful, coherent representations of knowledge
3	Construction of knowledge	The successful learner can link new information with existing knowledge in meaningful ways
4	Strategic thinking	The successful learner can create and use a repertoire of thinking and reasoning strategies to achieve complex learning goals
5	Thinking about thinking	Higher order strategies for selecting and monitoring mental operations facilitate creative and critical thinking
6	Context of learning	Learning is influenced by environmental factors, including culture, technology and instructional practices
7	Motivational and emotional influences on learning	What and how much is learned is influenced by the motivation. Motivation to learn, in turn, is influenced by the individual's emotional states, beliefs, interests and goals, as well as habits of thinking
8	Intrinsic motivation to learn	The learner's creativity, higher order thinking, and natural curiosity all contribute to motivation to learn. Intrinsic motivation is stimulated by tasks of optimal novelty and difficulty, relevant to personal interests, and providing for personal choice and control
9	Effects of motivation on effort	Acquisition of complex knowledge and skills requires extended learner effort and guided practice. Without learners' motivation to learn, the willingness to exert this effort is unlikely without coercion
10	Developmental influences on learning	As individuals develop, there are different opportunities and constraints for learning. Learning is most effective when differential development within and across physical, intellectual, emotional and social domains is taken into account
11	Social influences on learning	Learning is influenced by social interactions, interpersonal relations and communication with others
12	Individual differences in learning	Learners have different strategies, approaches and capabilities for learning that are a function of prior experience and heredity
13	Learning and diversity	Learning is most effective when differences in learners' linguistic, cultural and social backgrounds are taken into account
14	Standards and assessment	Setting appropriately high and challenging standards and assessing the learner as well as learning progress – including diagnostic, process and outcome assessment – are integral parts of the learning process

Source: Adapted from APA (1997).

The second shift is to be found in *the role of learning in performance enhancement*. Noe (2017) pointed to this shift by stating that training must evolve from being an event to learning. This new thinking focuses on learning and its ability to help organizations meet business challenges and gain a competitive advantage. Training programmes must ensure that employees learn strategically aligned competencies that would help organizations reach their strategic goals.

Thus, the focus is to better understand the links between learning and performance; for example, whether learners undergoing learning interventions demonstrate improved performance as seen in measurable indicators such as time-to-productivity or reduction in error rates in task performance.

Traditionally, training departments monitored metrics such as training expenditure; training hours and training participation. The point being that resources invested to monitor these metrics do not support understanding whether learning is occurring in the organization. Instead, training organizations should monitor learning outcomes more closely, such as observable behaviour changes and performance levels at the individual, group or organizational level. How can L&D as a function make an impact on performance? This is where technology has played a critical role in transforming the tools of the trade.

Table 13.2 summarises the key differences between training and learning in terms of features and metrics (standards of measurement).

Digital revolution in L&D

In line with the global trend of digital HR, there is also a similar revolution in L&D. Today's landscape in L&D is replete with learning techniques, tools and technologies that

Table 13.2 Comparing training with learning

Training	Learning
Features	
1 Employees are informed about training by their managers	1 Employees decide learning to meet their individual and team's needs and goals
2 Corporate 'owns' training and development	2 Corporate L&D curates development and creates learning experiences
3 Learning occurs via classroom methods, sometimes online methods	3 Learning occurs all the time, in micro-learning, online courses, classrooms and groups
4 Learning content is provided by L&D and experts	4 Learning content is provided by everyone in the organization and curated by employees as well as HRD
5 Learning technology focuses on compliance and course catalogues	5 Learning technology creates a collaborative, curated learning experience
Metrics	
• Expenditure per employee	• Amount of knowledge content acquired
• Learning hours per employee	• Application of knowledge
• Cost per learning hour	• Skills acquired
• Participation or attendance rates	• Degree of behaviour-change
• Training completion rates	
• Return on investment	

Features: Source: Adapted from Bersin (2017).

Metrics: Source: Adapted from Noe (2017).

are now ubiquitous. According to the 2017 Training Industry Report (Training Magazine, 2017), the most often used training technologies today are

- Learning management systems (LMSs) (86%)
- Virtual classroom/webcasting/video broadcasting (73%)
- Rapid e-learning tools (48%)
- Application simulation tools (38%)

Learning is also today driven by the individual, who is seen signing up for online classes, interacting with learners online on discussion forums and being assessed through online tests. These technology-enabled learning activities comprise e-L&D insofar as the underlying philosophy of the learning process and the aims of e-L&D are realized. There is a strong uptake of new L&D technologies in mid- to large-sized companies but whether the uptake in smaller companies increases in the future remains to be seen. However, according to Deloitte's Global Human Capital Trends Report (Bersin et al., 2016), only 38% of organizations surveyed were considering digital HR and only 9% were 'fully ready'. Similarly, another report concluded that only 25% of global companies surveyed showed that they were 'digitally-mature' (Kane et al., 2016), that is, the degree to which businesses have adapted to digital environments.

This slow adoption is attributed to hurdles in competencies, such as the ability to partner with IT, develop digital HR competencies in applying design thinking and performing predictive analytics on large data (Stephan et al., 2016), thus suggesting that technology advances at a faster pace than human beings' ability to acquire competencies and overcome fears and resistance. Bersin et al. (2016) encouraged L&D departments to adopt self-directed learning to create learning experiences that enable individuals at all levels in the organization to learn continually.

One of the major influences of technology on the HR function and its processes is the human resource information system (HRIS). HRIS is defined as 'integrated systems used to gather, store and analyze information regarding an organization's human resources' (Hendrickson, 2003, p. 381). The core purpose of HRIS is to present information in a user-friendly manner so that meaningful and appropriate interpretations can be made to support strategic decisions for the company. Capitalising on innovations from HRIS, the tools and techniques used for learning design, administration and delivery have changed. The main HRIS application for learning and development is the *learning management system* (LMS). Manual administrative tasks that were typically undertaken by trainers have also been transformed into modern technology-based LMS.

The LMS is an enterprise technology system for automating the administration of online training (Noe, 2017). It is a software application that allows instructors or training managers to create online training courses. It also allows instructors to track the progress of their learners taking online courses. The key features of a LMS are:

- Allows instructors or training managers authoring tools to create online training courses
- Allows instructors to track and report the progress of their learners taking the created e-courses
- Allows instructors and learners to interact in online classrooms and discussion forums
- Allows instructors to create and assign assessment tests
- Allows a link to other human capital management systems (such as performance management, career development and talent management)

Rapid instructional design is also being increasingly adopted with the creation of tools like rapid e-learning software to quicken the pace of converting PowerPoint slides to e-learning courses. Traditional LMS systems are being transformed today to focus more on managing learning performance (Davis, Carmean and Wagner., 2009). Bersin (2017) describes new learning tools that have entered the market such as Degreed, Pathgather, EdCast, Grovo and Axonify. At institutes of higher learning, learning tools such as Storify, Gnowbe and Perusall are used to engage students to actively learn with professors in online environments. These tools offer learning designers with the ability to create content, mobile learning solutions, micro-learning and video learning available on the internet.

One major advantage with LMS systems is that trainers have more time to focus on evaluation and gathering learning metrics. With e-learning, strain on training delivery is also reduced. Salas, DeRouin and Littrell (2005) recognized that the key benefits of utilizing e-learning systems to deliver training to employees include increasing flexibility and convenience, as well as lowering costs in using traditional training methods.

From the learner's perspective, tools for learning have been revolutionized by the internet and digital technology, for instance, in the use of computers, *social media* such as Facebook and Twitter, Google Docs and virtual classrooms for learning. These modes of learning contrast starkly with traditional training methods such as face-to-face, instructor-led classroom interactions. From the organizational perspective, the shift to digital has created new and powerful tools for *big data and predictive analytics* (see Chapters 5 and 6). Predictive analytics holds tremendous potential for organizations to make strategic decisions facing HR today, using data and analysis techniques. It goes beyond descriptive data like training participation rates and seeks to understand why things happen in the organization. Data would be used to answer questions such as why are learners failing to perform after attending training? To what extent do training programmes impact organizational performance? (Edwards & Edwards, 2016; Fitz-enz & Mattox, 2014). In e-L&D, HR information system databases such as SuccessFactors allow efficient management and aggregation of large amounts of data. Also known as *big data*, these systems provide a snapshot of all the employees' learning needs in an organization, sorted by location, employee management level and other variables (Manyika et. al., 2011).

These new technologies allow learning data to be captured live and monitored for swifter planning and intervention. The drivers for these new tools are the prospects of increasing productivity gains and the ability to save training costs. As aptly noted by Davis, Carmean and Wagner (2009: 2)

> Digital technologies continue to influence the way we find, create, share, and negotiate information and ideas – even influencing the ways that we think about knowledge itself. Learning, education, and training continue to extend the reach of classrooms and training rooms by including a more organic, integrated array of learning experiences and support – available 'anywhere, anytime, and just-in-time'.

The onus is on L&D professionals to upskill themselves to use these systems beyond simple monitoring and to drive interventions that make a difference on performance. The shifts identified in this chapter further suggest a real and urgent need for the learning and development profession to acquire new competencies in order to realize the transformative power of e-L&D. These competencies include a sensitivity to the learning needs of individuals, theoretical understanding of psychological mechanisms underlying learning processes and a proclivity for evaluation using learning and performance data. The latter involves understanding performance metrics and data analytic skills, so that evidence-based assessment of impact can be made. With these new competencies, e-L&D can have a transformative effect on organizations by impacting business strategy. Each new day brings about technological innovations that continue to shape the world of e-L&D; however, rather than being enamoured by glossy advertising of trendy software and dashboards, L&D professionals need to possess a firm grounding in the fundamental theoretical and methodological understanding of e-L&D (Short & Ketchen, 2011).

Methods of e-learning and development

In line with technology-intensive business processes and practices and the strategic orientation of learning, the e-L&D market is witnessing an increasing number of new tools, technologies and techniques. The focus of this section is on key methods that are effectively used to achieve learning outcomes today with a particular emphasis on learning purposes and processes that each method provides the instructional designer and the learner. This is in line with research by Johnson, Gueutal and Falbe (2009) and Colquitt, LePine and Noe (2000) that instrumentally focuses on learning effectiveness of technological characteristics and individual learner characteristics on e-learning outcomes. Accordingly, this section will introduce the main methods of e-L&D, including e-learning/web-based training/distance learning, social media, massive open online courses (MOOCs), e-mentoring, mobile learning and wearables.

As defined by Noe (2017), instruction could be synchronous, which means that it is conducted in real time, or could be asynchronous or time delayed. Most companies use a blend of several methods to achieve learning goals; some companies apply the 70:20:10 rule of blended learning, whereby 70% of learning is on the job, 20% is through social interactions such as mentoring or coaching and 10% is through formal instruction.

e-Learning/web-based learning/distance learning

e-Learning refers to training initiatives that provide learning material in online repositories and content is pushed to learners through via electronic media such as the internet, audio or video tape, satellite broadcast, interactive TV and CD-ROM (Kaplan-Leiserson, 2000; Johnson, Gueutal & Falbe, 2009). Besides text and graphics, the current generation of e-learning also utilizes video, video-conferencing, simulations/games, virtual classrooms and digital content libraries to deliver an interactive e-learning experience, with its contents tailored to the learners' business-driven learning needs, learning styles and continuous knowledge needs (Arth, 2011). e-Learning falls in the learning system posited by Noe (2017) under guided competency development purposes, which involves the company creating and guiding the learning, as compared with contextual learning guided by learners and is typically used in mandatory training, such as cybersecurity courses, occupational health and safety courses or new-hire orientation programmes. The term 'distance learning' is almost synonymous with e-learning, whereby 'distance learning' stresses on the ability of technology to bridge physical distances and connect learners with trainers in different locations locally and globally at reduced costs.

With respect to learning effectiveness of e-learning methods, Sitzmann et al. (2006) found no differences in the learning outcomes of those who took e-learning courses and face-to-face courses. Learner satisfaction with blended delivery methods (that includes both face-to-face and e-learning) have been found in both classroom and organizational sectors (Tang & Byrne, 2007).

There are clear advantages of e-learning over traditional classroom learning. Arth (2011) recognized that e-learning allows scalability, which is about meeting increased demands; learning agility, which is the ability of e-learning to facilitate an organization's ability to respond to change; and influences organizational learning culture, which encourages continuous learning among employees.

In contrast, traditional classroom learning is less scalable and is constrained by classroom space, location of classroom, scheduling and availability of instructors. e-Learning does not possess these limitations and is able to connect learners around the globe at any time, at reduced cost and more quickly than with traditional classroom learning. In addition, e-learning ensures consistency in delivery of learning content to multiple audiences, an essential principle for maintaining consistent performance and knowledge among learners (Forman, 1994).

Self-directed e-learning can be designed to become part of employees' busy schedules and learning styles, allowing learning to occur at their own pace; e-learning also eliminates administrative burden caused by scheduling rooms and coordination, allows companies to track employees' learning progress and monitors areas in need of intervention or further explanation. Furthermore, unlike traditional classroom learning, in which instructors are limited to when they can offer immediate feedback, e-learning allows for immediate feedback via online assessment to a wide range of learners.

Studies from Kulik (1994), Willett, Yamashita and Anderson (1983), Sivin-Kachala (1998) and Fletcher and Tobias (2000) suggest that learners learn more effectively using computer-based instruction than they do with traditional training methods. The content retention rate with e-learning was observed to be 25% to 50% higher (Adams, 1992). Clark (2002) attributed improved learning effectiveness to the higher level of interactivity in computer-based learning, which promoted learner participation and in turn led to higher levels of learner engagement and retention. In addition, self-paced learning played a role in increasing retention rate because learners had adequate time to analyse the information. Several studies (Kulik & Kulik, 1991; Kulik, Kulik, & Cohen, 1980) have indicated that learners using computer-based instruction learn faster, as seen in studies that showed that training time was reduced by up to 50% (Forman, 1994).

e-Learning systems with virtual simulations have been used to accelerate the acquisition of skills and expertise that are critical but not frequently practiced in reality (Clark & Mayer, 2016). For instance, when troubleshooting equipment, occurrences of failures are generally quite rare. However, computers can simulate a variety of failures and allow opportunities for workers to practice troubleshooting skills.

At the same time, there are significant disadvantages of e-learning. For example, organizations that may have been too expedient in converting traditional classroom training material, such as content-heavy PowerPoint slides or instructional manuals, into e-learning could have overlooked the need to restructure content to make it engaging for the learner on a e-learning platform (Salas, DeRouin & Littrell, 2005). The learner's potential lack of computer skills may create challenges for e-learning (Carr, 1999). Furthermore, individuals who may lack motivation and self-discipline may struggle to complete self-paced e-learning (Kearsley, 2000).

Table 13.3 summarizes the key advantages and disadvantages of e-learning.

Table 13.3 Advantages and disadvantages of e-learning

Advantages	Disadvantages
– e-Learning allows scalability, which is about meeting increased demands (Arth, 2011) – e-Learning connects learners around the globe at any time, at reduced cost and at increased speeds – e-Learning eliminates administrative burden caused by scheduling rooms and coordination, and allows companies to track employees' learning progress – e-Learning allows immediate feedback via online assessment – Learning is more effective using computer-based instruction than with traditional training methods – e-Learning systems accelerate the acquisition of skills and expertise (Clark & Mayer, 2016).	– e-Learning may be too content heavy and not engaging (Salas, DeRouin & Littrell, 2005) – Lack of computer skills by learners could create challenges for e-learning (Carr, 1999) – Self-paced e-learning requires learners' self-discipline and motivation, which may be absent (Kearsley, 2000) – Less social interactions might make learners feel isolated (Schott et al., 2003; Stonebraker & Hazeltine, 2004) – Problems related to bandwidth include internet connectivity, busy internet lines and internet traffic problem (Zhang et al., 2004) – Issues of trust, authorization, confidentiality, copyright and security on the internet – Influence of organizational time constraints outside of the learners' control may be at play that reduces learner motivation

Source: Author.

In summary, two major advantages were found with e-learning, including the increased retention rate and improved learning speed. The challenge for organizations is to apply *research-based guidelines* (see Table 13.4) to create interactive and meaningful e-learning that keeps the learner engaged and is not a simple conversion of lecture-based presentations into reading-based e-learning (DeRouin, Fritzsche & Salas, 2004; Salas, DeRouin & Littrell, 2005; Burbach, 2015).

Table 13.4 Research guidelines for e-learning design

When designing e-learning, the following guidelines should be considered:

1. Ensure that e-learning is a solution that meets the organization's learning and development needs.
2. Ensure that e-learning is developed in line with theories of information processing and human cognition.
3. Ensure that the learning experience is enhanced by using graphics and text, so that learners are primed to make meaningful associations that aid learning. Graphics should not distract the learner from understanding the text.
4. Ensure that learners are able to have control of some aspects of instruction, for example, provide choices for learners to choose the context of practice examples that is relevant to their experience or job.
5. Provide sufficient guidance to learners so that they are able to navigate easily within the e-learning program, for example, using organising tools such as cognitive maps.
6. Ensure that e-learning has sufficient interactive activities to keep learners engaged.
7. Allow opportunities for online interaction between learners and learners with their instructors.
8. Ensure that learners have the necessary basic computer skills training before embarking on e-learning.
9. Ensure that training methods suit the type of skills being trained. For example, e-learning is more suitable for knowledge outcomes and hard skills such as 'how to sort mail envelopes'. For soft or abstract skills like business ethics, face-to-face approaches such as role play or face-to-face facilitated discussions are advisable.
10. Provide a blended learning approach that combines both e-learning and face-to-face modes of delivery, so as to meet the needs of different learner preferences.

Source: Adapted from Salas, DeRouin and Littrell (2005) and Burbach (2015).

Massive open online courses

A new pedagogical phenomenon that emerged around 2012 to 2013 were the MOOCs. Stemming from the Ivy League universities in the United States, the use of MOOCs has also influenced corporate organizations (Savino, 2014). MOOC courses are typically delivered on the web and are free to access (although some courses have now started charging fees for some services, such as certification on successful completion). MOOCs are 'massive' because they allow a large number of learners to be enrolled in a course; 'open' because anyone with an internet connection is able to access the course; 'online' because course delivery involves videos, online lectures and interactive activities; and 'course' suggests that the learning has a fixed duration, typically terminating with an assessment and certification (Noe, 2017). Baturay (2015) characterised three main features of MOOCs as open, participatory and distributed.

1. Open: Participation in a MOOC is open to anyone who has access to the internet. The work that is generated through the course (both by the facilitators and learners) is shared and available publicly. Finally, there is openness in terms of the learner's role.
2. Participatory: The learning in a MOOC is enabled through active, voluntary participation. Learners create and share online and interact with others.
3. Distributed: The theoretical foundation of MOOC is based upon the connectivist approach; this suggests that knowledge should be distributed among a network of individuals. Learning activities occur in social learning environments, where participants interact with learning content such as videos and online lectures and share interpretations of it. Course readings serve to stimulate discussion and further thinking.

Current MOOCs in today's learning industry include Coursera (see 'Video learning resources'), edX and Udacity. The strengths of MOOCs are that learners can set their own pace and follow their own schedules in any location in the world. Courses may impose deadlines for coursework and assessments, but choices are available as to when to complete them. These features empower a learner to choose what to learn and have control over what additional learning would match one's progress.

In general, initial participation is high but dropout rates are equally high as many learners begin with initial euphoria lured by free offering but do not complete the courses (Brahimi & Sarirete, 2015). Nonetheless, there is high interest by organizations, as seen in a survey by Grossman (2013) reporting that 75% of chief learning officers were exploring MOOCs for their companies. This high interest in organizations is driven by a number of factors, including upskilling their workforce without having to develop their own materials and allowing employees to build a personal learning path or knowledge base (Pappas, 2016). This is especially important in contexts where skills are required to be imparted in a relatively short time.

Meister (2013) identified three elements that make MOOCs (such as Coursera) relevant for corporate training:

1. Semi-synchronicity: Allows students to proceed at their own pace.
2. Course design: A flipped classroom style whereby learning is not lecture-based but student analyse materials that lead to more in-depth discussions, role plays and case analysis.
3. Credentials: Provides learners with course completion certificates that may motivate employees to participate.

Social media

Social media utilizes mobile and web-based technologies to build interactive platforms for employees and groups to share, create and discuss content produced by users or learners. Prevalent examples of social media include Facebook and Twitter, as well as document sharing platforms such as Google Groups and blogs. Keitzmann et al. (2011) presented a framework that defines social media and the implications for organizations to consider regarding building relationships, sharing information and preserving identity among employees.

The advantages of social media in learning and development include the ability for learners to write and contribute to blogs and read others' blogs. Wikis refer to websites that allow users to create, edit and share knowledge on the internet, thus creating online communities. These activities can be classified as contextual-based learning, user-created and allows learning to occur informally in organizations (Noe, 2017). Companies and non-profit organizations have used social media to encourage collaborative learning. For example, Humana, a healthcare company, partnered a learning technology company, Pivotal, to create a social learning platform called Knowledge Exchange, for employees to share knowledge and collaborate to develop products (Melo, 2017).

Social media, while a popular choice of communication over traditional emails, can be potentially misused by employees (see Chapter 8). There are three forms of misuse (Taylor et al., 2016):

- Comments that potentially harm oneself
- Comments that potentially harm other people
- Comments that potentially harm the brand or reputation of the organization

Taylor et al. (2016) recommend organizations to have clear policies and statements over what is deemed acceptable to be communicated on all online platforms, whether company owned or personal. In addition, policies should be clear over employees' behaviours on the internet during and outside office hours.

e-Mentoring

e-Mentoring refers to the process of using electronic or technology to create a channel of communication between mentor and mentee (Hamilton & Scandura, 2003). Traditional mentoring requires face-to-face contact, whereas e-mentoring does not. Some examples for e-mentoring include electronic media, such as email, chat and web discussion boards. The advantages of e-mentoring are the greater flexibility provided for creating and maintaining relationships especially for employees in different geographic locations and for allowing employees on flexible work arrangements to connect with mentors without change to their work schedules.

e-Mentoring allows greater convenience and wider access to mentors around the world. While convenience is increased, there are potential disadvantages to e-mentoring such as a lack of personal touch in the relationship. This drawback can be overcome by blended mentoring, which comprises both face-to-face and e-mentoring. This recommendation is supported by research evidence that suggests that blended mentoring increases the amount of support received by the mentee, which then leads to positive outcomes such as satisfaction and intention to continue with the mentoring (Murphy, 2011).

Longitudinal research also demonstrated that frequency of interaction mediates the relationship between antecedents such as motivation to participate and outcomes such as self-efficacy and task-efficacy (Direnzo et al., 2010).

Mobile learning and wearables

Mobile learning refers to training delivered utilizing mobile devices such as smartphones, iPads and notebook or laptop computers. Mobile devices appeal to a new generation of learners who are constantly on the move and prefer to learn at their own time and pace. Mobile devices can store videos, online learning content and podcasts, all easily accessible to learners to view while they are on the move (i.e., away from their desktop computers in offices or at home) (see the case study at the end of this chapter).

Closely related to concept and benefits of mobile learning is the new invention of the 'wearable'. Wearables refer to technology that is worn on individuals' bodies. Common wearables include the watch or Fitbit device that is worn on the arm or the Apple Watch that is almost a mini computer and is referred to as the most 'personal' computing device that fits an individual's unique body anatomy (Mills et al., 2016). Security of these mini-computer systems are of concern and protecting the security of the devices and the personal data that they hold will prove challenging to organizations. In the learning and development setting, wearables have the propensity to provide immediate feedback and reminders to learners to complete learning tasks or even provide feedback on performance tasks. Wearables have the potential to collect important performance data (such as scan times in delivery settings) that can assist with the training function assessing performance gaps and identifying learning needs.

Technological advances such as wearable technology is bringing forth new opportunities for contextual learning and is transforming e-L&D beyond straightforward e-learning solutions. The *Experience API* or *Tin Can API* is a type of learning technology that allows the tracking of e-learning activity. Data is collected in real time about an individual's or team's offline or online learning experiences and statements are channelled back to the learner in the form of an action or activity, such as 'I did this' (Noe, 2017; Wroten, 2015). This technology offers the enticing prospect of closing the loop on learning and performance; and innovations such as IBM's Watson project hint at how intuitive, continual learning technology can support us in ways we never thought possible. It is a priority for L&D to create learning ecosystems (Pradhan, 2016) and link that to the business strategy of any organization, so that L&D as a function can continue to add value and impact organizational performance.

In the world of big data, analytics, social media, robotics, artificial intelligence and so on, organizations should strive to retain the human touch in e-L&D. For instance, in e-mentoring, whereby technology has created electronic platforms for improved frequency and quality in communication, successfully bridging gaps not only between vast physical distances but also creating connections between human experts and learners from all spectrums of life. The onus is on the L&D profession to maintain this balance of automation and human touch.

Summary

The landscape of e-L&D continues to change rapidly and intensely, both in breadth and depth, and accordingly, the L&D function must focus on staying abreast of developments in tools and methods without losing strong foundational understanding of learning theory and processes that motivate and engage a learner. New discoveries must continue in areas of learning with technology and meta-cognitive skills to enable cognitive flexibility and adaptability required to meet the demands of the changing nature of work. Research efforts should also be directed towards integrating computing and artificial intelligence with learning and development of employees as well as non-employees (such as flexi-workers, contract workers).

In summary, this chapter focused on e-learning and development – a field that is rife with constant change and rich with potential to transform employees and organizations. The chapter was divided into two main sections: the first section began by discussing the transformation from a historical perspective, tracing the transformation of 'training and development', which focused more on the *passive* administration of training activities to employees, to 'learning and development', which focused more on engaging cognitive and mental capacities for *active* learning within individuals. Learning and performance metrics have become a new focus for organizations. In the transformation of tools used in L&D, the digital revolution has played a significant role, with clear drivers such as lowering training costs, demonstrating business value in learning and creating social impact. The second half of the chapter focused on the methods of e-L&D and the important principles to apply when designing or selecting e-L&D solutions for organizations and the potential range of new learning methods available.

Case study: Wings Logistics' journey from training to learning organization

Wings Logistics entered the Asia-Pacific market in early 2000 and grew quickly in 15 countries with over 15,000 employees. The L&D department accordingly had a similar growth and now deploys 70 L&D professionals in the region covering multiple technical and management training functions.

It all started in 2012 when Rob Lowe, the Senior Vice President (VP) of HR from the global head office visited the Asia regional office in Singapore and met with Rachel, the L&D Director and her team. He said, 'How can we use new everyday technologies like mobile phones and iPads to help our employees work more effectively? People these days are constantly on their mobile phones and devices for most of the day; my kids even wouldn't talk to me over dinner!'. This was consistent with the learner profiles that the L&D team had recently discovered in their recent needs analysis initiative – increasing numbers of new staff were millennials and fresh school leavers who were used to using new technology to communicate informally with their social contacts.

Rachel was enthusiastic and had her own ideas on how to take this forward. In the next management meeting, she was to convince senior management to convert traditional classroom training to newer learning innovations using mobile technology and learning management systems. She was nervous as in her previous meetings with Marcell, VP – Finance and Josh, VP – Operations, both gave her a hard time. Marcel was concerned about return on investment (RoI), as there were significant development costs in hiring an IT company to develop a customized learning application on desktop and mobile devices. Josh was concerned about how this might affect business operations because turnover rates were fairly high in some major units. and new hires needed to become productive quickly. Josh was trained in the old school and was quite happy with the existing method of two weeks classroom training, followed by on-job-training.

Clearly, there were benefits in converting traditional classroom training to mobile learning, such as cost savings incurred from reduced travel costs by trainers and trainees. But what if this whole thing falls flat?

Case study questions

- What can Rachel do to convince management to adopt mobile learning and transform e-L&D?
- Who are the stakeholders involved in this transformation?
- What are the needs of a future workforce in terms of learning preferences?
- From an HR perspective, what future challenges could arise when this transformation is implemented? Discuss this question in terms of trainer competencies.
- As the L&D director, what should Rachel share about the learning effectiveness of mobile learning?

Debate: Does e-learning actually promote employee learning and development?

Introduction

It may be argued that e-L&D promotes employee learning through the use of technology. However, a counter argument against e-L&D suggests that learning is actually impeded by technology due to factors such as a mismatch with learning styles. Empirical evidence around this debate encourages learning professionals to understand what is fundamentally meant by learning, that is, cognitive and/or behaviour changes that occur in people and the underlying psychological processes that are influenced by e-learning.

Arguments in favour

- e-Learning allows for learning at the learner's pace, that is, learner control. e-Learning allows for flexibility in when and how a learner wants to engage with the material (Rao, 2011). Studies have shown an increased engagement and retention of material in learners (Clark & Mayer, 2016).
- e-Learning is able to disseminate learning content more consistently than instructor-led training (which varies across instructor's individual style).
- e-Learning allows immediate feedback that improves learning through well-designed online assessments.
- e-Learning allows learners to be connected to experts worldwide.

- e-Learning systems with virtual simulations have been used to accelerate the acquisition of skills and expertise that are critical but not frequently practiced in reality (Clark & Mayer, 2016).

Arguments against

- e-Learning is isolating and does not allow learners to collaborate in live, interactive discussion with other learners.
- Learning may be less conducive in e-learning environments because there are fewer opportunities for learners to seek clarifications or immediate feedback from instructors. This is especially so for learning outcomes that are skills-based.
- e-Learning works only with the assumption that learners are highly self-directed and motivated to learn (Rao, 2011).
- e-Learning programmes work only with the assumption that the learning content has been well-designed, for example, with learners' cognitive load taken into account. e-Learning that is overloaded with content actually impedes learning and mastery (Salas, DeRouin, & Littrell, 2005). Complex content (complex analytical concepts) and skills-based outcomes may be less appropriate for e-learning (Noe, 2017).
- National cultures have a powerful impact on learning pace, style and preferences. Some non-Western cultures prefer a more participative learning approach beyond what e-learning provides with instructor-led learning (Rao, 2011). In addition, countries with low internet usage may struggle with accessing e-learning easily.

Useful references

Clark, R. and Mayer, R. (2016). *e-Learning and the science of instruction: Proven guidelines for consumers and designers of multimedia learning*. 4th ed. Hoboken, NJ: Wiley.

Noe, R. (2017). *Employee training and development*. 7th edn. New York, NY: McGraw-Hill Education.

Rao, P. (2011). *Taking sides: Clashing views in human resource management*. New York, NY: McGraw-Hill.

Salas, E., DeRouin, R. E. and Littrell, L. N. (2005). Research-based guidelines for designing distance learning: What we know so far. In: H. G. Gueutal and D. L. Stone, eds., *The Brave New World of e-HR*. San Francisco, CA: Jossey-Bass, pp. 104–137.

Video learning resources

- What is a learning management system? LMS Software: Provides visual examples of various functionalities of a typical LMS software: www.youtube.com/watch?v=FAsdtwj00Uo
- SAP SuccessFactors learning overview: Illustrates a learning management system that is used by employees, customers and partners: www.youtube.com/watch?v=s1TPE5BFbaY&t=61s

- The future of learning: How Google transformed their L&D delivery: An example of how mobile learning has transformed learning and development delivery in an organization: www.youtube.com/watch?v=TSVI3Hs9Gfk
- Welcome to Coursera: An example of a Massive Online Open Course (MOOC) offered by the top universities: www.youtube.com/watch?v=PojLL3E-zk0
- e-Learning project management: www.youtube.com/watch?v=WURExExwxU2M
- e-Learning strategy secrets: www.youtube.com/watch?v=u29ZjZvSG2o
- Wearables at Work: Augmented reality solutions for enterprise: Shows the capabilities of wearables and how they can be applied to employees at work to enhance productivity: www.youtube.com/watch?v=TxzWJy1lAO0

References

Adams, G. (1992). Why interactive? *Multimedia and Videodisc Monitor*, 10, pp. 20–25.

Adobe. (2014). *Adobe employees get a strong start.* [online] Available at: www.adobe.com/content/dam/acom/en/customer-success/pdfs/adobe-adobe-connect-case-study.pdf [Accessed 6 January 2018].

American Psychological Association (APA). (1997). *Learner-centred psychological principles.* [online] Available at: www.apa.org/ed/governance/bea/learner-centered.pdf [Accessed 1 August 2017].

Arth, B. (2011). The business impact of next-generation e-learning. *Research Reports Bersin and Associates*, 1.

Baturay, M. H. (2015). An overview of the world of MOOCs. *Procedia – Social and Behavioral Sciences*, 174, pp. 427–433.

Bersin, J. (2017). *Rewriting the rules for the digital age: 2017 Deloitte Human Capital Trends.* [online] Available at www2.deloitte.com/content/dam/Deloitte/global/Documents/About-Deloitte/central-europe/ce-global-human-capital-trends.pdf [Accessed 21 March 2018].

Bersin, J., Mallon, D., Barnett, L. and Hines, J. (2016). *Predictions for 2017: Everything is becoming digital.* [Online] Available at www2.deloitte.com/content/dam/Deloitte/at/Documents/about-deloitte/predictions-for-2017-final.pdf [Accessed 21 March 2018].

Brahimi, T. and Sarirete, A. (2015). Learning outside the classroom through MOOCs. *Computers in Human Behaviour*, 51, pp. 604–609.

Burbach, R. (2015). Training and development: Issues and HRIS applications. In: M. J. Kavanagh, M. Thite, and R. D. Johnson (eds.) *Human Resource Information Systems.* 3rd edn. Thousand Oaks, CA: Sage.

Carr, J. (1999). The role of higher education in the effective delivery of multimedia management training to small and medium enterprises. *Educational Technology and Society*, 2, pp. 1176–3647.

Clark, D. (2002). Psychological myths in e-learning. *Medical Teacher*, 24, pp. 598–604.

Clark, R. and Mayer, R. (2016). *e-Learning and the science of instruction: Proven guidelines for consumers and designers of multimedia learning.* 4th ed. Hoboken, NJ: Wiley.

Colquitt, J., LePine, J. and Noe, R. (2000). Toward an integrative theory of training motivation: A meta-analytic path analysis of 20 years of research. *Journal of Applied Psychology*, 85, pp. 678–707.

Davis, B., Carmean, C. and Wagner, E. (2009). *The evolution of the LMS: From management to learning-deep analysis of trends shaping the future of eLearning.* Santa Rosa, CA: eLearning Guild Research.

DeRouin, R. E., Fritzsche, B. A. and Salas E. (2004). Optimizing e-learning: Research-based guidelines for learner-controlled training. *Human Resource Management Journal*, 43, pp. 147–162.

Direnzo, M., Linnehan, F., Shao, P. and Rosenberg, W. L. (2010). A moderated mediation model of e-mentoring. *Journal of Vocational Behaviour*, 76, pp. 292–305.

Edwards, M. and Edwards, K. (2016). *Predictive HR analytics: Mastering the HR metric.* London: Kogan Page.

Fitz-enz, J. and Mattox, J. (2014). *Predictive analytics for human resources*. Hoboken, NJ: Wiley.
Fletcher, J. D. and Tobias, S. (2000) (Eds.). *Training and retraining; Handbook of research on educational communications and technology. A handbook for business, industry, government, and the military.* New York, NY: Macmillan.
Forman, D. (1994). Benefits and value of multimedia learning systems. In: C. McBeath and R. Atkinson. *Proceedings of the Second International Interactive Multimedia Symposium*. Perth, Western Australia, pp. 140–146. [online] Available at: www.aset.org.au/confs/iims/1994/dg/forman.html. [Accessed 20 October 2017].
Grossman, R. (2013). Are massive online courses in your future? Organizational and Employee Development Special Report. *SHRM HR Magazine – August 2013*, 34. [online] Hrmagazine-digital.com. Available at: www.hrmagazine-digital.com/hrmagazine/201308?pg=34#pg34 [Accessed 10 October 2017].
Hamilton, B. A. and Scandura, T. A. (2003). E-mentoring: Implications for organizational learning and development in a wired world. *Organizational Dynamics*, 31, pp. 388–402.
Hendrickson, A. R. (2003). Human resource information systems: Backbone technology of contemporary human resources. *Journal of Labor Research*, 24, pp. 381–394.
Johnson, R. D., Gueutal, H. and Falbe, C. M. (2009). Technology, trainees, metacognitive activity and e-learning effectiveness. *Journal of Managerial Psychology*, 24, pp. 545–566.
Kane, G., Palmer, D., Phillips, A., Kiron, D. and Natasha, B. (2016). *Achieving digital maturity*. [online] DU Press. Available at: https://dupress.deloitte.com/dup-us-en/focus/digital-maturity/digital-mindset-mit-smr-report.html [Accessed 23 October 2017].
Kaplan-Leiserson, E. (2000). *e-Learning glossary*. [online] Available at: www.learningcircuits.org/glossary.html [Accessed 1 August 2017).
Kearsley, G. (2000). *Online education: Learning and teaching in cyberspace*. Belmont, CA: Wadsworth Publishing.
Keitzmann, J. H., Hermkens, K., McCarthy, I. P. and Silvestre, B. S. (2011). Social media? Get serious! Understanding the functional building blocks of social media. *Business Horizons*, 52, pp. 241–251.
Kolb, D. (1984). *Experiential learning*. Englewood Cliffs, NJ: Prentice-Hall, Inc.
Kolb, D. and Fry, R. E. (1975). Toward an applied theory of experiential learning. In: C. Cooper, ed., *Theories of Group Process*. New York, NY: Wiley, pp. 33–57.
Kulik, J. A. (1994). Meta-analytic studies of findings on computer-based instruction. In: E. L. Baker and H. F. O'Neil, eds., *Technology Assessment in Education and Training*. Hillsdale, NJ: Prentice Hall, pp. 9–33.
Kulik, J. A. and Kulik, C. C. (1991). Effectiveness of computer-based instruction; an updated analysis. *Computers in Human Behaviour*, 7, pp. 75–94.
Kulik, J. A., Kulik, C. C. and Cohen, P. A. (1980). Effectiveness of computer-based college teaching: a meta-analysis of findings. *Review of Educational Research*, 50, pp. 525-544
Manyika, J., Chui, M., Brown, B., Bughin, J., Dobbs, R., Roxburgh, C. and Byers A. H. (2011). *Big data: The next frontier for innovation, competition, and productivity*. [online] McKinsey Global Institute. Available at: www.mckinsey.com/business-functions/digital-mckinsey/our-insights/big-data-the-next-frontier-for-innovation [Accessed 23 October 2017].
Meister, J. (2013). *How MOOCs will revolutionize corporate learning and development*. [online] Available at: www.forbes.com/sites/jeannemeister/2013/08/13/how-moocs-will-revolutionize-corporate-learning-development/#568bd12d1255 [Accessed 1 August 2017].
Melo, A. (2017). *Enabling collaborative software development with Pivotal Cloud Foundry*. [online] Available at: https://content.pivotal.io/case-studies/humana [Accessed 1 August 2017].
Mills, A. J., Watson, R. T., Pitt, L. and Kietzmann, J. (2016). Wearing safe: Physical and informational security in the age of the wearable device. *Business Horizons*, 59, pp. 615–622.
Murphy, W. M. (2011). From e-mentoring to blended mentoring: Increasing students' developmental initiation and mentors' satisfaction. *Academy of Management Learning & Education*, 10, pp. 606–622.
Noe, R. (2017). *Employee training and development*. 7th ed. New York, NY: McGraw-Hill Education.

Pappas, C. (2016). *7 Tips for using MOOCs in corporate eLearning – eLearning industry*. [online] eLearning Industry. Available at: https://elearningindustry.com/tips-using-moocs-corporate-elearning [Accessed 8 January 2018].

Pradhan, A. (2016). *E-learning modules will die*. [online] Available at: www.elearninglearning.com/ibm/?open-article-id=4634975&article-title=elearning-modules-will-die--and-70-20-10-will-hold-the-smoking-gun&blog-domain=learnnovators.com&blog-title=learnnovators [Accessed 1 August 2017].

Salas, E., DeRouin, R. E. and Littrell, L. N. (2005). Research-based guidelines for designing distance learning: What we know so far. In: H. G. Gueutal and D. L. Stone, eds., *The Brave New World of e-HR*. San Francisco, CA: Jossey-Bass, pp. 104–137.

Savino, D. M. (2014). The impact of MOOCs on human resource training and development. *Journal of Higher Education Theory and Practice*, 14, pp. 59–64.

Schott, M., Chernish, W., Dooley, K. E. and Linder, J. R. (2003). Innovations in distance learning program development and delivery. *Online Journal of Distance Learning Administration*, 6, 1–7. [online] Available at: https://eric.ed.gov/?id=EJ1068367. [Accessed 1 August 2017].

Short, J. and Ketchen, D. (2011). The good, the fad and the ugly. *Business Horizons*, 54, pp. 7–16.

SHRM. (2017). *Keeping pace with a mobile workforce (Infographic)*. [online] Available at: www.shrm.org/hr-today/news/hr-magazine/0317/pages/keeping-pace-with-a-mobile-workforce-(infographic).aspx?_ga=2.66722538.559304530.1508747083-274057372.1508747081 [Accessed 23 Oct. 2017].

Sitzmann, T., Kraiger, K., Stewart, D. and Wisher, R. (2006). The comparative effectiveness of web-based and classroom instruction: A meta-analysis. *Personnel Psychology*, 59, 623–664.

Sivin-Kachala, J. (1998). *Report of the effectiveness of technology in schools, 1990–1997*. Washington, DC: Software Publishers Association.

Sloman, M. (2005). Learning in knowledge-intensive organisations: Moving from training to learning. *Development and Learning in Organizations*, 19, pp. 9–10.

Stephan, M., Uzawa, S., Volini, E., Walsh, B. and Yoshida, R. (2016). Digital HR: Revolution, not evolution. [online] Available at: http://diginomica.com/2017/01/05/hr-people-dont-just-digital-digital-2017/ [Accessed 1 August 2017].

Stonebraker, P. W. and Hazeltine, J. E. (2004). Virtual learning effectiveness. *The Learning Organization*, 11, pp. 209–225.

Szasz, F. M. (2006). Quotes about history. [online] Available at: http://hnn.us/articles/1328.html. [Accessed 1 August 2017].

Tang, M. and Byrne, R. (2007). Regular versus online versus blended: a qualitative description of the advantages of the electronic modes and a quantitative evaluation. *International Journal of E-Learning*, 6, pp. 257–266.

Taylor, M., Haggerty, J., Gresty, D., Wren, C. and Berry, T. (2016). Avoiding the misuse of social media by employees. *Network Security*, 5, pp. 8–11.

Training Magazine. (2017). *2017 Training industry report*. [online] Available at: https://trainingmag.com/trgmag-article/2017-training-industry-report [Accessed 5 January 2018].

Willett, J. B., Yamashita, J. M. and Anderson, R. D. (1983). A meta-analysis of instructional systems. *Journal of Research in Science Teaching*, 20, pp. 405–417.

Wright, A. (2017). *Technology allows cisco to work with the best, no matter where they are*. [online] SHRM. Available at: www.shrm.org/resourcesandtools/hr-topics/technology/pages/technology-allows-cisco-to-work-with-the-best-no-matter-where-they-are.aspx?_ga=2.65756906.559304530.1508747083-274057372.1508747081 [Accessed 23 October 2017].

Wroten, C. (2015). *The Experience API (xAPI): What you need to know - eLearning industry*. [online] eLearning industry. Available at: https://elearningindustry.com/experience-api-xapi-what-need-know [Accessed 8 January 2018].

Zhang, D., Zhao J. L., Zhou, L. and Nunamaker, J. F. (2004). Can e-learning replace classroom learning? *Communications of the ACM*, 47, pp. 75–79.

Part IV
Problems and prospects

14 Strategic evaluation of e-HRM

Ralf Burbach

Learning objectives

- To assess the potential benefits of using technology in terms of operational, relational, global and transformational aspects of HRM
- To highlight the potential drawbacks of e-HRM
- To discuss the key success factors in e-HRM implementation
- To differentiate between intended and unintended e-HRM outcomes
- To identify ways in which the use of e-HRM can be assessed strategically

---

Introduction

Enthusiastic proponents of technology view it as a 'nirvana' – a heavenly state of perfect peace and happiness. The detractors however view technology as a 'nemesis' – leading to ruin and destruction. The truth obviously lies somewhere in between. The sobering fact is that 70 per cent of software implementations can be considered a failure (Wright, 2016). In the specific context of e-HRM, the situation is no different. According to a survey of HR managers, the top five HR technology implementation challenges include:

- Difficulties in defining the future state of the HR organisation post HR technology implementation
- Added cost and time through necessary customisation
- Challenges in setting up and running of reports and analytics
- Lack of knowledge and experience of implementation team
- Internal resource constraints including people, time and money

Moreover, only about a fifth of organisations stated that they would be able to overcome these challenges (Wright, 2016).

Previous chapters in this book have already outlined in detail the broad range of potential operational, relational and transformational uses of e-HRM (Parry, 2011; Ruël, Bondarouk & Looise, 2004). Operational advantages focus on the attainment of additional efficiencies and effectiveness through the use of e-HRM and a commensurate reduction in HR transaction costs. Relational benefits can be gained by using e-HRM to improve communication between employees, line managers and the HR department as well as by increasing employee involvement in the HR process. e-HRM can also provide new ways of providing employees a voice through the more extensive use of social media by HR departments, especially for Generation Y employees (Holland, Cooper & Hecker, 2016). Transformational uses of e-HRM focus on facilitating HR departments to become involved in the strategic decision-making processes of their firms by providing better HR service, HR analytics and decision support. Yet, many organisations appear to fail to capitalise fully on the advantages of employing e-HRM technologies (Burbach & Charlier, 2017; Burbach & Dundon, 2005; Burbach & Royle, 2014).

This chapter aims to evaluate the strategic use of e-HRM with a particular focus on the possible pitfalls and barriers to capitalising on the potential of e-HRM, that is, its smart and its dark side (Holland & Bardoel, 2016). The benefits of digitalising HRM activities for organisations of any size are numerous and are amplified for multinational organisations (MNC) that operate across many sites and many countries (Svoboda & Schroder, 2001). Some of the strategic advantages of e-HRM include added value to the organisation, around-the-clock HR self-service, improved employee involvement and communication, employee empowerment, online training and development, talent management systems, better HR metrics and performance appraisals. This chapter outlines the benefits of e-HRM before discussing the potential barriers to e-HRM utilisation. Then, this chapter considers the key success factors in e-HRM implementation before exploring various ways and models in which the strategic benefits of e-HRM can be assessed. The chapter concludes with an e-HRM implementation case study and a debate on the subject matter.

Benefits of digitising HRM

Many authors refer to the potential of HR technology to transform the HR function by *adding value* to firms essentially by freeing up HR staff to engage more in strategic planning activities and by leveraging the global, transactional, relational and transformational uses of technology (Grissemann, Plank & Brunner-Sperdin, 2013; Hussain, Wallace & Cornelius, 2007; Martin, Reddington & Alexander, 2008; Parry, 2011). In a similar vein, Strohmeier and Kabst (2014) discuss three different categories of users of e-HRM – non-users, operational users and power users. Only organisations that can be classified as *power users* of e-HRM will be able to add strategic value to the organisation. The use of e-HRM allows HR practitioners to better manage organisational HR knowledge and the gathering and analysis of HR metrics to support evidenced-based HR management (Bassi, 2012; Falletta, 2014). Thus, e-HRM can add value to all HR related activities such as training and development activities, for example, the establishment of detailed training needs analyses or training plans even across the largest of firms (Burbach & Charlier, 2017). Advanced uses of e-HRM and HR intelligence are often associated with the use of decision support systems and artificial intelligence (Falletta, 2014).

Improved *HR analytics* can help identify pivotal talent in organisations and it is almost implicit in the talent management literature that large corporations ought to employ talent management systems to leverage this process (Collings, Scullion & Vaiman, 2015; Dries, 2013). Talent management systems form part of the broader e-HRM structure of an organisation and offer a number of strategic advantages, such as the identification, management and development of talent and talent pools in an organisation (Bondarouk & Ruël, 2010; Grant & Newell, 2013; Heikkilä, 2013; Parry, 2011).

Furthermore, the roll-out of e-HRM in an organisation allows employees to avail of HR services 24/7 as part of an *employee self-service system* (Marler & Fisher, 2013; Strohmeier, Bondarouk & Konradt, 2012), while the introduction of e-HRM and online recruitment has completely transformed the recruitment and selection process (Holm, 2014; Parry & Olivas-Lujan, 2011). Self-service applications also aid in the effective and efficient operation of HR shared services centres either as an in-house solution or as part of an outsourced provision (Farndale, Paauwe & Hoeksema, 2009).

In addition, *increased access to HR related information* will not only empower employees in terms of their access to HR services including training, recruitment and promotion, it will also *empower* line managers to carry out HR activities themselves, which in turn will free up HR staff to spend more time on more strategic activities (Parry, 2014).

e-HRM, especially if it utilises social media platforms, has the strategic potential to improve the recruitment and selection processes (Eckhardt, Laumer, Maier & Weitzel, 2014) as well as organisational communication and employee engagement (Bell, 2015). Increased employee *access to information* can also enhance *employee involvement* in the workplace. In fact, firms could use e-HRM to support employee relationship management in the same fashion as organisations utilise customer relationship management software to increase engagement and retention (Strohmeier, 2013). Some examples of the benefits of employing e-HRM are outlined in Table 14.1.

While, undoubtedly, e-HRM offers many strategic advantages to a firm, which have been discussed in detail in previous chapters of this book, few firms are actually able to capitalise on these (Burbach & Charlier, 2017). The potential barriers and drawbacks of employing e-HRM are discussed in the following section.

Potential barriers to and drawbacks of digital HRM

Information technology (IT), particularly as a result of the widespread use of mobile technologies, is an intricate part of people's private and professional lives. However, some authors have argued that the introduction of IT and in particular e-HRM may be driven by an effort in firms to increase their *control over employees* (Stanton & Weiss, 2003) and to carry out *employee surveillance* (Findlay & McKinlay, 2003; Holland & Bardoel, 2016; Ngoc Duc, Siengthai & Page, 2013). This in turn has led to employee concerns over the *invasion of privacy and data security* in firms that use e-HRM (Lukaszewski, Stone & Stone-Romero, 2008; Phillips, Isenhour & Stone, 2008; Stone, Lukaszewski, Stone-Romero & Johnson, 2013). These concerns may be unfounded in the majority of cases. However, the mere suspicion by employees will be enough to affect user satisfaction with and trust in e-HRM. Utilising e-HRM and the sharing of employee-related information can also give rise to legal issues, as data protection legislation varies from country to country. These are discussed further in the next chapter.

While clearly e-HRM has the potential to foster the relational aspects of HRM, for instance by *fostering the employee champion role* by allowing employees to remain in close contact with the (virtual) HR department (Guiderdoni-Jourdain & Oiry, 2011), one may also argue that the roll out of e-HRM and the digitalisation of communications with the HR department may lead to the *depersonalisation of the employee–employer relationship* and may make employees feel disenfranchised due to the lack of personal contact with HR staff.

A lack of *usability, user friendliness and user acceptance* will ultimately undermine the success of e-HRM technology. Usability and user friendliness will also determine users' satisfaction with e-HRM (Strohmeier, 2007). In other words, the degree of user acceptance is a function of users' reactions to this technology, their intention to use it, their actual use and the actual benefits gained from utilising e-HRM (Delone & McLean, 2003;

Table 14.1 Benefits of using e-HRM

Operational	• Facilitates the processing and management of all HR-related information • Increased accuracy of HR-related information • Production of timely and accurate HR-related information • Better HR metrics • Reduction of HR transaction costs and time • More efficient and effective recruitment and selection processes through the use of online assessment tests and centres, advanced algorithms to select applicants, direct link with job websites
Relational	• Improved communication with potential recruits through the use of social media • Enhance information sharing and knowledge management • Better relationships between organisational members and between the organisation and its external partners • Improved organisational culture and trust due to improved transparency • Increase the timeliness of transactions between managers and employees and other stakeholders • Higher HR service levels
Global	• Better data to identify talent and to create and maintain talent pools • Improved communication among HR departments in an MNC • Streamlined HR service provision in large multisite operations • Anytime-anyplace access for all employees to HR-related information • Supports new types of organisational forms such as born global or virtual organisations
Transformational	• Better HR analytics • Improved decision making • Freeing up HR staff for strategic decision-making purposes • Transformed training and development through the application of augmented and virtual reality technologies • Better matching of applicants with jobs due to improved decision support systems • Improved change management processes • Devolvement of HR responsibilities to line management and increased access to HR related information for line managers • Increased levels of employee involvement • Empowerment of employees in relation to managing their interface with the HR department including training and development, performance appraisals and rewards • Attainment of strategic organisational goals as a result of better alignment of HR activities with organisational objectives • Potential to augment employee hiring success, retention and performance, and to reduce employee turnover as a result of more strategic analysis and use of HR information • Ability to respond faster to changes in the firm's environment

Source: Author.

Stone & Davis, 2008; Venkatesh et al., 2003). If employees feel that the use of e-HRM is of no perceived benefit to them, they will simply not use it.

Of course, one of the key assumptions of e-HRM and perhaps also one of the biggest sources of user dissatisfaction is the presumption that all employees of a firm are IT and information literate and that they have continuous access to e-HRM, which of course cannot be ensured in all instances. In addition, it is implied in the terms of e-HRM that employees can, and in some cases are expected to, access e-HRM services anytime anyplace, as would be the case for many e-learning activities that firms offer their employees.

These need to be engaged with in order to meet key performance indicators for their next performance appraisal.

Thus, e-HRM can negatively impact on an employee's work-life balance. In addition, these can negatively impact an employee's trust in the organisation and its overall IT systems. An individual's *degree of trust* in e-HRM can be negatively affected by the interplay of their predisposition to trust, organisational trust, organisational culture, usability and utility of the technology as well as their sensitivity to privacy (Tate, Furtmueller & Wilderom, 2013). Employee trust can be improved if a firm focuses to a greater extent on the relational aspects of e-HRM (Guiderdoni-Jourdain & Oiry, 2011).

Stone and Davis (2008) argue that user acceptance equates to e-HRM implementation success, while Ruël, Bondarouk and Van der Velde (2007) purport that improving the perceived quality of e-HRM applications will lead to a commensurate increase in the effectiveness of HRM. Yet, many organisations fail to involve users in the rollout of e-HRM (Burbach & Dundon, 2005; Ruta, 2009). In addition to user acceptance, a number of other factors are critical in the e-HRM implementation success that are discussed next.

Key success factors in e-HRM implementation

The key success factors in e-HRM implementation include leadership and top management support, detailed planning, proper change management, an organisational culture that is open to change, communication, and training (Guiderdoni-Jourdain & Oiry, 2011; Stone & Davis, 2008). Moreover, Burbach and Royle (2014) put forward that e-HRM implementation success is contingent on a range of *institutional factors* of an organisation, that is,

- external factors (e.g. legal, educational, competition);
- relational factors (e.g. trust, culture, micro-politics);
- organisational factors (e.g. governance, other HR systems and processes, change management); and
- individual factors (e.g. user reaction, user satisfaction, usability, user acceptance).

Organisations have little influence on their external environment. However, e-HRM should be configured in such a way that it can be utilised to the same extent and in the same way across all subsidiaries of an MNC in any part of the world. The relational aspect must be managed carefully from the outset.

A *lack of trust* in e-HRM can develop very quickly and it is thus important to communicate with and involve employees in the implementation process from the start. *Micro-politics* in an organisation can affect the successful implementation of e-HRM (Tate, Furtmueller & Wilderom, 2013). Micro-politics are common in an organisational context and are often the result of internal struggles for resources and recognition particularly in MNCs where individual subsidiaries or regions compete for resources allocated by the headquarters. Organisations that are *open, transparent and change ready* are far more likely to implement e-HRM successfully.

Other organisational factors that are conducive to e-HRM success are strong management support, additional resources and a business strategy that marries existing HR processes and systems with the new e-HRM configuration. For example, many organisations introduce highly sophisticated e-HRM and decision support systems but fail to develop fully the necessary metrics or 'what if' scenarios to fully exploit their potential.

Table 14.2 Key success factors for e-HRM implementation

Project management success factors	– Identification of a project team and project champions – Detailed project planning with milestones – Implementation strategy – Leadership – Monitoring and evaluation of implementation – Ongoing training
Communication success factors	– Effective communication – Cooperation between IT and HR departments – Stakeholder involvement
System level success factors	– System and information quality – Compatibility with legacy systems – Business process adaptation and/or re-engineering – Advance testing and troubleshooting of the e-HRM system – Language support – User acceptance, user satisfaction, usability and user-friendliness of system
Organisational level success factors	– Organisational citizenship behaviour – Alignment with business, HR and IT strategies – Compatibility and organisational fit and readiness – Organisational trust – Organisational readiness – Organisational and national culture
Leadership level success factors	– Change management – Overcome/avoid resistance to change – Top management level support – Sufficient resources

Source: Burbach and Royle (2014).

Thus, firms ought to have a very clear *vision and strategy* for what they aim to achieve with the use of e-HRM. At an individual level, research has shown that there is a very strong correlation between the ease of use, attitude towards e-HRM, user satisfaction, a clear e-HRM strategy and user support (Yusliza & Ramayah, 2012). Therefore, organisations need to ensure a large degree of buy-in from their employees and that employees are trained and supported in their use of e-HRM from the outset. The key success factors of e-HRM implementation are summarised in Table 14.2.

Unintended outcomes of e-HRM utilisation

Many authors have highlighted that e-HRM introduction does not always lead to the expected positive outcomes or returns on investment (Burbach & Royle, 2014; Ruël et al., 2004). Even a successful e-HRM implementation process can lead to a broad range of 'functional' and 'dysfunctional' outcomes (Stone, Stone-Romero & Lukaszewski, 2003). Many of the latter are the result of a poor implementation process and a lack of vision or strategy for e-HRM, which in turn lead to low levels of user satisfaction and a lack of trust.

Martin et al. (2008) developed a very useful taxonomy that categorises these outcomes in four quadrants as either *intended positive or negative* and *unintended positive or negative*. Examples of unintended negative operational outcomes would be a lack of face to face communication of employees with HR staff and perhaps lack of trust as a result of perceived employee surveillance and the perceived invasion of privacy. Reductions in the

Table 14.3 Potential negative outcomes of e-HRM

Frustration with e-HRM due to lack of involvement in the implementation process, poor training, lack of IT skills of users and poor usability of system

Lack of trust as a result of perceived increased control, monitoring and surveillance in the workplace

Feeling of isolation and a perceived reduction in the level of HR service provided due to the reduction in face-to-face contact with HR staff

Reduction in headcount of HR staff and loss of intellectual capital in that area

Resistance to change caused by the introduction of e-HRM and the subsequent change of HR practices and routines

Disillusionment by management with e-HRM because expected productivity gains and transformation of the HR department could not be attained

Privacy concerns as employees have to input an increasing amount of personal information into an employee database

Changes in power relationships and shifts in the micro-political configuration of an organisation

'Technostress' (Tarafdar, D'Arcy, Turel, & Gupta, 2015) due to the overuse of information technology in all aspects of the employee's life

Financial losses for the firm as the return on investment on e-HRM could not be materialised

---

Source: Author.

HR headcount may well be an intended negative outcome (for the employees). An increased use of e-HRM may unintentionally lead to a loss of intellectual HR capital, an increased frustration and a feeling of powerlessness due to the high level of automation of HR processes and the increased workload of line managers who often need to compensate for the lack of HR staff dealing with issues.

At the transformational level, positive intended outcomes include the increased availability and data mining of HR-related information to support business processes and the freeing up of HR staff to focus on value added rather than transactional HR activities. Positive unintended outcomes could include more innovation due to improved knowledge sharing and the identification of talent and the formation of talent pools. Another example of unintended positive outcomes is what is referred to as 'reverse diffusion' of e-HRM practices, that is the adoption and rollout of e-HRM practices across the subsidiaries of an MNC that had been developed or adopted successfully first by a single subsidiary (Burbach & Royle, 2014). For example, a subsidiary might develop a new e-HRM practice such as e-recruitment or some aspect of online training and development, which is subsequently adopted by the entire firm.

e-HRM outcomes should be classified as intended or unintended contingent on an organisation's overall e-HRM vision and strategy. In other words, if an e-HRM outcome was not implicit in an organisation's e-HRM strategy, it must be considered an unintended outcome. However, it should be noted that some negative outcomes, such as the monitoring of online communication of staff or the changes of HR routines, may well be intended outcomes, particularly in a highly competitive business environment. Some of the negative and often unintended outcomes of e-HRM utilisation are summarised in Table 14.3.

Strategic evaluation models for e-HRM

The previous discussion has illustrated the need for and also the difficulties in trying to carry out a strategic evaluation of e-HRM. Clearly, e-HRM offers many advantages but also many pitfalls that firms ought to avoid at all cost. The extant e-HRM literature offers a number of different approaches and different angles to the strategic evaluation of e-HRM. For instance, this chapter has already alluded to the importance of the organisational context within e-HRM. Thus, it is important to assess the impact of *contextual factors* on the level of implementation of e-HRM (Heikkilä, 2013; Strohmeier et al., 2012).

Furthermore, this chapter has identified the importance of clear e-HRM goals and their integration with the overall strategy of the business. This is an issue that ought to be explored in more detail. It is also evident that even high-tech firms are not necessarily able to capitalise on the potential of e-HRM. Therefore, it is worthwhile exploring whether an organisation's IT capability is a necessary requirement for successful e-HRM utilisation.

Recent articles on e-HRM have somewhat moved away from using this term, as it can be somewhat limiting in terms of the types of technologies that are now available to firms and their HR departments, especially if virtual reality and other forms of artificial intelligence are considered. Therefore, the strategic assessment of e-HRM should incorporate an evaluation of the degree of digitalisation of an organisation's HR functions. These approaches to assessing e-HRM strategically are discussed in more detail below.

The organisational context assessment

A number of authors have highlighted the influence of institutional factors on the attainment of strategic potential of e-HRM (Guiderdoni-Jourdain & Oiry, 2011; Heikkilä, 2013; Holm, 2014; Strohmeier, 2007). Burbach and Royle (2014) suggest that expected e-HRM outcomes in MNCs are not only mediated by the various factors that make up the institutional context of the organisation but also the extent to which e-HRM is actually implemented, internalised and integrated within the firm and its existing systems and processes. They (Burbach & Royle, 2014) make the valid point that the fact that an e-HRM system is implemented (installed) will not necessarily lead to any of the advantages offered by it. e-HRM must be *internalised*, that is, it must be accepted by organisational members and it must ultimately be *integrated* and become part of the organisation and what it does.

Full integration and indeed the preceding step, internalisation, appear to be difficult to achieve without a proper strategy, organisational commitment and resources. That is why many organisations fail to capitalise on the advantages of e-HRM. Strohmeier (2007) also offers a framework for the assessment of e-HRM outcomes. In his framework, e-HRM outcomes are mediated by the *e-HRM configuration*, that is, the various actors using e-HRM, e-HRM strategies and activities and the actual technologies utilised. This e-HRM configuration is in turn affected by the micro and macro context of the organisation.

The strategic alignment assessment

This chapter has already alluded to the need to develop a clear e-HRM strategy for the organisation against which the outcomes of e-HRM ought to be measured (Bondarouk & Looise, 2009). Burbach (2012) states that a critical success factor in e-HRM implementation is the *degree of alignment* of the e-HRM strategy with corporate, HRM, other functional and subsidiary-level-strategies. It would be worthwhile for firms to ascertain the degree to which this is the case, as a misaligned e-HRM strategy is unlikely to support other business processes and decision making in the firm.

The IT capability assessment

Another useful way to assess whether e-HRM is used to its full potential is to consider an organisation's IT capability and to compare it with the manner in which e-HRM is utilised (Burbach & Dundon, 2009; L'Écuyer & Raymond, 2017). However, even organisations with limited IT capabilities will be able to use their existing e-HRM for strategic decision-making purposes. Yet, it is also possible that an organisation with very strong IT capabilities will not employ e-HRM to its full potential.

The digitalisation of HR activity assessment

In recent years, the HR technology debate has shifted from focusing on human resource information systems (HRIS), to electronic HRM and more recently to digital HRM (d-HRM) or smart HRM. This development is largely owing to the rapid developments in IT and the proliferation of mobile technologies, which have in many ways revolutionised the role of HRM in recruitment and selection, performance assessment or training and development.

Jooss and Burbach (2017) have developed a HR digitalisation model based on a continuum from no digitalisation to the application of Web 3.0 technologies, such as the Internet of Things (IoT), wearables and augmented reality, to HRM activities, which can be used to assess the degree of digitalisation of HRM activities in firms. While the case study organisations in their research employed e-HRM to varying degrees for different HR activities, it is evident that d-HRM or smart HRM is an ideal state that firms may never actually reach. However, it must be mentioned here that it may not be such a good idea to fully digitalise all of an organisation's HR activities. After all, it is implicit in the nature of HRM that it deals with people and that human contact is essential in that equation.

Continuous monitoring and evaluation of e-HRM

Any organisational process and system should be subject to continuous monitoring and evaluation in order to ensure prolonged success. The feedback loop should continuously compare the expected strategic outcomes with the actual outcomes of e-HRM utilisation. As part of this process, it will be crucial to take account of functional and dysfunctional, expected and unexpected outcomes, whereby the latter ought to be minimised as they are an indicator of poor alignment between e-HRM strategy and business strategy.

Summary

Despite the many advantages that e-HRM has to offer, many organisations do not capitalise on all of its advantages, often as a result of a flawed implementation process. This chapter has highlighted the smart as well as the dark side of e-HRM (Holland & Bardoel, 2016). In addition, the chapter suggested initiatives that should pave the way for the successful implementation of e-HRM. Moreover, the chapter outlined various ways in which the value of e-HRM can be evaluated strategically.

Case study: International Hotelco

International Hotelco is a large multinational hotel corporation with over 500,000 hotel rooms in over 100 countries. It employs over 150,000 people at all levels across the globe and is headquartered in the USA. Hotels typically use a broad range of information technology (IT) systems particularly for taking reservations, managing their revenues or to control their supply chain, most of which are common to the industry. Profits in the hotel industry have been increasing year on year and the hotel chain is expanding rapidly, particularly in Asia.

However, one of the main issues it is facing is the recruitment and retention of talent. International Hotelco is closely following the development of its competitors and their increased focus on nurturing talent. Following some conversations with their software suppliers, it emerged that most of its competitors were using a particular e-HRM package, which appeared to offer all bells and whistles as far as HR software was concerned. Particularly, the talent management system that was embedded within the software, which was completely cloud-based, appealed to the board of directors of the company. However, the organisation did not spend any time on developing any human resource (HR) metrics that could be used to identify talent.

Following some meetings at the corporate level, it was decided to purchase the software and to implement it across all of its hotel properties around the world. During the rollout phase, which commenced in the US, some initial e-HRM training was provided to the 'super users' of the system, which were located at the headquarters and regional headquarters offices. The default language of the system was US English and most of the default data fields in the system related to the US education and training system. Initially, the HR department was very fond of the software, as it its recruitment and selection tool integrated well with existing external recruitment websites, which streamlined the process greatly.

The e-HRM software also included an online training and development tool and the company purchased a bank of online courses that all employees had access to through the system. Employees were encouraged to enrol on these online courses in their out of office hours to minimise the impact on the operations. There was a big push from line managers for employees to undertake as much online training as possible in order to obtain a more positive performance appraisal. All performance appraisals and talent reviews had to be completed using the e-HRM system.

Quite a number of HR staff at headquarters and at regional headquarters were made redundant, as e-HRM had now replaced many of the activities that they used to undertake. Initially, the corporation experienced many cost savings due to the increased speed and reduced cost at which transactions could be processed. However, after a while it emerged that the e-HRM system was hardly used by the individual hotels and the managers of those hotels. In particular, individual employees felt that the system was not user friendly and some developed a certain level of mistrust towards the e-HRM system.

Case study questions

- How could the various issues with the e-HRM system arise?
- What steps were involved in the e-HRM implementation process?
- What could the organisation have done to prevent these issues from occurring?

Debate: Can technology really transform the HRM function?

Introduction

In a series of short articles in the *Digital Journal*, Sandle (2017) suggests that organisations that invest in technology can expect a complete digital transformation in a broad range of HRM related activities, such as performance management, recruitment, HR data analytics or learning, training and development. However, the e-HRM literature also suggests that many firms fail to capitalise fully on the many advantages that the digitalisation of the HRM function has to offer.

Arguments in favour

- According to a recent report by KPMG (2016), the future of HR technology lies in 'cloud HR'. Potential benefits of cloud HR comprise lower costs, better HR service, improved functionality, a more strategic role for HR and value added to an organisation.
- Novel uses of technology can lead to better engagement with existing employees and attract new ones.
- The digitalisation of HRM can facilitate improved HR analytics (Marler, Cronemberger, & Tao, 2017) and the talent management processes of an organisation, which are intricately linked and critical to its long-term success.
- The transformation of HRM through technology is multifaceted, that is, it can take many forms. Firms can hope to achieve operational advantages in terms of improved efficiency and effectiveness of processes; it can boost internal communication and knowledge sharing; IT can transform the HRM function by providing the tools and information for improved strategic decision making.

Arguments against

- The KPMG (2016) report mentioned above also, however, alludes to the fact that merely 24 per cent of the 854 executives surveyed felt that cloud HR alone can not provide greater value to a business.
- The implementation of HR technology alone will not lead to a transformation of the HRM function. It needs to be internalised and integrated within the organisation and its current systems and processes.
- The introduction of e-HRM can lead to a number of negative outcomes including loss of HR staff, security and privacy concerns with regard to the use and storage of personal information, increased pressure on line management due to the devolution of HR activities or diminution of the human touch amongst others.
- e-HRM success depends on quite a large number of contextual factors, such as the language, laws, culture, training systems, competition and the industry sector, most of which cannot be influenced by an organisation.
- Successful e-HRM implementation is also contingent on a broad range of internal factors, including good change management, open organisational culture, top level management support, adequate resourcing, user training and so on, which can make it difficult to get it right.

Useful references

KPMG. (2016). *HR transformation survey 2016: The future belongs to the bold*. Retrieved from https://assets.kpmg.com/content/dam/kpmg/pdf/2016/07/cloud-hr-the-future-belongs-to-the-bold.pdf.

Marler, J. H., Cronemberger, F., & Tao, C. (2017). HR Analytics: Here to Stay or Short Lived Management Fashion? In T. V. Bondarouk, H. J. M. Ruël & E. Parry (Eds.), *Electronic HRM in the Smart Era* (pp. 3–59). Bingley: Emerald Publishing Limited.

Sandle, T. (2017). *Increased take-up of digital technology by human resources – Digital transformation*. Retrieved from www.digitaljournal.com/digitaltransformation/2017/09/increased-take-up-of-digital-technology-by-human-resources/.

Video learning resources

- Cloud HR: The future belongs to the bold: www.youtube.com/watch?v=rTPHOGrFpz8
- Dr Dave Ulrich – The future of HR: www.youtube.com/watch?v=57PmDk73u7I
- Digital HR: Technology for HR teams | Global Human Capital Trends 2016: www.youtube.com/watch?v=W7XJvnWojl8
- Digital HR: Using digital tools to unlock HR's true potential: www.youtube.com/watch?v=RyZRtolpmmw
- Are robots, AI and augmented reality the future of HR? With Tom Haak: www.youtube.com/watch?v=xpjl7bGseb8
- Future of artificial intelligence | Arjun Pratap | TED×SMIT www.youtube.com/watch?v=u7c86oNUe4M

References

Bassi, L. (2012). Raging debates in HR analytics. *Human Resource Management International Digest*, *20*(2), 14–18. DOI: 10.1108/hrmid.2012.04420baa.010.

Bell, L. (2015). Transactional versus strategic use of HR software and technology. *Human Resources*, February/March, 6–10.

Bondarouk, T. V., & Ruël, H. J. M. (2010). The strategic value of e-HRM: Results from an exploratory study in a governmental organization. *CEUR Workshop Proceedings*, *570* (November 2013), 15–32. DOI: 10.1080/09585192.2012.675142.

Bondarouk, T. V., & Looise, J. K. (2009). A Contingency Perspective on the Implementation of E-Performance Management. In T. Torres-Coronas & M. Arias-Oliva (Eds.), *Encyclopedia of HRIS: Challenges in e-HRM* (pp. 197–202). London: Information Science Reference.

Burbach, R. (2012). Strategic Alignment: The Sine Qua Non of e-HRM Implementation? In C. Tansley & H. Williams (Eds.), *4th International E-HRM Conference: Innovation, Creativity and e-HRM* (pp. 103–127). Nottingham: Nottingham Trent University.

Burbach, R., & Charlier, S. D. (2017). Training and Development: Issues and HRIS Applications. In M. J. Kavanagh & R. D. Johnson (Eds.), *Human Resource Information Systems: Basics, Applications and Future Directions* (4th ed., pp. 289–324). Thousand Oaks, CA: Sage Publications.

Burbach, R., & Dundon, T. (2005). The strategic potential of human resource information systems: Evidence from the Republic of Ireland. *International Employment Relations Review, 11*(1/2), 97–118.

Burbach, R., & Dundon, T. (2009). Administrative vs. Strategic Applications of Human Resource Information Technology. In T. Torres-Coronas & M. Arias-Oliva (Eds.), *Encyclopedia of HRIS: Challenges in e-HRM* (pp. 56–62). London: Information Science Reference.

Burbach, R., & Royle, T. (2014). Institutional determinants of e-HRM diffusion success. *Employee Relations, 36*(4), 354–375. DOI: 10.1108/ER-07-2013-0080.

Collings, D. G., Scullion, H., & Vaiman, V. (2015). Talent management: Progress and prospects. *Human Resource Management Review, 25*(3), 233–235. DOI: 10.1016/j.hrmr.2015.04.005.

Delone, W. H., & McLean, E. R. (2003). The DeLone and McLean model of information systems success: A ten-year update. *Journal of Management Information Systems, 19*(4), 9–30.

Dries, N. (2013). The psychology of talent management: A review and research agenda. *Human Resource Management Review, 23*(4), 272–285. DOI: 10.1016/j.hrmr.2013.05.001.

Eckhardt, A., Laumer, S., Maier, C., & Weitzel, T. (2014). The transformation of people, processes, and IT in e-recruiting. *Employee Relations, 36*(4), 415–431. DOI: 10.1108/ER-07-2013-0079.

Falletta, S. (2014). In search of HR intelligence: Evidence-based HR analytics practices in high performing companies. *People & Strategy, 36*(4), 28–37. Retrieved from http://search.ebscohost.com/login.aspx?direct=true&db=bth&AN=94589558&site=ehost-live.

Farndale, E., Paauwe, J., & Hoeksema, L. (2009). In-sourcing HR: Shared service centres in the Netherlands. *International Journal of Human Resource Management, 20*(3), 544–561. DOI: 10.1080/09585190802707300.

Findlay, P., & McKinlay, A. (2003). Surveillance, electronic communications technologies and regulation. *Industrial Relations Journal, 34*(4), 305–318. DOI: 10.1111/1468-2338.00277.

Grant, D., & Newell, S. (2013). Realizing the strategic potential of e-HRM. *Journal of Strategic Information Systems, 22*(3), 187–192. DOI: 10.1016/j.jsis.2013.07.001.

Grissemann, U., Plank, A., & Brunner-Sperdin, A. (2013). Enhancing business performance of hotels: The role of innovation and customer orientation. *International Journal of Hospitality Management, 33*(1), 347–356. DOI: 10.1016/j.ijhm.2012.10.005.

Guiderdoni-Jourdain, K., & Oiry, E. (2011). 'Local universe' and uses of an HR intranet: Discursive results from the case of middle management. *Advanced Series in Management, 8*(2), 105–117. DOI: 10.1108/S1877-6361(2011)0000008010.

Heikkilä, J. P. (2013). An institutional theory perspective on e-HRM's strategic potential in MNC subsidiaries. *Journal of Strategic Information Systems, 22*(3), 238–251. DOI: 10.1016/j.jsis.2013.07.003.

Holland, P., & Bardoel, A. (2016). The impact of technology on work in the twenty-first century: Exploring the smart and dark side. *International Journal of Human Resource Management, 27*(21), 2579–2581. DOI: 10.1080/09585192.2016.1238126.

Holland, P., Cooper, B. K., & Hecker, R. (2016). Use of social media at work: A new form of employee voice? *The International Journal of Human Resource Management, 27*(21), 2621–2634. DOI: 10.1080/09585192.2016.1227867.

Holm, A. B. (2014). Institutional context and e-recruitment practices of Danish organizations. *Employee Relations, 36*(4), 432–455. DOI: 10.1108/ER-07-2013-0088.

Hussain, Z., Wallace, J., & Cornelius, N. E. (2007). The use and impact of human resource information systems on human resource management professionals. *Information and Management, 44*(1), 74–89. DOI: 10.1016/j.im.2006.10.006.

Jooss, S., & Burbach, R. (2017). Assessing the Degree of Human Resource Innovation: An Exploratory Analysis of Irish Hotel Corporations. In T. V. Bondarouk, H. J. M. Ruël & E. Parry (Eds.), *Electronic HRM in the Smart Era* (pp. 2–33). Bingley: Emerald Publishing Limited. DOI: 10.1108/978-1-78714-315-920161002.

KPMG. (2016). *HR Transformation Survey 2016: The future belongs to the bold*. Retrieved from https://assets.kpmg.com/content/dam/kpmg/pdf/2016/07/cloud-hr-the-future-belongs-to-the-bold.pdf.

L'Écuyer, F., & Raymond, L. (2017). Aligning the e-HRM and Strategic HRM Capabilities of Manufacturing SMEs: A 'Gestalts' Perspective. In T. V. Bondarouk, H. J. M. Ruël & E. Parry (Eds.), *Electronic HRM in the Smart Era* (pp. 137–172). Bingley: Emerald Publishing Limited. DOI: 10.1108/978-1-78714-315-920161006.

Lukaszewski, K. M., Stone, D. L., & Stone-Romero, E. F. (2008). The effects of the ability to choose the type of human resources system on perceptions of invasion of privacy and system satisfaction. *Journal of Business and Psychology*, 23(3–4), 73–86. DOI: 10.1007/s10869-008-9074-0.

Marler, J. H., Cronemberger, F., & Tao, C. (2017). HR Analytics: Here to Stay or Short Lived Management Fashion? In T. V. Bondarouk, H. J. M. Ruël & E. Parry (Eds.), *Electronic HRM in the Smart Era* (pp. 3–59). Bingley: Emerald Publishing Limited. DOI: 10.1108/978-1-78714-315-920161003.

Marler, J. H., & Fisher, S. L. (2013). An evidence-based review of e-HRM and strategic human resource management. *Human Resource Management Review*, 23(1), 18–36. DOI: 10.1016/j.hrmr.2012.06.002.

Martin, G., Reddington, M., & Alexander, H. (2008). Chapter 1 – Technology, Outsourcing, and HR Transformation: An Introduction BT – Technology, Outsourcing & Transforming HR. In G. Martin, M. Reddington & H. Alexander (Eds.), *Technology, Outsourcing & Transforming HR* (pp. 1–35). Oxford: Butterworth-Heinemann. DOI: 10.1016/B978-0-7506-8645-7.50006-4.

Ngoc Duc, N., Siengthai, S., & Page, S. (2013). A conceptual model of HRIS Trust: An understanding of suppliers'/customers' relationship. *Foresight*, 15(2), 106–116. DOI: 10.1108/14636681311321112.

Parry, E. (2011). An examination of e-HRM as a means to increase the value of the HR function. *International Journal of Human Resource Management*, 22(5), 1146–1162. DOI: 10.1080/09585192.2011.556791.

Parry, E. (2014). e-HRM: A Catalyst for Changing the HR Function? In F. J. Martínez-López (Ed.), *Handbook of Strategic e-Business Management* (pp. 589–604). Berlin: Springer-Verlag. DOI: 10.1007/978-3-642-39747-9.

Parry, E., & Olivas-Lujan, M. R. (2011). Drivers of the Adoption of Online Recruitment – An Analysis Using Innovation Attributes from Diffusion of Innovation Theory. In E. Parry & S. Strohmeier (Eds.), *Electronic HRM in Theory and Practice (Advanced Series in Management), Emerald Group Publishing Ltd* (Vol. 8, pp. 159–174). Bingley: Emerald Publishing Limited. DOI: 10.1108/S1877-6361(2011)0000008013.

Phillips, T. N., Isenhour, L. C., & Stone, D. (2008). Chapter 8 – The Potential for Privacy Violations in Electronic Human Resource Practices BT—Technology, Outsourcing & Transforming HR. In G. Martin, M. Reddington & H. Alexander (Eds.), *Technology, Outsourcing & Transforming HR* (pp. 193–230). Oxford: Butterworth-Heinemann. DOI: 10.1016/B978-0-7506-8645-7.50013-1.

Ruël, H. J. M., Bondarouk, T. V., & Looise, J. K. (2004). *E-HRM: Innovation or Irritation? Ecis*. Utrecht: Lemma Publishers.

Ruël, H. J. M., Bondarouk, T. V., & Van der Velde, M. (2007). The contribution of e-HRM to HRM effectiveness: Results from a quantitative study in a Dutch Ministry. *Employee Relations*, 29(3), 280–291. DOI: 10.1108/01425450710741757.

Ruta, C. D. (2009). HR Portals as Tools for Relational Resources Management. In T. Torres-Coronas & M. Arias-Oliva (Eds.), *Encyclopedia of HRIS: Challenges in e-HRM* (pp. 428–433). London: Information Science Reference.

Sandle, T. (2017). *Increased take-up of digital technology by human resources – Digital transformation*. Retrieved from www.digitaljournal.com/digitaltransformation/2017/09/increased-take-up-of-digital-technology-by-human-resources/.

Stanton, J. M., & Weiss, E. M. (2003). Organisational databases of personnel information: Contrasting the concerns of human resource managers and employees. *Behaviour and Information Technology*, 22(5), 291–304. DOI: 10.1080/01449290310001599733.

Stone, D. L., Lukaszewski, K. M., Stone-Romero, E. F., & Johnson, T. L. (2013). Factors affecting the effectiveness and acceptance of electronic selection systems. *Human Resource Management Review*, *23*(1), 50–70. DOI: 10.1016/j.hrmr.2012.06.006.

Stone, D. L., Stone-Romero, E. F., & Lukaszewski, K. (2003). 3. The Functional and Dysfunctional Consequences of Human Resource Information Technology for Organizations and Their Employees. In E. Salas (Ed.), *Advances in Human Performance and Cognitive Engineering Research* (Vol. 3, pp. 37–68). Bingley: Emerald Group Publishing Limited.

Stone, R. A., & Davis, J. M. (2008). Change Management: Implementation, Integration, and Maintenance of the HRIS. In M. J. Kavanagh & M. Thite (Eds.), *Human Resource Information Systems: Basics, Applications and Future Directions* (pp. 173–210). Thousand Oaks, CA: Sage Publications.

Strohmeier, S. (2007). Research in e-HRM: Review and implications. *Human Resource Management Review*, *17*(1), 19–37. DOI: 10.1016/j.hrmr.2006.11.002.

Strohmeier, S. (2013). Employee relationship management – Realizing competitive advantage through information technology? *Human Resource Management Review*, *23*(1), 93–104. DOI: 10.1016/j.hrmr.2012.06.009.

Strohmeier, S., Bondarouk, T., & Konradt, U. (2012). Editorial: Electronic human resource management: Transformation of HRM? *Zeitschrift Fur Personalforschung*, *26*(3), 215–217. DOI: 10.1177/239700221202600301.

Strohmeier, S., & Kabst, R. (2014). Configurations of e-HRM – An empirical exploration. *Employee Relations*, *36*(4), 333–353. DOI: 10.1108/ER-07-2013-0082.

Svoboda, M., & Schroder, S. (2001). Transforming human resources in the new economy: developing the next generation of global HR managers at Deutsche Bank AG. *Human Resource Management*, *40*(3), 261–263.

Tarafdar, M., D'Arcy, J., Turel, O., & Gupta, A. (2015). The dark side of information technology. *Sloan Management Review*, *56*(2), 59–70. DOI: 10.1111/isj.12015.

Tate, M., Furtmueller, E., & Wilderom, C. P. M. (2013). Localising versus standardising electronic human resource management: Complexities and tensions between HRM and IT departments. *European J. of International Management*, *7*(4), 413. DOI: 10.1504/EJIM.2013.055280.

Venkatesh, V., Morris, M. G., Davis, G. B., Davis, F. D., DeLone, W. H., McLean, E. R., ... Chin, W. W. (2003). User acceptance of information technology: Toward a unified view. *MIS Quarterly*, *27*(3), 425–478. DOI: 10.1017/CBO9781107415324.004.

Wright, A. D. (2016). *How to meet challenges when deploying new HR technology*. Retrieved from www.shrm.org/resourcesandtools/hr-topics/technology/pages/how-to-meet-challenges-when-deploying-new-hr-technology.aspx.

Yusliza, M., & Ramayah, T. (2012). Determinants of attitude towards E-HRM: An empirical study among HR professionals. *Procedia – Social and Behavioral Sciences*, *57*, 312–319. DOI: 10.1016/j.sbspro.2012.09.1191.

15 Information security and privacy in e-HRM

Shankar Subramaniyan, Mohan Thite & S. Sampathkumar

Learning objectives

- Understand the critical importance of information security and privacy
- Describe the critical steps under the information security management system
- Describe privacy principles and related statutory requirements
- Explain the critical role of HR in protecting information security and privacy, before, during, and after employment

Introduction

Consider this incident:

> Cybercriminals are posing as job applicants as part of a new campaign to infect victims in corporate human resources departments with GoldenEye ransomware … GoldenEye targets human resources departments in an effort to exploit the fact that HR employees must often open emails and attachments from unknown sources.
>
> (Palmer, 2017, p. 1)

The incident highlights the vulnerability of HR departments to attacks on sensitive information held by them. Now consider the following incidents as reported by von Ogden (2016):

- At Snapchat, a social networking firm, an employee with criminal intent posed as the CEO and sent an email to someone in the company's payroll department, resulting in the release of protected information about employees.
- An employee of the City of Calgary in Canada accidentally leaked the personal information of employees while sending the information via email in the process of asking for technical assistance.
- An employee at Whitehead Nursing Home in Northern Ireland took home an unencrypted work laptop, which was later stolen in a home burglary and in the process exposed protected data on employees and patients.
- At Revenue and Customs department in Great Britain, two password-protected digital disks containing the details of every child and family in Great Britain subject to benefits payments were mailed by poorly trained junior employees to another government agency but never arrived.

What is common in these incidents? As von Ogden (2016, p. 1) reports,

> In the past year, *77% of data breaches involved an insider,* according to Verizon. From disgruntled employees committing sabotage to innocent mistakes, humans are one of your organization's greatest information security risks. In fact, a shocking amount of high-profile data breaches in recent years have occurred because of employee behaviors.

Today, the mantra in management is to "work anywhere, anytime, using any device in a 24/7 work environment." With rapid changes in technology landscape, including big data, cloud computing, social media, use of personal devices for work purposes, outsourcing/offshoring of services, and daily release of new gadgets with weak security features, coupled with increasing sophistication in cyberattacks, ensuring information security has become one of the most critical challenges for today's organizations. Organizations implement various information security measures to protect against cyberattacks that include performing risk assessments and implementing information security framework and technologies to prevent, detect, and protect against cyber risks and attacks.

But the most critical need in ensuring cyber security is to understand the nature and severity of threats in the first place. Cybercrime costs the global economy a staggering 450 billion every year and according to The Hiscox Cyber Readiness Report 2017, "53 percent of the companies assessed were ill-prepared to deal with an attack" (Graham, 2017, p. 1). Another study by McAfee revealed that that among companies experiencing data breaches, internal actors were responsible for 43% of data loss in 2014, half of which was intentional, and half accidental (von Fischer, 2015). The findings from both studies highlight the fact that organizations need to be vigilant of not only external cyber threats, but also the potential for trouble within their workforce.

When implementing information security measures, the human resources (HR) function plays a critical role for two reasons. Firstly, HR is at the forefront of workforce planning, implementation, and management. Given that a number of cyber security problems emerge due to the actions of an organization's own workforce, HR functionaries, alongside information technology (IT) professionals, can play a crucial role in the fight against cybercrime at the workplace (GHRR, 2016). HR can implement effective security controls before, during, and after employment to ensure people-related security controls are in place.

Secondly, HR departments hold some of the most private, important, and sensitive information. Privacy data is sought most after credit card data by cyber criminals in the "dark web," a part of the world wide web that requires special software to access and where much of the illegal activities are supposed to take place. An HR database holds sensitive employee information such as bank details, dates of birth, social security numbers, home addresses, and many more. With skilled cyber criminals constantly looking for these sensitive data, HR becomes the main target for them. It also results in a serious breach of privacy laws and regulations. Therefore, it is crucial that HR departments not only understand how to protect their own data, but also comply with various information security and privacy laws.

In this chapter, we explain why this topic merits the utmost attention of HR professionals dealing with technology and describe the concept, principles, and framework of information security and privacy. We also emphasize and explain how HR can play a pivotal role in partnering with IT to design, apply, enforce, and monitor various control mechanisms in this regard.

Increasing importance of information security

With fundamental changes in business models, technology trends, and increasingly sophisticated cyberattacks, followed by complex statutory regulations, information security and privacy have become critically important. What is more, as Morgan (2014, p. 2) states, "the new rule for the future is going to be, 'anything that can be connected, will be connected.'" This raises the frightening possibility of the information economy becoming extremely vulnerable to criminal mischief with individuals, firms, nations, and the global economy having to pay a heavy price in the quest for a connected world.

Changing business models: With a view to "do more with less," organizations are now moving toward outsourcing and collaborative models to improve the supply chain and cost efficiency. They are also increasingly adopting flexi workforce, crowd sourcing, and Gig economy models that rely more on independent contractors and a casualized workforce rather than permanent employees. These trends result in lack of visibility and control over what work is done, when, where, and by whom, which make enforcement of information security controls more and more difficult and challenging.

Rapid technology changes: Technology has rapidly evolved from mainframe (one computer, many users) to desktop personal computer (one computer, one user) and now to ubiquitous computing (one user, many computers). Now users can login from their phone, tablet, or laptop and access the required application. More people, applications, and smart devices are getting connected to the internet. This refers to the concept of the "Internet of Things" (IoT), a giant network connecting virtually any device at home or work to the internet, resulting in a "relationship between people-people, people-things, and things-things" (Morgan, 2014, p.1). The IoT is expected to grow from 2 billion objects in 2006 to a projected 200 billion by 2020, powered by 26 smart devices per every human on earth.

Some of the risks posed by new technologies, such as mobile, cloud, and big data are:

1   Loss of control and visibility for the organization
2   Data leakage or loss
3   Increased risk with additional end points
4   Blurred data ownership due to personal and private usage
5   Volumes of data (big data) exposes organizations to more risks
6   Harder to predict vulnerabilities in new technologies

Rising sophisticated cyberattacks: Cyberattacks have evolved from worms and viruses to more advanced and organized attacks with the emergence of deception technologies. The rising number of attacks such as organized data intrusion and the fraudulent use and theft of the information assets of organizations and government agencies together with the theft of user credentials from a number of popular sites by "hacker" groups, in some cases instigated by state sponsored entities, are a major concern. Widespread attacks such as ransomware exploiting zero-day vulnerabilities and distributed denial of service attacks (DDoS) affect the organizations' business operations and impact their profitability and revenue growth.

Increasingly complex regulations: Previously, information security regulations used to focus more on data protection such as protecting financial data and intellectual property. But with recent concerns on privacy and national security, regulatory bodies are now focusing more on cyber disclosure and national security. The privacy definition, scope, data localization, and breach notification requirements vary widely from one country or region to another. These varying laws and regulatory requirements pose challenges for multinational organizations with a global network.

Information security management system

The primary *purpose/goals of information security* are "to protect Confidentiality, Integrity and Availability (CIA) of the information assets of the organization, in which

- Confidentiality refers to ensuring only the right people have access to the information,
- Integrity refers to ensuring data is accurate and not modified, and
- Availability refers to ensuring the data is available for the right people at the right time, that is, when needed."

Information security management system (ISMS) is the "management framework to initiate, implement and control information security within the organization." It typically follows the Plan-Do-Check-Act (PDCA) Cycle, that is,

- Plan: Define security policies and procedures
- Do: Implement and manage security controls/process
- Check: Review/audit security management and controls
- Act: Implement identified improvements, corrective/preventive actions

Organizations follow various information security frameworks to protect their information security assets such as the ISO/IEC 27000 family, COBIT (Control Objectives for Information and Related Technologies), and NIST (*National Institute of Standards and Technology*). In this chapter, we have adopted the "*ISO/IEC 27001*" approach as stipulated by the International Organization for Standardization (ISO) as it is considered the best-known standard in providing requirements for an information security management system (ISMS). ISO defines ISMS as "a systematic approach to managing sensitive company information so that it remains secure. It includes people, processes and IT systems by applying a risk management process" (www.iso.org/isoiec-27001-information-security.html). An overview of ISMS is presented in Figure 15.1 and the steps involved are briefly described below.

Security requirements: ISMS starts with identifying the information security requirements for the organization. Every organization is unique with its own set of information assets, requirements, and concerns. Security requirements are collected from the compliance and regulatory requirements applicable to the organization, contractual requirements, and business requirements. One also needs to identify the stakeholders of the ISMS and the scope of the ISMS.

Security policy and governance: The security organization structure is important to drive and implement the ISMS across the organization. Hence defining the security organization and assigning the responsibilities is the foundation for the ISMS.

Asset profiling: The key success factor of ISMS is through risk assessment and effective risk management. Risk assessment starts with asset identification, which involves identifying all the information repositories that need to be protected for running the

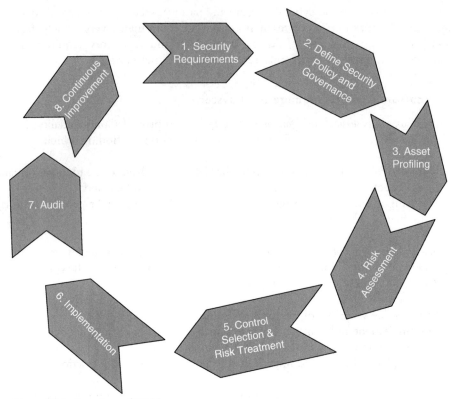

Figure 15.1 Overview of ISMS.
Source: Authors.

business. Information with higher value needs more protection and information with lower value needs less protection. All assets in the company can be classified as:

- People assets: Employees who are a part of the organization
- Paper-based information assets: Contracts, guidelines, company documentation, business results, HR records, purchase documents, invoices, etc.
- Electronic information: Databases, data files, system documentation, user manuals, training material, operational and support procedures, intellectual property, continuity plans, fallback arrangements, etc.
- Hardware assets: Computers, servers, IT Networking equipment, storage devices, etc.
- Software assets: Application systems, databases, development tools, and utilities.
- Support services/equipment: Safes, rooms, furniture, AC plant, DG sets, etc.

Once the assets are identified, they are then classified according to their business criticality such as public, internal purpose, confidential, or high confidential. These information assets need to be classified to indicate the degree of protection. The classification should result into appropriate information labeling to indicate whether it is sensitive or critical and what procedure is appropriate for copying, storing, transmitting, or destruction of the information asset. Thus, asset identification and classification give the organization the necessary knowledge about "what to protect."

Risk assessment: Risk assessment and risk management deal with "how to protect." Risk assessment phase determines the risks associated with each asset for various threats and vulnerabilities. Threats are the external agents that could act to malicious effects. Some of the *types of threats* are malware, hackers, attackers, BOTS (internet robots, also known as spiders, crawlers, and web *bots*), and so on. Vulnerabilities are the internal weakness in the system, such as an unpatched system. When the Threat acts on the Vulnerability, it results in Risk.

All the possible threats need to be identified, taking in to account the relevant vulnerability (e.g., no virus threat for paper-based information). Different *categories of threats* are

- *Natural causes*, such as flood, earthquakes, and cyclonic storms
- *Manmade*, such as intrusions/hacking, virus attack, theft, operator error, and deliberate destruction/sabotage
- *Emergencies*, such as civil strife/war, fire outbreaks, system crashes, disk failures, power outages, power glitches, communication link failure, and network component failure

The impact of a threat should be described in terms of loss or degradation of any, or a combination of any of the three security goals: Confidentiality, Integrity, and Availability. The impact can be measured by loss of system functionality, degradation of system response time, monetary losses, loss of public confidence, or unauthorized disclosure of data. Once the risk value is determined, risks are classified as High, Medium, and Low risks to determine the urgency and criticality of the actions to be taken to reduce the risks. High risks need immediate action.

Control selection and risk treatment: If it is decided to mitigate the risks, then appropriate controls should be selected to mitigate the impact of the risks. The goal of the recommended controls is to reduce the level of risk to the IT system and its data to an acceptable level. The various *types of controls* are

- *Technical controls*: Desktop security, network security, encryption, identification, authentication, etc.
- *Operational controls*: Physical access, security awareness training, personal security, etc.
- *Management controls:* Security policy and procedures, security organization, risk management, audit, etc.

Controls can also be classified, based on the *purpose*. For example, assume you would like to prevent the risk of an unauthorized person accessing the system.

- *Preventive*: Prevents the risk before it occurs, such as ensuring a strong password policy to access the system.
- *Detective*: Detects the risk after it occurs like system logs, which capture who accessed the system and when. By using a system log, one can identify if any unauthorized user accessed the system.
- *Corrective*: Corrects the risk after it occurs. For example, review the list of users to ensure only authorized persons have access to the system.
- *Compensating*: If any other types of controls cannot be implemented, then it is recommended to implement compensating controls. For example, if the application does

not contain the technical capability to configure a strong password policy, then compensating controls could be a more frequent user access review, as well as a log review to increase the oversight.
- *Deterrent*: Provides warning or deterrent messages for the attacker, such as a log-on message before accessing the system.

Once the types and purpose of controls are determined the *Risk Treatment* begins. Risk treatment involves prioritizing, evaluating, and implementing the appropriate risk-reducing controls, considering the risks and the existing controls. Based on the value of the risk, organizations can decide to take the any of the following risk treatment methods:

- *Accept*: Accept the risk if the cost of treating the risk is more than the impact
- *Avoid*: Avoid the risk by changing the process or technology or assets involved
- *Mitigate*: Mitigate the risks by implementing the appropriate controls
- *Transfer*: Transfer the risks to a third party, such as insurance providers

Implement/audit/improve: After the controls are selected and implemented, they need to be continuously monitored and improved to increase the effectiveness of the controls. Periodic audits assist in finding any gaps and improving the effectiveness of controls. Third-party validation by external auditors and certifications like ISO27001 increase the credibility of the system protections adopted.

Benefits: Thus, ISMS forms the backbone of information security infrastructure. The key benefits of implementing ISMS are

- Increases security awareness within the organization
- Enables identification of critical assets via the business risk assessment
- Provides a framework for continuous improvement
- Boosts confidence internally as well as to external business partners
- Enhances the knowledge and awareness of security-related issues at the management level

Role of HR in information security

Building awareness is the starting point for a stronger information security culture. The HR team plays a major role in building security awareness and a strong information security culture. Alert and well-trained employees who are aware of what to look for can prevent several major security breaches. Human errors, negligence, and greed are responsible for most thefts, frauds, or misuse of facilities. Various proactive measures that should be taken such as background verification, confidentiality agreements, terms and conditions of employment, and information security education and training, are grouped under the "personnel security" domain. The HR team is involved in these safeguard measures/controls that apply to before, during, and after employment as outlined below.

Before employment

- *Background verification check*: At the time of recruitment, verification checks are performed to identify any potential fraud or malicious user. Verification checks vary based on the type of industry, role, and responsibility. Generally, they include a reference

check, confirmation of claimed academic and professional qualifications, independent identity checks, medical test, criminal background check, and so on.
- *Confidentiality/non-disclosure agreement*: A confidentiality agreement legally binds the employee/contractor from disclosing any company-owned confidential or proprietary information without appropriate approval to unauthorized persons. It is to be noted that a confidentiality agreement binds the employees even after they leave the organization.
- *Declaration form*: A form signed by all employees that signifies that the employee has read and understood the information security and privacy policy and will abide by the same.
- *Inclusion of information security in job responsibilities*: Information security is the responsibility of everyone. Hence general responsibility for implementing and maintaining security policy, responsibility for protection of assets and execution of specific security process or activities should be included in the job description and responsibilities.

During employment

- *Security awareness training*: Security awareness training educates employees about the organization's security policy and procedures. Incident reporting process and guidelines on secure use of company resources are also covered in security awareness training so that employees are alert and perform their duty securely.
- *Security incident management and violation history*: The HR department plays the critical role in handling security incidents, especially when it involves disgruntled employees. Any violations or incidents by the employees/contractors invites disciplinary action and HR is responsible for handling the disciplinary process and maintaining the records for any future verification. e-HRM or a human resource information system (HRIS) plays a critical role in maintaining the records for compliance purposes.

After employment

- *Clearance process to revoke user rights/accounts during employee exit*: In the event of an employee leaving the organization due to resignation, termination, or absconding, all associated access of the employee should be terminated and "no dues clearance" process should be followed to recover any company owned assets.

Apart from these general controls, there are some specific controls required as part of regulatory and compliance requirements. These controls might vary based on the type of industry and compliance. For instance, the *Sarbanes Oxley Act* was passed by the US Congress in 2002 to enforce financial accountability and control. It is aimed at protecting investors of US-based public organizations. The act helped in setting new standards for corporate governance, auditing, and financial reporting. Ensuring compliance with this Act is a critical objective for public companies. According to the mandate of the Act, public companies need to perform a *SOX compliance audit* periodically and provide the management attestation during financial reporting each year. The risks of non-compliance range from significant financial penalties to the possibility of damage to an organization's reputation. Therefore, organizations need to adhere to certain best practices/guidelines to meet the set objectives. Section 404 (management assessment of internal controls) ensures that internal control processes are in place so that the company can effectively control its processes and outcomes.

Table 15.1 Role of IT and HR in mitigating data breaches and cyber security threats

Know your data	The first step in protecting organizational data is in knowing where it is, and who has access to it. Organizations should document and understand what and how data enters, stored, processed/modified, transmitted, used, shared, and destroyed.
Information security and privacy policy and guidelines	– It is critical for HR and IT to "develop and disseminate" comprehensive and robust policies and guidelines on information security and privacy. – They need to be periodically "updated" in line with changing technologies, threats, and regulatory requirements. – It is equally important to review the policies adopted by "third-party providers" associated with the organization to make sure they are compliant and vigilant as well.
Top management support	The top management needs to walk the talk and make sure senior managers lead the way and act as role models to convince employees that the organization is dead serious about information security and privacy matters.
Staff training	– Training all HR staff and employees on cyber security protocols is one of the critical roles of HR. Cyber security training should be a central component of any on-boarding process, with new employees schooled in issues pertaining to accessing and using confidential data, alongside basic security training. There should also be a focus on email security and learning to spot signs of potentially malicious activity. – The training programs should be held on an ongoing basis and made a "mandatory component" of the performance appraisal process.
Regular audits	Conduct regular information security audits and publish anonymized results of audits. Seeing that policies are being enforced and policed can be a powerful deterrent.
Secure digital assets	– Physically secure IT equipment to immovable fixtures and store sensitive assets – including paper documents – in a separate, secure area. – Apply patches supplied by vendors promptly.
Password policies	– Ensure employees use strong (difficult to guess) passwords that are compulsorily changed periodically. – Where possible, use "two-factor authentication" (e.g., password and a one-time security code.)
Encrypt devices	While encryption will not affect the chances of an asset going missing, it will protect the data it stores.
Back up	Regular backups can prevent the loss of valuable data, reduce downtime, and help with forensics should you be breached.
Review user accounts	Having identified who has access to sensitive data, implement a process for revoking access when employees leave or change role.
Former employees	It is necessary to close the online accounts of any former employees as soon as possible because research shows that well over half of former employees have stolen confidential company data upon departing.
Disciplinary actions	HR should stress the disciplinary repercussions, including termination, for employees that do not comply with security guidelines.

Source: Adapted from GHRR (2016) and Lewis (2014).

People-related costs, such as salaries, benefits, and incentives and training, are nearly half of the budget for most employers. Hence, controls and related processes are needed in the HR department to prevent any errors or fraud in people-related costs such as ensuring that a worker's compensation claims are reasonable and benefits and stock options to employees are calculated accurately. Also, the HR department should define policies and processes to avoid conflict of interest and ensure segregation of duty to avoid any collusion or fraud possibilities.

In addition, Section 306 (insider trades during pension fund blackout period) of SOX mandates that employees cannot exercise their stock options during a "blackout period." Another section of SOX, Section 301 deals with the *employee grievance* system and mandates that SOX-related complaints should be treated with discretion and without fear of retaliation. All SOX- related claims should be protected and retained as per compliance requirements. e-HRM can be an effective tool to comply with any regulatory or compliance requirements such as SOX in terms of ensuring accuracy of data, retaining the records for the retention period, and implementing effective work flows or decision paths to avoid any collusion or fraud.

In summary, the security policy should be comprehensive enough to encompass "personnel, physical, procedural and technical" aspects and should be specific to the organizational environment and requirements. Verizon (2017, p. 7) advises organizations to "be vigilant; make people first line of defense; only keep data on a 'need to know' basis; apply security patches promptly; encrypt sensitive data; use two-factor authentication and don't forget physical security." Table 15.1 summarizes the key roles that IT and HR can play in mitigating data breaches and cyber security threats (GHRR, 2016, p. 3; Lewis, 2014).

Privacy: Concept, principles, and regulations

Information privacy is widely regarded as a fundamental human right in all democratic societies. Privacy comprises ethical, moral, and legal dimensions. It is defined in many ways. For example, some view privacy as the "fundamental right to be left alone." Others define privacy as the "right of an individual to be protected against intrusion into his personal life or affairs by direct physical means or by publication information." According to Kovach, Tansey, and Framinan (2000), privacy is "a human value consisting of four elements, namely,

- Solitude: The right to be alone without disturbances
- Anonymity: The right to have no public personal identity
- Intimacy: The right not to be monitored
- Reserve: The right to control one's personal information including the methods of dissemination of that information"

In general, data privacy can be defined as an "individual's expectation that one will use their personal data as intended and protect it from disclosure to unauthorized parties." Every organization has a legal responsibility to protect their employees' and business partners' personal data.

Personal data are also called *personal identity information* (PII). It refers to "any information which can be used to identify, contact, or locate an individual, either directly or indirectly." Some PII data is considered as sensitive personal data. Sensitive personal data is a subset of personal data that requires special protection because it could cause harm to the individual if compromised. Examples of sensitive personal data include personal profile and contact information, bank account number, government identification (social security number or tax file number), information regarding the race, ethnic origin, religious or philosophical beliefs, political opinions, trade union membership, sexual lifestyle or orientation, criminal checks, and the medical history of a person, called PII Principal. The harm caused by unauthorized exposure of PII data could be financial, such as identity theft, or physical or psychological harm such as discrimination or criminal activity.

It is worth noting that some of the attributes may not be directly identifying an individual. But when they are combined, they can identify an individual. Whether a person is identifiable based on a combination of attributes might also be dependent on the specific domain. For instance, the combination of the attributes "male," "25," and "manager" can be sufficient to identify a person within a particular company but will often be insufficient to identify that person outside of that company. Also, it is worth noting that confidentiality requirements of PII might vary from country to country. For example, criminal records are public information in the USA whereas it is confidential information in Europe.

In order to protect the PII, organizations implement a *privacy framework*. As part of the framework, they first identify the privacy safeguarding requirements based on legal and regulatory requirements, contracts, and business requirements. Some examples of legal requirements include data protection laws, consumer protection laws, breach notification laws, data retention laws, employment laws, and relevant international laws affecting cross-border transfer of PII, some of which are described later in the section. Safeguarding requirements can relate to many different aspects of PII processing, for example, the collection and retention of PII, the transfer of PII to third parties, the contractual relationship among PII controllers and PII processors, and the international transfer of PII.

Once the privacy requirements are identified, an organization should:

- Develop privacy principles based on established standards, such as ISO29100.
- Conduct the privacy risk assessment to identify the gaps.
- Develop and implement specific privacy controls based on standards such as ISO27002 and ISO27018. Privacy controls include encryption of PII data, data masking, privacy awareness training, privacy notification process, etc.

Privacy principles

Privacy principles are safeguards to be followed while collecting, using, storing, transferring, or deleting personal data. These privacy principles should be used to guide the design, development, and implementation of privacy controls. Some of the common privacy principles are given below.

Consent and choice: PII principals should be given an opportunity to choose how their PII is handled and to allow them to withdraw consent easily and free of charge. There are two types of consent and choice: "Opt-in" and "opt-out." Opt-in consent occurs when the PII principal affirmatively and explicitly indicates his/her desire to have their data processed by the organization. Opt-out consent occurs when the PII principal implicitly consents by not indicating their disapproval of requested processing. Opt-in consent is generally required for more intrusive processing such as handling sensitive personal information. While opt-out consent is appropriate for less intrusive forms of processing like signing up for marketing emails.

Purpose legitimacy and specification: Organizations should have a legitimate reason to collect personal data and use it only for that purpose. The purpose for which personal data is collected should be specified at or before the time of data collection and subsequent use should be limited to the fulfilment of that purpose or compatible purpose.

Collection limitation: There should be limits to the collection of PII data and any collected data should be obtained by lawful and fair means and, where appropriate, with the knowledge or consent of the PII principal.

Data minimization: Collect only the minimum amount of personal data needed for the purpose. Data minimization is closely linked to the principle of "collection limitation" but goes further than that. While "collection limitation" refers to limited data being collected in relation to the specified purpose, "data minimization" strictly minimizes the processing of PII.

Use, retention, and disclosure limitation: PII data should not be used, retained, or disclosed for the purpose other than those specified, except with the consent of the data subject or by the authority of the law.

Accuracy and quality: Organizations that collect data should ensure that they are accurate, complete, and up to date. This principle is particularly important in cases where the data could be used to grant or deny a significant benefit to the individual (PII principal) or in which inaccurate data could otherwise result in significant harm to the person.

Openness, transparency, and notice: An organization should inform individuals what personal data are collected and why before they collect the data. They should make their privacy policies and practices relating to processing of PII easily accessible to PII principals. In order to be transparent, these policies and practices, including general information on the logic underlying the PII processing, can be made available to PII principles, particularly if the processing involves a decision impacting on the PII principal.

Individual participation and access: Organizations should give individuals the ability to review their personal data and correct factual inaccuracies. Organization should apply appropriate controls to ensure that PII principals only access their own PII and not that of other PII principals.

Accountability: The responsible unit or person in the organization (called the PII controller) should be accountable for effectively complying with measures adopted to implement the organization's privacy policies and procedures.

Security: Organizations should protect personal data with adequate security and ensure that they address physical security and information security.

The World Information Technology and Services Alliance (WITSA) summarizes the key dimensions of privacy principles, which are detailed in Table 15.2 (WITSA, 2017).

Table 15.2 Key dimensions of privacy principles

Transparency	To ensure individuals have the right to be informed when their personal data is being collected, stored, or processed.
Legitimate purpose	Personal data can only be processed for specified explicit and legitimate purposes, and not processed further in a way incompatible with those purposes.
Proportionality	Personal data may be processed only insofar as it is adequate, relevant, and not excessive in relation to the purposes for which the data are collected.
Accuracy	The data must be accurate and, where necessary, maintained up to date, with inaccurate data removed or corrected; and destroyed when no longer needed.
Specificity	Data protection also incorporates the practice of collecting and retaining personal data for a specific objective and period.

Source: Adapted from WITSA (2017).

Table 15.3 Privacy principles listed in Australia's Privacy Act 1988

1. Open and transparent management of personal information
2. Anonymity and pseudonymity
3. Collection of solicited personal information
4. Dealing with unsolicited personal information
5. Notification of the collection of personal information
6. Use or disclosure of personal information
7. Direct marketing
8. Cross-border disclosure of personal information
9. Adoption, use, or disclosure of government related identifiers
10. Quality of personal information
11. Security of personal information
12. Access to personal information
13. Correction of personal information

Source: Australian privacy policies – Public information sheet; www.oaic.gov.au/resources/agencies-and-organisations/guides/app-quick-reference-tool.pdf

Privacy laws and regulations

Different countries have various laws to address their unique privacy concerns. Some of them are given below.

- *USA*: While there is no single, comprehensive national law regulating the collection and use of personal data in the USA, a number of federal and state laws exist (Jolly, Loeb, & Loeb, 2017), including: Health Insurance Portability and Accountability Act (HIPAA); Genetic Information Nondiscrimination Act (GINA); Fair Credit Reporting Act (FCRA); Gramm-Leach-Bliley Act (GLBA); Telemarketing Sales Rule (TSR); Electronic Communications Privacy Act; USA PATRIOT Act
- *Canada*: The Privacy Act; The Personal Information Protection and Electronic Documents Act (PIPEDA) (www.priv.gc.ca/en/privacy-topics/privacy-laws-in-canada/02_05_d_15/)
- *European Union (EU)*: The General Data Protection Regulation (GDPR), which comes into effect from May 2018, brings a new set of "digital rights" for EU citizens and provides for a harmonization of data protection regulations throughout the EU
- *Australia*: Privacy Act 1988

These privacy laws typically incorporate the privacy principles outlined above. For example, Australia's Privacy Act 1988 specifies 13 Privacy Principles as listed in Table 15.3.

As a HRIS contains personal data, the above requirements will also be applicable to HRIS applications. Hence, the HR team along with IT should review the above requirements and ensure their compliance. Meeting some of these requirements such as data subject access rights, right to have data erased, data portability, data anonymization, timely data breach notification, and data deletion after the objective is met could be challenging in legacy applications (which refer to outdated computer systems) and might need major changes or upgrades.

Role of HR in privacy

Generally, the HR department handles PII data as part of various HR functions and processes in the organization, such as recruitment and selection, performance management, health and wellness program, learning and development, payroll, and termination. While handling PII data, HR should ensure it is strictly handled as per the organization's privacy policies and procedures. Any violation should be taken seriously and reported. Incidents such as misplacing a document, losing a laptop or mobile media, improperly sharing documents, or accidentally sending an email to the wrong person can result in privacy risks. Hence protecting the personal information form privacy risks is the responsibility of the organization. Privacy incidents could impact the reputation of the organization, customer trust, and possible legal fines.

Generally, invasion of privacy in the workplace from unreasonable conduct by an employer includes:

- *Intrusion into seclusion*: This occurs when an employer intentionally intrudes, physically or otherwise, upon the solitude or seclusion of another or their private affairs or concerns. For example, conducting video surveillance in a locker room or rest room may constitute an intrusion into seclusion.
- *Public disclosure of privacy facts*: This occurs when an employer gives publicity to a matter concerning the private life of an employee. Example would be an employer issuing a press release indicating a specific employee has a serious life-threatening medical condition.
- *Portrayal in false light*: This occurs when an employer gives publicity to a matter that places the employee in a false or bad light. It is similar to defamation. While false light requires dissemination to the public at large, defamation may occur when the false statement is published to only a single third party. For example, terminated employees may file claims for defamation and/or false light over their employer's release of information surrounding their termination.

Some of the key HR activities and processes where HR should be extremely cautious in adhering to organizational privacy policies and procedures to avoid any privacy incidents are given below.

- *Pre-employment practices*: It is critical that anti-discrimination practices are reviewed and prevented in job posting, pre-employment screening, and the test and interviewing process. As a best practice, the information obtained and requested through the pre-employment screening process should be limited to those essential for determining if a person is qualified for the job. Any inquiry or question should be justified by some business purpose and questions related to personal information should be avoided.
- *Monitoring and investigating the conduct of an employee*: Employers must be careful to protect the results of drug and alcohol tests and background screening results. They should use extreme discretion when disciplining employees for drug- or alcohol-related misconduct. Also, they should know the applicable legal practices for monitoring telephone calls, email monitoring, video surveillance, and intercepting wire or oral communications. An employer should inform employees of these surveillance and monitoring activities in advance and document the need for such surveillance.
- *Post termination activities*: Employers must ensure that any information provided about former employees, for example, during reference checks or recommendations, are accurate to protect against defamation and/or false light claims by terminated employees. Another major concern is to protect the files and records related to former employees. Various data breach laws mandate that organizations are required to protect the personal information and notify the individuals affected by the data breach.

The e-HRM system is best placed to protect the personal information and to ensure accuracy and validity of the information. It should have features to easily locate and provide the PII data so that access rights of the PII principles are ensured. The system should be enabled with adequate logging and monitoring to detect any data breaches and violations.

Summary

It is now well established that organizations everywhere and of all types and sizes are vulnerable to data breaches and the security threats are only going to increase and intensify as the digital economy becomes all pervasive. The commonly held perception is that the threats mostly originate from outsiders and that it is basically an IT issue. In this chapter, we have highlighted the critical importance of information security and privacy, described their key principles within the information security management system architecture, and outlined the regulatory environment. We have also reinforced the key role that HR can play to secure the digital assets with people as the first line of defense and the measures that it can take before, during, and after employment. Safeguarding information security and privacy is not a one-off exercise but an ongoing effort aimed at continuous improvement where people treat data as seriously as money and make it a personal commitment.

Case study: How silly mistakes become serious problems

Sally is a HR manager in a medium size IT company that provides software services. One day, she was told that the company was expecting a major project from a key client and that the HR department needed to launch a major recruitment drive to hire 50 IT personnel within three months. Sally understood the urgency and importance of the task and immediately convened a meeting of HR personnel to initiate the hiring process, using employee referrals, walk-in interviews, and university graduate recruitment.

A few days later, a senior project manager in charge of the new project called Sally to say that he personally knows and worked with a very good candidate with highly relevant experience. Sally said she will call him for an interview. But the project manager said he already interviewed the candidate and insisted that the candidate should be on boarded immediately because this candidate was earmarked for a critical lead role and the client was eager to meet key project members. Sally was initially hesitant to hasten the recruitment process but realizing the urgency of the matter she agreed to issue the appointment letter without background verification.

As it was late evening, Sally decided to work on the offer letter from home. When she went home and logged into her office laptop, it had some technical issue and she could not login. She called her colleague in the office and shared her password and asked her to login to the HR portal to generate the offer letter and email it to her personal email ID. Upon receiving the letter, she wanted to print, sign, and scan it, then send it to the candidate. Unfortunately, the printer at her home was not working.

So she uploaded letter from her personal laptop into the USB drive that she normally used for office work and went to a nearby internet kiosk. She took the printout, signed the letter, and then scanned and sent it to the candidate. She was happy that she finished her task quickly and supported the business effectively. She came home and forgot to bring the USB drive that had the offer letter and other personal identity information about company employees. The USB drive was neither encrypted nor password protected.

The next day she realized that she did not have the USB drive. She rushed to the internet kiosk only to find that somebody else had taken it. Sally did not think much about it and thought she would buy another USB. She did not report this to her company. The company found out a few days later through an IT security agency that the information in the USB drive was uploaded to the dark web.

Case study questions

- List the mistakes that Sally made that resulted in data theft.
- What actions would you recommend to the company to prevent such occurrences in the future?

Debate: Is an internal IT auditor a watchdog or a blood hound?

Introduction

Research shows that there is a significant confusion between auditors and stakeholders as to the former's role and contributions (Lenz, 2016). IT internal audits are performed to assess the effectiveness of the security measures implemented to protect the organization from cyber threats and to meet various compliance requirements. Auditors use various methods and techniques to make their assessment. These are typically long-drawn processes involving information gathering from a variety of sources. Some of these audit findings have very high visibility and impact in the organization when the reports are sent to external parties such as customers or regulatory bodies. One may argue that auditors are the watchdogs and they help us to improve the overall compliance of the organization by finding the gaps and areas of improvement. One may also argue that auditors are like blood hounds because audit objectives are not clear and they use biased or subjective methods, resulting in unnecessary harassment of employees.

Arguments in favor of "the IT auditor is a watchdog"

- Audits help to improve the overall effectiveness of the process and safety measures
- Audits boost customer confidence and provides a competitive advantage
- Auditors act as change agents and audits should be used as a tool for improvement.

Arguments in favor of "the IT auditor is a blood hound"

- The value and relevance of an internal audit are questioned by many and IT audits run the risk of becoming a marginalized function (Lenz, 2016)
- Sometimes major audit findings result in disciplinary action and adversely affect the career of the auditee

- Audits can take a lot of time and effort
- Audits can sometimes be biased and subjective
- Sometimes audit documentations are too onerous, cumbersome, and affect the productivity and flexibility of the process
- Auditors may not be transparent in the way they gather and interpret evidence

Useful references

Cohen, F. (2006). *Internal IT audit: Friend not foe*. [Online] www.gartner.com/doc/1404981/internal-it-audit-friend-foe (Accessed 12 January, 2018).

Lenz, R. (2016). *Internal auditors as change agents: What a difference a year makes!* [Online] www.kppsearch.com/news/the-open-auditor-edition-3/ (Accessed 12 January, 2018).

Rojas, J. (2016). *Auditors: Friends or foes*. [Online] www.accountingtoday.com/news/auditors-friends-or-foes (Accessed 12 January, 2018).

Video learning resources

- HRIS security: www.youtube.com/watch?v=4bkobskp8q0
- Human resource security requirements in ISO 27001 implementation: www.youtube.com/watch?v=Z0hXiLm8X1c
- Audit of human resources and payroll: www.youtube.com/watch?v=fqfukGeRRdU
- Information security: Anish Bhimani at TEDxUConn 2013: www.youtube.com/watch?v=UPmVTPyE5DM
- Human resources – Domain 5 – Information security & privacy program: https://youtu.be/J2jHjA94CQ0

References

GHRR (2016). *The role of HR in mitigating cyber security threats*. Global HR Research. [Online] www.ghrr.com/the-role-of-hr-in-mitigating-cyber-security-threats/ (Accessed 11 January, 2018).

Graham, L. (2017). *Cybercrime costs the global economy $450 billion: CEO*. [Online] www.cnbc.com/2017/02/07/cybercrime-costs-the-global-economy-450-billion-ceo.html (Accessed 11 January, 2018).

Jolly, L., Loeb & Loeb. (2017). *Data protection in the United States: Overview*. [Online] https://uk.practicallaw.thomsonreuters.com/6-502-0467?transitionType=Default&contextData=(sc.Default)&firstPage=true&bhcp=1 (Accessed 12 January, 2018).

Kovach, K. A., Jordan, J., Tansey, K., & Framinan, E. (2000). The balance between employee privacy and employer interests. *Business and Society Review, 105*(2), 289–298.

Lewis, R. (2014). *What HR can do prevent data breaches and cyber threats*. [Online] www.humanresourcesonline.net/hr-can-help-prevent-data-breaches-cyber-threats/ (Accessed 11 January, 2018).

Morgan, J. (2014). *A simple explanation of "The Internet of Things."* [Online] www.forbes.com/sites/jacobmorgan/2014/05/13/simple-explanation-internet-things-that-anyone-can-understand/#7c7255571d09 (Accessed 10 January, 2018).

Palmer, D. (2017). *This ransomware targets HR departments with fake job applications.* [Online] www.zdnet.com/article/this-ransomware-targets-hr-departments-with-fake-job-applications/ (Accessed 9 January, 2018).

Verizon (2017). *2017 data breach investigations report.* Executive Summary. [Online] www.verizonenterprise.com/verizon-insights-lab/dbir/2017/ (Accessed 12 January, 2018).

von Fischer, S. (2015). *Data exfiltration in five easy pieces.* [Online] http://vonfischer.com/blog/2015/12/07/data-exfiltration-in-five-easy-pieces/ (Accessed 9 January, 2018).

von Ogden (2016). *8 Examples of internal-caused data breaches.* [Online] www.cimcor.com/blog/8-examples-of-insider-internal-caused-data-breaches (Accessed 9 January, 2018).

WITSA (2017). *WITSA's statement of policy on privacy, security and data protection.* [Online] https://witsa.org/wp-content/uploads/2013/10/Privacy-Security-Data-Protection-final-1.pdf (Accessed 11 January, 2018).

16 Future directions in electronic/digital HRM

Mohan Thite

> **Learning objectives**
> - Identify different milestones in the evolution of the HR function, in terms of external environment, functional and technology focus
> - Study futuristic technology trends
> - Study HR technology trends and related HR initiatives
> - Present a framework of digital HR strategy

Introduction

The US based Society for HRM (SHRM), the world's largest HR professional society, features a technology section on its website (www.shrm.org/ResourcesAndTools/hr-topics/technology/Pages/default.aspx). The following is an illustrative list of topics that it has covered in recent times:

- Gig economy, technology changing the future of work
- AI (artificial intelligence) won't kill all the jobs
- Predictive assessments give companies insights into candidate potential
- EU (European Union): Covert surveillance is prohibited
- Data – friend or enemy?
- Office desk sensors can cause employee anxiety (hot desking)
- Job seekers are frustrated with automated recruiting; high-tech doesn't replace high-touch in recruiting: Why traditional methods still matter
- What HR can do about cyberbullying in the workplace
- Social media mistakes can cost you the job
- Public enemy no. 1 for employers? Careless cloud users
- Cybercriminals strike ADP
- The future of work – augmented intelligence hits HR
- Is open source HR the next big thing?

These topics capture some of the major issues, challenges, and strategies of digital HR. While they point to promising digital technologies that can aid and augment the efficiency and effectiveness of HR service delivery, they also caution us about the challenges, such as the concerns and statutory restrictions pertaining to information security and privacy, and the ill-effects of 24/7 digital connectedness, including analysis paralysis due to information overload, increasing employee stress levels, and social isolation. Strategically aligned technology can augment employee performance but sometimes, short-term technology-mediated patchwork solutions can turn into long-term structural problems. Most importantly, we need to be mindful of the dangers of excessive and misdirected use of technology in managing people, at the cost of long-term focus and investment in people, based on trust and transparency (Thite, 2004, p. 50-67), and ignoring the importance of well-defined and aligned processes, managerial competency, intuition and insights. In other words, 'high-tech. doesn't replace high-touch'.

As pointed out in Chapter 1, in the business context, digital technologies essentially refer to intelligent processes that use continuous real time feedback in order to make constant improvement in the efficiency and effectiveness of work design, processes and outcome (Thomas, Kass and Davarzani, 2013, p. 2). In the process, they directly influence and enhance customer value and organisational revenue. This means, it is not 'doing digital' but 'being digital' that is most important. This requires a fundamental change in organisational mindset and culture to be a true learning organisation, underpinned by systems thinking, personal mastery, mental models, building shared vision and team learning (Senge, 1990).

Before undertaking any organisational change/renewal, we need to ask *Three Big Questions*:

- *Where are we now?* Refers to the degree of alignment between external environmental demands and internal capabilities, such as McKinsey's 7-S framework of hard elements (strategy, structure and systems) and soft elements (shared values, skills, style and staff).
- *Where do we want to go?* Refers to the future-focused organisational strategy, vision and mission, keeping in mind emerging disruptive technologies and best-practice management trends.
- *How will we get there?* Refers to organisation-specific and fit-for-purpose 'implementation strategies' that are constantly monitored and fine-tuned, in line with changing environmental characteristics, demands and responses.

To answer where we are now, we need to have a keen sense of the past and the present. Accordingly, in this chapter, we begin with the evolution of the HR function in terms of the changing environmental demands, functional focus and technology focus. To answer where do we want to go, we need to look at futuristic trends in strategic management, technology and HR. Here, 'voices from the ground' by way of data collected from practitioners by consultancy organisations can be very useful. Therefore, we will examine the survey and interview data collected by reputed management consultancy firms, including:

- Gartner hype cycle for emerging technologies (Panetta, 2017) and the top 10 strategic technology trends for 2018 (Gartner, 2017);
- The 2017 Deloitte global human capital trends (Deloitte, 2017); and
- The Sierra-Cedar 2017–2018 HR systems survey (Harris and Spencer, 2017).

Finally, to answer the question, how we will get there, this chapter will present a road map in the form of an evidence-based strategic framework of digital HR strategy.

Evolution of the HR function

Before we explore the future directions of HR technology and the HR function in the digital world, we need to examine the historical evolution of the HR function over the last century. This analysis helps us understand why HR has taken so long to transform from a support/administrative function to being the critical and strategic function that it is today, and during this journey, how it has suffered from an identity crisis and why it has been somewhat slow in adopting technology-enabled evidence-based management.

As illustrated in Table 16.1, the HR function has slowly but steadily evolved from labour welfare to personnel administration to strategic HRM (SHRM) in response to external environmental changes and in the process, its functional and technology focus has undergone similar transformation.

Just as the external environment has evolved from being domestic and stable to being global and highly uncertain, the focus of the HR function has shifted from being passive and reactive to being strategic and proactive. Similarly, HR technology has rapidly transformed from being primitive, expensive and monolithic to being highly advanced, disruptive, agile and relatively affordable. As summarised by Cohen (2015, p. 205), 'HR's past is relatively long and humble. The present is both positive and challenging, and the future of HR presents the profession with opportunities and even more thought-provoking challenges'.

At the same time, the world is also characterised by 'digital divide' with uneven and inequitable access to information and communication technologies between and within countries. Similarly, in many countries, industries and organisations, the HR function is still reactive and confined to administrative support role. We will discuss the implications of this unevenness in environmental, HR and technology foci towards the end of the chapter. Let us turn our attention to the key emerging technologies of the future.

Futuristic technology trends

The Gartner hype cycle for emerging technologies (Panetta, 2017, p. 2-3) highlights three 'emerging technology mega trends', namely,

- *Artificial intelligence (AI) everywhere*, such as cognitive computing, machine learning, smart robots and smart workspace that enable organisations 'to harness data in order to adapt to new situations and solve problems that no one has ever encountered previously';
- *Transparently immersive experiences*, such as augmented reality, brain–computer interface and human augmentation that 'introduce transparency between people, business and things' with technology becoming more human-centric; and
- *Digital platforms*, such as 5G, quantum computing and software-defined security, with digital businesses 'moving toward inter-connected ecosystems' and technology moving towards 'ecosystem enabling platforms'.

Further, according to Gartner (2017), the top 10 strategic technology trends for 2018 with substantial disruptive potential are:

1 **AI foundation**: Creating systems that learn, adapt and potentially act autonomously will be a major battleground for technology vendors through to at least 2020.

Table 16.1 Evolution of the HR function

Period	State of HR function
Up to the 1940s	**Labour welfare** – *Environment*: Minimum government intervention. Mostly guided by owner's beliefs and attitudes. Labour exploitation rife – *Functional focus:* Passive; reactive; influenced by Taylorism (scientific principles of management) – *Technology focus*: Primitive. Manual record keeping
1950s to 1960s	**Personnel administration and industrial relations** – *Environment*: Unprecedented economic and job growth – *Functional focus:* Realisation of employee motivation and morale; evolution of job classification and analysis; development of occupational categories; growth of trade unions – *Technology focus*: Technology primitive (by today's standards) and costly. Advent of transactional electronic data processing (EDP) using mainframes
1970s to 1980s	**Human resource management** – *Environment*: Rapid growth of labour legislation; increasing competition from Japanese manufacturers leading to cost consciousness – *Functional focus:* Considered a mainstream function; increasing professionalism across all HR functions; shift in focus from employee maintenance to development – *Technology focus*: Increased requirements for legislative compliance and associated data; employee record system; technology becomes cheaper and more efficient; advent of management information system (MIS) using personal computers
1990s to 2000s	**Strategic human resource management** – *Environment*: Increasing globalisation and competitiveness; global movement of capital, production and labour leading to business process re-engineering, outsourcing and offshoring; focus on cost reduction and productivity improvement to do 'more with less' – *Functional focus:* Strategic business partner and change agent as key roles for HR; centres of expertise/excellence; integrated talent management system; increasing pressure on HR to deliver technology-enabled HR services better, faster and cheaper; increasing adoption of flexi-labour, outsourcing, self-service and shared services in HR; increasing awareness about data-driven evidence-based management of HR functions; balanced scorecard – *Technology focus*: rapid world wide web-enabled software advances leading to decision support systems (DSS); rise of enterprise resource planning (ERP) with enterprise wide networking of IT infrastructure and business functions
2010 to today	**Smart/digital HRM** – *Environment*: Further push for globalisation leading to hyper-competition and extremely uncertain business environment; innovation, creativity, ambidexterity (simultaneous focus on competition and collaboration, flexibility and sustainability) and agility as key competitive advantages; push for all-inclusive stakeholder focus, including employee well-being, societal well-being and environmental well-being – *Functional focus*: World of work becoming anytime, anywhere 24/7 environment; future-focused; learning organisation focus in a knowledge-intensive environment; increasing need for HR business case (cost justification, return on investment, gestation, utility analysis etc.) leading to adoption of HR metrics and analytics; managing multigenerational and highly diverse workforce – *Technology focus*: Rapid introduction and advancement of social, mobile, analytics and cloud (SMAC) technologies; focus on apps, AI and robotics; executive information/support systems (EIS/ESS) for high-level prescriptive and predictive analytics (what-if scenarios); disruptive technologies destroying old businesses and creating new ones; rapid technological obsolesce; highly networked and connected world

Source: Author.

2 **Intelligent apps and analytics**: Over the next few years, virtually every app, application and service will incorporate some level of AI. Augmented analytics is a particularly strategic growth area that uses machine learning to automate data preparation, insight discovery and insight sharing.
3 **Intelligent things**: Intelligent things are physical things that go beyond the execution of rigid programming models to exploit AI to deliver advanced behaviours and interact more naturally with their surroundings and with people (e.g. autonomous vehicles, robots and drones).
4 **Digital twin**: Refers to the digital representation of a real-world entity or system. Well-designed digital twins of assets have the potential to significantly improve enterprise decision making.
5 **Cloud to the edge**: Refers to a computing topology in which information processing, and content collection and delivery, are placed closer to the sources of this information.
6 **Conversational platforms**: Will drive the next big paradigm shift in how humans interact with the digital world. The burden of translating intent shifts from user to computer.
7 **Immersive experience**: While conversational interfaces are changing how people control the digital world, virtual, augmented and mixed reality are changing the way that people perceive and interact with the digital world (e.g. video games and 360-degree spherical videos).
8 **Blockchain**: Evolving from a digital currency infrastructure into a platform for digital transformation.
9 **Event Driven**: Central to digital business is the idea that the business is always sensing and ready to exploit new digital business moments. Business events could be anything that is noted digitally.
10 **Continuous adaptive risk and trust**: Security infrastructure must be adaptive everywhere to embrace the opportunity – and manage the risks – that comes from delivering security that moves at the speed of digital business.

In analysing these future-focused reports, we need to keep in mind that as pointed out by the Gartner hype cycle for emerging technologies (Gartner, 2018, p. 1), emerging technologies typically go through the following five key *phases of a technology's life cycle*:

Innovation trigger: A potential technology breakthrough kicks things off. Early proof-of-concept stories and media interest trigger significant publicity. Often no usable products exist and commercial viability is unproven.

Peak of inflated expectations: Early publicity produces a number of success stories – often accompanied by scores of failures. Some companies take action; many do not.

Trough of disillusionment: Interest wanes as experiments and implementations fail to deliver. Producers of the technology shake out or fail. Investments continue only if the surviving providers improve their products to the satisfaction of early adopters.

Slope of enlightenment: More instances of how the technology can benefit the enterprise start to crystallise and become more widely understood. Second- and third-generation products appear from technology providers. More enterprises fund pilots; conservative companies remain cautious.

Plateau of productivity: Mainstream adoption starts to take off. Criteria for assessing provider viability are more clearly defined. The technology's broad market applicability and relevance are clearly paying off.

What do these trends mean for HR? In the background of Gartner's report, Wright (2017, p. 1), quotes a technology leader as saying that,

> continual changes to the workforce and technology advancements will give HR teams an overt opportunity to be strategic advisors in their organizations ... HR will play a pivotal role in aligning company culture, talent, structure and processes to make sure that businesses select the right tools for delivering the best employee digital experience.

Futuristic HR trends

The 2017 Deloitte Global Human Capital Trends (Deloitte, 2017, p. 5–9), 'identify 10 areas in which organisations will need to close the gap between the pace of change and the challenges of work and talent management':

1 *Organisation of the future* (88%): As organisations become more digital, they face a growing imperative to redesign themselves to move faster, adapt more quickly, learn rapidly and embrace dynamic career demands. Leading organisations are moving past the design phase to actively build this new organisation.
2 *Careers and learning* (83%): As companies build the organisation of the future, continuous learning is critical for business success. The new rules call for a learning and development organisation that can deliver learning that is always on and always available over a range of mobile platforms.
3 *Talent acquisition* (81%): Recruiting is becoming a digital experience as candidates come to expect convenience and mobile contact. Savvy recruiters will embrace new talent acquisition technologies to forge psychological and emotional connections with candidates and constantly strengthen the employment brand.
4 *Employee experience* (79%): Rather than focus narrowly on employee engagement and culture, organisations are developing an integrated focus on the entire employee experience. A new marketplace of pulse feedback tools, wellness and fitness apps, and integrated employee self-service tools is helping.
5 *Performance management* (78%): Across all industries and geographies, companies are re-evaluating every aspect of their performance management programs, from goal setting and evaluation to incentives and rewards. They are aligning these changes to business strategy and the ongoing transformation of work.
6 *Leadership* (78%): Today, as never before, organisations do not just need more strong leaders, they need a completely different kind of leader – younger, more agile, and 'digital-ready'.
7 *Digital HR* (73%): HR leaders are being pushed to take on a larger role in helping to drive the organisation to 'be digital', not just 'do digital'. As digital management practices and agile organisation design become central to business thinking, HR is focusing on people, work and platforms.
8 *People analytics* (71%): No longer is analytics about finding interesting information and flagging it for managers. It is now becoming a business function focused on using data to understand every part of a business operation and embedding analytics into real-time apps and the way we work.
9 *Diversity and inclusion* (69%): Fairness, equity, and inclusion are now CEO level issues, but continue to be frustrating and challenging. Training and education are not

working well enough. The new rules focus on experiential learning, process change, data-driven tools, transparency and accountability.
10 *The augmented workforce* (63%): Automation, cognitive computing and crowds are paradigm-shifting forces reshaping the workforce. Organisations must experiment and implement cognitive tools, focus on retraining people to use these tools and rethink the role of people as more and more work becomes automated. However, as Panetta (2017, p. 1) argues, '(while) human augmentation has the potential to use technology to enhance bodies and minds, (it) also raises ethical and legal questions'.

HR technology trends and initiatives

Finally, we look at the Sierra-Cedar HR Systems Survey, which is arguably 'a global benchmark of HR technology adoption and the value achieved from the use of these technologies, seen through the eyes of HR Information Technologists (HRIT) and Information Technologists (IT)' (Harris and Spencer, 2017, p. 1). According to the Sierra-Cedar 2017–2018 HR systems survey, the top 10 HR technology initiatives are:

1 Business process improvements and innovations (67%)
2 HR systems strategy: Establishes or refines an HR application strategy that supports business strategy (40%)
3 Talent management applications: Implement or change applications including recruiting, performance, learning, compensation or succession planning (35%)
4 Service delivery improvements: Improve the user experience (UX) through employee self service (ESS)/manager self service (MSS) or implement portals or help desk solutions (34%)
5 Business intelligence/workforce metrics initiatives (19%)
6 Systems integrations (19%)
7 Mergers and acquisitions (17%)
8 Workforce management (17%)
9 Mobile enablement (17%)
10 Social enablement (16%)

In further analysing the above initiatives, Harris and Spencer (2017, pp. 2–5) highlight the impact on strategy, culture and technology as below:

Strategy has become a key issue for top performing organisations, as well as those organisations evaluating their HR technology environments; 40% of organisations have a major HR systems strategy initiative, however, only 17% of organisations have a strategy for integrating HR applications; 70% of the organisations with the highest HR talent and business outcomes have a risk and security strategy that includes HR systems.
Culture: Data driven, talent driven, socially responsible and top performing organisations provide statistically significant insights into their unique approach to HR systems. The increasing focus on initiatives such as diversity, pay equity, employee engagement and leave policies requires organisations to take both a technical and human approach.
Technology: Currently, 50% of organisations have at least one major HR system in a cloud environment. HR technology buyers have been the beneficiaries of a highly

competitive HRMS market. Next generation technology is designed to inform our decisions and simplify our activities; it is meant to be invisible and ubiquitous in our lives. The line between what organisations want and what they can do may come down to intelligent platforms.

Framework of digital HR strategy

Over the last 20 years, work has become more distributed and driven by collaboration. This has resulted in 'the importance of *connectedness*, an emphasis on *modularity, less reliance on authority*, and an accelerating shift from *input control to output control*' (Evans and Rodriguez-Montemayor, 2016, p. 68). The very purpose of a digital strategy is to proactively respond to external environmental demands that are constantly and sometimes radically changing, by adopting an 'outside-in perspective' as well as 'inside-out perspective' in optimally reconfiguring its internal capabilities and resources. In the context of HR, this requires organisations to ensure that there is a horizontal and vertical 'strategic alignment/fit' between the business strategy, HR or talent management (TM) strategy and the digital HR strategy with the external and internal environments.

Based on available research evidence (Andersson, Lanvin and Van der Heydon, 2016, p. 56; Deloitte, 2017, p. 91; Lanvin and Evans, 2016; Kane, Palmer, Phillips, Kiron and Buckley, 2017, p. 3; Gothelf and Seiden, 2017), this chapter proposes a framework of digital HR strategy. The strategic components and considerations underpinning the digital HR strategy are listed in Figure 16.1.

Let us briefly explore the key concepts and principles behind the digital HR strategy:

External influencing factors

Globalisation and information and communication technology (ICT) have united the world like never before. This has led to ever increasing global spread and the movement of production, services, capital and talent. Accordingly, *global economic competitiveness* has intensified with a direct influence on national and firm competitive advantages, built primarily on innovation and creative capabilities.

In the specific context of technology, the *breadth and depth of technology intensity and penetration* are unevenly spread across the globe. This has implications particularly for multinational firms as their technology policies and practices have to take cognisance of technological readiness and adoption in the countries they operate. Similarly, firms in emerging economies need to be realistic about their technology agenda and ambitions.

Another important external consideration is that technologies have serious *implications for national cultures, social and political freedom*. For example, in many countries, governments restrict freedom of thought and expression, limiting the ability of people to freely express themselves. Their national cultures also may restrain them from exercising their rights. Further, most countries have strict laws governing information security and privacy.

In Chapter 1, we discussed how an ageing population and lack of e-skills and digital fluency have contributed to serious skill shortages in the *labour market*. While many firms may therefore want to adopt global, rather than local or regional talent sourcing policy to attract the digital workforce, government restrictions, political pressures and local employee resentment may restrict their ability to recruit foreign talent.

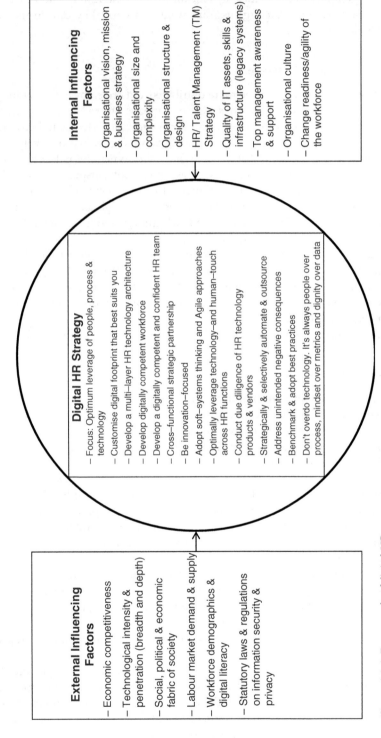

Figure 16.1 Framework of digital HR strategy.

Source: Author.

Internal influencing factors

Organisations need to develop a 'customised digital footprint' that specifically addresses the unique organisational demands, keeping in mind their strengths, weaknesses, opportunities and threats (SWOT). Some of the internal factors that determine the role and nature of a digital strategy are as follows:

- *Organisational size*: The bigger an organisation, the better it is likely to be in its ability to deploy state of the art technologies; however, historical baggage, legacy technologies and bureaucracy may restrict its ability to successfully implement it.
- *Organisational structure and complexity*: As explained in Chapter 3, the more the complexity and bureaucracy in an organisation, the more challenging is technology adoption.
- *Organisational culture*: As seen in Chapter 4, agile and adaptable organisations that constantly reinvent themselves by allowing employees freedom to experiment and express themselves are more likely to be digitally mature.
- *Leadership*: The digital world requires leaders at all levels of the organisation to lead from the front and be visionary, inspiring, competent, capable and supportive of digital initiatives, investments and experiments.

Research by Andersson et al. (2016, p. 55) revealed that the *key success factors for digital initiatives* are:

- A clear vision
- Support from senior leadership
- Right technology in place
- Seen as a priority
- Good planning
- Strong internal collaboration
- Strong collaboration with partners
- Appropriate level of investment
- Strong organisational capabilities
- Buy-in from the board
- Clear expectations of contributors

Core elements of digital HR strategy

As Ulrich says in his Foreword to this book, 'HR is not about HR, but about delivering value to employees, organisations, customers, investors, and communities … By understanding technology, HR professionals may help shape both a business and the HR digital agenda'. One of the transformative roles of HR in the digitalised learning organisation is to instil and institutionalise *digitally minded and agile organisational cultures, structures and workforce practices*, such as cross-functional collaboration and risk tolerance. It should develop tomorrow's leaders who are digitally literate and mature.

Digital thinking and practice demand appropriate *digital skills and competencies* referred to in Chapter 1, and these skills need to be developed both in-house as well as sourced from outside in an optimum combination. The talent management strategy should serve as a talent magnet and be capable of attracting, deploying, developing and retaining top talent by addressing the unique characteristics and requirements of knowledge workers referred to previously.

HR is often accused of being slow and sloppy in understanding and embracing evidence-based management that harnesses the potential of digital technologies, including big data, analytics and social media. To be true strategic business partners, HR leaders should first become what they expect the rest of the organisation to be – agile, future-focused, innovation-driven, systems thinkers, cross-functional collaborators and curators of knowledge. While HR has been somewhat successful in using technology to automate and streamline administrative work, access information and innovate some HR practices, such as applicant tracking systems and learning management systems, it should now move to the next critical phase of using technology to 'create social experiences and connections', as Ulrich recommends in his Foreword to this book.

Summary

Huselid (2011, p. 311) observes that,

> the world is an ever more complex and challenging place to work and live. As a consequence, the workforce, workforce management systems, and the people who design and implement them have never been more important determinants of a firm's strategic success. Indeed, at the end of the day, the only truly sustainable source of competitive advantage is talent.

Harnessing the full potential of the digital world is a long-term game and is always a work-in-progress, focusing on continuous experimentation, business process re-engineering and improvement.

The final message of the book is that HRM is first and foremost about being 'people-centric' before it becomes 'business-centric and technology-centric', and as such needs to place

- people over process;
- mindset over metrics; and
- dignity (privacy) over (intrusive) data.

Case study: University of the future

ABC university is a 40-year old public university in Australia. By Australian standards, it is a medium-size university with 4,000 academic staff offering 200 degrees to 50,000 students, across its five campuses spread around a major Australian city. It is ranked in the top 3% of universities globally. Its vision is to be one of the most influential universities in Australia and the Asia-Pacific region.

The university recognises that information technology (IT) is now ubiquitous within higher education, which has created both challenges and opportunities. It has led to potentially 'game changing' initiatives in higher education, such as massive open online courses (MOOCs). By leveraging on emerging technologies, it aims to gain a distinct competitive advantage in a highly competitive global knowledge economy.

Accordingly, it wants to broaden and deepen its commitment to IT to make it the very essence of the university's functions of knowledge creation, preservation, synthesis and dissemination. It believes that innovative development, use and application of IT in research, and learning and teaching could be a strategic advantage. However, it is cognisant of the fact that the emerging global digital world is about 'connection rather than location' and that innovation in university practices and processes, not IT itself, will offer strategic differentiation with its local, regional and global competitors.

To meet the challenges of the unfolding digital world, the university aims to overhaul its processes and systems to facilitate agility, connectedness and sustainability. It also aims to put its people at the centre of the change process and wants its academic workforce to be flexible and adaptable, as well as undertake deliberate experimentation in the application of IT in their teaching and research. In other words, its aim is to be an agile university of the future.

Case study questions

- Explain how the external environment has an impact on the university's way of working.
- Explain how the university's internal environment needs to respond to external demands, in terms of McKinsey's 7-S framework of hard elements (strategy, structure and systems) and soft elements (shared values, skills, style and staff).
- As the head of HR of this university, design an appropriate HR digital strategy in line with its external realities and strategic intent.

Debate: Is managing people an art or a science?

Introduction

According to one blogger, 'Art is reason applied without limits, geared towards an ideal and guided by the practical. Science is reason applied within a framework, geared towards the practical and guided by an ideal' (Philosophy Forums, 2017). One may argue that science deals with black and white, something that is empirically proven whereas arts deal with grey, something that is fuzzy in nature. One may also argue that art is essentially about creativity, creative freedom and experimentation, individuality and non-conformity, whereas science is all about empirical reasoning based on hard data or evidence, well defined structure, stability and conformity.

Arguments in favour of 'managing people is an art'

- HRM is about people who do not come in one size fits all. It is the intangibility of people as an asset and the fuzzy nature of managing people that makes it an art. 'It requires perfection through practice, practical knowledge, creativity, personal skills etc' (Wikiversity, 2017).
- Context is paramount in the practice of people management. It is not about best practice but best fit – whatever suits the circumstances. As such there cannot be a standard set of operating procedures that can be 'prescribed'.

- The key outcomes in HRM are employee motivation, productivity, performance and engagement. What works at one time, in one place and for one set of people may not work elsewhere.
- People management is less about rational decision making and more about managing emotions (winning the hearts and minds) that cannot be easily captured, measured or managed. It requires an artistic/creative way of management rather than the scientific way.
- Scientific management can only tap into explicit knowledge, not the hidden tacit knowledge that requires the development and harnessing of informal social networks.

Arguments in favour of 'managing people is a science'

- 'Science is a systematic body of knowledge pertaining to a specific field of study that contains general facts which explains a phenomenon. It establishes cause and effect relationship between two or more variables and underlines the principles governing their relationship. These principles are developed through scientific method of observation and verification through testing' (Wikiversity, 2017)
- 'The main reason for the inexactness of science of management is that it deals with human beings and it is very difficult to predict their behavior accurately. Since it is a social process, therefore it falls in the area of social sciences. It is a flexible science & that is why its theories and principles may produce different results at different times and therefore it is a behaviour science' (Wikiversity, 2017)
- Evidence-based management means one has to formulate and implement HR policies based on scientific data and analysis. According to Rousseau and Barends (2011, p. 221), 'Evidence-based HR (EBHR) is a decision-making process combining critical thinking with use of the best available scientific evidence and business information'.
- Google provides the best example of data and analytics driven people management. Its HR head, Bock (2016) explains how Google uses data and analytics to take people management decisions on hiring, employee engagement, performance and reward management based purely on scientific principles of management.

Useful references

Bock, L. (2016). *Work rules! insights from inside Google that will transform how you live and lead.* London: Hodder and Stoughton.

Boettinger, H. M. (1975). Is management really an art? *Harvard Business Review*, January.

Devinney, T. M., Donald, S. and Siegel, D. S. (2012). Perspectives on the art and science of management scholarship. *Academy of Management Perspectives*, 26(1), 6–11.

Gothelf, J. and Seiden, J. (2017). You need to manage digital projects for outcomes, not outputs. *Harvard Business Review*, 6 February.

Philosophy Forums (2017). *Definitions of art and science.* Philosophy Forums. [Online] http://forums.philosophyforums.com/threads/definition-of-art-and-science-29402.html

Rousseau, D. M. and Barends, E. G. R. (2011), Becoming an evidence-based HR practitioner. *Human Resource Management Journal*, 21: 221–235.
Wikiversity (2017). Talk: Is management a science or an art? [Online] https://en.wikiversity.org/wiki/Talk:Is_management_a_science_or_an_art%3F

Video learning resources

- The changing world of work: https://news.microsoft.com/features/the-changing-world-of-work-2/
- The responsive organisation: https://news.microsoft.com/features/the-responsive-organization/
- Unlocking creativity: https://news.microsoft.com/features/unlocking-creativity/
- Human resource technology trends for 2017: www.youtube.com/watch?v=-Z_sxg_V9Q4
- Australian HR professionals unprepared for the future: www2.deloitte.com/au/en/pages/human-capital/articles/global-human-capital-trends-2017.html
- Future proof: www.abc.net.au/4corners/future-proof-promo/7562184

References

Andersson, L., Lanvin, B. and Van der Heyden, L. (2016). Digitalisation initiatives and corporate strategies: A few implications for talent. In B. Lanvin & P. Evans (Eds.) *The global competitiveness index 2017: Talent and technology*. Fontainebleau: INSEAD, pp. 51–57.

Cohen, D. J. (2015). HR past, present and future: A call for consistent practices and a focus on competencies. *Human Resource Management Review*, 25: 205–215.

Deloitte (2017). *Rewriting the rules for the digital age: 2017 Deloitte global human capital trends*. [Online] www2.deloitte.com/content/dam/Deloitte/us/Documents/human-capital/hc-2017-global-human-capital-trends-us.pdf (Accessed 3 April 2018).

Evans, P. and Rodriguez-Montemayor, E. (2016). Are we prepared for the talent overhaul induced by technology? A GTCI research commentary. In B. Lanvin & P. Evans (Eds.) *The global competitiveness index 2017: Talent and technology*. Fontainebleau: INSEAD, pp. 67–83.

Gartner (2017). *Gartner identifies the top 10 strategic technology trends for 2018*. [Online] www.gartner.com/newsroom/id/3812063 (Accessed 26 January 2018).

Gartner (2018). *Gartner hype cycle*. [Online] www.gartner.com/technology/research/methodologies/hype-cycle.jsp (Accessed 30 January 2018).

Gothelf, J. and Seiden, J. (2017). You need to manage digital projects for outcomes, not outputs. *Harvard Business Review*, 6 February.

Harris, S. and Spencer, E. (2017) *Sierra-Cedar 2017-2018 HR systems survey*. [Online] www.sierra-cedar.com/wp-content/uploads/sites/12/2018/01/Sierra-Cedar_2017-2018_HRSystemsSurvey_WhitePaper.pdf (Accessed 26 January 2018).

Huselid, M. A. (2011). Celebrating 50 years: Looking back and looking forward: 50 years of human resource management. *Human Resource Management*, 50(3): 309–312.

Kane, G. C., Palmer, D., Phillips, A. N., Kiron, D. and Buckley, N. (2017). *Achieving digital maturity*. MIT Sloan Management Review and Deloitte University Press, July. [Online] www.technologypeople.com.au/wp-content/uploads/2017/09/Achieving-Digital-Maturity.pdf (Accessed 23 January, 2018).

Lanvin, B. and Evans, P. (Eds.) (2016). *The global competitiveness index 2017: Talent and technology.* Fontainebleau: INSEAD.

Panetta, K. (2017). *Top trends in the Gartner hype cycle for emerging technologies,* 2017. [Online] www.gartner.com/smarterwithgartner/top-trends-in-the-gartner-hype-cycle-for-emerging-technologies-2017/ (Accessed 29 January 2018).

Senge, P. M. (1990). *The fifth discipline.* London: Random House.

Thite, M. (2004). Management philosophy: Foundation of people-centric culture. In M. Thite (Ed.) *Managing people in the new economy.* New Delhi: Sage, pp. 50–67.

Thomas, R. J., Kass, A. and Davarzani, L. (2013). *How digital technologies are changing the way we work.* Accenture. Outlook, No. 3. [Online] www.accenture.com/t00010101T000000Z__w__/au-en/_acnmedia/Accenture/Conversion-Assets/Outlook/Documents/1/Accenture-Outlook-How-Digital-Technologies-Are-Changing-The-Way-We-Work.ashx#zoom=50 (Accessed 28 January 2018).

Wright, A. (2017). *Top HR technology trends for 2018.* Society for HRM. [Online] www.shrm.org/resourcesandtools/hr-topics/technology/pages/top-hr-technology-trends-2018.aspx (Accessed 26 January 2018).

Index

Tables are indicated by the page number in bold, and figures by the page number in italics

absorptive capacities of multinational organizations 30
abstinence in project management **43**
accountability 257, 261
accuracy 33, 261, **261**
ActiveRain (social media platform) 125
Acumatica ERP (cloud solution) 107
adaptive multinational organizations 29
adaptive security infrastructure as future trend 272
administrative expert role 11
Adobe Systems, Adobe Connect 214
ADP 157
Agile project management: Agile Manifesto (2001) 58–9, **59**, 61; Agile Scrum methodology 60–1, *62*, **63**, 69–70; approach 13, 15, 57–71; implementation challenges 67–8; key characteristics 59–60; principles 58–9, **59**; role of HR 61–7; and technology projects 69
agility, or stability debate 70–1
Airbnb 1
algorithms 80–1, **81**, 101–2, 162
Amazon 32, 33; EC2 (cloud-based service) 111, 112
American Psychological Association 216
America's Army (game) 140, 189
Andersson, L. 3–4, 5, 16, 277
Angrave, D. **81**, 90, 99, 101, 102, 103
Apple Retail 134
Apple Watch 225
applicant tracking system (ATS) 9, 12, 176, 179, 187
applicants. *See* jobs
application forms 181–2
applications for e-HRM: e-learning and development (e-L&D) 16, 214–28; e-performance management system 15–16, 196–210; e-recruitment and e-selection (e-R&S) 15, 172–93; e-talent 15, 153–68
approaches to e-HRM: Agile project management 15, 57–71; soft systems thinking 15, 42–55; strategic management 14–15, 25–39
approval seekers (social media users) **126**
apps, intelligent 272
arrogance in project management **43**
Arthur, J.B. 26–8
artificial intelligence (AI) 1–2, 5, 32–3, 270, 272
asset profiling 253–5
AstraZeneca **91**
attributes in performance assessment 199–200
augmented workforce as future trend 274
automation, HRM 32, 35–6, 77
availability, and information security 253

background verification checks 256–7
Bates, Rachel 172
Becker, B.E. 29, 30, 94, 99, 100, **100**
benefits: of e-HRM 236–7, **238**; of ISMS 256; of social media 125–6
bias: in e-performance management 206; and performance assessment 199–200; and social media 127–8; and talent acquisition 160; when using algorithms 101–2
big data: and algorithms 80–1, **81**; applications 80–3; and capable personnel 75–6; critical perspective 76–9; definition 76; direction 15, 75–85; and e-learning and development 219; and HRM 83; literature review **81**; in management 79–80, **80**; need for literacy 77–9; opportunities 109; wrong use of 79
Biohax 33
blockchain 272
BlueGranite 37
Bluvision 33

Boudreau, J.W. 82, 89, 90, 100, **100**
Boyles, T. 26–8
Brilliant U (online learning platform) **10**
business models 252
business process re-engineering (BPR) 9
business strategies, vs. corporate strategies 26, **27**

Calvard, T. S. **81**
Canada, privacy laws 262
capability management 51
CareerBuilder (online job board) 130, 177
careers 5–7, 273
Carnegie Mellon University, Software Engineering Institute (SEI) 49
Cascio, W.F. 31–2, 33
'Cellular' organisational structure 6
Ceridian (talent management product) 157
change agent role 11
change management 51–2
changelings (social media users) **126**
Chartered Institute of Personnel and Development (CIPD) 175
Checkpoint (digital tool) **10**
China 2, 5, 14
CHIP (digital tool) **10**
Cisco 214
cloud computing: architecture 110–11; case study 117–18; debate 118–20; deployment models 112; direction 15, 106–20; and e-HRM 106–8, 109–10, 116–17; enterprise 115–16; and HRM 112–15; key features **110**, 111; measures for success 116; service models 111; and SMEs 107, 110; and technology costs 156
cloud to the edge, future trend 272
cognitive ability tests 184
collaboration 30, 115, 252, 275
collective ownership, as Agile characteristic 60
commercial off the shelf (COTS) 46
compensation 114, 200, 202–3
competencies 65–6; for Agile project management **65**; analytic 92, 99–100, **100**; big data 75–6, 78–9; digital 5, **6**, 188, 277; learning and development 219–20; management 51, 65–6
competitive advantage 30
compliance 257–9
CompTIA, Fifth Annual Trends in Cloud Computing 115–16
computational thinking 78
computer-adaptive testing (CAT) principles 184
confidentiality 253, 257
consent 260

continuing professional development (CPD) 114
conversational platforms as future trend 272
coordination flexibility 29
corporate governance 257–9
corporate strategies, vs. business strategies 26, **27**
corporate websites 175–7
Crisp, Samuel 134
cross functional team, as Agile characteristic 59
Crowdsourcing (digital tool) **10**, 112–13
cultures, and technologies 274, 275
Curtis, B. 50–2
customer relationship management (CRM) 107
customer services, social media for 123–4
customers, as Agile characteristic 60
customized off-the-shelf HRM cloud products 114–15
cybercrime 250–1, 252, **258**

"dark web" 251
data: breaches 250–1, **258**, 263; definition 76; minimization 261; privacy concept 259; security 116, 237; visualisation 100–1
data collection limitation 261
data protection issues 190, 237, 262. *See also* privacy
data quality 261
DataRobot (digital tool) **10**, 93
decision support systems (DSS) 9
Deloitte 9, 13, 14, 34–5; Digital Centre for Immersive Learning 164; Global Human Capital Trends 11, 218, 273; Leadership Academy 164
Deloitte Insights, Tech Trend Report (2017) 109–10
deniers (social media users) **126**
design: and Agile project management **66**; as phase of SDLC 46, *48*
digital footprint 160, *161*, 277
digital HR strategy: case study 278–9; core elements 277–8; external influencing factors 275, *276*; framework 275–8, *276*; future trend 273; internal influencing factors *276*, 277; unintended outcomes 240–1
digital HRM. *See* e-HRM
digital immigrants 127
digital initiatives success factors 277
digital natives 127
digital platforms as future trend 270
digital skills 5, **6**, 188, 190, 277
digital tools and technologies 1–4, **10**, 92, 189, 268–9
digital twin as future trend 272

digital workforce 4–7, **6**, 11
digital workplace 34–5
digitalisation model of e-HRM 243
dippers (social media users) 126, **126**
directions in e-HRM: big data 15, 75–85; cloud computing 15, 106–20; gamification 15, 140–8; HR metrics and analytics 15, 89–104; social media 15, 123–37
discipline, social media for 133–4
disclosure limitation 261
discrimination 127–8, 181, 199, 263
Disney 153
distance learning 220–2
diversity **95**, 97–9, 273–4
documentation, minimal as Agile characteristic 60

e-compensation systems 202–6
Edwards, K. 90, 92, 97–9, **97**, 101–2
Edwards, M.R. 90, 92, 97–9, **97**, 101–2
e-HRM: barriers and drawbacks 237–9; benefits of 236–7, **238**; core elements 277–8; definition 7–11, 35; and digital technologies 268–9; emergence 10–11; implementation 243; introduction 1–19; issues and challenges 268–9; key approaches to 25–72; key success factors 239–40, **240**; negative outcomes **241**; positive outcomes 241; and SHRM 35–6; strategic evaluation models 241–3; strategic use of 235–6; strategy. *See* digital HR strategy unintended outcomes
elasticity in cloud computing **110**, 111
e-learning and development (e-L&D): advantages and disadvantages **222**; application 16, 214–28; case study 226–7; change and development 225–6; debate 226–7; digital revolution in 217–20; learning speed 221–2; methods 220–5; overview 214–15; retention rate 221–2; and talent development 164
electronic data processing (EDP) 8
electronic/digital HRM. *See* e-HRM
emails 14
Embark (digital tool) **10**
e-Mentoring 224–5
emotional maturity, and project management **43**
employee champion role 11
employee experience as future trend 273
employee referrals 175–6, 177, 178, 189
employees/employment: attrition 47, 80; benefits options 202; clearance process on departure 257; contract employees 6; core employees 6; core labor pool 30; development 132–3; e-HRM concerns 237–9; engagement 13–14; flexible arrangements 33–4; flows 94, **95**; and gamification 146–7; impact of technology on 33–5; and information security 256–7; and microchips 75; monitoring 263; non-disclosure agreement 257; post termination activities 263; pre-employment privacy practices 263; relationship management 5–7, 206, 237; retention 82–3; and social media 133, 135–6; surveillance 237, 263; temporary employees 6; turnover **95**, 96–7
employer branding 176
engagement **95**, 98
enterprise resource planning (ERP) 7–8, 107, 108–9, 156
e-performance management system: adoption factors 203–5; application 15–16, 196–210; case study 207–9; debate 209–10; evaluation of 205–7; potential and pitfalls 207; role of technology 201–3
e-recruitment and e-selection (e-R&S): and applicants 179; application 15, 172–93; and corporate websites 175–7; data protection issues 190; evaluation of system 187; introduction 172; job analysis 174–5; key steps, processes and considerations **180**, **186**; opportunities and challenges 187–90; process 174; processing applications 179; technology-enabled 173–81
e-talent: application 15, 153–68; challenges of 165; management products 157–8; and talent acquisition 158–60; and talent development 164; and talent identification 160–3, **162**; and talent management 156–8; and talent retention 164–5
ethical issues, social media 127–8, 131–2
European Community Data Protection Directive and regulation (25 May 2018) 190
European Union (EU), privacy laws 262
evaluative methods for selection 182–7
event driven as future trend 272
everybody as talent **155**
evidence-based HR analytics 102
evidence-based management 79–80, 84–5
executive information systems (EIS) 9
Experience API (learning technology) **10**, 225
experiential learning theory (ELT) 215–16
Expert as a Service (EaaS) (cloud-based expert service) 114
'Expert Cloud' (cloud-based expert service) **10**
exportive multinational organizations 29
external fit of SHRM 29
external influencing factors 275, *276*

Facebook (social media platform): for customer services 123–4; different patterns of use 127; and discipline 133, 134; for employees 35; evolution 125; for learning and development 224; for marketing 123; numbers using 4; pattern recognition software 2; purpose 125; for recruitment and selection 130–1, 177; for retaliation 128; stories 125
face-to-face interviews, for employee selection 183
FC Midtjylland 82
feedback, as Agile characteristic 60
firm-specific skills 30
First Direct Banking 126
Fitbit 82, 225
flexibility: SHRM 29; in work arrangements 33–4
Formaposte 144
Fortune 500 companies 4, 189
'fourth industrial revolution' 2
fraudulence in project management **43**
Friendster 125
fully participating customer, as Agile characteristic 60
future trends 16, 268–81, 270–4

Galagan, P. **81**
gamification: building blocks of 142; concept 141–3; debate 147–8; direction 15, 140–8; and employee productivity 146–7; and employee referrals 189; growth of 140–1; and HRM 143–6; numbers playing games 4; for recruitment **10**, 12, 189; for selection 189; strategic and operational approaches 144–5
Gartner hype cycle for emerging technologies 270–3
GE **10**, 13
ghosts (social media users) **126**
Gieles, H. 61, 64
gig economy 4, 34
Glassdoor (social media platform) **10**, 125
globalisation, and digital HR strategy 275
Gnowbe (learning tool) 219
goals 113, 198
GoldenEye (ransomware) 250
Gollub, U. 1–2
Google: and gamification 143, 144; Google AppEngine (cloud-based service) 111, 112; Google Docs 111; Google Groups 224; Google Mail 111; Google+ 4, 125; mobile phones 188; for recruitment and selection 12, 82; use of big data 85
Great Britain, HM Revenue and Customs 250

Harris Poll 186
HCL Technologies 13
health technology 2
Hefley, B, 50–2
Heineken **10**, 159
Hiscox Cyber Readiness Report 251
horizontal fit of SHRM 29
HR: activities 8–10; climate **27**, 28; and cybercrime 250–1, **258**; digital strategy 275–8, *276*; and digital technology **10**, 274–5, 277–8; futuristic trends 273–4; and information security 256–9; outsourcing 9–10; and performance management 198; philosophy **27**, 28; policies, practices and programs **27**, 28; and privacy 262–4; role in Agile project management 61–7; skills and competencies **100**, 188; sustainable competitive advantage 30; technology-enabled 11–12
HR analytics: benefits of digital technology 236; and big data 82; cloud-enabled 115; competencies 99–100, **100**; conceptualisations **155**; and data visualisation 100–1; definition 90; differing models 102–3; and digital technology 92; direction 15, 89–104; and e-learning and development 219; evidence-based 94, 102; examples of projects 96–9; as future trend 273; and HRIS 94; and key HR metrics 94–5, **95**; for management decisions 95–6; in practice 90–2; as a specialism 89–90, 101–2, 103–4; and statistical software 92–4; turnover analyses **91**
HR functions: evolution 270, **271**; future 35–7; and social media 128–34; and technology 106–8, 245; technology-enabled 12–14
HR metrics. *See* HR analytics
HRM. *See* human resource management (HRM)
HR Systems Survey *See* Sierra-Cedar
human capital theory 30
human resource information systems (HRIS): and cloud computing 116–17; evolution 7–8; and gamification 145; and HR analytics 94; and learning and development 218; manager role 44–5; need for 109
human resource management (HRM): and big data 83; changing technological environment 31–5; cloud-based 112–15; evolution of technologies 108–10, **108**; and gamification 143–6; "hard" or "soft" 38; HR function **271**. *See also* strategic human resource management (SHRM)
human resources (HR). *See* HR
human resources (HR) analytics. *See* HR analytics

Humana, Knowledge Exchange 224
Huselid, M.A. 94, 99, 100, **100**, 278
Hyatt (hotels) 114
Hybrid Agile 59
hybrid cloud 112

IBM **10**, **28**, 94; Queensland Health payroll crisis 53; Watson 1–2, **10**, 225
ignorance in project management **43**
immersive experiences as future trend 270, 272
implementation: and Agile project management 67–8; of e-HRM 239–40, **240**, 243; of information security controls 256; measures for successful cloud 116; as phase of SDLC 46–7, *48*
inclusion as future trend 273–4
inconsistent management 50
Indeed (social media platform) 125
India 5
individuals: access to data 261; as talent **155**
industrial relations **271**
information overload 14
information security: case study 264–5; controls 255–6; declaration form 257; frameworks 253; HR role in 256–9; importance 250–1, 264; inclusion in job responsibilities 257; increasing importance of 252–3; problem 16, 250–66; role of IT and HR **258**; standards 253
information security management system (ISMS) 253–6, *254*
information technologies (IT): auditors 265–6; capability 242, 243; and cybercrime **258**; evolution of HRM 108–10; recruitment and selection 190; and talent management 154
informers (social media users) 126, **126**
Infrastructure as a Service (IaaS) (cloud-based service) 111
innovator & integrator role 11
Instagram (social media platform) 4, 124, 125, 177
institutionalised metric-oriented behaviour (IMOB) 101
integration of e-HRM 242
integrative multinational organization 29
integrity: for employee selection 185; and information security 253
intelligent apps and analytics as future trend 272
intelligent things as future trend 272
interactive voice response (IVR) 182
internal actors and data loss 251
internal fit of SHRM 29

internal influencing factors, on digital HR strategy *276*, 277
internal operations, strategic international HRM 29
internalisation of e-HRM 242
International Hotelco 243
internet: and e-learning and development 219; for employee selection 186–7; job boards 177–8; numbers with access to 140; and talent acquisition 158–9
Internet of Things (IoT) 109, 252
interunit linkages, strategic international HRM 29
ISO.IEC 27001 253

JASP (statistical software tool) **93**
J.D. Power 123
jobs: advertising *173*, 175–6, 177–8, 188; analysis 174–5; applicants 174–9, 183; application forms 181–2; information security responsibilities 257; realistic job previews (RJPs) 182. *See also* employees/employment
Jobvite 130
John Neilson Software 69–70

Know Your Worth (digital tool) **10**
Knowledge Exchange 224
knowledge workers 4, 7
Kodak 1
Kolb, D. 215–16
Kryscynski, D. 90, 100, **100**

labor/labour: human capital theory 30; market restrictions 275; online platforms 34; welfare **271**
LAMP framework 100, **100**
leadership 60, 273
learner-centred psychological principles **216**
learning and development: and cloud-based HRM 114; compared with training **217**; digital revolution in 217–20; as future trend 273; historical developments in 215–17; learning goals 220; overview 214–15; social media for 132–3; talent development 163–4; technology-enabled 13; through games 143
learning management system (LMS) 9, 218–19
learning organisations, and Agile project management **66**, 69
learning speed in e-learning 221–2
legal issues: and privacy framework 260; and social media 127–8, 132
LinkedIn (social media platform): costs and benefits 125–6; different patterns of use 127;

288   Index

digital tool **10**; m-recruitment 188; numbers using 4; and processing job applications 179; purpose 124; Recruiter Mobile 188; for recruitment 130, 177; for selection 130–1; and talent acquisition 158–9; and talent development 164; and talent retention 165
Lowe, Rob 226
lurkers/observers (social media users) 126, **126**, 164

machine learning 33, 92–4
maintenance and support, as phase of SDLC 47, *48*, 49
management: management information systems (MIS) 9; use of big data 79–80, **80**; use of HR metrics 95–6
Marriot (hotels) 144
Massive Open Online Courses (MOOCs) **10**, 13, 223
McDonalds 107
McKinsey, People Analytics 165
MDE framework (mechanics, dynamics, emotions) 141
measured service in cloud computing **110**, 111
mentoring, social media for 132
Meta4 (talent management product) 157
micro politics and e-HRM 239
microchips implants 75
Microsoft 214; "Hit Refresh" paradigm 37; Office Teams product 35
Miller, M. **81**
Miller, S. 50–2
minimal documentation, as Agile characteristic 60
Minitab (statistical software tool) **93**
mobile phones 188–9, 225
Mondelez International 123
Moneyball case **80**
monitoring and evaluation 115, 243
Monster (online job board) 177
Montealegre, R. 31–2, 33
MOOCs. *See* Massive Open Online Courses (MOOCs)
Morton's Steakhouse 123
motivational-enhancing HR practices 199
m-recruitment 188–9
multinational organizations 29
multiple ownership, as Agile characteristic 60
multiple supporting platforms of cloud computing **110**, 111
musicals 25
Mya (chatbot service) **10**
MySpace (social media platform) 125

Netflix (film streaming service) 33
'Networked' organisational structure 6
Nordstrom 133
notice, as privacy principle 261

Oakland Athletics **80**
Occupational Information Network (O★Net) 174–5
O'Connor, Melanie 196
off-the-shelf HRM cloud products, customized 114–15
onboarding, social media for 132
online learning. *See* e-learning and development (e-L&D)
Ontame.io 178–9
openness: as Agile characteristic 60; as privacy principle 261
opportunity-enhancing HR practices 199
Oracle 94, 113, 114–15, 156, 157
organizations/organisations: context assessment 242; culture 63; digital 83–4; digital footprint 277; and e-performance management systems 204–5; and e-talent 165; of the future 273; and gamification 144–5; structure 6; and talent management 154–5, 164
outsourcing 53–5, 252
overambition in project management **43**

passive jobseekers 175
passive selection procedure, social media screen as 131
pay, and performance assessment 200
P-CMM. *See* people capability maturity model (P-CMM)
peacocks (social media users) **126**
people analytics. *See* HR analytics
people capability maturity model (P-CMM) 49–52, *50*
people management 50–1, 204, 279–80
people-centric HRM 278
people-related costs and controls 258
Perez, Hernan 128
performance: appraisal 113, 196, 197; assessment 197–8; enhancement 217; feedback 197–8, 200–1, 205; and talent identification 163; use of HR analytics **95**, 97, **97**
performance management: and Agile project management 66–7; definition 197; future trend 273; overview 197–201; potential and pitfalls 196–7, 207; purpose 197–8; role of technology 201–3; social media for 133–4; system design 200–1; and talent identification 160; technology-enabled 13; use of big data 82

personal data 101, 259–60
personal identity information (PII) 259–64
personal social media platforms 125
personnel administration as HR function **271**
Perusall (learning tool) 219
Pier Sixty 128
Pinterest (social media platform) 4, 125
Pivotal, Knowledge Exchange 224
Plan-Do-Check-Act (PDCA) Cycle 253
Platform as a Service (PaaS) (cloud-based service) 111
'platform mediated contracting' 34
platforms: conversational 272; digital as future trend 270; labor/labour 34; multiple supporting **110**, 111; social media 124–5
playing, and learning 143
portfolio-centred staffing 6
PowerPoint (software) 219, 221
predictive analytics. *See* HR analytics
privacy: and cloud computing 116; concept 259–60; drawbacks of e-HRM 237; framework 260; importance 250–1; laws and regulations 262; principles 260–2, **261**, **262**; role of HR in 262–4; and social media 128, 133
Privacy Act (1988) (Australia) 262
private cloud 112
problems and prospects of e-HRM: future directions 16, 268–81; information security and privacy 16, 250–66; strategic evaluation 16, 235–46
productivity 14, **95**
project closure, as phase of SDLC 47
project management **43**, 44–5, 57–8, 69, 70–1
project planning, as phase of SDLC 46, *48*
proportionality, as privacy principle **261**
'protean' 7
public cloud 112
purpose legitimacy, as privacy principle 260, **261**
Python (statistical software tool) **93**

quality management framework 49–52, *50*
Queensland Health payroll crisis 52–3
quizzers (social media users) 126, **126**

'R' (statistical software tool) **93**
Ramstad, P.M. 100, **100**
ransomware 250, 252
ranters (social media users) **126**
rapid elasticity in cloud computing **110**, 111
rapid feedback and action, as Agile characteristic 60
rapid instructional design 219
realistic job previews (RJPs) 182

Recruiter Mobile (digital tool) 10
recruitment and selection (R&S): and Agile project management 65, **65**; applicant attraction 175–9; benefits of e-HRM 236–7; of candidates 187; case study 190–1; and cloud-based HRM 112–13; communication with applicants 179; computer-based tests 184; contingent methods 185–7; definition 172–3; evaluative methods 182–7; and gamification 12, 189; and HR analytics **95**, 98–9; identification of applicants 174–5; job analysis 174–5; key steps, processes and considerations **180**, **186**; knowledge tests 184; locating applicants 175; multinational organizations 29–30; online interviews 183; personality tests 184–5; process 173–4, **173**, 179; recruitment messages 175; recruitment sources 175–8; screening methods 181–2; situational judgement tests (SJTs) 185; smartphones for 189; and social media 129–32, **131**, 191–2; technology-enabled 12, 173–90; telephone interviews 183; telephone screens 182; use of big data 82
Reddit (social media platform) 125
regulations, information security 252–3
relational HR 8–9
reliability in performance management 199
remote working 34
request for proposal (RFP) 46
requirement analysis, as phase of SDLC 46, *48*
ResearchGate (social media platform) 125
resource flexibility in SHRM 29
resource pooling in cloud computing **110**, 111
resource-based view (RBV) in SHRM 30
retaliation, and social media 128
retention: and e-learning 221–2; as privacy principle 261
retrospection, as Agile characteristic 60
revenue, HR metrics **95**
reverse diffusion, of e-HRM practices 241
reward management 197–207
rewards and recognitions (R&R) 67, 113–14
Richardson & Company, LLP **27**
risk assessment 253–4, 255
risk treatment 255–6
RoadWarrior (game) 143
robotics 5, 32
Royal Bank of Canada **10**

S3 (cloud-based service) 112
SalesForce.com (cloud-based service) 111, 112
SAP 143, 156
Sarbanes Oxley Act 257–9
SAS (statistical software tool) **93**

Savage, Robert 207–9
Scholz, T. M. 81, **81**
science, technology, engineering and mathematics (STEM) 4–5
score card tools 13
screening methods for selection 131, **131**, 181–2
security: awareness training 257; incident management 257; ISMS policy 253; ISMS requirements 253; as privacy principle 261
self driving cars 2
self-assessment, and gamification 189
self-leadership approach 13
self-organising team, as Agile characteristic 59
self-selection, and corporate websites 177
self-service: applications 9; benefits of e-HRM 236–7; and e-compensation schemes 206–7; and e-learning and development 221; as key feature of cloud computing **110**, 111; and processing job applications 179; procurement services 115
servant leadership, as Agile characteristic 60
service level agreement (SLA) 47
'shamrock' organisation 6
Shankman, Peter 123
shared services centres (SSCs) 9
SHRM. *See* strategic human resource management (SHRM)
SHRMConnect (social media platform) 124
sickness absence **95**
Siemens 144
Sierra-Cedar: HR Systems Survey 109–10, 269, 274
skeptical thinking, and big data 78–9
skill-enhancing HR practices 198–9
skills: for Agile project management 65–6, **65**; analytic 44–5, 99; big data 75, 77–8; digital 5, **6**, 188, 190, 277; firm-specific 30; and talent management 155, **155**; tests for 184, **186**
small and medium enterprises (SMEs) 8, 107, 110
smart HRM. *See* e-HRM
smartphones 188–9, 225
Smith, Adam 133
SnapChat (social media platform) 125, 177, 250
social, mobile, analytics and cloud (SMAC) technologies 4, 8
social exchange theory (SET) 30–1
Social Index (digital tool) **10**, 160
social media: costs and benefits 125–6; for customer services 123–4; for development 132–3; different patterns of use 126–7; differentiating between platforms 124–5; direction 15, 123–37; for discipline 133–4; for e-learning and development 219; for employee development 132–3; for employee selection 186–7; and employment decisions 135–6; evolution of platforms 125; in an HR context 124–8, 134; and HR functions 128–34; and HRM 109; implications 134–5; for learning and development 224; legal and ethical issues 127–8; for marketing 123; for onboarding and socialization 132; for performance management 133–4; policy 128, **129**, 133–4, 224; professional platforms 124–5; for recruitment and selection 129–32, **131**, 177, 191–2; and talent acquisition 158–60; types of user **126**
social networking sites (SNS). *See* social media
socialization, social media for 132
Society for Human Resource Management (SHRM) 128, 174–6, 183, 187, 268
Society for Industrial and Organizational Psychology (SIOP) 130
soft systems thinking approach 15, 42–55. *See also* systems thinking
software development projects 42–3
Software Engineering Institute (SEI) 49
software-as-a-service (SaaS) 8, 110, 111, 113
Sontech Pharmaceuticals 207–9
specificity, as privacy principle **261**
SPSS (statistical software tool) 92, **93**, 94
stability, or agility 70–1
Standish Group, CHAOS reports 42, 58
Starbucks 27
Stata (statistical software tool) **93**
statistical analyses tools 92–4, **93**
statistical thinking, and big data 78
STEM (science, technology, engineering and mathematics) 4–5
Storify (learning tool) 219
strategic alignment assessment, of e-HRM 242–3
strategic business partner role 11
strategic evaluation: models for e-HRM 241–3; problem of e-HRM 16, 235–46
strategic HR competency framework **100**
strategic human resource management (SHRM): changing technological environment 31–5; definition 25–6; and e-HRM 35–6; fit vs. flexibility 28–9, **28**; future 35–7; HR function **271**; international 29–30; levels 26–8, **27**; theories 30–1; vs. traditional human resource management 26
strategic international human resource management (SIHRM) 29–30
strategic management, approach to e-HRM 14–15, 25–39

Index   291

strategy: framework of digital HR 275–8, *276*; and HR technology 274; and implementation of e-HRM 240
subject matter experts (SMEs) 174
SuccessFactors (digital tool) **10**, 113, 114, 157, 219
Switch (recruitment app) **10**
systems development life cycle (SDLC): approach 7; evaluation of waterfall model 49; key success factors *48*; SDLC for IT Projects *45*; using waterfall methodology 45–9, *45*, 57
systems thinking: definition 44–5; and project management 44–5; for technology projects 43, 52. *See also* soft systems thinking approach

talent: acquisition 112–13, 158–60, 273; analytics, *see* HR analytics conceptualisations; development 163–4; identification 160–3, **162**; outsourcing 53–5; retention 164–5
talent management: and Agile project management 63–4, *64*; application 15, 153–68; benefits of e-HRM 236; case study 166–7; debate 167–8; definition 154–5; HR metrics **95**; importance 153–4; and information technologies 154; software 157–8; technology-enabled systems and products 156–8; use of big data 82
talent management system (TMS) 156–60
Taleo (recruitment software) 115
teams 30, 59
technology: and adoption of e-performance management systems 204; development 1–2; and e-learning and development 217–20; evolution of HRM 108–10, **108**; futuristic trends 270–3; and HR activities 8–9; and HR functions 12–14, 106–8, 245; and HR roles 11–12; and HR technology 274–5; and HR trends and initiatives 274–5; and HRM environmental trends 31–5; impact on work 33; intensity and penetration 275; jobs 4; life cycle 272; and managing people 269; and performance management 201–3; rapid changes in 252; and reward management 201–3; skills 4–5; and talent identification 160–3, **162**; and talent management 154, 156–8; unintended consequences 14
Technology Acceptance Model (TAM) 68
technology projects: and Agile project management 69; need for systems thinking approach 43, 52; project management 57–8, 69
technology proponent role 11

threats: identification of 255; risk assessment 255
3D printing 2
360-degree feedback system 13, 113, 202, 206
time-boxed iterations, as Agile characteristic 59
Tin Can API (learning technology) **10**
traditional human resource management, vs. SHRM 26
training: compared with learning **217**; shift to learning 215–17; social media for 132–3
transformational HR 9
transparency: as Agile characteristic 60; as privacy principle 261, **261**
transparently immersive experiences, as future trend 270
'Tricorder' (medical device) 2
TripAdvisor 82
Triple-T 109
truck industry, use of big data 82
trust, of e-HRM 239
turnover analysis, and HR analytics 96–7
Twitter (social media platform): for customer services 123–4; for discipline 133; for learning and development 224; numbers using 4; purpose 124, 125; for recruitment 177

Uber 1, 5, 144
ubiquitous computing 31–2, 252
Udacity (MOOC) 223
Ulrich, D. 11–12, 100, **100**, 277, 278
Ultimate Systems 157
ultras (social media users) 126, **126**
unintended outcomes, of e-HRM utilisation 240–1, **241**
uniqueness of HR 30
United States: Army **10**, 140, 144, 189; Department of Defense 45; dominance 14; Equal Employment Opportunity Commission 181; Navy **28**, 175; privacy laws 262
usability, lack of 237
use limitation of data, as privacy principle 261
user acceptance: of e-HRM 237–9; and performance management 200, 204
user friendliness, lack of 237

validity in performance management 199
valuable, rare, difficult to imitate, and non-sustainable resources (VRIN), competitive advantage 30
van der Meer, R. 61, 64
vendor lock-in, and cloud computing 116
verification checks 256–7

vertical fit of SHRM 29
video conferencing 183
video games 140–1, 144
virgins (social media users) **126**
virtual HRs (V-HRs) (digital tool) **10**, 114.
    See also e-HRM
virtual machines (VM) 111
virtual private cloud (VPC) 112
virtual simulations, and e-learning 221
vision, and implementation of
    e-HRM 240

Wade and Wendy (chatbot service) 107
Walmart 35
waterfall methodology 45–9, *45*, 57
Watson Analytics 93
wearables 225
web browsing time 4
web-based HR. *See* e-HRM
web-based learning 220–2
websites 175–7
weighted application forms 181–2

Whitehead Nursing Home 250
wikis 224
Wings Logistics 226–7
work: flexible arrangements 33–4; impact of
    technology on 33
Workable 172
Workday 114, 157, 165
work-flow engine, cloud-enabled 115
workforce, augmented 274
workplace, digital 34–5
workplace of the future 17–18
World Economic Forum 77
World Information Technology and Services
    Alliance (WITSA) 261
www.nurse.com 177–8

Xerox 80

YouTube 124, 125, 130, 159

Zappos **27**
Zoho CRM (cloud solution) 107

PGMO 07/03/2018